LANGUAGE AND LITERACY SERIES

Dorothy S. Strickland and Celia Genishi, SERIES EDITORS

ADVISORY BOARD: RICHARD ALLINGTON, DONNA ALVERMANN, KATHRYN AU, EDWARD CHITTENDON, BERNICE CULLINAN, COLETTE DAIUTE, ANNE HAAS DYSON, CAROLE EDELSKY, JANET EMIG, SHIRLEY BRICE HEATH, CONNIE JUEL, SUSAN LYTLE

(Continued)

THE
BOOK CLUB
CONNECTION

→ ←

Literacy Learning and Classroom Talk

Edited by

Susan I. McMahon and **Taffy E. Raphael**

with

Virginia J. Goatley and Laura S. Pardo

FOREWORD BY BERNICE E. CULLINAN

International
Reading
Association

Teachers College
Columbia University
New York and London

Published simultaneously by Teachers College Press, 1234 Amsterdam Avenue, New York, NY 10027 and the International Reading Association, 800 Barksdale Road, Newark, DE 19714

Library of Congress Cataloging-in-Publication Data

The book club connection : literacy learning and classroom talk /
  edited by Susan I. McMahon and Taffy E. Raphael with Virginia J.
  Goatley and Laura S. Pardo ; foreword by Bernice E. Cullinan.
      p. cm. – (Language and literacy series)
    Includes bibliographical references (p.   ) and index.
    ISBN 0-8077-3615-5 (cloth : alk. paper). – ISBN 0-8077-3614-7
  (pbk.)
    1. Group reading–United States. 2. Book clubs–United States.
  3. Reading (Elementary)–United States. 4. Action research in
  education–United States.   I. McMahon, Susan I. II. Raphael, Taffy.
  III. Series: Language and literacy series (New York, N.Y.)
  LC6651.B63   1997
  372.41′62–dc21   96-52792

ISBN 0-8077-3614-7 (paper)
ISBN 0-8077-3615-5 (cloth)
IRA Inventory Number 9111

Printed on acid-free paper
Manufactured in the United States of America

04 03 02 01 00 99 98 97   8 7 6 5 4 3 2 1

Contents

Section III: Teacher–Researchers in the Book Club Program

Foreword

Seeds of change lead to unexpected growth. The seeds of thought that teachers generate produce new ideas and change the world. They empower teachers to become researchers, collaborators, and members of learning communities.

In the past, we gathered students into reading groups to ask them to take turns reading aloud: It was the way we taught reading–or at least it was a way we checked to see if students were learning to read. Such groups differed markedly from the Book Club described here. In reading groups, teachers were in control. Teachers chose what students would read, planned when they met, led the discussions, and decided when to end the sessions. Teachers also did most of the talking.

But seeds of today's knowledge and research force us to change reading instruction and teaching practice. Through classroom research, Taffy Raphael and Susan McMahon found that students talk more in Book Club when teachers are not members of the group. They found that talk in Book Club clarifies interpretation and expands students' concepts about literature. Because of what students learn, teachers share with them social and interpretive authority about literature. Teachers now find that they want to talk about talk and to encourage their students to talk with one another.

Susan McMahon and Taffy Raphael began experimenting with Book Club as a way to get books into classrooms, to give students choices about what they read, and to encourage meaningful conversations. The seeds of thought they planted broke open in classrooms and caused new ideas to germinate other new ideas. This book records the widening circle of participants. Section I recounts their conceptualization and the theoretical foundations of Book Club. McMahon, Raphael, Goatley, and Boyd explain reading and writing components as well as whole-class and student-led discussions. In Section II, the researchers explore the use of Book Club among special education students, second-language learners, and cross-aged groups. They also describe assessment and allow students to describe their perspective. Teachers in the Book Club program speak for themselves in Section III. They reflect upon their teaching with Book Club, they describe the way Book Club works in primary grades, early elementary school, and content areas. They show how portfolios help to guide and monitor student growth. Commentaries by noted scholars follow all these excellent pieces.

The seeds that Raphael and McMahon plant bear fruit because they are theory-based and tested through research. Researchers and practitioners here recognize the social nature of language learning, and they know the role language plays in the development of thought. They are aware of the influence of peer talk on students' learning, and they know that students internalize new concepts and make them their own by talking about them. Ideas planted in fertile fields begin to grow and change the world around them.

In this book, we hear the voices of teachers, the voices of researchers, and the voices of students as they experience the joy of Book Club. When teachers and students become involved, Book Club changes the contexts of classrooms. Students begin to see themselves as active contributors to a learning environment and change that environment in the process. The rich language context enables learners to express their thoughts, often shaping them at the point of utterance. The context provides teachers opportunities to observe learners, to monitor student thinking, and to modify instruction.

Talk leads to more talk. Teachers, once isolated in self-contained classrooms, are now collaborators—fellow researchers. They find that in Book Club students are active participants in their own learning and create a literate community. They learn that seeds of change continue to grow in the fertile ground of literate communities.

Bernice E. Cullinan
New York University

Preface

This book describes the research underlying a six-year effort to explore an alternative to conventional reading instruction. Our decisions throughout the project were influenced by: (1) changing theoretical perspectives and definitions of literacy, (2) changes in the curriculum used in reading instruction and related interest in increasing opportunities for meaningful talk about text, and (3) the potential afforded through close collaboration between university- and school-based teachers and researchers. Since 1989, the Book Club project researchers and teachers have asked the fundamental question, What implications does adopting a sociocultural perspective have for literature-based reading instruction?

This book reflects the multiple voices involved in the project, which provide different insights into the Book Club program and related research. When we initially conceptualized writing a book about Book Club, we realized that no one person or group was in a position to convey all that the project had come to represent. While we, as project codirectors, had initially framed the Book Club program in 1989–90, the program today reflects significant contributions and developments through extensions classroom teachers have made to such areas as assessment and subject matter connections, as well as to new populations of students, from early elementary through high school. The program today also reflects extensions by former classroom teachers who had returned to the university as doctoral students, extending Book Club as they worked with students for whom English was their second language or who had been labeled learning-disabled. Within each extension, the Book Club program's integrity was maintained, but we learned new ways to support and document a diverse range of students' literacy development.

We organized this book with three audiences in mind – literacy researchers, teacher educators, and teachers, hoping that despite the multiple perspectives in such an audience, our readers would find connections within and across the different sections and chapters. Our decisions were guided by our theoretical assumptions, based in sociocultural traditions that underscore the active and social nature of learning, as well as the important role of language in the process of literacy learning. Our assumptions included the following:

- Literacy acquisition and development are grounded in connections between oral and written language.

- Literacy acquisition and development must be grounded in the use of authentic reading materials and authentic oral and written activities related to the reading.
- Reading is a social process.
- Learners should be actively engaged in constructing meaning as they read, write, and discuss texts.
- Learners should be actively engaged in meaningful literacy activities that provide opportunities for more knowledgeable "others" to advance their literacy abilities.
- Learning to read should occur through interactions around *literature*, not texts created simply to teach reading.

After a one-year pilot study, Susan McMahon and Taffy Raphael developed the framework for the Book Club program that included four contexts for instruction and participation in language and literacy:

1. *Community share:* This is the large-group context in which students participate as a member of the classroom community–sharing ideas from their reading and small-group discussions, observing their teacher and peers in interaction around textual ideas, and making connections across the texts in their lives.
2. *Reading:* This is the context in which students engage in reading across a range of circumstances: alone, with partners, and in small groups. It is also where they have the opportunity to apply skills and strategies for: (a) personal response, (b) building fluency, (c) comprehending, (d) interpreting, and (e) critiquing the literature they read. Further, it is the context in which students interact with a range of literary works over the academic year.
3. *Writing:* This is the context in which students engage in writing to support both reading and discussion. Students write in response logs and in more structured "think-sheets." They write informally in response to their reading, and they develop their ideas in more formal writing pieces. Thus writing activities provide opportunities for both brief response and the creation of extended texts.
4. *Book Clubs:* This is the context in which small groups of three to five students meet to discuss a common reading, including specific chapters from longer trade books, folk tales and picture books, articles and short stories. They share their personal responses, help one another clarify potentially confusing aspects of their reading, create interpretations and critiques of their texts, discuss authors' intent, and so forth. This is the context at the center of the program, from which the program takes its name, and to which all other components contribute.

Fundamental to all four contexts is the instruction that helps students participate successfully with a repertoire of strategies. Thus, in the Book Club program, instruction is contextualized to meet the particular needs of students' acquiring and developing literacy abilities (i.e., reading and writing) and oral language abilities (i.e., as speakers and listeners in meaningful discussion).

Our learning process began in 1989, as we developed the original project team: Taffy Raphael and Susan McMahon were codirectors, conceptualizing the Book Club framework and serving as participant observers throughout the first year of the research. Laura Pardo and Deb Woodman were classroom teachers who not only helped flesh out the program's framework as members of the project team, but also served as the primary instructors throughout the first year. Ginny Goatley, Jessica Bentley, and Fenice Boyd were research assistants in that first year, using their background as former classroom teachers as they supported and recorded Laura's and Deb's teaching activities and their students' responses, and helped in ongoing data analysis. Our weekly Wednesday project meetings began in the context of one of the classrooms, moved quickly to a restaurant for dinner meetings, and eventually became weekly potluck dinners in our homes. The transition in context is a metaphor for the evolution of camaraderie that made the project a very special one.

At these weekly meetings, we planned instruction in reading, writing, and discussion that was critical to successfully talking about books in meaningful ways. We developed repertoires of strategies useful in reading, writing, and discussion and considered ways of creating opportunities for practice in the four Book Club program contexts. We debated "big issues" such as tensions between student choice and curriculum demands, disparity between the limitation of report cards and the range of literacy areas in which students were learning and developing, effective grouping practices from factors that contribute to heterogeneous groups to optimal group size, and so forth (see Raphael et al., 1992). These weekly meetings were critical for moving the Book Club program from a general framework and set of principles to a concrete and workable instructional program.

Our learning continued as others heard about Book Club and began to work with us, many of them students in Michigan State University's Master's program in Literacy Instruction. Kristin Grattan and Pam Scherer, both teaching early elementary students, began to explore ways of extending Book Club to younger students. Kathy Highfield and Julie Folkert spent their weekly 90-minute commute to graduate school classes talking about ways to connect the original Book Club focus to social studies. Later, in an assessment class taught by Tanja Bisesi, Julie, Tanja, and Sara Fries began to explore performance-based and portfolio assessments. Over the years, original participants such as Ginny and Fenice began to explore their own extensions as they researched Book Club as a context for working with students who had not succeeded in traditional mainstream settings. Similarly, doctoral students such as Cindy Brock studied second-language learners' experiences in Book Club. Tanja helped direct the Book Club Assessment Project in 1994–95, as an outgrowth of her earlier work with Julie and Sara. In short, what we began in our role as project directors was an exciting journey of learning that we hope to convey in the pages of this book.

Our volume is organized in three sections. In Section I, Susan and Taffy describe the theoretical basis of the program in Chapter 1. In Chapters 2 through 5, we focus on each of the four Book Club program components. Taffy and Ginny detail *community share* in Chapter 2; Susan discusses *reading* in Chapter 3, Taffy and Fenice describe *writing* in Chapter 4, and Susan presents the student-led discussion component, *book club*—for which the program is named—in Chapter 5. The section concludes with a commentary by Gordon Wells of the Ontario Institute for Studies in Education.

In Section II, there are five chapters that extend the original Book Club program to new populations or new areas. Ginny's work with students with special needs is described in Chapter 6; Cindy's work with students for whom English is a second language is described in Chapter 7; Fenice's Cross-Aged Literacy Project for high school students struggling to develop literacy is presented in Chapter 8. Tanja and Taffy share their work on developing the Book Club performance-based assessment in Chapter 9. The section concludes with a chapter written by three former Book Club students—Christi Vance, Justin Ross, and Jenny Davis—who worked with Cindy for three years to develop a chapter on what they thought teachers needed to know about the program from the students' perspective. Each chapter is followed by a commentary from a leading scholar in a related area of literacy education.

Section III describes the work of five elementary classroom teacher-researchers who explored Book Club's implementation in light of their particular settings. In Chapter 11, Laura focuses on the importance of teacher inquiry as she modified and extended Book Club over a five-year period. In Chapters 12 and 13, Pam and Kristin, respectively, describe their research modifying Book Club for younger students. In Chapter 14, Kathy and Julie describe their interdisciplinary connections, bringing research in social studies into the Book Club program's format. Chapter 15 presents Julie and Sara's development of a portfolio system that aligned with the Book Club program's goals. As in Section II, each chapter is followed by a commentary from a leading scholar in a related area of literacy education.

We have many people to thank for their contributions to the Book Club project overall as well as specifically for the development of this book. While each of the project team participants named above deserves recognition and thanks, special acknowledgments are due to Ginny Goatley (Section II editor) and Laura Pardo (Section III editor). We appreciate the support of the Center for the Study of Elementary School Subjects, Michigan State University, which provided the much-needed financial base for our beginnings from 1989 to 1992, and the support from Simon & Schuster, which funded research assistantships at different phases of the research. Further, assessment work was supported by internal grants from Michigan State University's All University Research Initiative Grants. We have had help from our secretaries, Kathy Galloway and Kathy Lessard, and project assistants, Jennifer Carlson and Janice Strop. In moving from the research and curriculum development to the publication of the book, we gratefully acknowledge the support from reviewers, and from our editors, Carol Collins, Sarah Biondello, and Karl Nyberg.

Finally, we wish to thank all the students who have actively participated in the Book Club classrooms for the past six years, represented in this volume by Christi, Justin, and Jenny. Their insights, participation, and enthusiasm made the project a success and greatly contributed to our journey in developing an alternative context for literacy instruction.

T.E.R.
S.I.M.
7/1/96

SECTION I

The Book Club Program
Foundations and Components

In Section I, we describe the conceptual foundations of the Book Club program and detail the four program components:

- Community share (i.e., *whole-class setting*)
- Reading
- Writing
- Book club (i.e., *small student-led discussion groups*)

The section concludes with a commentary by Gordon Wells, a scholar interested in classroom discourse, the integration of the language arts, and collaborative research.

In Chapter 1, Susan I. McMahon and Taffy E. Raphael develop the Book Club program framework in terms of sociocultural theory, theories of reader response, and pedagogical implications for building literacy communities. This chapter is critical for understanding how the component programs interrelate. Each of the remaining four chapters is devoted to one of the four program components, focusing first on the conceptual underpinnings specific to each component, then describing the curricular goals and pedagogical methods related to the specific components. In Chapter 2, Taffy and Virginia J. Goatley describe the whole-group setting, community share, the site for community building as well as whole-group instruction. In Chapter 3, Susan characterizes the reading component of the program, explaining how Book Club facilitated students' development of this aspect of literacy. In Chapter 4, Taffy and Fenice B. Boyd describe the writing component, drawing on research conceptualizing writing as a tool for thinking, as well as research into the writing process. In Chapter 5, Susan illustrates the issues related to fostering a context in which students can successfully lead their own discussions.

The commentary that follows places the Book Club program re-

1

search into the broader context of helping develop literate children and adults. Gordon Wells discusses the broader contexts of literature-based reading instruction, of theoretical bases for instruction, of the important instructional roles teachers play, and of the relationship between convention and invention in literacy education and how all of this applies to Book Club.

CHAPTER 1

The Book Club Program
Theoretical and Research Foundations

SUSAN I. McMAHON and TAFFY E. RAPHAEL

It's September and in Laura Pardo's fifth-grade students are participating in a student-led discussion known as a "book club." Crystal, Joshua, and their peers have been engaged for a few weeks in an integrated approach to literacy instruction known as the Book Club program. Within this approach, they read literary selections, write responses in their reading logs to text sections, and engage in both small-group and whole-class discussions. Below is an excerpt from a relatively successful early "book club" conversation.

In this excerpt the students discuss their response to Winnie's dilemma in Babbitt's (1975) *Tuck Everlasting*: Should she drink the water from the spring, granting eternal life? Crystal opens this exchange by asking her peers to place themselves in Winnie's situation. (See the Appendix to this chapter for an explanation of the typographic conventions used in dialog.)

Crystal: Would you drink water from the spring?
Joshua: If I had to drink the spring water I would pick to drink the water when I am 25 because I can do more things when I'm 25 than when I'm in my teens. I can get my degree, my diploma, and I can get married. I could do anything I want and I could stay out as late as I want and I could party all night long.
Latrice: [And you wouldn't have to get whoopings.
Joshua [and I could have my own house . . . I don't get whoopings.
Latrice: You did at Alabama.
Joshua: Yeah, in Alabama.
Latrice: And you wouldn't go back to Alabama.

Joshua: I could have my own house and I can go to college and I can have a
    roommate and I can start dating. *(At this point, Camille shifted the focus
    slightly, back from when to whether or not to drink the water.)*
Camille: Well, if you could drink the spring water, or can't drink the spring
    water, which one would you pick?
Latrice: Do you mean if I could drink the spring water today?
Camille: Would you want to drink it today or would you never want to
    drink it?
Latrice: Never. I would like to die because I haven't seen my grandfather
    since I was 7 years old. I would rather go to heaven. I want to see Jesus,
    too. I would like to live the natural living. I wouldn't like to be alive for-
    ever.
Camille: Are you scared to die?
Latrice: Yeah. You wouldn't even know the experience of getting old if you
    took the spring water – you wouldn't know how it is, but in a way I
    would like to take the spring water because you could depend on your-
    self and you wouldn't have to get your diaper changed when you're so
    old and stuff.
Camille: The problem is we are not going to die the way we think we are go-
    ing to die.
Crystal: If I had to drink the water, the spring water, I would drink it at age
    10 because I wouldn't have to worry about paying taxes or paying any-
    thing like that.

This conversation reveals many of our goals for the Book Club program.
Our primary goal was to create a context within which students could engage
in meaningful conversations, on their own, about the texts they read. To that
end, this conversation illustrates how successfully the students engage in
conversation without their teacher's presence. It also shows their ability to
identify interesting conversational topics. Both Camille and Crystal invite
students to think about whether or not they would drink water from the
spring at all, while Joshua considers the age at which he might drink the
water. These topics are relevant to both the text – the plot revolves around
one family who drank the water to live forever and a young girl who must
choose whether or not to join them for eternity – and to the students' own
lives. Latrice considers her implicit beliefs about life after death, as well as the
more practical considerations of what it might be like to depend on others as
she ages. Finally, the conversation shows how the students, through their
questions and responses, encourage one another to participate.

Such interactions, encouraged within school settings, reflect our sociocultural perspective of literacy learning, one that suggests "human learning
presupposes a specific *social nature* and a process by which children grow into

the intellectual life of those around them" (Vygotsky, 1978, p. 88, emphasis added) and that leads us to rethink instructional approaches which ignore or downplay this critical component. The content of the students' discussion reflects current trends toward basing literacy instruction in "real" literature available through full-length literary selections. Further, the interaction around the literature provides a window into current approaches that argue for integrating the language arts, weaving together instruction in reading, writing, and oral language. In this book, we explore the development and extensions of the Book Club program, an instructional intervention based in sociocultural theory that guides thematically organized literature-based instruction in reading, writing, and oral language. Despite the success of Crystal, Camille, and their peers in participating in the conversation about eternal life, the conversation also provides a window into areas in which they might improve, highlighting the need for instructional support through programs such as Book Club.

Their conversation, upon closer analysis, is actually a set of paired exchanges, first between Latrice and Joshua, then between Latrice and Camille. We never hear from Trenton, a fifth member of the group. Further, while Crystal asks the question about *whether* to drink the water, Joshua actually responds by talking about *when* he would drink it. Yet Crystal does not ask for clarification. On the other hand, when Joshua finishes his contribution, Camille returns to Crystal's question, allowing no follow-up or probing of others' stance toward Joshua's decision to drink the water at age 25. While their conversation left no doubt in our mind that they brought many strengths to this discussion, it also revealed the potential benefits of instruction.

Throughout this book, we explore issues related to creating an instructional environment in which students would develop the necessary literary knowledge and literacy tools to participate fully and effectively in talk about text. We begin Section I with this chapter outlining the theories behind Book Club and discussing the work of scholars who contributed to our thinking as we developed the program. We discuss these influences in terms of: (1) conceptual issues, (2) community building, and (3) curricular design.

CONCEPTUAL ISSUES

We began our professional careers as teachers, Susan in secondary English and Taffy in elementary classrooms. Thus our experiences have provided us a considerable basis on which to build a literacy curriculum. At the same time, through university study and teaching, we had undergone changes in our thinking about teaching and learning, bringing us to a sociocultural perspective on learning. As we reflected on the design of a literature-based reading program, we wanted to incorporate practices grounded in our developing beliefs about literacy learning. The writings of Vygotsky (1978, 1986) influenced us greatly, as did those of others who were complementary to or extended Vygotsky's ideas (e.g., Bakhtin, 1986; Gee, 1990; Mead, 1934; Wertsch, 1985). We examine these influences in terms of key concepts from Vygotskian perspectives on learning and development, then turn to a discussion of the social construction of self, meanings, and discourse patterns.

Key Concepts from Vygotskian Perspectives on Learning and Development

While many scholars contributed to our thinking about sociocultural perspectives as they related to designing the Book Club program, Vygotsky was paramount. His studies and descriptions of the vital role of language in the development of thought provided the basis for the development of multiple opportunities—as individuals, in small peer-led and in whole-class settings—for both written and oral language use within the Book Club program.

Vygotsky was one of the earliest theorists to question long-accepted assumptions about learning and development. First, early scholars had suggested that learning followed development, that

> processes such as deduction and understanding . . . mastery of logical forms of thought and abstract logic all occur by themselves, without any influence from school learning. An example of such a theory is Piaget's extremely complex and interesting theoretical principles, which also shape the methodology he employs. (Vygotsky, 1978, p. 80)

Vygotsky argued that such assumptions ignore the role learning plays in promoting the development of students' intellectual abilities; ignore the way language use can help students frame problems in ways that make them meaningful and, hence, solvable; and call into question such methods of evaluating students' learning and learning potential as asking them questions that are clearly beyond the sphere of meaningful events in their lives. In terms of Book Club, such a theory might suggest that Camille, Crystal, and their peers would become more facile at literary discussion when they matured—leaving to middle school, high school, or college teachers the work of helping refine their language and literacy abilities.

Second, other early scholars argued that learning and development may be related, that "the process of maturation prepares and makes possible a specific process of learning. The learning process then stimulates and pushes forward the maturation process" (Vygotsky, 1978, p. 81). Vygotsky noted that proponents of this theory, while moving forward in their thinking about the relationship between learning and development as mutually dependent and interactive, leave "the nature of the interaction . . . virtually unexplored," which leads to questions about transfer of what is learned in one domain to other areas of learning. In short, according to Vygotsky (1978), early proponents of this belief argued for teaching the disciplines so that general learning might occur, leading to intellectual maturation or development across a variety of areas, so that "regardless of the irrelevance of these particular subjects for daily living, they were of greatest value for the pupil's mental development" (p. 82). In terms of Book Club, such a theoretical view might lead us to assume that as students had more opportunity to engage in disciplined thinking, in analysis, and in general training in memory and attention, they would transfer this knowledge to create more effective and interesting talk about text.

In rejecting these earlier perspectives on learning and development, Vygotsky proposed a theory that focused directly on students' learning within specific contexts, that examined the disparity between what children may be able to accomplish independently in contrast to what might be accomplished with support of more knowledgeable others, and that stressed the importance of language for the development of thought. In terms of Book Club, this theoretical lens leads us to examine students' earlier experiences with language and literacy and to build upon them in our instruction; to build a system that supports the kind of thinking and engagement with text that leads to interesting discussions, which, in turn, leads students to view their texts in different ways; and to create multiple opportunities for students such as Camille and Latrice to hear and use the language of literacy, literature, and critical thinking. Three concepts related to Vygotsky's theory of children's learning and development were critical to us as we created the Book Club program: (1) the role of language in the development of thought, (2) the zone of proximal development, and (3) the process of *internalization* of newly learned concepts.

The role of language in the development of thought. Vygotsky argued that the essence of humans as unique biological creatures stems from the higher-order thinking that characterizes our species, thinking made possible through our symbol systems and their use. Wertsch (1985) explains Vygotsky's distinction of higher mental functions from elementary ones in terms of four criteria. First, higher mental functions reflect a shift in control from the environment to the individual; they are characterized by voluntary regulation. Second, higher mental functions are characterized by a conscious realization of mental processing. Third, higher mental functions are social in their origins, learned first through interaction with others. Fourth, higher mental functions are mediated by the use of sign systems such as language. Our language reflects a system of signs and symbols that we can use as psychological tools to organize, reflect upon, and modify our thoughts and actions. The notion that an individual's use of signs and symbols leads to the development of higher-order thinking contributed to our thinking as we developed the Book Club program (Vygotsky, 1978; Wertsch, 1985).

Based on Vygotsky's writings, we believed that learners develop the ability for logical memory, selective attention, decision-making, and language comprehension as they use signs and symbols within a social context. The more opportunities they have to use signs or symbols as tools to construct and communicate meaning, the greater the development of higher-order thinking. While many such signs are a part of human activity, one major manifestation is language; in Western cultures higher-order thinking is associated with language use and is heavily dependent on literacy. Therefore, as we thought about Vygotsky's ideas, we saw that our instructional design would have to provide learners with multiple occasions to use language and signs as tools to construct and communicate meaning so that such use could facilitate their development of higher-order, literate thinking. In subsequent chapters, we detail the nature of students' engagement and related instruction with written language through reading, writing, and oral language use in whole-class and small peer-group settings.

The zone of proximal development and the role of more knowledgeable others. As noted above, a Vygotskian perspective on learning does not assume that children learn naturally on their own. Instead, it assumes that someone more knowledgeable guides their learning. The appropriate point for teaching is related to what Vygotsky called the zone of proximal development (ZPD). In Vygotsky's (1978) words, the ZPD is "the distance between the child's actual developmental level as determined by independent problem solving and the level of potential development as determined through problem solving under adult guidance or in collaboration with more capable peers" (p. 86). In other words, the ZPD is that area in which children can achieve a goal with the support and guidance of a more knowledgeable other. Thus the ZPD is defined by both children's level of development and the form of instruction, and it can be determined by how children seek help, how they use various aspects of the environment, and how they ask questions. Using this information enables the knowledgeable one to tailor instruction for the learner.

In successful interactions in which the teacher considers the learners' ZPD, instruction precedes development, much as a scaffold precedes the building of a house, providing temporary and adjustable support. For example, in interactions between parents and children, the parent continually assesses the child's progress. In the case of the classroom, teachers and other students assume this role. The teacher who considers each student's ZPD arranges the environment and creates a "scaffold" so that learners are able to attain a higher or more abstract perspective on the learning task. The children benefit from the conscious awareness of this more knowledgeable other who understands their current capabilities, the end goal, and the means to help them reach it.

Bruner (1989) elaborates on Vygotsky's ideas about the ZPD by identifying two important conditions that must be present for successful learning. First, learners must be willing to try; teachers cannot provide instruction on concepts associated with literacy if children are not already engaged in the processes in some way. For example, teaching specific ways to engage in talk about text, to respond in a variety of ways, and to invite peers' participation is more likely to be successful in the context described at the opening of this chapter. Students such as Joshua and Camille are more able to understand specific guidelines from their teacher, and their teacher is more likely to provide meaningful help in "teachable moments," when students are actively engaged in meaningful literacy processes.

Second, teachers must provide a scaffold that narrows the task sufficiently for the learner. This task must be neither too easy nor too difficult. As Laura's students participated in the Book Club program in September, their small-group, peer-led discussions were short (i.e., five to seven minutes). Further, students had an opportunity to record in their reading logs ideas they wanted to share in their small groups prior to the discussion. Finally, Laura often wrote a general prompt on a chart in the front of the room for those students who were not sure where to begin. All of these structures served to scaffold students' early participation in small-group discussions. As Dixon-Krauss (1995) noted, when working within students' ZPD, (1) teachers mediate learning through social interaction, (2) their roles remain flexible, and (3) their support is based on students' needs.

Internalization. Vygotsky (1978) suggested that individuals are guided by their own mental processes as they participate in social acts, but these processes are influenced by social experiences. He argued that mental functions begin first on a social, interpsychological plane, then move to an inner, intrapsychological plane, a process he called "internalization." This internalization is not a matter of simply copying the external reality of a social interaction on some preexisting plane. Instead, it is a process in which the internal plane of consciousness is formed. Further, the social context in which the individual participates plays a primary role in determining how the internal plane functions.

As with the previous ideas related to the social formation of the mind, Vygotsky's notions about internalization contributed to our thinking about how to design the Book Club program. If individuals are regulated by their own mental processes as they participate in social contexts, then classrooms can be powerful settings in which learners develop their thinking about the texts they read. Such contexts must provide forums in which students actively participate, reflect, critique, and reformulate their thinking. We hoped to provide such arenas in Book Club. However, we also realized that the ability to become active readers and writers who can thoughtfully respond to texts, critique various ideas, and synthesize these into a new understanding required literate thinking, not simply skill acquisition. Vygotsky facilitated our thinking about these issues as well in his articulation of the role of language in the development of higher-order, literate thinking (see Chapter 2 for a model of the internalization process).

Thus Vygotsky's writings on learning and development provided a strong basis from which to reimagine the context for literacy instruction that would characterize classrooms using the Book Club program. These classrooms would emphasize language and thinking, with written and oral language forming the psychological tools supporting students' literacy development. The teachers and peers would act as more knowledgeable others, sharing leadership roles across a variety of contexts. Finally, students would internalize language strategies and tools as they developed their ability to establish their own literacy goals and work together to meet them.

Social Construction of Self, Meanings, and Discourse Patterns

While Vygotsky was critical to our evolving understanding of the Book Club program and its components, we were also influenced by related scholars who both complemented and extended his theory as they explored the construction of self, of meanings, and of discourse patterns.

The social construction of self. Mead (1934) was among the first to formulate a sociocultural approach to philosophy and psychology. Like Vygotsky, he believed that learning—or more generally, consciousness—begins within social acts. Mead described language as being a creation of the social world and of the individuals in that world. Thus, for Mead, meaning is constructed within the context and act of communication. An important part of Mead's perspective on meaning construction includes how participants create a perception of self. He argued that in a social group, individuals try to assume the attitude of the others. That is, they attempt to take on the role of the other person with whom they are talking and, thus, in a way, come to know themselves as others may see them. Through this process, individuals can become self-critical. They imagine others' responses to their comments and modify their own statements as they deem necessary for communication.

Individuals in any group assume the attitudes of the others so that they can direct and modify language and behavior in ways appropriate for the group. These individuals are not only self-conscious but also self-critical. In Mead's terms, this process results in the "generalized other," or the self-perception of others' construct of them.

Mead's ideas are echoed in Gee's (1990) description of classroom interactions. Gee argues that participation in any group leads individuals to integrate language and behaviors into a sort of "identity kit" for being a member of the group. This kit includes rules about membership and conduct. Historically, participants in classrooms have constructed this identity kit in ways that obligate the teacher to assume responsibility for directing the content and flow of all interactions, using particular curricular goals as the guidelines. Thus both teachers and students have constructed roles related to these interactions, most often implicitly, as they participate in classrooms. Teachers learned these roles when they were students, and they often continue the pattern in their role as teachers. Students often have learned that their role in discussions is to answer the teacher's questions correctly.

As we considered both Mead's and Gee's ideas about the social construction of identities and roles in a classroom context, we considered a key aspect of the curriculum to be the type of interactions in which students participated and the potential roles open to them. We believed that given students' histories in schooling, they may have to reconstruct their own identity kits to include themselves as individuals who have ideas to share with others, who encourage peers to participate, and who assume responsibility for their own learning. This suggested that instruction in the Book Club program would extend beyond a focus on language and literacy curriculum to include new ways of interacting in social groups and various opportunities to construct new aspects of their identities as they interact with peers in small and whole-class groups.

The social construction of meanings. Like Mead, Bakhtin (1986) saw both the context and the act of communication as important in the development of mental processes. However, his ideas furthered our thinking by suggesting two important concepts: (1) Word meanings are constructed in social contexts and (2) interactions occur within particular speech patterns or "speech genres."

Bakhtin proposed that the meanings of words or signs resulted from both experience and consciousness. That is, to construct meanings for words, the individual has to be a participant in multiple social contexts (Sinha, 1989). Bakhtin and his associates identified four social factors that make understanding of written and oral speech possible: (1) words materialize within experience, (2) the experience occurs within a social context, (3) word meanings are thus constructed within discourse, and (4) any study of language must consider the social context (Clark & Holquist, 1984).

Bakhtin's first social factor, that both the word and its influence emerge in some outer experience, suggests that words do not exist without a social context; words come about as the result of a need to refer *to* something. Second, this outer experience must be organized socially; that is, individuals must be part of some social group in which each helps to create the discourse and, thus, the meaning. Third, Bakhtin argued that word meanings do not come from dictionaries but, instead, are derived from some memory of a previous usage in discourse; individuals' prior experiences with a word influence their understanding of its meaning and use in discourse. Fourth, he argued that any study of language and our resulting beliefs about meanings must consider this social context. Language cannot be studied independent of the social circumstance in which it takes place.

We found Bakhtin's ideas about the social construction of meaning helpful because they focused our attention on the importance of the types of discourse in group settings. While his ideas about groups, and identities within the groups, reiterate Mead's and Gee's ideas about the social construction of self, Bakhtin's contribution related to the *effect* of these interactions on the construction of meaning. Like the other two scholars, he argued that each social group has its own: (1) ways of interacting, (2) set of values, and (3) sense of shared experiences. However, he carried these ideas further by stating that since no two individuals are members of the same set of social groups, no two will have exactly the same meanings of language. This argues for the importance to students—who are members of a variety of social groups and who differ in their combination of memberships—of having frequent and sustained opportunities to participate actively in their school-group settings. Further, they need to participate not only in daily whole-class interactions but also in daily small-group ones as well. Within the smaller settings, students have greater opportunities to speak, to tune in to multiple others, and to critically evaluate how they communicate their ideas. Doing so facilitates their constructions of meaning and of themselves as literate members of a community.

The social construction of discourse patterns. In addition to the construction of word meanings in social contexts, the second contribution Bakhtin (1986) made to our thinking about our literature-based program was his argument that, when interacting with others, we adopt various speech genres. That is, as we move from one social setting to another, we modify our speech patterns to fit the new context. Much like literary genres, each speech genre has particular characteristics that set it apart from others. Participants in the social group often adjust to new speech genres subconsciously and without effort. This idea seems parallel to Gee's (1990) position that we adopt an identity kit for each group interaction. As part of our kit, we determine how we converse within particular groups.

Our review of research analyzing discourse patterns in classrooms showed a pattern consistent with Bakhtin's ideas. Several researchers found that classroom discourse is dominated by one type of speech genre – teacher *i*nitiation, student *r*esponse, and teacher *e*valuation, or I-R-E (Cazden, 1988a; Edwards & Mercer, 1987; Tharpe & Gallimore, 1988). This pattern often begins with a teacher's question. Students raise their hand to bid for turns. The teacher then selects a student for response, the response occurs, and the teacher evaluates the response before repeating the process. The teacher controls the topic, speakers, and pace. The result is that students construct their identities as being passive agents who merely react to the teacher's directions. Teachers and students become adept at this genre as they participate in classroom "discussions."

These descriptions of classroom discourse patterns indicated necessary changes to incorporate in the Book Club classrooms. If students and teachers develop their sense of self in social contexts, if this results in a type of identity kit, and if meaning is constructed in interactions, we would create multiple contexts in which students could construct self-identities and meaning through language use. Thus we would develop instructional plans that altered the dominant, apparently well-established, interactional patterns to provide students more opportunities to interact and express their ideas. Further, we would provide occasions in which children could either learn new speech genres or apply ones they already knew to classroom use. Since such learning is often implicit and difficult for children as they struggle with new expectations, we anticipated that we might need to provide explicit models of the new expected discourse patterns until the students internalized them.

Our examination of the sociocultural perspective helped us understand how the social context and the "knowledgeable other" facilitate children's development of self, of meanings, and of higher-order, literate thinking. While the theory provided guidelines for curriculum development to support some aspects of the learner's growth, it left us wanting in terms of other areas specifically related to a literature-based reading program. We knew language use was essential, but we needed more information about language use related specifically to literature. Thus we turned to the scholarship related to literary criticism and reader response.

The Role of Reader Response in a Literature-Based Reading Program

The writings of scholars in the areas of literary criticism and reader response provided a rich body of ideas for considering the content of a literature-based reading program, specifically the work focusing on the role of the reader. This research provided the basis for insights into reader–text relationships, the types of response in which readers engage, and the process of response to literature.

Reader–text relationships. The perspectives adopted in response to literature have varied throughout history (Eagleton, 1986). Phenomenologists focused on literature as an object separate from its historical context, its author, its conditions of production, and its readers. Structuralists thought that the forms of literature and how they work should be the focus of response. Those interested in the psychoanalytical stance viewed literature in terms of how it evolved–studying the author and the context of the work. Others have focused on the role of individuals in the reading process. In general, almost from the time readers began discussing texts, debate has raged about where the meaning resides–within the text or within the reader. What limited many of these earlier theories was the view that meaning exists in either one place or the other–the reader or the text. Further, none of these perspectives were consistent with our sociocultural perspective on learning. We connected more closely to beliefs about response grounded in the view that meaning results as an interaction between the reader and the text.

Rosenblatt (1938/1976) was one of the earliest authors to articulate an integrated relationship between reader and text. In what she identified as a transactional theory, she argued that meaning existed as the *result of the interaction* between the reader and text and not solely within one or the other. She explained the literary experience as the synthesis of what the text presents to the reader and what the reader brings to the act of reading. The reader brings meanings to the symbols on the page; the text guides the reader's meaning-making through its structure. This theory provides an image of an active reader, constantly working to achieve meaning with the guidance of the text. Thus both the reader and the text are essential elements in the process of constructing meaning.

Echoing Vygotsky's notion of a ZPD, Rosenblatt stressed that the reader's initial reaction to a text is the essential beginning of instruction. Children often react in terms of their own experiences and affective stance, much as Joshua did, in the conversation that opened this chapter, when he responded to Winnie's choice by considering when he would drink the water from the eternal spring, or as Latrice did when she rejected the idea of drinking the water at any age. The teacher needs to begin instruction with the child's initial reactions to further these responses and to enable readers to consider the opinions of others while returning to the text for further reflection. Rosenblatt argued that personal response must be elaborated through a social exchange of ideas.

Iser (1978), another scholar interested in the relationship between the reader and the text, supported Rosenblatt's ideas. His theory of text–reader interaction is based on the distinction between those variables of influence found in the text and those found in the reader. For him, each literary work has two sides – the artistic and the aesthetic. The artistic side is created by the author, while the aesthetic is the realization accomplished by the reader. These two aspects come together to create a literary work that results from the combination of the text and the reader's experience with it. The role of the text is to engage the imagination of the reader so that reading becomes active and creative. The reader's role is to fill in the inevitable gaps in any literary work by making inferences or creating metaphors to construct meaning. This construction, while it may create a complete understanding for one reader, will differ for every other reader. There is no one "correct" interpretation of any text. Instead, there are interpretations that are complete in that they incorporate the information the author explicitly states.

Iser argued that since the reading process is selective, the potential for any text is greater than what may result from an individual reading. Any text must leave opportunities that evoke the imagination of the readers or they will never become actively involved in the reading process. At the same time, the text must create challenges for readers by presenting unforeseen events lest readers become bored. There must be a balance between images the text provides and those readers create. Thus the reading process involves readers entering a world of visions and oscillating between the creation of these illusions and the observation of them.

Iser argued further that readers will not maintain a perfect balance, for then the text would become predictable. Instead, this balance is occasionally tipped as the text challenges readers' expectations. Active readers are constantly working to maintain a balance that is never fully achieved. Each time readers attempt to impose a consistent pattern on a text, the text creates discrepancies that readers must accommodate. The text creates an anticipation of events in its readers, who then assess these in retrospect. Readers enter the world of the text, observing events as they unfold, but do not necessarily anticipate the involvement the text requires. Frequently, readers feel the need to discuss a book in which they have been very involved. This need to talk about the text is the result of their need to understand more fully the reading experience. Thus three aspects of the reading process affect how readers construct meaning from text: (1) the actions of anticipation and retrospection, (2) the consequent unfolding of the text, and (3) the resulting impression of reality.

Iser's description of the meaning-making process is consistent with Rosenblatt's and with a sociocultural perspective, since it recognizes the active role of the reader in the construction of meaning; however, both of these scholars addressed meaning-making without noting the role of the social context in the construction of knowledge. Others who have studied reader response are consistent with Iser and Rosenblatt. Both Scholes and Fish have highlighted intertextual connections, Scholes in his discussions of connections among texts and Fish in his discussions of connections among readers of the same texts. Scholes (1985) based his argument on the notion of readers developing power over the text to guide their own understanding. One means of assuming this control is to connect new texts with others previously read. Response, therefore, is the result of ongoing compositions created in the social context in which they are read, since all texts are related to other texts. Fish (1980) underscores the role of community in a single reader's construction of meaning. He argues that interpretations are constructed within groups as a result of their interactions with one another.

These ideas highlighted the need for Book Club to incorporate students' prior knowledge and experiences into the act of reading to shape the meaning-making process. Traditional skills-based approaches to reading instruction frequently minimize this in favor of the text and the skills associated with successful reading. Further, the context in which readers interact with text also influences the meaning constructed. This context includes facilitating readers' abilities to make intertextual connections on multiple levels and building a community of literate individuals whose interactions help them develop interpretations of texts. Changing to a literature-based approach required us to design a program that attended to the readers, to what they bring to the act of reading, and to the context in which reading occurs. With our focus on readers, we found the research on the range of complexity of reader response to be relevant.

Types of reader response. Types of reader response have been of interest to researchers over the past two decades, with studies that have identified a range and variety of readers' responses. For example, some researchers examined the ranges of responses by categorizing the final written or oral comments readers made after completing the reading (e.g., Odell & Cooper, 1976; Purves & Beach, 1972). In their classic text, Purves and Beach (1972) delineated five types of responses: (1) the personal statement, (2) descriptive responses, (3) interpretative responses, (4) evaluative responses, and (5) miscellaneous responses. They found a connection between readers' understanding and their interest in the text, which, not surprisingly, focused more on content than on form. They also found that readers were influenced intellectually, emotionally, and attitudinally by what they read.

Later, Odell and Cooper (1976) amended Purves and Beach's categories by adding subcategories. They divided personal statements into those about the reader and those about the text. Descriptive responses could be narrative or could focus on particular aspects of the work referenced. Interpretative statements could allude to parts of the work or to the entire work. Finally, evaluative statements could refer to the evocativeness, the meaningfulness, and/or to the construction of the work.

As a body of work, this research on response to literature helped us envision all that students are capable of and the multiple dimensions the instructional program could include. At the same time, the very nature of the data—responses collected after completing the reading—represents a "final product," a response after reading has ended. The research did little to inform us about the *process* of response, which was important to us, given our socio-cultural framework and its emphasis on the *development* of thought.

Exploring the process of student response. Research on the process of reader response has attempted to capture response throughout the reading process as well as to identify various factors that potentially influence it during the course of reading. For example, Squire's (1964) findings indicated that response develops and changes during the reading process. Similarly, Langer (1990a) documented very different responses that evolved during the reading process. In her research, Langer made three assumptions about reading: (1) Reading is an interpretive act, (2) readers follow certain conventions signaled by the text, and (3) readers need to personalize or objectify their reading experience with the text. While primarily focusing on the reader, these assumptions do not negate the role of the text that guides readers' experiences as they enter the world of the text. At the same time, it is the readers' purposes for reading that also guide their experience and interpretation. These purposes might be efferent (Rosenblatt, 1938/1976), resulting from a quest for scientific knowledge (Bruner, 1986), or aesthetic (Rosenblatt, 1938/1976), resulting from a quest for narrative experience (Bruner, 1986). Approaching text from an efferent stance, the reader is seeking logical, rational meaning: approaching from an aesthetic stance, the reader is seeking a more emotional experience.

Langer's (1990a) research detailing the stances readers assume throughout the response process expanded our understanding of readers' constructions of meaning and responses to that meaning. While noting that readers' goals within a stance vary as a function of the nature of the text, Langer identified four recursive stances readers assume: (1) being out and stepping into an envisionment, (2) being in and moving through an envisionment, (3) stepping back and rethinking what one knows, and (4) stepping out and objectifying the experience.

While a sociocultural perspective raised questions for us about the universality of these stances, we felt they had instructional potential. Vygotsky's arguments about the role of language on the development of thought and Bakhtin's notions that meanings are constructed in social contexts influenced our decision to adopt Langer's stances to provide teachers and students with explicit language for classroom use. This language not only helped teachers make a hidden, mental process explicit for students to understand, it also helped students develop a language to discuss their developing responses to texts.

In addition to research that attempted to characterize the process of response, scholars have also explored potential factors that influence the types of response and the response process. For example, some identified developmental, personal, and social factors as being highly influential (e.g., Hickman, 1983). Others noted that reading ability influences the response process (e.g., Eeds & Wells, 1989). Still others noted the influence of differences in the ways readers elect to process text (Langer, 1990a; MacClean, 1988); that is, how much they balance their own prior knowledge with knowledge presented in the text. Despite the complexity, research suggests there are many ways to encourage response and deepen readers' understandings of the multiple texts that they read (e.g., Pappas & Brown, 1987; Strickland, Dillon, Finkhouser, Glick, & Rogers, 1989).

Summary of Theoretical Concepts

As we considered how a sociocultural perspective contributed to our design of the Book Club program, we identified four key principles. First, language develops thinking and learners construct meanings–which are eventually internalized–in their interactions with others. Second, learning is best facilitated as more knowledgeable others guide the learner with appropriate tasks. Third, individuals construct a sense of self as they participate in social contexts; this identity includes their own and others' roles in the group. Fourth, individuals construct meanings for language within their experiences and develop speech genres particular to given social contexts.

The research exploring reader response provided the basis for three additional principles. First, we believed readers interact with texts within a social context and that meaning results from this transaction. Second, readers respond to texts in multiple ways, so a reading program should promote variation in the kinds and ways students represent their responses. Third, since response varies depending on readers' stances and points of progression through a text, students should have opportunities to respond throughout the reading process.

Given our belief in the importance of the social context and reader response, we shifted our focus to the classroom learning environment. In the next section, we describe the basis of creating a social context in which students saw themselves as members of a community of learners.

COMMUNITY BUILDING

Book Club explicitly changes traditional classroom contexts in three ways. First, students construct concepts of themselves and their peers as active contributors to the learning environment (see Chapter 10 for a description of Book Club from participating students' perspectives). Second, a context rich in language enables learners to express their developing thoughts. Third, the context provides opportunities for the teacher to monitor student thinking and provide instruction within the learners' ZPD. The targets for change from more traditional practices include: (1) students' opportunities for interactions, (2) students' opportunities to respond to texts in multiple ways, (3) an expansion of the nature of interactions, and (4) the teacher's role in these interactions. The goal for all of these adjustments was to facilitate students' constructions of themselves as members of a literate community. Each of these is developed further in subsequent chapters, so we summarize them here.

Opportunities for Student-to-Student Interactions

In classrooms, children are part of a community larger than most other social groups. While in more traditional classrooms students do talk and are frequently aware that others are listening to what they are saying, they cannot talk often nor do they get regular feedback because of the size of the group and the need for many children to participate. Tharpe and Gallimore (1988) note that most interactions in classrooms consist of teacher-directed questions that require only convergent, factual response. Such a process, often only probing for a "correct" response, does not value student thinking nor does it provide the assistance students need to develop literate thought.

Teachers frequently believe that they must direct all interactions because: (1) They are responsible for meeting curricular goals, (2) they must monitor student learning, and (3) they believe students will not assume responsibility for their own learning. Thus, even if they include small-group discussions as a regular part of their instruction, they maintain leadership and control of the discussion (McMahon, 1996). While these reactions are understandable, a sociocultural framework suggests that such interactions hamper student learning and the development of literate thinking since the discourse does not promote optimal use of language among all students, does not encourage students' efforts to clearly articulate ideas for one another without teacher interference, and does not afford the teacher maximum opportunities to monitor student thinking. Thus, to provide occasions for students to articulate, clarify, and expand their developing ideas, teachers need to increase students' opportunities to interact with a meaningful audience (e.g., peers) (see Chapter 5).

Opportunities to Respond in Multiple Ways

In addition to providing forums for oral discourse, Book Club provided ways to encourage children to represent their ideas in a variety of written formats. Bakhtin noted that there are two primary ways teachers traditionally ask students to respond to texts: (1) to memorize and (2) to retell text in one's own words (Emerson, 1986). These place very different demands on learners, but they also result in various attitudes toward texts. When asked to memorize another's words, students may think the words have taken on an authoritarian mode because they cannot doubt the words or change them. To modify a text in such a situation constitutes making a mistake. This approach leads children to construct an understanding of texts as documents with a single interpretation. Their role as readers, then, becomes discovering that meaning. Children constructing such a concept about reading eventually devalue their own response in favor of the "correct" one. Certainly, one of the goals for Book Club was to guide learners in understanding that response is related to information in the text and that some interpretations may appear to be more reasonable than others; however, we also wanted to elicit student response and the thinking behind it. Clearly, from our perspective, a focus on memorizing texts or "main" ideas within texts was not satisfactory. Such a focus removes the power from readers and places it totally within the text. This led us to reflect on Bakhtin's second mode of interacting, retelling.

According to Bakhtin, the second way children are asked to learn text in school is to retell it in their own words. This is a more flexible and responsive approach since the speaker can illustrate originality in how he or she retells the text. One aspect of community we wanted to incorporate was to encourage more flexible ways of interacting with texts. Retelling is particularly valuable for examining initial response to and comprehension of text, so instruction could begin here and move beyond by teaching readers how to base these responses in the events of the text. Learners then realize that both the texts and they, as readers, contribute to meaning construction and appreciation of literature (see Chapter 4).

The Role of the Teacher

In more traditional classrooms, the teacher's opportunities to monitor student thinking is severely limited. Written work is often confined to single-answer responses to questions on worksheets, and oral language is restricted to responding to teacher-generated (Edwards & Mercer, 1987), text-based (R. C. Anderson, Hiebert, Scott, & Wilkinson, 1985) comprehension questions. Such instructional designs do not provide for a community of learners with multiple opportunities to interact in a variety of ways leading to literate thinking. Instead, communication is controlled, restricting learners' language use and teachers' abilities to build instruction on what children already know.

We felt strongly that teachers using Book Club would have a critical role in creating the classroom community in which Book Club would thrive and in explicitly teaching a range of language conventions, comprehension strategies, literary elements, and literature response (see Chapter 2 for further discussion of the teachers' roles and the content of instruction). In taking this stance, we aligned with researchers who have argued that, like the more traditional language conventions that have long been a part of the instructional curriculum, both comprehension and response can and should be taught (e.g., Dole, Duffy, Roehler, & Pearson, 1991; Lucking, 1976; Purves & Beach, 1972). However, we also firmly believed that teachers need not always place themselves in the role of explicit instructor. Rather, there are several roles that they may assume, depending on their students' background and ability to achieve important goals on their own (see Chapters 2 and 3).

CURRICULAR DESIGN

The Book Club program expands elementary children's daily experiences with language in terms of both the amount and kinds of interactions in which they participate to strengthen their literacy capabilities. First and foremost, it facilitates students' capabilities related to literacy. While more traditional reading programs teach the "mechanics" of reading, we know that such programs often fail to teach an appreciation for and enjoyment of reading (Walmsley & Walp, 1989). Therefore, Book Club not only enables children to develop their literacy capabilities, it also encourages a desire to read and an appreciation of texts because children have extended opportunities to read, write, and discuss their texts.

Reading

In more traditional classrooms, reading is bounded both in terms of the kinds of texts children read and the amount of time they spend reading. What they read is frequently limited to texts required by the curriculum without consideration of the students' interests or prior knowledge. Historically, these texts have been found in commercially prepared basal readers written to teach reading and, as such, containing constrained language with limited vocabulary (K. S. Goodman, Shannon, Freeman, & Murphy, 1988). In addition to limitations on what students read, the time provided for reading is measurable in terms of minutes a day (Walmsley & Walp, 1989).

In the Book Club program, we were committed to literature, to texts written to convey meaning. These provide better models of language use than texts written to facilitate reading instruction and, thus, are more likely to contribute to literate thinking. Second, we were committed to texts that related to students' interests and helped build students' knowledge. Third, we were committed to extended periods of time each day devoted to interacting with texts; that is, for a minimum of 15 minutes each day during Book Club, students read books. (While 15 minutes may not seem long, we recognized that in traditional programs, students often read one day per week, then spent the remaining four days engaged in skill lessons and workbook activities. Further, students read throughout the day, in addition to the time spent during Book Club.) This occurred through reading aloud or silently, reading with a partner or alone, or having the teacher or a peer read aloud to the class. By designing a program with these considerations for reading instruction, we incorporated multiple opportunities for students to interact with texts in which authors had organized language in a variety of ways to convey meaning (see Chapter 3).

Writing

Just as we defined standards for the reading component, we developed standards for writing to ensure that students used writing to engage in (1) personal reflection on and response to their daily reading, (2) contextualized comprehension and response strategies, and (3) extended thinking as they synthesized, analyzed, and expanded upon ideas prompted by their daily reading, writing, and discussion activities. At a minimum, students engaged in daily writing of extended texts (i.e., beyond simple one-word and short answers to given questions) that related to the texts they had read. There were two main writing opportunities within Book Club: (1) daily writing in their reading logs and more focused writing using "think-sheets," and (2) extended writing through participation in the full process of planning, drafting, revising, and publishing as students developed essays or created content-area reports. Together, these writing experiences served important functions for both students and teachers. For students, daily writing enabled them to become engaged in extended written activities, allowing them to use language in a variety of ways to construct their own meaning. For teachers, the written student texts provided a window into the way in which students were appropriating taught response strategies and transforming them in ways that they found personally meaningful (see Chapter 4).

Discussion

The Book Club program devoted attention to the learners' use of oral language in the classroom. To this end, we designed two different contexts in which children discussed daily the texts they had read and ones they had written: community share, the whole-class discussion context; and book club, the small peer-led discussion groups for which the program was named.

Community share was the site for the teacher-led whole-class discussion. It provided an important forum for creating the discourse community to which all students in the class belonged, bringing together the smaller book clubs to form a single, coherent unit. In this setting, the teacher modeled conversational strategies and ways of responding and constructing meaning; helped students make connections across their different book club discussions; raised issues that might have been important to the story but did not emerge during book clubs; clarified issues peers were unable to explain on their own; and helped bridge to the thematic content in which the book club discussions were embedded. Further, through observing students in the small-group and whole-class discussions, teachers acquired important information to guide their decisions about instructional focuses to bring into subsequent sessions (see Chapter 2).

Book clubs were the small, student-led discussion groups in which students had the opportunity to discuss with peers the issues and ideas they found interesting, relevant, challenging, and exciting in the text that they had read. Such a setting was critical to students' language and literacy development. Guided by their reading log entries, students in this context controlled both the content and the flow of the discussion. They were responsible for introducing ideas, clarifying one another's comments and questions, balancing talk among the participants, and so forth—behavior and activity that, within more traditional classrooms, lies primarily within the teacher's domain. For the teacher, book clubs provided a window similar to that of the reading logs. By observing and listening to the students' discussions, the teacher gained insights into the way students had appropriated and transformed conversational strategies, discussion techniques, and strategies for constructing meaning (see Chapter 5).

The reading, writing, and discussion opportunities had the potential to provide students with multiple experiences manipulating signs and symbols associated with language. With these components defined, we then considered how to embed instruction within them.

Instruction

Vygotsky's argument for the important role of the more knowledgeable other underscored the opportunities for instruction within the components of Book Club. Both teachers and peers served in an instructional capacity within the program, enhancing students' abilities to read, to use writing as a tool for thinking as well as a means for expression, and to discuss important issues related to the texts that they read. Instruction was closely connected to students' needs in each of the components, so subsequent chapters describe instructional focuses. Since any discussion of instructional decisions in this chapter would be redundant with what readers can find elsewhere in the book, let us finish by saying that all instructional decisions were grounded in Book Club's overarching goals of fostering literate discourse among elementary children who willingly participated in reading, writing, and discussing texts. Further, all instruction was also based on the needs of the particular students in a given context. After all, effective literacy instruction begins with where children are and what they need, and it maintains the goal of enhanced literacy development for all.

CONCLUDING COMMENTS

In summary, the Book Club program was designed as an alternative approach to literacy instruction, and consisted of four interrelated components: reading, community share, writing, and book club. Instructional support guaranteed that all students in the classroom had access to the texts and opportunity to participate as members of the community in all program components. Justin Ross, one of the graduates of Book Club (see also Chapter 10), shared the students' perspective on Book Club with teachers at the 1995 annual meeting of the Michigan Reading Association. He summarized features critical to his own literacy development:

> One of my favorite things about Book Club is that we get a chance to talk with our peers. When we talk with our peers we find out about other people's ideas, have a chance to say something really important, get to tell what the author should do better or different, ask questions about the book, and express our feelings and ideas. Also, sometimes books were hard for me to understand. In Book Club, other students, or the teacher, helped one another to understand the story. So, a big advantage of Book Club was talking with friends. Talking is important because you can have a say in what you feel about a story or a certain topic, and your peers will listen. This helps you get better knowledge

about the story or a certain topic. What I mean is, you get to say what you want to say. This is important because kids have important things to say. Also, Book Club discussions let teachers know if kids are doing better or learning more about books.

What we hope is that through Book Club, students such as Justin will see themselves as and become members of the community of lifelong readers, writers, and critical thinkers.

APPENDIX

Throughout this volume, the following typographic conventions are used for dialog:

///	Indicates pauses within the speaker's turn. Each note (/) indicates one second.
[	Indicates overlappping talk.
. . .	Indicates the speaker's thoughts were interrupted by talk, but the other speaker might have begun during a slight pause in the first speaker's turn.
italic	Indicates the speaker stressed this word. For example, "I want you to do that *now*."
( )	Indicates author comments, including interpretation of how someone stated something, or what other group members were doing at the same time.
" "	Indicates the speaker was reading from a log or book.
,	Indicates slight pauses in speech.
(?)	Indicates the speaker said something that was not distinguishable on the tape.

CHAPTER 2

Classrooms as Communities

Features of Community Share

TAFFY E. RAPHAEL and VIRGINIA J. GOATLEY

When we walked into Laura Pardo's fifth-grade classroom (March 1995), we were struck by the sense of community among Laura and the students. They were beginning a Book Club unit about the Civil War, thematically related to their year-long study of our nation's development. Their discussions underscore their classroom community's shared knowledge, including:

- Our nation's history
- Debatable issues that have divided our country historically and presently (e.g., economic disparities, freedom of choice)
- Relevant literature (e.g., Avi's [1984] *The Fighting Ground*, portraying characters' views of war and willingness to fight for their beliefs)
- Classroom activities (e.g., a whole-class project simulating a wagon train heading west)
- "Intertextual" connections (e.g., relating Jethro's farm in I. Hunt's [1964] *Across Five Aprils* to science text topics about the southern Illinois glacier-formed, rich farmlands)

This sense of community—with numerous examples of shared understandings—demonstrates the importance of community share, Book Club's whole-group component. Early in the year, Laura and the students had learned the significance of sharing their ideas, responses, and questions in a community where it was safe to take risks. Further, they developed a shared language with which to talk about the issues, ideas, and information they encountered in each unit. This shared level of knowledge provides a sound basis for their current area of study. During community share, students interact with their classroom peers in ways that lead to a rich and varied basis from which their talk about text develops.

Since community share is primarily teacher-led, it provides teachers with critical opportunities for instructing, modeling, building intertextual connections among different book clubs within a unit or across units over time, initiating "repair activities" when interpretations of story events conflict with conventional knowledge, and, in general, helping students participate as active members of their educational community. Community share is also critical to building community in the classroom, inviting students to share with the entire class thoughts and ideas that emerged in their book clubs. Through this component, students maintain their connections with classroom peers, become "visitors" to the content and issues raised in other book clubs, and are comfortable forming new book clubs for each thematic unit. In this chapter, we focus on community share in terms of its conceptual foundations and curricular content.

CONCEPTUAL FOUNDATIONS OF COMMUNITY SHARE

Community share developed from three lines of theory and research in the sociocultural perspective. First, scholars (e.g., Harré, 1984, 1986; Vygotsky, 1981) have described the importance of social interactions from which individual's learning develops. Community share is one of the key social contexts of the Book Club program in which such learning occurs. Second, scholars (e.g., Edwards & Mercer, 1987; G. Wells, 1993) have articulated the dual functions of schooling as a site for encouraging invention while simultaneously teaching what our culture has determined as conventional knowledge. Community share provides an opportunity to convey both the multiple interpretations texts evoke and our culture's conventional knowledge and understandings that may influence and shape individuals' interpretations. Third, scholars (e.g., Gee, 1990; Swales, 1990) have argued that discourse communities function as important groups within which ideas are developed, shared, and refined. Community share creates an important context for students' development of a discourse community within which conceptions and beliefs can be developed, articulated, supported, and challenged.

Community Share as Context for Learning and Sharing

The sense of community and students' active participation within it are critical because all higher psychological processes originate in social interaction. That is, "any function appears on the social plane, and then on the psychological plane. First, it appears between people as an interpsychological category, and then within the child as an intrapsychological category" (Vygotsky, 1981, p. 163). The concept of movement from the *inter*psychological to *intra*psychological planes in learning suggests that whatever a child is able to do as an individual comes from and begins with those experiences that arise out of social interactions. Community share is a primary site for students to engage in social interactions with their teacher. While "more knowledgeable others" include both teachers and students, community share is the teacher's opportunity to generate discussion around specific topics. However, it is more than simply a site for interactions among teacher and students. The nature of these interactions reflects a "community-of-learners" model of development. Rogoff (1994) argues that a community-of-learners model assumes "that learning is a process of transforming participation in shared sociocultural endeavors" (p. 210). In Book Club, these shared endeavors relate to language and literacy development, and discourse is the primary means of participation and transformation. Therefore we must consider the role of discourse in communities and change instruction to reflect our language use in the learning process. Classroom talk is critical to learning the conventions and purposes of our written symbol systems (Corson, 1984; Florio-Ruane, 1991; Goldenberg, 1992/93; G. Wells, 1990b).

Harré (1984, 1986) has developed a useful representation of the inter- to intrapsychological processes by which learning occurs. Figure 2.1 is Gavelek and Raphael's (1996) modification of what Harré termed the "Vygotsky space." The figure displays two planes, the *public–private* and the *social–individual*. These two planes are a continuum that, when crossed, form four quadrants depicting different ways in which language is used in the learning process. Discourse along the *public–private* plane includes, at one end, language use that is visible, external, and open and, at the other end, language use that is invisible, internal, and thus unavailable for observation. Discourse along the *social–individual* plane represents, at one end, language use among individuals within a social setting and, at the other end, language use by an individual working independently.

Movement among the four quadrants depicted in Figure 2.1 involves four processes:

- Appropriation
- Transformation
- Publication
- Conventionalization

Learners engage in these processes throughout their formal and informal schooling as they develop and learn language conventions, concepts, and the

FIGURE 2.1.   The Vygotsky Space

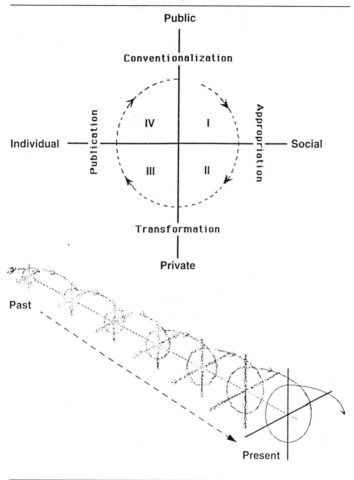

This figure first appeared in Gavelek & Raphael, 1996. Reprinted by permission of *Language Arts*.

knowledge of our society. Students acquire this knowledge to use "as is," as well as transform the knowledge in unique ways. Taken together, these processes describe "internalization." The four processes of the Vygotsky space can be applied to children's literacy learning and inform the type of discourse that might occur in our literacy communities (Gavelek & Raphael, 1996).

Appropriation. Appropriation is the process by which students adopt concepts, strategies, ideas, and language that have been introduced and shared within the social and public discourse of quadrant I (Q_I). The discourse of Q_I occurs publicly and socially as teachers engage in instructional strategies such as thinking aloud while reading to students, explicitly teaching (Roehler, Duffy, & Meloth, 1986), facilitating student discussions (Gilles, 1990; Roller & Beed, 1994; Wiencek & O'Flahavan, 1994), and so forth. Within Q_I, students hear the language of literacy as they participate in and raise questions about the concepts, strategies, and conventions associated with literacy.

One goal of schooling is to help students develop their abilities to engage in and use the social discourse associated with literacy to pursue individual goals. During the appropriation process, students learn about strategies, knowledge, and concepts through discussion in public contexts. In doing so, they begin "internalizing" the public knowledge as it was originally learned or experienced so that it becomes a useful and meaningful tool for their own individual activities. Since these appropriations are private, they are not observable, but they can be inferred when teachers observe students' products (e.g., written reading log entries) created within quadrant II.

For example, when Laura leads community share activities, she models ways of constructing personal response to literature, making intertextual connections, and engaging in critical evaluation. During many of her units, she leads discussions that help students learn about literary elements (e.g., plot, character) and initiates activities that invite discussion from different points of view. Throughout the Civil War unit, she read aloud from *Across Five Aprils*. When she came to a section that described the Battle of Shiloh, she used this event to model intertextual connections. She thought aloud about how the mention of Shiloh in this book reminded her of the report one of the students, Katrina, had written and presented a few weeks earlier. Laura conveyed the language of intertextual connections, identified what had prompted her to make the connections, and, simultaneously, encouraged recognition that the texts produced by the students were valuable resources from which students might draw ideas.

In addition to modeling the use of intertextual connections, Laura encourages the students to share their own connections with one another. In the Civil War unit, students participated in one of four different book clubs, each reading a different historical fiction trade book whose story took place during the Civil War era, thus providing many opportunities for connections across the stories. For example, during one of the community shares following students' book club discussions, Charles explained an exciting event from *Turn Homeward, Hannalee* (Beatty, 1984), the book his group was reading. The two main characters, Hannalee and her brother, had been sent by the northern army, against their will, to work in the Indiana and Ohio mills and had escaped to find their way back to Georgia. Charles described an event in which a peddler helped the two main characters during their journey home.

Katrina's book club was reading Reit's (1988) *Behind Rebel Lines* and knew that their main character, Emma, had disguised herself as a peddler during a spy mission to the Confederate states. After Charles described Hannalee's experience, Katrina and her group connected the two books as they conjectured that if the timing were right, the peddler helping Hannalee and her brother could have been Emma, the main character from their book, in disguise. The public and social discourse during community share set the context for building the classroom community's knowledge about the Civil War and the importance of drawing connections among various novels.

Similarly, another teacher, Deb Woodman, had conducted minilessons on literature response throughout her units in her fourth/fifth-grade classroom. For some community share sessions, she explicitly taught students how to engage in personal response, drawing connections between story events and their own lives as well as encouraging them to share and support their reactions to texts. She taught them strategies and forms of response and encouraged them to invent new types of responses. In one particular lesson, she helped students construct a new personal response, one they called "in the character's shoes" (see Chapter 11 for further discussion). Through both modeling and explicit discussion within the social and public discourse of community share, Deb taught students how to *use, construct,* and *value* response. Thus students could appropriate specific response strategies as well as the very concepts of constructing and valuing response.

In the previous examples, evidence that students appropriated what they had learned in Q_1 was inferred from public oral and written forms. When listening to students' discussions during the public and social discourse of book club and community share, Laura heard examples of intertextual connections, suggesting that students had appropriated this form of text engagement. During private and social discourse, such as writing in their reading logs, students wrote personal responses reflecting formats they had been explicitly taught, some introduced by their teacher and others (e.g., "in the character's shoes") constructed as a class. Such written responses provided further evidence of students' appropriation.

Community share is a critical public–social space within which the language of literacy is modeled, used, and exchanged among teachers and students, and among peers. It is also a context in which ideas that were initially introduced, then transformed by students in their own literate activities, become public once again. To see how this function of community share evolved, consider the processes of transformation and publication noted in Figure 2.1.

Transformation. We do not want students simply to appropriate what they have learned in order to reproduce particular strategies, concepts, or interpretations. Rather, one of the goals of education is to help students modify, adapt, or transform what they have learned to achieve their own goals. Like quadrant II, evidence of transformation suggested by the private-individual space of quadrant III must be inferred from students' individual and independent literacy activities. For example, entries from students' reading logs provide evidence that they not only appropriate but also make changes, or transform, what they have learned and used in more social spaces.

For example, Dana, a student in Laura's classroom, invented a new form of response she called a "picture prediction." This example reflects her transforming two types of responses learned earlier in the year: drawing a picture of an important or favorite text event and making a prediction of an upcoming event. By combining the two categories, Dana showed evidence of transformation. Similarly, Kami described a form of author's craft that she and Charles had called a "picture sequence." Kami described how during reading, she thinks of a series of mental pictures that are created by the author's words. Kami then explained that she drew these pictures in her reading log. During community share, Laura highlighted how Kami had invented a new form of response by combining author's craft, pictures, and sequencing. The transformations that Dana, Kami, and Charles conveyed during community share are not directly observable but can be inferred by reading their logs and listening to their discussions. Through the process of "publication," we are able to infer their transformations.

Publication. In the public–individual space represented by quadrant IV (Q_{IV}), we have access to the private thinking that characterizes Q_{II} and Q_{III}. Dana's and Kami's logs provide public evidence of their new response forms transformed from more social–public and social–individual language use. During community share, they presented their new categories to their peers. They engaged in the process of publication as they shared their new ways of responding and as they talked about how these forms of response can be used with other chapters or books. The publication process reflects movement from the private–individual language use that characterizes Q_{III} to the public–individual discourse (i.e., personal transformations presented in a social realm) that characterizes Q_{IV}. Thus community share is not only important for initial social interactions associated with Q_I, but is also a critical site for engaging in language use that makes public one's individual approaches and forms of literate behaviors. It is through community share that such individually transformed literate activities become part of the conventional activity within the classroom.

Conventionalization. As Dana's and Kami's response forms, "picture sequence" and "picture prediction," became accepted and encouraged, the forms were added to the response categories chart on the classroom wall, a process of conventionalization wherein concepts that emerge through individual activities become part of the public and social discourse of the classroom.

Thus the public–social space of quadrant I is foundational to the entire learning process. The discourse within this quadrant (1) introduces concepts, (2) encourages the disposition to work creatively with the concepts, and (3) validates students' emerging inventive ways of modifying and transforming what they have learned. Dana's, Kami's, and Charles's transformations of reading log response entries would not have happened without a history of public and social discourse about response forms. It would also have been unlikely without a history of teachers sharing their own innovations in response and encouraging students to do so as well. As G. Wells and Chang-Wells (1992) note:

> Vygotsky considered the development of cognition to result from participation with others in goal-directed activity, in the course of which the learner encounters particular problems and comes to understand and be able to resolve them with the aid of the intellectual tools inherited from previous generations and with the assistance provided by the members of his or her immediate community. (p. 31)

Community share provides the public contexts that are fundamental to students' individual cognitive development, the means by which literacy can continue to develop and build upon past histories of the culture, the community, and the individual.

Community Share and the Functions of Schooling

In building upon past histories, schooling serves two critical functions: convention and invention. As Edwards and Mercer (1987) note:

> Schools serve many social and cultural purposes, . . . but their institutional *raison d'etre* is always their function of passing on a part of the accumulated knowledge of a society, and evaluating students' success in acquiring this knowledge. . . . But it consists of much more than given "facts"; it includes ways of operating on the world, and of making judgements. . . . The boundaries of educational knowledge are continuously marked out, and reinforced, in classroom discourse. (pp. 2–3)

Edwards and Mercer describe the two critical functions of schooling. One of these functions – helping young learners acquire the *conventional* knowledge of our culture and society–may actually come into conflict with the second purpose of schooling, *invention*.

Invention speaks to educating our children to be more than what society currently can offer. It emphasizes their learning to use their own creativity, imagination, and other resources to invent new ways of thinking, interpreting the world, or making "things" work. Schooling must balance the transfer of the conventional knowledge of our society with the development of learners who are able to evaluate critically and construct new knowledge as well as to recognize how that knowledge is culturally and socially bound. This distinction gets to the heart of philosophical debates about the nature of knowledge, whether it is something "out there" that can be identified, quantified, and passed on to future generations or whether it is socially negotiated among the individuals within a society–to be questioned, interpreted, and changed over time. Within a sociocultural perspective, the emphasis is on the socially negotiated nature of meaning, which, when applied to classroom literacy instruction, raises questions about what constitutes the boundaries of interpretation. Community share is critical in providing a balance between these two goals of schooling, for it is there that students learn the conventional knowledge of our society and, at the same time, are encouraged to evaluate, interpret, and critique the texts they read to construct their own meaning.

The nature of the convention–invention conflict is illustrated in an example drawn from Gavelek and Raphael (1996):

> students in Ms. Woodman's room had elected to read and discuss Lowry's (1989) Newbery award winning book, *Number the Stars*, in winter, 1991, shortly after the award had been announced. A group of students had read one of the chapters in which the Danish king was tormented by German forces. In the small group, one student asked, "Why would Hitler want to take over Denmark?" . . . (Tron) responded authoritatively that the Danish king had a lot of oil and wouldn't share it with his neighbors, so they went in to get the oil. . . . (He) had applied his knowledge of the Persian Gulf War (which was in progress at this time) to his reading of Lowry's novel. (p. 190)

In this example, Tron certainly integrated his personal experience with the text they were reading. However, his interpretation was based on faulty information. While knowledge may be constructed, no credible person would accept the reasoning behind Tron's explanation of Hitler's actions.

Community share served as an important context for building students' knowledge of World War II history. In the community share that followed this book club, a series of whole-group activities helped students access or acquire important background knowledge about Germany and Denmark during the World War II era. After learning this conventional knowledge, students are able to better understand, make judgments about, and interpret text events. With such knowledge, students understand that while Tron's interpretation may have shown creativity, it is in conflict with our conventional knowledge.

This illustration underscores how our language and school cultures promote both particular ways of thinking and students' perspectives of what "counts" as learning. As Barnes (1976) suggests:

> A school in its very nature is the place where communication goes on: that is what it is for. Education is a form of communication. . . . As the form of communication changes, so will the form of what is learnt. One kind of communication will encourage the memorizing of details, another will encourage pupils to reason about the evidence, and a third will head them towards the imaginative reconstruction of a way of life. (pp. 14–15)

Community share activities enable teachers such as Laura and Deb to help balance and maintain the multiple goals of schooling: developing conventional knowledge while encouraging invention and interpretation beyond the "givens."

Community Share to Establish a Discourse Community

Students are members of various communities where they engage in social situations with others to develop their definitions and uses of literacy. Within these communities (e.g., home, school, work), they build and value both conventional knowledge and the importance of invention and interpretation. These literacy interactions enable students to become integral members of our literate society, one in which we define literate thinking in terms of both oral and written abilities (see Langer, 1991; G. Wells, 1990b). We want to encourage our students to think of themselves as members of this literate society, to value literate thinking, and to have the tools for engaging in it. One of the goals of schooling is to help students acquire these tools and the knowledge needed to be a full participant in the broader society.

At the same time, students are also a part of smaller communities that develop around them. Bloome (1986) suggests:

> In every community, whether a classroom, home, or work community, literacy is constantly being built and rebuilt. People are continuously using literacy to signal their membership in a community, to accomplish goals within a community, and to structure their community. The nature of literate activity within a community will depend, in large part, on the nature of that community's goals, how it structures itself, and its history. (p. 5)

In Book Club, the students are using language and literacy by talking with each other, sharing ideas, and building upon their shared knowledge in developing their community. There are daily routines and forms of discussion unique to their classroom, as they build upon conventions while inventing new forms of response and means of discussion.

A line of scholarship useful for conceptualizing what it means to be a participant in a literate society is the study of discourse communities (e.g., Swales, 1990). Swales (1990) distinguishes between speech and discourse communities, noting "speech communities are centripetal (they tend to absorb people into that general fabric), whereas discourse communities are centrifugal (they tend to separate people into occupational or specialty-interest groups)" (p. 24). The Book Club community did both: enabling students to incorporate the larger literacy ideals of society while creating a special interest group in which students defined their own versions of literacy and literacy ideals through participation with their teachers and peers.

Swales outlined six criteria of a discourse community that helped shape the way in which we conceived community share's role in the Book Club program. These six criteria are:

1. A broadly agreed upon set of common public goals
2. Mechanisms for intercommunication among community members
3. Participatory mechanisms primarily for providing information and feedback
4. One or more genres in the communicative furtherance of the community's aims
5. Some specific lexis
6. A threshold level of members with a suitable degree of relevant content and discoursal expertise.

In the following description, we explore each criteria as it relates to community share.

Common public goals. A goal is what is common, not simply the topic under study. There can be a number of communities studying a topic such as the Civil War, yet they can have very different goals for doing so. Community share is built on the assumption that students who participate in a Book Club classroom share common goals of developing their literacy abilities, engaging in literature discussion, making connections from their own lives to the texts that they read, learning theme-related content, and so forth. Teachers and students generate these goals, which evolve over the year as the students mature in their literacy reasoning.

Mechanisms for intercommunication. Students in Book Club classrooms communicate with one another and with their teacher through defined mechanisms, including book club discussions, reading logs, and community share. Community share is critical as the most public and social context during which communication occurs among all community members.

Participatory mechanisms. Information and feedback within the Book Club community focus on a range of areas, including "what to share" (i.e., the content of the texts read and the focuses within the texts) and "how to share" (i.e., conventions of communication). In short, by participating in the Book Club community, students use participatory mechanisms for learning about language and literacy conventions, literary elements, response to literature, and strategies for comprehension. Through their logs, discussions, questioning, clarifying, and responding, students continually develop and refine their language and literacy practices. The Book Club program is designed to ensure that participatory mechanisms are multiple and varied to provide access for students across ages (see Chapters 12 and 13 for participatory mechanisms specific to younger students' participation), across ability levels (see Chapters 6 and 8 for discussion of participatory mechanisms for students who had been labeled as having learning problems), and across cultures (see Chapter 7 for examples of participatory mechanisms that allow participation among students for whom English is not their native language).

Genres in the communicative furtherance of the community's aims. Not any classroom involved in literature-based discussion is a Book Club classroom, nor is any classroom a Book Club classroom simply because teachers involve students in written and oral response to literature, reading logs, or small-group discussions. In Book Club, there are specific genres for communication, *in a specific framework and for a specific set of goals*, that are used consistently and effectively among participating members of the classroom. These genres include book club discussions drawn from reading log entries; community share discourse genres of instructing, modeling, sharing, and so forth. These genres are public and shared among members of the classroom.

Specific lexis. The lexis, or specialized vocabulary of Book Club, relates to its components, activities within the components, and conventions for interaction within the components. For example, within the lexis related to reading long entries, "titles" (creating titles for untitled chapters) has a specific meaning for a specific form of reader response and log entry. Students also share a lexis of strategies and frameworks used within their classroom during Book Club but drawn from the research literature on literacy education (e.g.,

Ogle's [1986] K-W-L, referring to knowledge–wonder–learn; inquiry charts based on Hoffman's [1992] I-Charts).

Threshold level of members. Swales notes that discourse communities have changing memberships and thus the ratio of novice to experts is important. Book Club classrooms are similar in a key respect to any other class-room–turnover from year to year is usually close to 100%. However, each year, teachers begin building community in the classroom and students understand this aspect of schooling. Further, in some schools Book Club is used across grades (e.g., Laura's fifth-grade students came from two fourth-grade classrooms, one of which uses Book Club). By distributing experienced Book Club students across the small discussion groups, and by their very presence in the community share setting, the less experienced students can draw on their more knowledgeable peers (McMahon & Goatley, 1995).

With these six features of a discourse community in mind, the role of community share in establishing and maintaining the Book Club context becomes clear. It is designed to help students obtain access to the lexicon and genres of Book Club, to participate and receive information and feedback, to engage in literacy as a means toward the common goal of literate thinking and lifelong literate activities, and to share in literature discussions with peers through the participatory mechanisms that characterize the program. These special features enable the shared knowledge of the community to grow and to support students' entrance into the larger literate society.

CURRICULAR ASPECTS OF COMMUNITY SHARE

Given the three lines of research upon which community share is based, it is not surprising to find it a complex context serving multiple purposes: (1) a public–social space within which the language of literacy, literature, and literate thinking may be used for meaningful purposes, (2) a context with rich instructional opportunities for enhancing conventional knowledge, and (3) a site for community building among students. In this section we explore the curricular aspects of community share in terms of its instructional functions and the varying roles teachers assume in leading the sessions.

The Curricular Content of Community Share

In a study of community share's curricular content, we examined Deb's and Laura's community share sessions from 1990 to 1992 (Raphael & Goatley, 1994). Our findings suggest two distinct functions of community share: instructional activities and text discussion. These vary depending on when during the Book Club session community share occurs (see Figure 2.2). When community share occurs at the beginning of daily Book Club events, it is largely instructional, emphasizing the following elements:

- Introducing and teaching about new strategies for reading (e.g., comprehension, vocabulary), writing (e.g., log entries, synthesis activities), and discussion (e.g., how to share during book club, identifying topics for discussion)
- Reviewing and synthesizing previously read chapters or texts and setting the stage for the upcoming reading.

In contrast, when community share occurs as a closing activity, the focus is primarily on discussion, including sharing personal responses, making connections across book club discussions, and clarifying confusions that have emerged in the small groups. For example, instruction about reading log entries occurred when community share was an opening activity, while the peddler discussion during the Civil War unit occurred as a closing one.

The instructional content of community share can be framed in terms of four categories: language conventions, comprehension, literary elements, and response to literature (see Figure 2.3). Within community share, when instruction occurs as an opening activity prior to writing or book clubs, it focuses on one of these four areas.

FIGURE 2.2.   Curricular Purposes of Community Share

Community share prior to book club discussions	*Community share following book club discussions*
Set Stage for Day's Events	Connecting Across Book Club Groups
• introduce new strategy or literacy "tool" for use during reading or reading log activities	• sharing ideas, responses, confusions; clarifying; and using "built-in repair structure"
• summarize previous day's story events—recap	• theme related discussion
• read-aloud from thematically related book	• raise questions and make predictions
• modeling	• intertextual links (e.g., when reading multiple-book sets; to past texts; to personal experiences)
• add to community's knowledge base on which to draw during theme discussions	

FIGURE 2.3.   Book Club Curriculum Chart

Language Conventions	Comprehension	Literary Elements	Response to Literature
Sound Symbol • spells conventionally • reads with fluency	Background Knowledge • prediction • draws on prior knowledge • builds knowledge if needed • context clues • intertextual connections	Theme • author's purposes • connections to life	Personal Response Impressionistic response to literature, one's own writing, or the writing of peers • shares experiences • shares personal feelings • places self in situation • compares self to characters

Grammatical Conventions
• uses appropriate language choices:
  verbs
  syntax
  punctuation
in oral reading, discussion, and writing
	Processing Text
	• summarizing
	• sequencing
	• vocabulary
	• organizing and drawing on text structure knowledge
	• analyze/develop characters, setting, plot sequence, and so forth
		Point of View
		• characters' POV
		• author' POV
			Creative Response
			"Play" in response to literature
			• "What?" (change event in story plot and explore impact)
			• dramatizing events, characters' attitudes or actions
			• illustrations of events, characters

Interaction Conventions • works with peers to set goals • interacts with peers in literacy contexts: • writing conferences • literary circles • author's chair	Monitoring • asking questions • clarifying confusions	Genre/Structures • story structure • expository structures • types of genres Authors' Craft • style • text features	Critical Response Analytic response to the "effectiveness," "purpose," or "coherence"; intertextual connections • explain changes in beliefs or feelings • evidence from text to support ideas • critique texts using specific examples • discuss author's purpose • identify author's craft • discuss author's purpose • uses text as mirror of one's own life and as window into the lives of others

Language conventions include how our language works, its symbol system, its written forms and genres, the language of literary response and literate thinking, and appropriate ways of using that language in interactions with others. During the Civil War unit, Laura focused on a particular language convention related to questions, specifically how to distinguish inquiry questions that lead to research, reading, and discussion from questions that are less probing or less likely to prompt extended interactions.

In an opening community share, she introduced the idea that not all questions are suitable for prompting productive discussions and asked students to think about qualities of good inquiry questions. On the overhead, she wrote the question, "How many people died in the war?" When students volunteered that the question did not seem to be a good one, she asked them to explain why. Students offered a range of reasons: They could find the answer easily in the book, too many people died in the war but it did not matter about the exact number, or it is hard to pinpoint the answer. Throughout the conversation, Laura elicited criteria for judging the quality of the question.

Continuing to work from examples, Laura asked students to discuss the quality of two questions: "Which side won the war?" and "Did the North fight the South?" Lenny described them as "stupid," saying "We already know [the answer]." Laura elaborated, making a distinction between *important* and *inquiry* questions. Some questions are important but may not require enough information to warrant inquiry.

Laura asked Derek to read another question from the overhead, "What was an average soldier's life like during the Civil War?" As he read, students began to comment that this was a good inquiry question. Julianne noted that "You could write a lot about what his life was like," then one of her peers added that it would be "like a diary entry." Laura modeled several subquestions related to the soldier's life and noted that "A good question makes you think of more questions such as, What did he wear? What were his weapons? Did he have a horse?" After several more minutes of discussion about inquiry questions, Laura asked the students for volunteers to describe a good inquiry question. Roger said that "One question would lead to more questions," while another student mentioned that "You have a lot to write about." Thus one curricular focus of community share involves teaching the conventions of our language, from those related to sounds and symbols to those we use in promoting discussion and interaction.

A second area of curricular content is comprehension. This focuses on the knowledge, strategies, skills, and dispositions that help readers construct meaning. There are many instances when the students must rely on their prior knowledge, with Laura helping them to build this knowledge as the unit progresses. Specific comprehension strategies she teaches during the Civil

War unit involve applying the concept of sequencing to tracking main events of the war, which unfold as students read their books. She scaffolds their sequencing by using wall charts such as a timeline. Students add relevant important events (e.g., specific battles). To aid in their monitoring, she provides a think-sheet (see Chapter 4) for each book club to plan their strategy for completing their book within the 15 sessions provided and to check on their progress both daily and weekly. To help them consider the issues underlying the books and how they relate to one another, Laura uses another wall chart to record issues that emerge during community share discussions: (1) states' rights: the right of the southern states to secede from their own country, (2) rightness of the war and what side to choose to support, (3) desertion and what to do with those who did desert, and (4) human rights: how the North treated immigrants and the South treated slaves. These tools to aid comprehension are intentionally created to help students share conventional knowledge, while eliciting monitoring processes such as asking questions, clarifying confusions, and tracking progress through the books.

The curricular content related to literary elements includes how literature works. A literature-based reading program is obliged to be cautious about abusing the literature. It is not simply a vehicle for teaching students to read, write, and construct knowledge; it is a craft in and of itself and, as such, worthy of study. For example, during the Civil War unit, Laura includes explicit instruction on *point of view*, including the author's and the story characters' points of view. For instance, points of view relevant to the Civil War are generated and recorded on a wall chart, including: North and South, slaves and immigrants, different family members, women and men/boys and girls, generals and average soldiers, and political leaders such as Lincoln. Further, Laura continues to highlight previously taught literary elements (e.g., setting, plot) through a chart she and the students maintain throughout the Book Club phase of the unit. The chart is ostensibly to help students keep track of the content of the four novels. Each column heading names one of the four books while each row notes characters, places, and events that were critical to the story. This chart serves as a tool to help the students learn from all the books, draw intertextual connections, and keep in mind issues related to the various points of view associated with a particular text.

The curricular content related to "literature" includes a range of ways of responding, from the personal to the creative to the critical. Through community share, students acquire much-needed skills and develop the dispositions, abilities, and attitudes that support their classroom literacy activities and lead to lifelong literacy. In the Civil War unit, Laura includes response opportunities in each of these areas through her encouragement of students' oral and written responses. For example, she encourages students to place themselves in the characters' situations, to share their personal feelings related to the events of the time period, and to imagine different events by asking "What if?"

These four categories of instructional content facilitate students' understanding of the texts and their ability to share ideas with one another. The focus on all four areas furthers their entrance to membership in a literate society.

Community Building During Community Share

The community plays an important role in furthering students' literacy processes and shared knowledge and reflects the teacher's instructional and curricular decision-making. The examples from Laura's thematic unit during the Civil War illustrate an atmosphere that encourages students to build upon one anothers' ideas, ask questions about confusions, and relate several ideas to one concept. The use of a thematic unit means the community merges ideas across time periods, texts, and conventional knowledge. That is, the theme unit helps students to group connecting ideas together from numerous and related sources of information. During the Civil War unit, the community building seemed to be a direct result of: (1) organizing thematic connections among issues, books, and discussions and (2) promoting intertextual connections across various texts and ideas.

Laura organized thematic connections in two ways. First, in designing the unit, she selected literature texts that complemented one another. While all took place during the Civil War era, the characters' roles, settings, and story time length differed greatly. This allowed students to learn about numerous views (e.g., North versus South), important battles and places (e.g., Gettysburg), and other conventional knowledge of the Civil War. Laura read aloud one book to the whole class (i.e., *Across Five Aprils*), thus providing a common text as a resource. Second, as a community, the students developed certain themes they frequently returned to for debate (e.g., the "rightness" of the war, human rights).

For example, after reading a chapter from *Across Five Aprils* in which Eb, one of the main characters, deserted and tried to return to his family, Laura started a conversation in community share about soldiers becoming deserters. Students built their comments on one anothers' ideas, relating both sides of the issue of desertion and expressing a range of opinions. Brett began the conversation by stating that he was not sure that desertion is right since soldiers are supposed to stay with their groups and fight the enemy. David then said that the soldiers from the North and the South might feel differently about deserters, that they might have different views about whether it was okay to desert or not and about how to treat those who did desert. Charles pointed out that Eb was sick and that is a good reason not to go back to fight.

When Laura asked the students what they would do if they were in Eb's situation, Julianne pointed out that if a soldier deserts, he has to hide in places like the woods, be on his own, and maybe die. She said that might be even worse than the punishment if he turned himself in for deserting.

During this conversation, several ideas were established:

- There are different reasons behind desertion.
- Students disagreed on whether desertion could be justified.
- There are potential punishments for deserting regardless of the justification.

Charles noted that the deserters were a lot like the character, Brian, in Paulsen's (1987) *Hatchet*, since Brian also had to hunt for food, though he did not worry about being "caught." Laura commented that Brian was also healthy. As a class, they realized that the soldiers had a rough life and some had been fighting for two years. Laura and the community share context encouraged debate over these issues and helped the students value connections across texts to clarify and understand events and themes.

These theme-related aspects of community share play a vital role in furthering both the criteria of discourse communities and the teacher's role in establishing such a community.

The Teacher's Role in Community Share

Raphael and Hiebert (1996) describe four different roles that teachers can assume during their interactions with students: (1) explicit instructor, (2) instructional scaffolder, (3) facilitator, and (4) participant. During the Civil War unit, Laura assumes each of these roles to achieve particular outcomes within community share. For example, one of her unit goals is to build students' understanding of point of view, developing the concept in terms of author's point of view, character's point of view, and the point of view from which we might read and discuss a text. To begin the thematic unit, Laura introduces students to point of view, explicitly teaching them what the phrase means, why it is important, and how they might discover point of view in the texts that they read. Given the content of the unit, the different perspectives about war in general, and the different sides fighting this particular war, point of view arose frequently throughout the unit. In addition, Laura selects five novels that have characters with contrasting points of view (e.g., North/South, soldier/worker, adult/child).

Laura *scaffolds* students' use of point of view throughout the unit, using questions, charts, reading log prompts, and so forth to encourage students' understanding of point of view. As students become more aware and able to draw on this concept in their text discussions during book club and community share, she exerts decreasing amounts of control and less guidance over time. For example, midway through the unit, Charles wrote an entry in his reading log about his views of his book club book, *Turn Homeward Hannalee*:

> I feel this book is a good book and I would reckomend it to teachers of kids who were studieing the civil war. A lot of books have the point of view of the north. This book has the point of view from the south. I like this book.

During book club and later, during community share, he told the class that he really liked how his book was written from a southern perspective. He described how much Hannalee loved the South and that, as a young girl, she did not seem to have strong feelings about the Southern issues, unlike Will in Reeder's (1989) novel *Shades of Gray*, who firmly believed in states' rights and who thought it reasonable to maintain slaves. Hannalee simply loved her home and loved the South and unquestioningly hated the "blue bellies" of the North. Laura acted as *facilitator*, inviting other students to comment on how they thought the characters' perspectives in their respective books might share or disagree with Hannalee's point of view. At other times, Laura served as facilitator by simply orchestrating turn taking, calling on one group, nodding to particular students, and inviting students to participate.

In other discussions, Laura's role was as *participant* in the discussion—but with no greater responsibility for orchestrating the flow of conversation or the control over content than any of the students. For example, as Laura read from *Across Five Aprils*, Alan asks what the phrase "fairly fought" meant. Students in the class began sharing their ideas, without guidance from Laura. Julianne said that both sides had weapons, while Charles said that they had "even odds." Students exchanged their ideas until Alan appeared to be satisfied with the possibilities. Laura participated much as did the students, maintaining eye contact with whomever was speaking, nodding occasionally to express her agreement with the idea. When the spontaneous discussion ended, she returned to reading aloud from the story without summarizing or indicating that some sets of responses were more appropriate than others. In short, she was a participant in a meaningful and authentic conversation that emerged in response to the text being read.

CONCLUDING COMMENTS

Community share is a complex and critical component of the Book Club program, providing a public and social forum within which students hear and use the language of literacy and of literary discussion. In this forum, teachers introduce students to conventions and conventional knowledge of our culture while valuing and encouraging students' use of this knowledge to invent new ways of thinking and responding to the texts that they read. It is the context in which the individual students and their independent book clubs come together to form a discourse community with shared knowledge, language, and goals. Wolf (1993) describes the move from traditional reading programs to conversationally oriented literature-based instruction as reflecting "a polar swing from teacher as dominant force to teacher as silent facilitator" (cited in Raphael & Goatley, 1994, p. 536). The curricular content of community share underscores the reality that we have more to teach, not less, in our current approaches to literacy education. Community share provides the context for teachers and students to learn the range of curricular content while assuming multiple ways of interacting to value the students' potential as well as the teacher's to support one anothers' literacy development.

CHAPTER 3

Reading in the Book Club Program

SUSAN I. McMAHON

> Based on what we now know, it is incorrect to suppose that there is a simple or single step which, if taken correctly, will immediately allow a child to read. Becoming a skilled reader is a journey that involves many steps. Strengthening any one element yields small gains. For large gains, many elements must be in place. (R. C. Anderson, Hiebert, Scott, & Wilkinson, 1985)

The ideas expressed above in the now landmark text, *Becoming a Nation of Readers*, were of paramount importance when expanding our basic model for a literature-based reading program. Reading is an active, complex, meaning-making process that cannot be simplified into a set of subskills and strategies. To be successful fostering literacy and literate thought in upper elementary grades, we considered many elements of the reading process. First, teachers needed to address the basic skills and strategies that foster comprehension and fluency, such as background knowledge, text structure, and metacognition (Beck & McKeown, 1986). At the same time, reading should not be limited to these since the reading process also includes other essential elements, such as motivation (Holdaway, 1979), lifelong reading (R. C. Anderson et al., 1985), social contexts (Bloome & Green, 1984), and the empowerment of literacy (Shor, 1992). Literacy involves not simply being *able* to read and write but also the *willingness* to engage in literate behaviors (Au, 1993). For students' successful literacy development, we needed to address all of these elements of the reading process. In this chapter, I briefly describe the conceptual issues related to the reading component, the ways in which community influenced it, and the curricular decisions most salient to reading in Book Club.

CONCEPTUALIZING A COMPLETE READING PROGRAM

Changes in reading research reflect a deepening understanding of the reading process (Beck & McKeown, 1986) that was key to the conceptualization of the reading component of Book Club. The program facilitates increased reading capabilities and develops readers who are members of a community engaging with texts on multiple levels for a variety of purposes. Because literacy is a set of complex social and cognitive processes, envisioning a more complete view of reading facilitates our continued efforts to maintain balanced instruction that sustains an emphasis on constructing meaning, responding to texts, and engaging in literate discourse.

Constructing Meaning

Current views of reading acknowledge the need for readers to make connections between oral and written texts, so teachers should continue to stress the need for phonemic awareness, word identification, and vocabulary development. At the same time, readers must also be able to construct meaning, which requires (1) the ability to make sense of the text's structure and organization, (2) prior knowledge related to the content, and (3) metacognitive awareness and monitoring of one's reading process. Our literature-based reading program fosters instruction that emphasizes these and stresses that meaning construction is the result of a complex process involving the *text*, including the author's craft and use of literary elements; the *reader*, including prior knowledge, strategy use, interests, and motivation; and the *social context*, or community in which reading occurs.

Three factors are key as children learn to construct meaning: (1) the ways they learn about comprehension, (2) the types of interactions in which they participate, and (3) the texts they read. Pearson and Fielding (1991) noted that students learn more about constructing meaning while engaged in reading complete texts and while participating in interactions in which they have some degree of control over the learning by initiating questions and topics of discussion. Instead of direct, procedural instruction, teachers focus on *how* students are developing literate thinking, which requires the teacher to use student input and constructed meanings as guides for further discussion and instruction. In addition, the texts influence the meaning constructed. Even though basal series may efficiently provide a framework for learning how to read, trade books provide richer language, imagery, and genre variety. For many children, particularly those struggling to become literate, literature encourages them to enjoy reading, to be willing to read more, to understand the multiple purposes for reading, and to develop a deeper understanding of literary structures (Tunnell & Jacobs, 1989). The most positive influence on increasing readers' capabilities is reading books (R. C. Anderson, Wilson, & Fielding, 1988), yet many classrooms are filled with children who do not read because they are not motivated to respond to textbooks (Wilson, 1992).

Consideration of these important aspects of meaning construction led to several conclusions about the nature of reading in Book Club. First, the teachers provide explicit comprehension instruction for all students that is embedded within the reading and discussion of trade books. Further, this instruction recognizes the need for students to have time and opportunity to practice what they are learning, to ask questions, and to internalize what they have learned. In addition, texts need to provide a range of content, genres, and styles that enable learners to make intertextual connections over time. Teachers use the log entries as vehicles for students' questions, ideas, and demonstrations of strategies to construct meaning. The logs allow for student selection of topics for conversation and/or personal response. Teachers use the logs and classroom discussions as means through which to assess student learning and scaffold instruction for individuals, groups, and the total class.

Responding to Texts

Since meaning results from an interaction between any reader and the text, instruction addresses both the individual and social basis of meaning-making—each person brings prior knowledge and experiences to the act of reading; in turn, each text brings a particular structure, setting, set of characters, and events to the printed page. Thus, to foster literary thinking and talk, contexts in which learners engage with texts need to support students' meaning construction, to provide occasions in which they share their developing interpretations with others, and to include opportunities to revise their thoughts.

Engaging in Literate Discourse

Discourse surrounding texts is key to fostering individuals who are able and willing to engage in literate acts. Armed with a repertoire of reading materials and an understanding of the author's craft, students are empowered to critically analyze what they read. For Book Club, two aspects of the program supported students in their attempts to participate in literate discourse: (1) well-written, interesting texts and (2) instruction on various literary elements.

Students prefer reading texts with characters and events that are similar to themselves and their experiences (Purves & Beach, 1972). In today's diverse schools, teachers trying to address this preference must not only consider texts that represent their students in terms of race, ethnicity, gender, and economic class, but they must also be certain that such texts are culturally authentic and that classroom sets are balanced in terms of the groups represented (Sims Bishop, 1992). Thus the inclusion of quality texts that authentically represent all students in the class and larger culture presents students a wide variety of books they are likely to read. Further, such a collection provides a variety of perspectives, creating a basis upon which to discuss differences, similarities, and inequities, leading to critical literacy (Giroux, 1988). Thus text selection became one important aspect of fostering increased discourse about texts in Book Club. A second important component became instruction focused on literary elements.

Literary elements refer to those aspects of literature often not explicitly taught until middle or high school. That is, plot, character, setting, point of view, tone, and symbolism are aspects of texts frequently not included in the elementary curriculum. Yet, as Eeds and Peterson (1995) point out, these are essential aspects of reading narrative texts and even the most novice reader discusses them at some level. For example, very young children will announce whether or not they like a particular character and explain why (see Chapters 12 and 13). The teacher can expand and develop these responses to foster more literate thinking among *all* students, not only the more experienced readers. They can prompt young readers to move beyond simply sharing their ideas to analyzing the text and their experiences more closely.

Therefore instruction on literary elements is important for two reasons. First, it makes authors' decision-making and its influence on readers' responses explicit. That characters develop in a particular way or plots unfold with slight twists of unexpected events is no accident. Authors craft their texts to evoke responses. Thus instruction on these elements and the author's decision-making process facilitates students' literacy development. Second, the more readers understand how the language and structure of a text can influence their the response, the more power they have over their own literacy process.

Our hope was to align our program to meet our three literacy goals of constructing meaning, responding to texts, and engaging in literate discourse. Together, these address the complexity of the reading process and support efforts to foster readers who perceive themselves as members of a literate community in which they willingly participate.

BUILDING A COMMUNITY OF READERS

A sociocultural perspective on learning stresses the key role of the social context in a student's literacy development and the literate thinking associated with it. Community facilitates literacy development because interactions surrounding ideas and knowledge related to texts is empowering. Literate individuals compare texts and ideas, sequence ideas within and across texts, argue with ideas presented in texts, and interpret and create texts of their own (Heath, 1991). To learn community norms as they relate to these literacy activities, learners must actively participate in interaction focused on texts. Thus, as a function of participation in the community, individuals develop a taste for and appreciation of what the larger community defines as literary (Purves, 1990). It is within this community of readers that the teacher is able to present opportunities for students to make connections between their own experiences and the text. The ability to engage in such social activities motivates individuals to practice lifelong reading and to become empowered over texts and, in many ways, over their lives. Students participating in Book Club needed to experience this empowerment by participating in a community of literate individuals. Research investigating existing literacy environments in elementary schools helped shape Book Club to be successful in elementary classrooms.

It can be argued that in some way all classrooms are social environments in which children participate as readers; however, the degree of help students offer one another and the depth of the sense of membership within a community are dependent on the teacher (Hepler, 1992). The contexts of many more traditional classrooms do not provide experiences that enable learners to construct concepts of themselves and their peers as literate members of a community. To foster the analysis and synthesis that leads to literate thinking, more classroom time should be devoted to student discussions about the texts they are reading. The purposes for literacy outlined earlier (constructing meaning, responding to texts, and engaging in literate discourse) will help clarify the role community can play in the construction of meaning.

Constructing Meaning

One purpose for becoming literate is to increase our knowledge about any topic. Certainly reading a text without discussing our constructed meaning with anyone else is possible. Traditional classroom practice that has focused on this mode of constructing meaning has resulted in many of us becoming literate. However, what happens when we are not able to construct meaning or the meaning we construct clearly differs from that of many others? A community of readers can support greater understandings of texts. Examining some students' interactions can help clarify this idea.

In the following discussion, fifth graders are in the middle of a conversation about the chapter book *Sadako and the Thousand Paper Cranes* (Coerr, 1977). One student questions why the book refers to the atomic bomb that destroyed Hiroshima as a "thunderbolt." Through their conversation, students are able to clarify what happened when the bomb was dropped.

Lissa: But why did they call the bomb a thunderbolt?

Mondo: 'Cause what if a thunderbolt hit, 'cause when it lands it makes some thunder.

Bart: 'Cause lightning is *very high* in electricity and so is a bomb.

Lissa: That's what happened. I saw it in the book the same story (hitting the desk).

Bart: Yep.

Lissa: I saw it in my book and it it made a [mushroom-shaped cloud . . .

Bart: [Mushroom-shaped like, like

Lissa: . . . and it killed almost every one around.

Bart: Yup, like that. *(Moving his hands up, illustrating an explosion.)*

Lissa: No it goes like this. It goes shh . . . *(Moving her hands higher in the air and tracing the form of a mushroom.)*

Bart: Yeah, that's what I did I went like . . . *(Moving his hands like before except in a more exaggerated way.)*

Chris: When the bomb hit poof!

Bart: The bomb could travel. The gas could travel up, 'cause when the wind, 'cause when the gas is in the air the wind blows it and it goes to country, to country, to country and they all die. (McMahon, 1994, pp. 115–116)

While their description of the atomic bomb is not scientifically accurate or totally complete, these fifth graders help one another construct a better understanding of events referred to in the book—an understanding that no individual may have had sufficient prior knowledge to construct alone. As a group, these members of a community of readers constructed identity kits that include helping one another comprehend a text by orally describing their own constructed meanings and helping one another clarify meanings, resulting in everyone's building a knowledge base.

Thus, one goal for the entire classroom community in both small and large groups is to help one another construct meaning. This is not the only form of discourse related to meaning construction, though, since readers sometimes construct slightly different meanings from the very same texts, as the next transcription reveals.

The following conversation occurs at the end of the class's reading of *Tuck Everlasting* (Babbitt, 1975). Two members of the group, Camille and Crystal, debate their different perspectives on whether the main character, Winnie, will drink from the spring that grants eternal life. Even though they had read the same book and participated in the same small-group discussions throughout the reading, each girl adopts a different interpretation.

Camille: I think she will drink the water before she is 17.

Crystal: When she is 17?

Camille: *Before.*

Crystal: *When* she's 17 because they are gonna like take all the water when she is 17. She drinks the water. She goes and marries him or something like that.

Camille: She's gonna do it before she said she was 17 though. That's what I think.

Crystal: But Winnie is going to go into the woods and, I think that Winnie is gonna to go into the woods and drink the water 'cuz she thinks it won't work. She thinks that they're just a bunch of crazy people, but they're her friends still. I said she thinks they're just a bunch of crazy people. I bet cha' she'll go in and check it when they leave. Fifteen? Thirteen? Fifteen? Somethin' like that?

Joshua: Yeah.

Crystal: Not, not old enough to drink or nothing like that.

Latrice: I think she will take it when she is 17 because, Tuck told her to. (McMahon & Goatley, 1995, p. 30)

Crystal and Camille do not interpret the character of Winnie in the same way because their knowledge of her differs. Other members of the group contribute their ideas as well, while these two girls debate, thus revealing multiple interpretations of the text. Clearly, members will construct richer meanings of this character and book events as a result of this conversation. Since the art of debate often leads to more convincing arguments, members will either become more firmly committed to an original interpretation or will modify their initial ideas. Without a community of readers who have developed a set of common experiences related to the text, these students might never cultivate their knowledge bases by questioning their interpretations, thus depriving themselves of an opportunity to generate the critical thinking associated with analyses and argumentation. Thus creating a context in which students define their roles as being active participants in a literate community supported this goal for constructing meaning.

Responding to Texts

Responding personally to texts empowers readers by building understanding and ability to communicate a perspective. In the following discussion, fifth graders are wrestling with the feelings evoked by reading the book *Faithful Elephants* (Tsuchiya, 1988), which recounts factual events surrounding the need to destroy zoo animals in cities being bombed during World War II. The English version of the book displays realistic pictures of animals suffering and dying. On one hand, the children understand the potential threat zoo animals may cause if their cages were destroyed by bombs; on the other, they mourn the deaths of innocent victims of a war.

Lissa: But they couldn't kill the people.

Chris: And those dumb folks up in the air coulda stopped that war. Why do they always drop it on the people that know they can't do anything back.

Bart: They shouldn't 'a put 'em through misery like that. If they really did wanna kill 'em, they shoulda just did it fast, 'cuz they made 'em suffer. And it really hurt 'em. And if that happened to them, I betcha they wouldn't like it at all; they would be beggin'.

Mondo: They shoulda just shoot, shot 'em with the elephant gun.

Chris: They tried to. They broke the middle.

Mondo: No, but a gun.

Bart: An elephant gun, and shoot 'em.

Mondo: The bullet's about that big.

As this brief section of transcript demonstrates, these students are not just trying to understand the events in a book, but wrestling with real happenings. The book evokes powerful responses that they need to discuss. The lack of fluidity in their talk reveals the emotion they feel and their attempts to understand within this community of readers how and why such events occur. By having time and opportunity to discuss how they personally feel about the events described in the book, these students are constructing a deeper understanding of the authentic dilemmas present on both sides of the issue. Being members of a literate community enables them to communicate their developing responses.

Engaging in Literate Discourse

The third goal for the reading component of Book Club is to create a social context in which children engage in literate discourse prompted by the texts they read. To foster this, teachers often select books set in the same time period, written by the same author, or representative of the same genre. Reading texts that are connected in some way enables students to engage in discourse that links books, events, and ideas. In the following conversation, two close friends, Bart and Chris, debate the virtues of war. This discussion occurred a few days after the one above. Students begin with a focus on Japan during World War II; however, their emphasis shifts quickly to the Gulf War (which was then frequently in the news).

Bart: I wrote about survival *too* and I wrote about Japanese. I was speaking about Japanese people and their culture. That's what I was really thinking about. But I wrote . . .

Chris: (Unclear.)

Bart: I know but I was thinking, if you can't bomb Americans,
Chris: It's war. They bombed us and we bombed 'em back.
Bart: I know, but still.
Chris: *(Unclear.)*
Lissa: Yeah, but the Americans had the the war.
Bart: Yeah, but if Japan bombs a part we don't have the right to go back and bomb them. Two wrongs don't make a right.
Chris: Japan bombed Pearl Harbor.
Bart: I know, but still,
Chris: Americans had to go bomb them back.
Bart: It doesn't make sense to go back and bomb them. That's like President Bush. He makes a mistake, like really uhm if they if they make a move on us, we have a war. Two wrongs don't make a right. That's wrong. I would say run me over, if they do something . . .
Martisse: Bomb them back.
Lissa: No!
Bart: No! Just *leave*, leave it. [Just leave.
Lissa: [Let it be. (McMahon, 1994, pp. 121-122)

Respected by his peers, Bart was a strong leader in this classroom. Chris looked up to Bart and usually followed his lead, adopting the same perspective Bart did as they discussed books. In the instance above, however, Chris quietly debates Bart's ideas. Using information from the readings and his personal experience, Chris espouses a nationalistic stance, arguing that war under the circumstances surrounding the bombing of Pearl Harbor was justified. Perhaps because of Chris's softly articulated responses or because of Bart's established leadership, Bart fights back valiantly, supporting his pacifist position. Occasionally the other two participants, Lissa and Martisse, join in articulating their support for one of the two sides. This discussion reveals the empowerment each student feels as a member of a literate community. No student personally attacks another. Instead, they firmly stand by their convictions, voicing an argument based on meaning constructed through reading and discussing texts. In this community, members are entitled to voice opinions that differ from those of others as long as they connect to events in the text. Such discourse reveals students' ability and willingness to engage in literate discourse.

Thus community played an essential role in our efforts to create a classroom context that reflected our literacy goals. That is, membership in a community can facilitate individual efforts to construct meaning, to respond personally to texts, and to engage in literate discourse. Once we had conceptualized the role of community in our reading program, we then considered the prevalent curricular issues.

BUILDING THE READING CURRICULUM

Conceptualizing the reading component of Book Club and identifying the need for a community of readers in the classroom were essential aspects of the Book Club framework. As mentioned earlier, key aspects of the program included both text selection and instruction on literary elements. This section of the chapter focuses on issues related to reading texts and instruction on literary elements. Both of these were key to students' constructing meaning, responding to texts, and engaging in literate discourse.

As the research team began the decision-making process related to the reading component, we realized that several factors influenced students' engagement with texts and the quality of the related discourse. Therefore, this section addresses issues of text selection, opportunities for reading, contexts for reading, provisions for all learners, and reading–writing connections.

Text Selection

Selecting appropriate books is just the first of many instructional factors all teachers must reflect on. Book Club is committed to the use of trade books and other publications created to communicate meaning (e.g., newspaper, magazines) because a sociocultural perspective recognizes the important role that language conveying meaning, engagement, and evocation of strong personal response plays in readers' constructions of meaning. Publications written to convey meaning can envelop readers and provide them models of enticing language use. Further, interest in the book is an important condition for constructing meaning. If the teacher or most students are not interested in the genre, setting, or character, getting students engaged in the texts and literate discourse is difficult for teachers. Since the students in Book Club represented the diversity of our society, books reflecting this were more interesting and meaningful. Finally, because it was an integral part of the literacy program, Book Club needed to address the district's curricular goals. Thus, four criteria applied to all texts considered for inclusion within the program: (1) quality of the literature, (2) teacher and student interest, (3) characters reflecting diversity in terms of gender, race, class, and ethnicity, and (4) curricular needs.

Quality texts. Defining "quality" in terms of literature is complex, so the research team based our decisions on three factors: (1) recommendations by others knowledgeable about children's literature, (2) the reputation of the author, and (3) the focus of the book.

We consulted several knowledgeable others about book selection. Since award-granting groups, such as Newberry and Caldecott, are well informed about children's literature and many of the complex issues related to text selection and because these individuals spend considerable time reviewing existing literature, their criteria proved helpful and their selection lists were an excellent place to begin. Second, consultation with colleagues provided valuable information. For example, librarians and language arts coordinators in the school district were knowledgeable about children's interests and selections that were already available either in the district or through loans from neighboring libraries. Buyers at local bookstores also proved helpful since they know about new books, the easiest way to order them, and the prices. Other university faculty who are experts on children's literature also were valuable resources to identify quality books. Another resource became the published reviews in journals such as *The Reading Teacher*, *The Horn Book* and *The New Advocate*. Finally, a major resource was the classroom teachers who best knew the students, their needs, and their interests. Not all books some outside expert identified as "quality" will necessarily spark student interest and/or discussion. Teachers know which texts will be best for their classes.

In addition to consulting with knowledgeable others, teachers selected books written by established authors because such texts are often well written. They also looked for literature presenting interesting, timely, and/or debatable topics and/or complex issues because such books are more likely to evoke strong personal response and controversy, which often motivate readers to engage in literate discourse (see Chapter 11).

With these resources available, we sorted through multiple titles of books designated as "quality." While helpful in beginning our process of identifying books to include, such factors were just our initiating point for literature selection. We had several other measures.

Teacher and student interests. While teachers enjoy reading, discussing, and providing instruction on some genres, authors, and/or topics, they may avoid others. While teacher preference should not stifle student interest, teacher choice was an important consideration because, if teachers were interested in the book, they were more likely able to kindle students' interests (see Chapter 11). At the same time, if a large number of students expressed interest in a particular book, the teacher needed to pursue this, if not for Book Club, then certainly as a free-choice selection. Thus, while teacher interest was key, it was not always the most important determining factor.

To meet the standard of student interest, teachers surveyed students to determine what they were interested in reading in terms of authors, titles, genres, and topics. Often they used this to narrow the options before bringing books to the students, providing book talks, and holding a class vote for which books to include. In addition, teachers often talked about book selection with one another. These discussions led them to identify books popular with one group of students (see Chapter 11). As with teacher preferences, students' interests varied within and across classes. Therefore, as with the other standards, student interest was important—but only when combined with the other factors.

Characters and settings representing diversity. We chose to address diversity through literature selection that mirrored the lives of children in the classroom and also expanded their knowledge about other cultures, nationalities, and backgrounds (Harris, 1992). Thus a third criteria for text selection was finding books that included strong characters reflecting our students in terms of age, gender, race, class, and/or ethnicity. Because prior knowledge and interest are key to constructing meaning and developing personal response, our text selection represented the students' own backgrounds, including strong female characters of ages similar to the students in the classes and from a variety of ethnic, racial, and class backgrounds. In addition, students expanded their awareness of other cultures in our larger society through literature about children in other countries, such as Japan, China, Vietnam, Denmark, and Russia, as well as books about American children from various ethnic and social groups.

Curricular needs. Before beginning any unit in Book Club, we considered the curricular goals for the literacy program. The particular school district in which Book Club began required the use of a basal series program because administrators believed that basal instruction focused on the specific skills and strategies identified in the program. We received permission to teach without the basal only if we included these skills and strategies. For example, both "comparing" and "contrasting" were listed as important skills. Therefore, we incorporated not only books students could compare and contrast but also ones that enabled them to understand how comparison and contrast can facilitate their meaning construction. The goal was to embed instruction on these requirements within the context of increasing students' capabilities to construct meaning from texts.

We agreed to match the curriculum guide with our program as long as students' needs matched the particular skills and strategies identified; however, the teachers did not teach aspects of reading that students had already mastered or ones that might have been beyond their zones of proximal development (see Chapter 1). For example, when planning a unit, the collaborative team considered several factors related to the established curriculum: (1) the reading needs of the students, (2) the skills and strategies required in the curriculum guide, (3) the available books, and (4) the match among all of these. If teachers decided their students had already mastered specific skills or strategies listed in the curriculum guide, they did not include them for instruction but drew on them for extended writing activities to provide practice. Most important was the integration of students' needs, the best books available, and the curriculum guidelines.

While text selection using the above criteria took considerable planning time at the beginning of each unit, it was essential. Since both (1) engaging students in the reading and responding process and (2) providing good models of language use and engaging topics were important to foster the literate discourse of Book Club, the books formed the basis of the program. If students did not find a book engaging, if they could not read it, if they did not find anything interesting to write about or discuss, if the teachers were not engaged in reading, responding to, and providing instruction based in the books, then Book Club for that unit would fail. Thus the time invested at the beginning helped insure long-term success.

Opportunities and Contexts for Reading

Regardless of the books or instructional focus, Book Club included a variety of opportunities for students to read. Drawing upon Vygotsky's principles by recognizing the role of language use on the development of thought, the need for learners to construct meaning within their own zones of proximal development (ZPDs), and the role of the more knowledgeable others in the room, the teachers incorporated reading on a variety of social planes. Further, readers need help within their ZPDs to construct meaning; text selection and the means through which students engaged with texts accommodated this. Finally, teachers must actively engage in monitoring student reading and meaning construction, in facilitating student growth, and in providing instruction as necessary. To meet these goals, the teachers provided students numerous opportunities and contexts in which to read.

During Book Club, as in many other classrooms, teachers and students sometimes read their texts aloud. To provide a model of fluent reading, the teacher read a selection to the class, often at the beginning of a text to acquaint the students with the author's voice, word choice, and setting of the book. Frequently, silent reading followed so that students engaged with the book on their own. Another read-aloud activity included paired reading in which students read to a peer. Occasionally, teachers asked students to read aloud a section of the book in their book clubs. Thus students had several opportunities to hear others read and to read aloud themselves. In addition to reading aloud, students also read sections of their texts silently. Teachers varied the reading experiences and the time allotment accordingly, allowing additional time for silent reading as needed.

Book Club was not the only time during the day when students read. Each day the school practiced DEAR (drop everything and read). Students read whatever they wanted at this time, but the teachers encouraged some of the slower readers having difficulty completing sections for discussions to use this time to read for Book Club. Teachers also encouraged students to keep their Book Club books handy so that if they had extra time during the day they could read. Finally, some students elected to take their Book Club books home. The message teachers tried to convey was that an important literacy goal was to read and participate in a literate community. To participate, all students must have read the same sections of the book. To complete this, they had to plan their reading. If Book Club time was not sufficient, they needed to schedule additional time.

While students were indeed encouraged to use whatever time they had between lessons, at lunch, or during DEAR to complete the reading for Book Club, they were also encouraged to read other texts. The teachers did not dictate the specific books, so to provide for optimal free choice while still supporting meaning construction and intertextual connections, the classroom library had several books selected from the school and local libraries or purchased specifically for the unit of study. Each time teachers began a unit, they found other books by the same author, with a similar theme, and/or of the same genre as the book they were currently reading in Book Club and included these in the classroom library.

In addition to providing students choice and flexibility in how they read the books, teachers also provided them choices about where to read. Practiced primarily during silent reading, the teacher permitted students to read their books anywhere in the room or in the adjacent hallway as long as they read while in their chosen place. They could sit on the floor, under a table, in a corner—anywhere they felt comfortable and where they could complete their reading.

Provisions for All Learners

Since Book club was designed and implemented in "real" schools, each classroom housed a diverse group of students. This diversity was noted not only in race, class, and gender differences, but also in facility with literacy. As already mentioned, teachers selected texts that reflected student interests and diversity in terms of culture, class, and gender. They also considered texts students could read either with teacher support or on their own. In addition, teachers identified students experiencing difficulties with certain texts and provided them with additional support, either through additional time or through individual or small-group instruction focused on particular needs. For example, during a biography unit, some students were not attending to details in the texts. Laura Pardo placed these students in a small group and provided them with some instruction and guided practice on noting details.

Once they demonstrated that they were doing this while reading, Laura no longer met with them as a group (see Chapter 11 for more detail about Laura's teaching). Such flexibility required teachers to monitor students' reading abilities continuously, identify weak areas, and plan instruction to meet their needs. Although this was not easy, it was easier than in more traditional settings because students were revealing their thinking through their talking and writing. As they communicated their thinking, they also uncovered problems in constructing meaning, thus clarifying for teachers what their instruction should address.

Reading–Writing Connections

Finally, we wanted students to see that reading and writing are related processes. Important to note here is that all written activities during Book Club were related to students' reading, responding to, and elaborating ideas related to books. Further, students wrote every day as a result of reading and in preparation for discussions. This provided records of students' developing reactions and responses to texts. Chapter 4 expands on this, explaining the writing component of the program; however, examples provided in the final section of this chapter demonstrate this as well.

Instruction on Literary Elements

As mentioned earlier, teachers often assume that instruction on literary elements belongs in middle or high school. However, children build understandings of plot, characterization, and metaphorical language as soon as they begin interacting with texts. For example, they construct knowledge about how stories are structured through reading (Lehr, 1991). Not only do they build these meanings, but they are likely to want to discuss or write about them if they think they are important (Eeds & Peterson, 1995). At the same time, even though children do consider these important aspects of texts, teachers must facilitate this meaning-making. That is, without the teacher's intervention, children do not always make connections between their reactions to a story and the very conscious effort of an author to evoke such responses (Eeds & Peterson, 1995).

In Book Club, teachers focus on multiple literary elements, such as plot, characterization, setting, point of view, tone, and symbolism. Students engage in a variety of written and oral responses designed to enhance their developing thinking about all the literary elements as they related to texts they read. Teachers implement a variety of written activities, including character maps, sequence charts, book critiques, and papers comparing and contrasting particular aspects of texts. Frequently, students discuss these in their book clubs so their multiple perspectives are more visible. A few examples, such as characterization, sequencing, and synthesis of themes, help demonstrate how we include instruction on literary elements within the reading program.

Characterization. When reading books with strong central characters, children may take for granted the information the author presents. That is, because major characters are key to the unfolding of events, children may assume they are real people, failing to appreciate the author's skillful ability to provide sufficient, vivid details that make fiction come to life. Further, authors choose to include characters who are not relevant to the story's unfolding but who serve a purpose for a few scenes. For example, the aunts in *James and the Giant Peach* (Dahl, 1961) are one-dimensional characters whose only purpose seems to be as motive for James to run away. The reader knows nothing of them, except that they are mean. Young readers may need help understanding why the author makes such choices. In Book Club, many books have strong central characters of ages and backgrounds similar to those of the students in the program. Thus many students identify with the characters on some level. It is important for their reading development to understand how authors create such vivid images and why they choose to elaborate some characters more than others.

Book Club teachers often begin a book by focusing on the main character and initial events leading to the conflict. Frequently, after having read several chapters, they ask students to represent one of the main characters in some way. For example, they might use a character map, ask children to draw a character, or ask them to describe verbally what the character is like. These activities provide occasions in which the teacher can monitor (1) students' constructed meanings of the characters, noting whether they are attending to key details that foreshadowed later events, (2) the character's traits each student is responding to, and (3) the discourse they use to communicate their understandings. Some examples of character maps help illustrate this.

When asked to construct a character map of Sadako, the main character in *Sadako and the Thousand Paper Cranes* (Coerr, 1977), both Lissa and Bart reveal they are constructing meanings consistent with events in the book. At the same time, their maps convey very different approaches. Lissa uses relatively simple discourse to communicate her ideas, with single words listing Sadako's qualities, such as "spirit," "courage," and "faithful" (see Figure 3.1). She also includes vague references that need elaboration to understand the connections she is making between the character and events. For example, her notation about culture and leukemia are less clear to someone who has not read the book. Thus Lissa's discourse reveals an abbreviated writing style. In contrast, Bart's character map (see Figure 3.2) contains more detail since

FIGURE 3.1. Lissa's Character Map

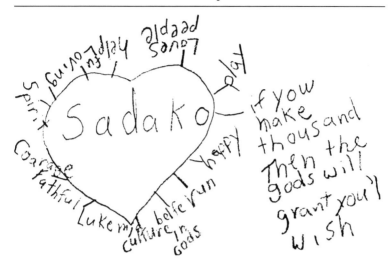

he chooses to write his ideas as more complete thoughts. While neither map proves to be a complete indicator of these students' constructed perceptions of Sadako, both provide a wealth of information about each student's constructed meaning, written discourse style, and the details they respond to. As such, they indicate the basis upon which each student develops a greater understanding of Sadako.

Having students represent their constructed perceptions of main characters facilitates the teacher's understanding of each student's meaning-making process. Activities like this not only provide the teacher with information but also stress to students that character development is an important aspect of reading to consider and discuss. Authors include particular details to evoke particular images in the reader's mind. These images are not consistent across readers, but each student understands why another might emphasize one quality over another. Further, the teacher leads instruction focused on which qualities are important in understanding the interactions between the characters and the events in the book. Sadako's courage, superstitious nature, and battle with leukemia are important; her enjoyment of running may be less so. Such activities also enable teachers to lead discussions on more minor characters. For example, after finishing the book some of the boys in Laura's class expressed frustration that Sadako's brother was not described more. They wanted to know about him, what activities he was interested in, and how he

FIGURE 3.2.   Bart's Character Map

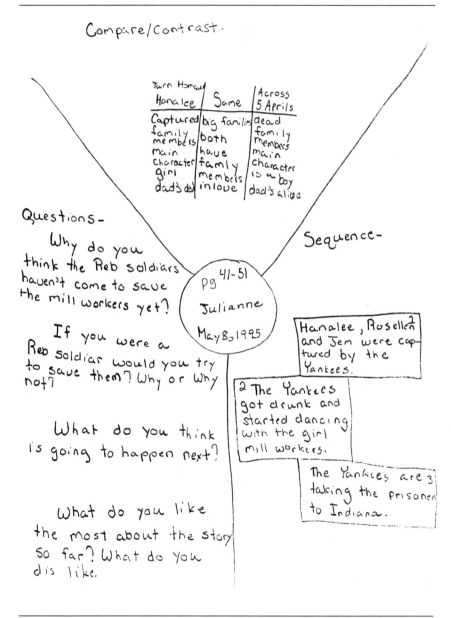

reacted to Sadako's death. This enabled Laura to provide a lesson on the role of minor characters. Thus, through such written and oral activities, students begin to understand the role of characters in books. Further, teachers understand their constructed meanings, personal responses, and preferences for discourse formats.

Sequencing. The sequence of events in a text is a powerful factor in a reader's meaning construction. In fiction, some readers enjoy texts with flashback scenes that gradually reveal the opening events. Others prefer chronological order. Also, some events are pivotal to the unfolding of the plot. If the reader forgets an event, the solution at the end may be confusing. In exposition, sequence is key to the argument being presented. In both narrative and expository texts, some events/facts are more important than others. Thus sequence is an important aspect of reading any text, so activities asking students to sequence major events reveal their meaning-making. Further, readers' choices about what to include may indicate which scenes are evoking personal responses and how students choose to communicate this.

One such activity designed to uncover students' meaning construction is the creation of a sequence chart, which reveals much to the teacher about children's constructed meaning. For example, Mondo's chart demonstrates to Laura that he is not keeping up with the assigned reading and that he is having difficulty separating topics discussed in his book club from text events (see Figure 3.3).

Mondo's chart begins with the relay race in which Sadako participates early in the book. His second picture represents the paper cranes, a factor mentioned in the title but not explained until later in the book. Mondo places the bombing of Hiroshima, an event predating those in the book but one discussed frequently in his book club, third. Finally, he includes a drawing that is hard to interpret because he has not written any explanatory note below.

Mondo's chart provided Laura considerable information about his knowledge construction. For example, at the time Laura asked students to construct this chart, they had not yet read about the origami cranes and the Japanese folk beliefs related to them. Therefore his second picture referred to the title but not to events disclosed at that point in the class's reading. His third picture indicated he was confusing book club discussion topics with text events. Laura correctly concluded that Mondo was struggling with completing the daily reading assignments; therefore he could not distinguish between book events his peers discussed and the events in the book itself. Such confusion was hampering his meaning construction related to the text. As he participated in the discussions constructing meanings related to Japan during World War II, he developed constructions that confused topics of conversa-

FIGURE 3.3.   Mondo's Sequence Chart

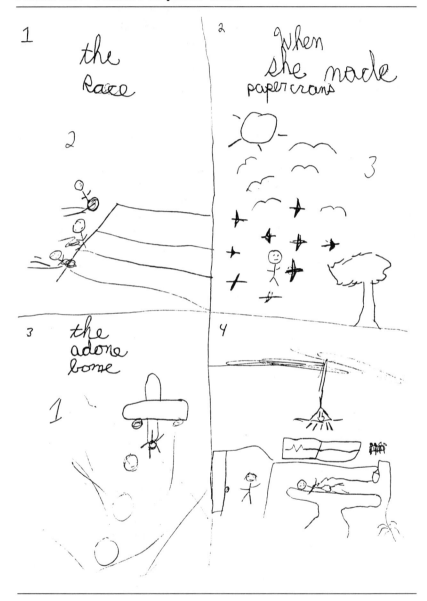

tion with actual text events. As a result, Laura provided instruction for Mondo about how to distinguish relevant events and to help him with the required reading.

Synthesis of themes. In addition to daily assignments highlighting various literary elements, Book Club teachers also include extended writing activities that enable students to make broader connections across texts. One such example is a final activity in which students selected one of many themes that connected *Sadako and the Thousand Paper Cranes, Faithful Elephants*, and *Hiroshima No Pika* (Maruki, 1980). This activity spanned several days as the class engaged in the writing process of brainstorming and drafting ideas, conferencing with peers, revising, and finalizing their papers. Bart's draft demonstrates his understanding of a theme related to innocents dying because of war.

Bart's Synthesis Paper

I am going to talk about 3 really good books that are Japanese. These three books are about Inoccent people and Elephants dying from the bomb.

The first book Im going to talk about is *Sadako and The Thousand Papper Crains*. Sadako died from the poisen which was the lukemea the lukemea was from the Itommic bomb. Sadako was Inoccent she was only 5 or 3 years old when the bomb hit. Sadako did not deserve to die.

The second book I'm going to talk about is *Hiroshima No Pika*, that means the flash in Japan. That also was about the bomb. Many people died in Hiroshima all those people were Inoccent. The only ones that weren't Inoccent were the ones who dropped the bomb on Perl Harbor. The main charecters in the story were the mom, father, and the little girl. After a few days the father dies from the Ingeries he had. He was Inoccent.

The third story Im going to talk about is *Faithful Elephants* that had something to do with the bomb. The two Elephants were Inoccent ones the owner of the zoo wanted to kill the Elephants because he was afraid that the bomb would hit and make the elephants run loose they tired to kill the elephants with needles but it would not work so they starved them and the Elephants died.

Clearly written by an elementary child, Bart's draft, written before he had made editorial changes, is a prime example of the literate discourse that results in the Book Club program. In this draft, Bart demonstrates his ability to analyze and synthesize book events to understand the broader thematic links across them. He selects relevant events from each book, identifies major characters, and synthesizes these to construct an argument that one thematic link across books is that innocent beings suffer during wars. This paper reveals his constructed meanings, his personal response, and his willingness to engage in literate discourse.

CONCLUDING COMMENTS

The reading component of Book Club is designed to facilitate and motivate elementary children's participation in a literate community by emphasizing meaning construction, personal response, and engagement in literate discourse. Key to this is providing children interesting texts and instruction on the role literary elements play in the reading process. Without engaging and interesting books, opportunities to read and respond to them, and time to develop their thinking, students cannot participate successfully in the community Book Club provides.

CHAPTER 4

When Readers Write

The Book Club Writing Component

TAFFY E. RAPHAEL and FENICE B. BOYD

Book Club was designed as an intradisciplinary reading program in the tradition described by Lipson, Valencia, Wixson, and Peters (1993). Lipson and colleagues suggest that students benefit greatly from thematic instruction that connects across what have traditionally been seen as separate subject areas. We have found it particularly troublesome that such separations occur even in the language arts—with reading, writing, and oral language activities taught as individual subjects. In this chapter, we focus on writing and the ways in which it was integrated into the students' Book Club activities. As in the other chapters in this section, we focus on the conceptual and curricular developments that underlie the role of writing in the Book Club program.

CONCEPTUAL BASES FOR WRITING IN THE BOOK CLUB PROGRAM

In developing the writing component, we drew on sociocultural perspectives emphasizing the relationship between language and thought as we focused on writing as a tool to enhance readers' learning about text. Students used writing to engage in (1) the processes of literary understanding, (2) meaningful, contextualized comprehension strategy use, and (3) extended and sustained opportunities to develop thoughts, knowledge, and positions.

Processes of Literary Understanding

A main program goal of the Book Club program is to help young readers develop dispositions and abilities to engage with text in ways that enhance their understandings about and response to literature as well as their dispositions toward valuing literary experiences. We drew on the writings of scholars such as Rosenblatt (1938/1976, 1985, 1991b; see also Clifford, 1991) who argue for the importance of both aesthetic and efferent responses. We found Langer (1990a, 1995) helpful in her articulation of stances readers assume as they engage with literature. We found the writings of Probst (1988, 1991), P. Hunt (1991), and B. E. Cullinan and Galda (1994) important for thinking about the literature's content. Through writing, we hoped to engage students in critical thinking and in opportunities to respond personally, creatively, and critically throughout their reading process.

Rosenblatt notes the importance, for those engaged in research and teaching of literary response, of offering "a satisfactory differentiation between the reading process that results in poems, stories, or plays and the process that characterizes other kinds of reading" (1985, p. 33). She uses the term *transaction* to convey the inherent balance in the contributions of both the reader and the text to meaning construction and text interpretation: Simple marks on the page become text because of their relationship to a particular reader, while "the reader brings to the text a network of past experiences in literature and in life" (1985, p. 35). She contrasts results of transactions that potentially create a "poem" (i.e., the "lived-through process or experience" [1985, p. 35])–an aesthetic response–with transactions focusing on more efferent readings. In the efferent response, the focus is on the "residue," what remains *after* the reading event, whether in the form of information to be remembered, actions to be conducted, conclusions to be formed, or judgments to be made. The aesthetic and the efferent transactions are the endpoints of a continuum, and it is on the continuum itself–rather than at the anchor points–that most transactions occur. In describing her theory almost 50 years ago, Rosenblatt (1938/1976) foreshadowed current sociocultural perspectives on response, arguing that any reading involves a particular reader who is situated culturally and historically. Thus any text may invite different readings–by the same reader at different times or in different contexts, or by different readers with their own unique literature and life histories.

Rosenblatt (1985) describes the concept of "stance" during literary readings, a notion that is key to Langer's description of the process of literary understanding (1990a; 1995). Rosenblatt and Langer each suggest that readers' stances shape the nature of the responses in which they are likely to engage. We found the four stances Langer proposed to be useful as we considered ways to involve students in a range of responses throughout their reading. Langer suggests that whether reading expository or narrative texts, readers create an envisionment and relate to that envisionment as they (1) step in, (2) move through, (3) step back, and (4) step out of it. We drew on the notion of stances not as part of a universal response process but in terms of what each stance might suggest for the kinds of writing in which students might elect to engage as they read. Together, the stances provide a framework to integrate readers' responses and their use of comprehension strategies.

The "stepping-in" stance invites students' personal response in terms of their predicted enjoyment based on the genre, their knowledge of the author, or their sense of the plot. Further, it invites attention to the role of background knowledge and experiences both in students' lives and as they relate to other texts. It draws on inferencing strategies, specifically the ability to predict, and on identifying important information such as that about author, genre, and topic.

When explaining the stepping-in stance to their students, teachers talk about the world created when readers engage with a text. Readers enter, or step into, the world that is created by the reader, the text, and the experiences readers bring to the situation. As they step in, they think about everything they know about the text's author, its genre, its focus or content, and their own relevant experiences in order to make sense of the text. Further, readers may predict what the text world might hold and how they might feel as they read the text. For example, as Julianne's book club began reading Beatty's (1984) *Turn Homeward, Hannalee*, she wrote predictions about the story in her reading log based on the cover of the book, the book jacket information, her knowledge of the genre, and a report one of her peers had presented about Civil War prisons:

> I predict that this girl will be captured and taken prisoner by the Union. I think she won't have it easy in the prison, but I think she'll get out of prison and return to her family in the end. I think this book is going to be an *excellent* book.

Teachers describe the "moving-through" stance in terms of the *reader's* influence on the *text*. That is, in the transaction between reader and text, moving through the newly created world is characterized by readers using everything they have available to make sense of and interpret the textual material. This stance reflects the merging of research in comprehension strategy instruction (e.g., using background knowledge, summarizing, sequencing) and literature (e.g., developing concepts of theme, point of view, knowledge of literary elements) with literary response.

The moving-through stance invites creative response, such as readers placing themselves in characters' situation in order to understand their moti-

FIGURE 4.1.   Julianne's Reading Log Entry

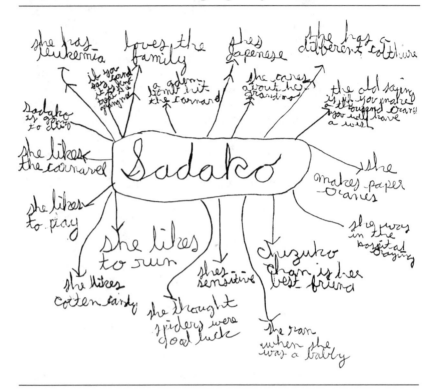

vations and feelings. It invites critical response in the form of judgments about how well the author conveyed important ideas and how easy it was to understand the story. Further, it invites students' use of comprehension strategies traditionally taught for sequencing, summarizing, inferring, and monitoring comprehension. Therefore, as readers move through a piece of text, they become involved in the story's narrative and work to construct meaning while continuing through the text. Julianne's reading log entry, illustrated in Figure 4.1, reflects her use of sequencing and comparison strategies to understand the relationship of two main characters, Rosellen and Hannalee, and her own response to their experiences as she makes sense of the story's events.

Teachers describe the stance of "stepping back" in terms of the *texts'* influence on the *reader*. In the transaction between reader and text, not only does the reader influence the text, but the text leads to changes within the reader. This stance invites more personal response and reflection than does comprehension-oriented response. Personal responses are characterized by comments about how the story impacts their feelings and beliefs. Creative response is illustrated when students place themselves in the story to consider how they might respond in such a situation. For example, when students read about the Tuck family in Babbitt's (1975) *Tuck Everlasting*, they begin to see the complexities of eternal life. What often initially seems to be a wonderful idea is complicated by the Tucks' experiences, as the characters become increasingly alienated from the times in which they still live, having lost friends who aged in ways they did not, and as the Tucks learn they needed to hide or else be regarded as "freaks." In response, Bianca wrote:

> I would not want to live for ever because I promised my dog Trixie I would see her again. Any way who would want to live forever. Your friends would get older and you would stay the same age. If you had kid your kids would grow older and you won't. People would think your a witch or warlock. . . . I think every one should live a happy and wonderful life and die. People should be able to chooce though. But me I would not want to live forever. . . . I would not want to go through all the suffering and hurtness in my hart.

Bianca drew on the characters' experiences as well as her own beliefs about mortality and an afterlife to develop her view on eternal life.

The fourth stance, "stepping out," describes metaphorically how readers leave the text world. It is in the departure that readers distance themselves from the events of the text and are in a position to critique the experience. In stepping out, readers may engage in an immediate aesthetic response, respond efferently in terms of something they have taken away to be remembered, respond creatively as they "play" with text ideas, or engage in a critical examination of the text and the effect the author has attempted to create. The stance invites comprehension strategies such as summarizing or inferring. After reading Paterson's (1988) *Park's Quest*, Eva composed an elaborate response of the text to critique the content and her own reading experience. She wrote:

> I think that It's weird the way that Thanh turned up to be Parks half sister. I mean It's crazy the way they came together. And another thing that I don't get is why did Frank marry Thanhs mother? It was his brothers girlfriend and child for crying out loud! Then the story gots an stupid ending! That dumb the way. . . . It's all about the bird and It hardly has anything to do with the grail. I did like the story but just not the ending. I would do the ending like Grandfather ends up dying because he got another stroke. And Thanh and Park go around and tell Frank what they

learned and how. Then Park will go back to Randy or better yet Randy will go down to grandfathers house and want to live there. Maybe the grandfather got his stroke from Park's dad going down to Vetenam [Vietnam] for another year to see Thanhs mother. That's what I think.

Eva stepped back from the text to take a critical perspective of some of the events in the story and the manner in which the author ended the story. Her stance enabled her to respond creatively with an alternative ending to the text, while simultaneously drawing on comprehension strategies as she summarized and interpreted story events.

As the examples illustrate, response is not independent of the literature's content. Bianca's reflections on eternity were tied directly to her lived-through experience in reading *Tuck Everlasting* and reflected an experience different from that she had reading other books. Eva's response emerged directly from the content of *Park's Quest*, integrated with her knowledge and experiences across a range of texts. These differences reflect the difference in content between these books in particular, as well as the highly evocative content that characterizes literature in general.

Probst (1988, 1991) suggests that the content of literature reflects big issues of society, culture, and humanity, including, but not limited to, love, hate, greed, justice, generosity, friendship, revenge, growing up, dying, and facing challenges. Young readers have experienced friendship before they ever encounter the friendships in *Tuck Everlasting* or Paterson's (1977) *Bridge to Terabithia*. They have had to rely on their own resources to succeed before encountering Brian and his struggles in Paulsen's (1987) *Hatchet*.

Like Probst, B. E. Cullinan and Galda (1994) describe literature's content as revealing the human experience, as both a mirror reflecting our lives and a window into the lives, times, events, and places that we may never personally experience. Thus, as children read realistic fiction, they often confront a mirror into their own lives as characters similar to themselves interact, form friendships, exact revenge, grow up, and so forth. Such literature encourages readers to reflect on their lives, to step back and think about how these reflections influence their beliefs, behaviors, and goals in life. However, realistic fiction may also take young readers into areas they never have experienced, into the lives of children whose cultures and histories differ dramatically from their own (see Harris, 1992).

Similarly, historical fiction and science fiction may take young readers to faraway places and times. Such literature serves more as a window than a mirror, giving young readers glimpses and views of life not as they know it. Such vicarious experiences are crucial to children's development as human beings. Young readers' experiences, feelings, and thoughts may be shaped by literature, just as they, in turn, shape the literature they read. The content of the literature and the stances readers assume form the basis for the transactive quality of literary response that Rosenblatt describes. The writing in which students engaged throughout the Book Club program was designed to provide opportunities to evoke a range of response to the literature they read.

Comprehension Processes

Text comprehension within a sociocultural framework raises interesting questions related to distinctions between *convention* and *invention*, between *understanding* and *interpretation*. These distinctions arise from questions of epistemology: What counts as knowledge and what boundaries exist for interpretation? Edwards and Mercer's (1987) description of the multiple goals of schooling, discussed in Chapter 3, are relevant to the issue of text comprehension. Just as there is conventional knowledge of a society that we wish our students to acquire, there are conventional meanings within texts that we want our students to understand. Research has helped to identify strategies useful to acquiring conventional text meanings and information a text may have been written to convey.

As educators, we wanted to challenge students' thinking that information is located "in" the text, to encourage them to think about what the information means, and urge them to negotiate meaning socially in personally relevant ways. However, we believe that students' interpretation and response to literature assumes that comprehension, at some level, has occurred. That is, to respond to the text requires that readers have the tools available to construct meaning and monitor their success in doing so. Thus, in addition to emphasizing response, a second purpose of the writing component was providing opportunities to learn about and use a range of comprehension strategies. These included building upon background knowledge, processing textual ideas, and monitoring comprehension.

Researchers have documented the important relationships between reading and writing in terms of underlying cognitive and social processes (e.g., Kucer, 1985; Tierney & Shanahan, 1991), text structures (e.g., Moore, 1995), and strategies for comprehending and constructing texts (e.g., Englert, Raphael, & Anderson, 1992; Tierney & Pearson, 1983). In their review of research on comprehension instruction, Dole, Duffy, Roehler, and Pearson (1991) argue for a shift from comprehension *skill* to comprehension *strategy* instruction. Defining strategies as "conscious, instantiated, and flexible plans readers apply and adapt to a variety of texts and tasks" (p. 242), they suggest five sets of strategies warranting instruction. The first set involves determining important information in text, with importance defined in terms of both the readers' purposes and the text's structure. The second set involves summarizing information within and across texts, both for the readers' own purposes (i.e., to remember or recall information) or for purposes that extend to other audiences (e.g., synthesizing information, writing essays to share with peers, teachers, etc.). Both categories are critical—while determining importance is necessary, it is not sufficient, for effective summarizing.

A third set of strategies focuses on drawing inferences "to fill in details omitted in text and to elaborate what they read" (Dole et al., 1991, p. 245). Such strategies help readers think about connections between their background and experiences, their expectations for the text, ideas from other texts, and the information in the text they are currently reading.

The fourth set of strategies involves generating questions. Dole and colleagues suggest that the ability to generate questions is critical to deep engagement with texts. Others, such as Beck, McKeown, and Worthy (1995), have found that students benefit greatly from "questioning the author," an important step in critical analysis and response to literature. Further, questions that seek to clarify text information have been an important part of multiple strategy programs, such as Palincsar and Brown's (1984) Reciprocal Teaching.

The fifth set of strategies encompasses the range of ways in which readers monitor comprehension, "being aware of the quality and the degree of one's understanding and knowing what to do and how to do it when one discovers comprehension failures" (Dole et al., 1991, p. 247). Thus the strategies in this category share the dual focus of providing tools for students to determine whether or not they need help, then helping them identify ways to attain the help they need.

With these five categories in mind, we created opportunities in the Book Club program for students to learn a range of strategies for using background knowledge, processing information from the texts they read, and monitoring their comprehension. Learning such tools through writing in response to literature, rather than as isolated practice activities, encouraged students to see the relationship among reading, response, comprehension, and interpretation.

Engaging in the Writing Process

A third area of research valuable in developing Book Club's writing component focused on the writing process. This work was distinguished from the role of writing for response and for comprehension in three ways. First, process writing involved opportunities sustained across time. Students engaged in activities from planning through going public to developing a piece of writing. Second, process writing focused on a theme or concept developed over time. That is, students engaged in writing about an idea that encouraged them to draw from multiple sources, to make intertextual connections, to respond to feedback, and to revise their thinking in ways that were not possible within their shorter reading log entries. Third, process writing created opportunities for studying and applying knowledge of literary elements – from genres to author's craft – as tools for students' own use as they created texts across themes and genres and for a variety of audiences.

We explored ways to integrate sustained writing that was thematically related to the Book Club texts. Many books, chapters, and articles have been written about the writing process detailing the existence of various aspects, including planning, drafting, revising, and going public (see, e.g., Calkins, 1986; Flower & Hayes, 1980; Graves, 1983). Scholars have argued for the importance of creating an environment in which students can socially engage around their ideas throughout the writing process (e.g., Dyson, 1993; Graves & Hansen, 1983). Scholars have also argued for the importance of instructional support as students acquire the skills, strategies, and dispositions needed for engaging in sustained writing (e.g., Hillocks, 1984; Smagorinsky, 1986). Thus, within the Book Club curriculum, we designed opportunities for students to become engaged in drawing upon the literature, their response log entries, their book club discussions, and their whole-class discussions to create their own extended texts. Sometimes the texts reflected their study of a genre, such as creating their own folktales after reading and discussing several during Book Club. At other times, the texts they created reflected issues they had struggled to understand, such as the essays Bianca and her peers wrote on eternal life after reading and discussing *Tuck Everlasting*.

WRITING AND THE BOOK CLUB CURRICULUM

Writing within the Book Club curriculum took two primary forms: (1) short, focused writing opportunities and (2) extended writing opportunities. These writing opportunities were designed to encourage students to appropriate and transform a variety of responses, comprehension strategies, and process writing tools to achieve their own goals within a range of literacy events.

Drawing on the research in response (e.g., Eeds & Wells, 1989; Raphael et al., 1992; Rosenblatt, 1991b), we defined three broad response categories: personal, creative, and critical. Personal response emphasizes readers' initial reactions to the readings: the thoughts, experiences, and feelings the text evoked. Creative response emphasizes interactions with the text that extended students' thinking and encouraged them to play with the ideas it raised. Critical response involves analyses about a text's meaning, effectiveness, and the effectiveness of the author's craft in creating the text. Figure 4.2 provides specific examples introduced to students through think-sheets, reading log prompts, and within their extended writing activities.

FIGURE 4.2.   Response to Literature in the Book Club Program

Response Emphases	Focus	Category-Specific Response Suggestions
Personal response	Valuing text read	Feelings evoked
		Degree of enjoyment
	Sharing personal stories and memories	From related texts
		From class experiences
		From family experiences
		From personal experiences
Creative response	Engaging creatively with text	Placing self-in-situation
		Altering text event(s)
		Extending the text
	Engaging creatively with author	Writing letters to author
		Asking the author questions
		Imagining self as author
Critical response	Text analysis	Of literary elements
		Of author's message
		Of effect

Complementing the teaching of literature response is instruction that drew on research on comprehension strategies. Teachers emphasize specific strategies within the five categories defined by Dole and colleagues (1991). They teach specific inferencing strategies, such as using background knowledge to make predictions; text-processing strategies, such as identifying important ideas, summarizing, and sequencing; and monitoring strategies, such as asking clarification questions. Reading logs and think-sheets provide focused writing opportunities that support students' use of response and comprehension tools.

Reading Logs

Numerous researchers have described reading logs, drawing on their work with students from first grade (e.g., Wollman-Bonilla & Werchadlo, 1995; see also Chapter 13) through middle and high schools (e.g., Atwell, 1984; Fulwiler, 1986). The reading logs integral to the Book Club program are used as daily journals inviting students to respond to the literature they read and encouraging specific comprehension strategy use.

The presence and kinds of prompts teachers use to encourage students' written response varies over the school year. Early in the year, teachers frequently use prompts to encourage students to practice particular response and comprehension strategies, often ones they recently have taught. For example, after Deb's and Laura's students read the first five chapters of Coerr's (1977) *Sadako and the Thousand Paper Cranes*, they taught students a way to illustrate key story events. The students' entries in their response logs become the basis for their book club discussion focusing on their understanding of the story (see Figures 3.1–3.3). Both teachers feel this is important for students to make sense of the events that follow Sadako's hospitalization. Similarly, when students in Laura's class begin to read *The Sign of the Beaver* (Speare, 1983), Laura prompts them to make a prediction about the upcoming story, drawing on information they had about the genre, the setting for the historical fiction, and information available by reading the information on the covers of the book. While both teachers invite students to record other responses that their reading had raised for them, in the early weeks of Book Club students tend to "try on" the various responses and strategies as their teachers introduce them (Raphael, Boyd, & Rittenhouse, 1993).

As students develop broader repertoires for response, teachers introduce them to a multiple-response format called "spokes" (see Julianne's log, pictured in Figure 4.1). The format invites students to engage in a range of responses both during and after they read specific chapters from their books. Students use a range of formats for developing their multiple responses. For example, Eva's speech from her reading log, in response to Chapter 10 from *Park's Quest* (see Figure 4.3), illustrates a variation from Julianne's spoke format in (Figure 4.1). Yet both maintain the key features.

When students use the spokes, they are to identify the chapters or pages to which they are responding, the date, and the response types they use. Further, they are encouraged to include at least three different responses. Figure 4.3 illustrates the range of Eva's responses. She uses imagery twice. First she creates a scene of Park on the telephone with his mother, Randy,

FIGURE 4.3.   Eva's Critique of *Park's Quest*

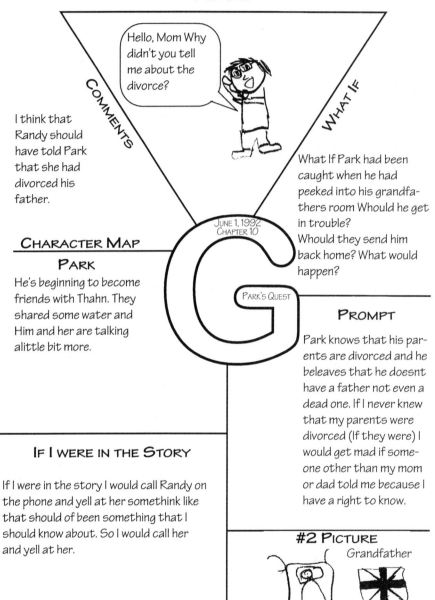

PICTURE

Hello, Mom Why didn't you tell me about the divorce?

COMMENTS

I think that Randy should have told Park that she had divorced his father.

WHAT IF

What If Park had been caught when he had peeked into his grandfathers room Whould he get in trouble? Whould they send him back home? What would happen?

JUNE 1, 1992
CHAPTER 10

PARK'S QUEST

CHARACTER MAP

PARK

He's beginning to become friends with Thahn. They shared some water and Him and her are talking alittle bit more.

PROMPT

Park knows that his parents are divorced and he beleaves that he doesnt have a father not even a dead one. If I never knew that my parents were divorced (If they were) I would get mad if someone other than my mom or dad told me because I have a right to know.

IF I WERE IN THE STORY

If I were in the story I would call Randy on the phone and yell at her somethink like that should of been something that I should know about. So I would call her and yell at her.

#2 PICTURE
Grandfather

after he found out his parents had divorced before his father was killed in the war; the imagery is consistent with her "comment" that Randy should have been more open with Park about the divorce. Second, she draws the grandfather in his bedridden state (part of a character description). In addition to focusing on the grandfather, she adds to her ongoing descriptions of Park, the main character of the story. She engages in creative response—"If I were in the story" and "What if . . . "—and she addresses the prompt that her teacher had on the wall chart. While her form varies from Julianne's, the essential features of the spoke format are the same across these two entries and both students show more than one stance in their log entries.

Focused Writing Opportunities: Think-Sheets

Think-sheets, a second form of short and focused writing, draw on the concept of procedural facilitation (Bereiter & Scardamalia, 1987; Raphael & Englert, 1990) in which specific models or prompts support students' contextualized use of newly acquired strategies or remind them of particular focuses within their reading. Sometimes the think-sheets frame particular comprehension and analysis strategies. These take forms such as providing frameworks for comparing and contrasting (see Figure 4.4), identifying interesting words for study (see Figure 4.5), critiquing, asking questions of peers or the author, and so forth.

Figure 4.4 shows the general format students use when learning about parallel traits for discussing similarities and differences within and across texts. Students learn that it is helpful to be explicit about the trait, then to talk about how they are alike or different. They use the think-sheet to compare characters, elements of plot, and other features across texts and sometimes text/film versions of stories over the course of the year. Julianne's reading log (Figure 4.1) shows her transformation of the think-sheet format to compare the two books, *Turn Homeward, Hannalee* and *Across Five Aprils*. She lists traits the two books shared in the center column (e.g., big families, both have family members in love), then lists differing traits under the respective book titles in the first and third columns. Julianne understands the concept of comparison, and she shows ownership and control of the concept as she transforms the think-sheet structure to fit her needs.

Similarly, Deb introduces critiquing to her students using a think-sheet that asks them to identify both what they thought the author had done well and what the author might have done to improve the story. Randy had used this think-sheet to critique Coerr's writing in October. In February, he draws on the format (note his paraphrasing of words from the think-sheet, indicated in italics below) to critique a specific chapter from Lowry's (1989) *Number the Stars*:

FIGURE 4.4.   Comparison/Contrast Think-Sheet

NAME _____   DATE _____

Planning for Compare/Contrast

I am going to compare and contrast _____ and
_____

First, I'll compare/contrast on _____

Alikes	Differences

Second, I'll compare/contrast on _____

Alikes	Differences

FIGURE 4.5. Crystal's Vocabulary Think-Sheet for *Island of the Blue Dolphins*

Name _Crystal_ Story/Article _Island of the Blue Dolphins_

Moving Through: Vocabulary

11-11-91 – 11-15-91

Date	Word	Page	Meaning
11-11	Island	title	Piece of land surrounded by water
11-11	Dolphin	Cover	Mammal that lives in the sea
11-11	Aleut	1	other indian tribe leader Russian
11-11	Cormorants	2	large Black sea bird
11-11	mesa	4	a hill with steep sides and a broad flat top that is similar to a
11-11	ravine	4	a deep narrow valley or gorge
11-11	toyon	4	a brush with white flowers + Red Berries
11-12	befell	12	happened
11-12	idle	12	avoiding work
11-12	rejoice	14	to feel express joy
11-13	kelp	15	a large brown seaweed
11-15	shipwreck	24	Not forward, tending to live

I think the author did well was the way she made it very funny but at the same time it is serious. *I think the author can improve on* is she needs to tell why they put dead people in the middle of the floor and she needed to tell more about the aunt

Randy's entry, like Julianne's, illustrates control over the concept of critique, modified to serve his purpose of seeking clarification of his confusion about an event in the story, a fake funeral that he had assumed was real. The critique invites his peers to clarify the confusion during their book club discussion, while at the same time conveying his belief that the author should have made this section more clear.

The vocabulary think-sheet illustrated in Figure 4.5 presents Crystal's first page of think-sheets about words, maintained during the reading of O'Dell's (1960) *Island of the Blue Dolphins*. This book, with many low-frequency words, invited a focus on word meanings in the context of the reading. Guided by the think-sheet, Crystal identified and defined key words important to comprehension (e.g., *island, Aleut*), as well as words she found interesting (e.g., *cormorants, kelp*).

As students develop their own repertoire of responses and strategies learned from both their teacher and their peers, they bring increasingly varied voices and perspectives to their book club discussions. The variety in their small-group discussions, in turn, enriches the community share sessions that follow.

Extended Writing Opportunities

While the short, focused writing plays a critical role in day-to-day reading and discussions during Book Club, extended writing opportunities are important for developing other writing skills and for enhancing the community's knowledge base. Students engage in extended writing including all aspects of the writing process for three purposes: (1) developing theme-related essays, (2) developing stories within the genre tradition of the Book Club unit book(s), and (3) connecting subject area-study and literacy instruction through informational writing.

Theme-related essays provide opportunity for students to think about the big issues raised within their discussions and to "step back" to reflect about how the readings and discussions influence their beliefs. For example, when Bianca, Eva, and their peers read *Tuck Everlasting*, they talked about their fantasies about everlasting life, what that might mean, and how societies and cultures change over time. In their reading logs, they wrote their thoughts. During book club and community share, they shared their views. An extended writing opportunity related to this unit involved asking Eva,

Bianca, and their peers to identify a "big issue" that had emerged over the course of the unit; review earlier log entries and brainstorm ways that they now think about this issue; connect their current beliefs to personal experience, ideas from the text, and ideas from earlier logs; and develop an essay to share their beliefs about the issue. Bart's synthesis paper in Chapter 3 is an illustration of the extended essay. Similarly, Stephen's essay on prejudice in Chapter 11 provides a second example of thematically related writing activities. He wrote this after reading Taylor's *Song of the Trees* (1975), *The Friendship and the Gold Cadillac* (1989), and *Mississippi Bridge* (1988). Others described how war affects ordinary people, after reading books from Avi's (1984) *The Fighting Ground* detailing events during the American Revolution to *Sadako and the Thousand Paper Cranes* detailing life in Japan following World War II.

A second form of extended writing connects to books' genres. For example, students in Deb's fourth grade read and listen to folktales representing the stories of a range of cultural groups, then talk about shared features of folktales. They compare and contrast two versions of the same folktale. For example, they read two versions of a tale of a mother whose dream was to create the most beautiful tapestry in the world and her three sons, two selfish and one generous. One version was San Souci's (1987) *The Enchanted Tapestry*; the other, Heyer's (1986) *The Weaving of a Dream*. They noted similar features such as relatively "flat" characters who are not richly developed by the author, the way magic plays an important role in the story, and the triumph of good over evil and selfishness. In another instance, they compared two versions of Cinderella, one on videotape, one a picture book. They used the two versions to make explicit the story's "essence" and potential ways it could vary and still be a Cinderella tale. After several such experiences, students created their own folktales, containing features such as characters facing difficult problems who overcome their difficulties through goodwill and magical intervention.

The third form of extended writing emphasizes informational writing for several purposes. At times, it helps prepare for reading upcoming fiction, such as studying relationships between European settlers and Native Americans prior to reading books such as *The Sign of the Beaver* or studying aspects of the Civil War prior to reading historical fiction set during that era (see Chapter 14). For example, students in Laura's fifth grade participated in a unit linking their study of the Civil War era with a set of historical fiction novels set during that time period (Raphael & Hiebert, 1996). Prior to reading the historical fiction, students engaged in a two-week research unit that begins with whole-class discussions using a modification of Ogle's (1986) K-W-L framework generating the community's knowledge base about the era and raising questions. Students then created Inquiry Charts (Hoffman, 1992), working in small research teams to address the four main questions. They then listed questions they still had as a class and as individuals, and each student identified a question to pursue individually. For example, Julianne developed a plan to learn more about Abraham Lincoln's death, including identifying resources she would use, the format for her report, and the means she would use to share the information with her peers (see Figure 4.6). She took notes, drafted, and revised until she completed the following report:

> Abraham Lincoln was the President of the United States during the Civil War. After the Civil War a tradgedy came to Lincoln, and his family, and the White House. That was the death of Abraham Lincoln.
>
> Abraham Lincoln was happy on April 14th, 1865, the war was finally over and the slaves were free. He went downstairs to eat breakfast, there he told his wife they were going to a play with major Henry R. Ratbone and his fiancee Clara Harris. They were late . . . but a box was still waiting for Lincoln, his wife, Mary, and their guests. While they were watching the play, the gaurd casualy snuck out to watch the show also. It was soon after that when someone walked through the doors pointed a Derringer Pistol, (wich is a gun) and pulled the trigger. Then he jumped out of the box onto the stage.
>
> Some people from the crowd recognized him, it was the former actor John Wilkes Booth a Confederate from Virginia. He was so mad at Lincoln for starting the war, that stopped slavery, and he didn't like the way Abe thought or acted, so he decided to kill him. The doctors came to help. . . . But at 7:22 on April 15, 1865 he died. After that John Wilkes Booth was cornered in a barn and was shot until he died.

Based on this report, Julianne developed a series of posters that she used during her oral report to frame her presentation and to help her remember the main points.

Armed with the knowledge generated from these extended writing opportunities, students are well prepared not only to read and understand novels such as Reeder's (1989) *Shades of Gray* and Beatty's (1984) *Turn Homeward, Hannalee*, they are in a position to make intertextual connections across novels and among novels' events, their own knowledge of history, and issues and themes that had emerged.

At times, the informational writing occurs after a unit, taking the place of more traditional testing. A primary goal is determining what students have learned from the unit, and a second goal, as a segue to the next unit. For example, in a unit on early exploration of North America, students in Laura's classroom read a biography of Christopher Columbus and Dorris's (1992) novel, *Morning Girl*. They developed a fundamental understanding of the complexities of exploring North America and were beginning a unit about

FIGURE 4.6.   Julianne's Plan for Her Report on Abraham Lincoln

---

Inquiry Question Planning Sheet

Name _Julianne_

Inquiry Question:

Who killed Abe, where did it happen,
when did it happen, what was the reason for the person
killing Abe, what weapon was used, and why?

Here is my **plan** for my inquiry question.

I. I will use these **resources**:

I will use a Social
Studies book, talk to
my parents, or mabey
find a whole book about Abes death, or movies.

II. This is how I will take **notes**:

I will use as many
note cards I need.

III. This is how I will show what I have learned (**written form**):

I will put together all the information
from my notes on lined paper, I
will have words up to 200 or over.

IV. This is how I will **present** the information to the class:

I am going to dress up as a
teacher and explain to them
about Abes death.

V. Here are the **enrichment** activities I will do:

I am going to use some
poster boards.

This **plan** will be accomplished by _April 21, 1995_, and if followed, I will earn a grade of
_A_.

Julianne   _4/7/95_
　　　Signature   Date

colonizing what would become the United States. The informational writing activities following the unit on early exploration were designed to reveal what students had learned about issues involved in exploration as well as what they had learned about the genre of biography.

Each student selected an explorer involved in the early exploration of North America, read at least two sources of information about the explorer, then created a biography of that person's life to share with peers. Some students wrote essays or reports, while others created posters or other visual representations. Laura was able to evaluate their understanding of conflicts in exploration as well as their knowledge of the biography genre, and students were prepared to begin studying colonization armed with a wide range of knowledge about the people involved, knowledge that was valuable as they read historical fiction related to that era.

CONCLUDING COMMENTS

The writing component of the Book Club program is a critical means for building students' comprehension abilities, their knowledge of literature and of content related to the literature, and their repertoire of response to literature. This component makes visible and meaningful a range of critical aspects of literacy development, from the study of words and the conventions of language use to the imagery and imagination that underlie effective communication through writing. Further, it helps students prepare to be active participants in their book club groups as well as within the community share events. It makes visible individual students' progress in ways that helped teachers continually modify and adapt their instructional approaches. Finally, it underscores for students that writing is a tool, one that is powerful for thinking, planning, learning, remembering, and engaging with literature.

CHAPTER 5

Book Clubs
Contexts for Students to Lead Their Own Discussions

SUSAN I. McMAHON

In November 1991, a group of students in Laura Pardo's fifth-grade class-room gathered for their book club discussion of O'Dell's (1960) *Island of the Blue Dolphin*. The segment that follows illustrates some of Book Club's goals. That is, students ask for (lines 1, 3, 5) and receive (lines 2, 4, 7) clarification when needed; make connections between their own lives and events in the text (lines 9, 10, 11); encourage others to participate (lines 8, 13); and share ideas as they occur to them, not in some preestablished order—all within the context of a conversation:

1 *Andy*: Why have the Aluits come to the island?
2 *Stark*: They came to the island to hunt.
3 *Jean*: So what did they come to hunt?
4 *Stark*: Sea otter.
5 *Mei*: They hunt sea otter?
6 *Jean*: [They come to hunt sea otters. It says so right here (*pointing to a page in the book.*)
7 *Stark*: [Uhh uh probably for fur and food.
8 *Jean*: And what problems do you think they'll cause?
9 *Stark*: [A battle.
10 *Jason*: [There might a fight because the other people don't want to have a fight. I mean, they like these animals and stuff and they want these animals because they just gonna come out and blow it up. It doesn't affect

any of the sea otters. Right now, if it was real life, there's only like a hundred thousand sea otters left in the world.

11 *Jean*: You know how they would be hunting sea otters? What if they don't catch sea otters and their nets start killing the dolphins?

12 *Stark*: Nobody probably knows. I mean it could be like a surprise.

13 *Jean*: You think that the problem will be . . . you see a battle, right?

14 *Stark*: [Yeah.

15 *Jason*: [Sort of because the Indians love their island and their animals and the islands have been there for many years. And they could just get whipped out and these other Indians could get real mad and start a fight.

As we began the Book Club project, one of our goals was to create a context in which elementary children conducted their own small-group discussions about literature. Through such discourse, students help one another construct meaning, fill in missing background knowledge, analyze and synthesize information, and solve problems. As the above section of transcript reveals, students *can* conduct meaningful conversations and create a sense of community in their groups. What this does not demonstrate, however, is that such conversations do not happen naturally. Half of the students in this group had participated in a traditional basal program in fourth grade, but the other half had participated in Book Club during fourth grade. As "second-year" students in Book Club, Jason, Mei, and Jean helped their less-experienced peers, Andy and Stark, participate (McMahon & Goatley, 1995). (For a more detailed description of Stark's progress, see Chapter 6. For a more detailed description of Mei's experiences in Book Club, see Chapter 7.) Further, Laura provided explicit instruction on literate conversations, including both modeling and scaffolding, and she provided multiple opportunities for students to engage in meaningful discussions of literature.

In this chapter I focus on the small, student-led book clubs, the core of the Book Club program. I begin with the conceptual issues on which we based our commitment to peer-led small-group discussions. Next, I discuss issues related to community building. Third, I describe the instructional process adopted during the first year in Laura Pardo's and Deb Woodman's classrooms.

CREATING CONTEXTS FOR STUDENT TALK

Book Club alters the social context of classrooms to provide multiple occasions for students to interact with their peers and teacher, to articulate their developing thoughts, to revise their thinking while reading, and to make intertextual connections. Including small-group discussions was one method of altering the social context to provide arenas for literate talk. Using small groups during reading instruction is not new. Traditionally, elementary teachers grouped students based on management issues: (1) instructional time allotted to reading, (2) perceptions about student ability, and (3) the size of the class and resulting groups (Eder, 1986). Historically, basal series often attempted to meet teachers' needs by providing a framework that allowed for the management of three reading groups. That is, they provided suggestions for pre- and post-reading activities and suggestions for instruction, enabling the teacher to assign worksheets that students completed in isolation while the teacher met with individual groups. Teachers provided leadership in the small groups by focusing attention on accuracy, fluency, skill development, and text-based comprehension questions. Students were often passive in this context—one student reading while peers waited silently for their turn. While this practice indeed included the use of small groups, the focus was on the development and monitoring of reading capabilities, not on engaging in literate talk.

While the practices outlined above facilitated the management of reading instruction, they did not provide students opportunities to engage in language use in a variety of ways as they reflected on the texts they read. Barnes (1993) notes two types of oral language use: (1) language of performance and (2) exploratory language. Language of performance dominated the practices described above. In contrast, we designed Book Club to provide a social context in which learners value one another's developing thoughts, provide feedback on one another's ideas, and revise thinking that was undeveloped or unsubstantiated by texts and personal experiences. That is, students participating in Book Club engage in exploratory talk reflecting "literate thinking" (G. Wells & Chang-Wells, 1992). When engaged in such thought, individuals make their positions explicit, connect their arguments to their position and that of others, consider alternatives, and reflect on previous arguments and their own work. Thus Book Club is not simply encouraging *more* student talk but a high quality of student discourse related to texts. The small, student-led book clubs became the sphere to encourage such discourse among peers for three reasons. First, we were committed to student-led discussions to create a social context in which learners practiced engaging in literate talk without the teacher's constant presence and intervention. Second, literate language use is a positive predictor for becoming literate (Galda, Shockley, & Pellegrini, 1995). Even though we were not initially in classrooms serving emergent readers and writers, we knew that literate talk fosters greater engagement with texts, higher motivation to read, and more meaningful interactions surrounding texts among older children. Third, creating a community in which members engage in daily discourse associated with texts not only enables them to bring their own ideas to the forefront, to be active contributors to the conversation, and to become invested in their own learning; participation in such a community also leads members to assume some responsibility for the learning of others (Krogness, 1989).

STUDENT-LED DISCUSSION GROUPS

Fostering a context in which students led their own discussions relating to texts in ways that enhanced and revealed their literate thought allowed several conversational aspects to occur in the teacher's absence: (1) Students were less likely to adopt the I-R-E interactional pattern established in most classrooms (e.g., Edwards & Mercer, 1987); (2) they engaged in more "exploratory" talk (Barnes, 1993); and (3) they assumed responsibility and ownership for their conversations because they were pursuing their questions (Freire, 1973). Instead of the I-R-E pattern, the discourse during book club resembled conversations that occur outside schools in which topics shift, ideas ebb and flow, and all discussion is prompted by participants' ideas and questions (D. Wells, 1995). This was more likely to occur without the teacher present, since the teacher may derail students' chosen topics for those more closely related to the curriculum (McMahon, 1996). Further, because they were talking with peers, students engaged in exploratory talk, resulting in a greater number of alternative interpretations, more elaborate and complex talk, and more student-generated questions (Almasi, 1995). Therefore we included student-led discussion groups in our literature-based reading program because children can learn many things from one another (Cazden, 1988a; Dyson, 1987). We based our development of the student-led discussion groups on three areas of research: (1) types of groups, (2) intended learning, and (3) representations of learning.

Types of Groups

Historically, teachers determined grouping based on perceptions of reading ability and the preference to manage no more than three groups of approximately 7 to 10 students, each group completing a different phase of the reading process at the same time: pre-reading, practice reading, and post-reading (Eder, 1986). Recently, educators have questioned such practice on multiple levels:

- The rigidity of established reading groups based on perceptions of ability
- The limitations imposed by ability grouping on student choice, interest, and motivation

- The extreme influence of management over optimal learning contexts
- The size of the groups
- The time invested in decontextualized worksheets
- The lack of student empowerment

This critique of ability grouping has led practitioners to experiment with alternatives that range from cross-age or cross-ability reading buddies (e.g., Morrice & Simmons, 1991) to heterogeneous groups reading a common text (e.g., Atwell, 1987; Keegan & Shrake, 1991), to flexible grouping from pairings to large groups (e.g., Berghoff & Egawa, 1991) to whole-class models (e.g., Cunningham, Hall, & Defee, 1991). Each of these may provide students more ownership over their reading and greater opportunities to use language to express their developing ideas; however, some argue that students need time and opportunity to articulate ideas in contexts in which they encourage one another to explain their thinking, expand it, and connect it to other concepts (Villaume, Worden, Williams, Hopkins, & Rosenblatt, 1994). Such "collaborative talk" is most likely to occur when participants are of equal status (G. Wells & Chang-Wells, 1996). Thus, to design an instructional program providing students more voice, time, flexibility, and ownership, we examined two factors related to increasing student participation: (1) mixture of students and (2) prominent roles within active communities.

Mixture of students. Book Club includes heterogeneous grouping for three reasons. First, factors other than ability influence student interactions. For example, Cohen (1986) identifies differential statuses students hold in classrooms that influence their participation: (1) social, (2) academic, (3) expert, and (4) peer. In sum, students include these statuses in their identity kits (Gee, 1990) in terms of how they define both themselves and others. This identity influences when and how each student interacts and how peers may respond. Thus a student whom the teacher identifies as a good reader with sound leadership skills may have low peer status, so other students may not follow his direction. At the same time, peers may follow another student, whom the teacher classifies as a weak reader, because they perceive her as someone with good ideas. Thus Cohen's four statuses reveal the need to look very closely at peer interactions to determine the appropriate mix for the student-led groups.

A second reason for incorporating heterogeneous groups is our goal of creating a context in which students engage in literate discourse. To be successful, a literature-based reading program combines interpretation, criticism, and response in a variety of ways, such as evaluating, reflecting, and sharing multiple responses (O'Brien, 1991). Placing students of like ability and language skills in the same groups leads to less diversity of response. Since learners profit from being able to turn to a variety of peers for knowledge and support (Dyson, 1996), students participating in Book Club need to see their peers and themselves as equal contributors in a community of discourse. In such a context differences in language ability, ethnicity, gender, and economic class become advantages since they encourage a variety of stances toward a single text. In such settings, notions of "ability" are questioned since all can participate in reading and responding. Therefore we want students of various backgrounds who exhibit multiple reading, writing, and oral language capabilities to be in each book club to contribute to the richness of the discussion, helping one another perceive the multiple stances a group of readers may adopt.

A third reason for heterogeneous grouping is the differences between the strengths students exhibit during whole-class discussions compared to those they display interacting with peers. Since meaning construction depends on purposes, texts, interests, knowledge, style, and audience (Dyson, 1996), changes in any of these may alter an individual's ability to construct meaning. This became visible as Deb and Laura noticed that some students who were perceived as "average" or "weak" readers were quite articulate when orally expressing their ideas related to texts. At the same time, some of the "good" readers were too closely tied to text-based answers to connect their reading to other texts, to their experiences, or to peers' experiences. Therefore the ability to articulate personal responses orally and make connections are other factors to consider when grouping students. Thus teachers have to observe students frequently, in multiple contexts, to understand how to best constitute the groups.

Students' roles in book club communities. Teachers provide assistance to students so they can assume leadership and responsibility for conducting their own conversations about texts. Participants in book discussions outside classrooms have legitimate reasons to speak and listen. Members clarify unclear ideas, organize the discussion, or encourage others to participate by asking sincere questions. Participants step into these roles as necessary to contribute to the conversation, not because of assigned responsibilities. Since Book Club provides an authentic context in which to discuss texts, students need opportunities and instructional support to develop the tools for engaging in literate thinking and oral response.

Readers will see in many of the transcripts throughout this book that students do indeed assume numerous roles as necessary in their discussions. Some become leaders in every book club, while others are leaders sometimes. Some accept responsibility for getting all to participate or for recording important ideas. Despite the variability among groups and within any individual student's behavior, leadership emerges and fluctuates based on the needs of the group (Goatley, Brock, & Raphael, 1995). Students assume multiple, beneficial roles in their book clubs, once the teacher has provided essential instruction, some of which is described later in this chapter.

Intended Learning

Research investigating the effectiveness of small-group interactions among students reveals that the teacher's stated goal for the group highly influences the interaction and learning that result (e.g., Johnson & Johnson, 1990). Successful Book Club teachers understand that, if the more immediate goals do not match the overarching ones supporting Book Club – providing a context in which students engage in literate thinking and talk – then the student-led discussions will fail. Therefore, teachers need to articulate carefully to students the program's goals of encouraging conversations that enable all participants to explore the multiple perspectives each one brings to the discussion. Then they can evaluate, critique, and revise their own responses in light of the perspectives their peers share in an oral discussion. Thus several aspects of reading and responding become the intended learning goals through participation in both the total program and in the student-led book clubs: (1) developing personal response, (2) articulating developing ideas, (3) analyzing and synthesizing ideas within and across texts, (4) critiquing texts and ideas, (5) developing problem solving strategies, (6) developing comprehension strategies, and (7) constructing meaning. Throughout the program, teachers emphasize each of these as purposes for reading, reacting to, and discussing texts. Further, they stress how book clubs are forums in which students engage in discourse related to these goals.

Representations of Learning

The third influential factor on the interaction in student-led groups is what the teacher defines as representations of learning. Book Club's goals include the creation of environments in which children are members of a community engaged in conversations that result in explorations of developing responses, analysis and synthesis of ideas, and critique of texts. Students articulate their own ideas, listen to others expressing their views, and revise their thinking as necessary. Therefore book club discussions are best when the representations of student learning lead to these goals. As one means of accomplishing this, teachers encourage students to record their responses in logs and use their entries as a resource during book club. Since, in addition to language, children often use drawing to respond to texts and organize their thinking (Dyson, 1996), the teachers also encourage students to represent their ideas through sketches or diagrams. Thus, to stimulate diversity of thought from the beginning, the teachers incorporate multifaceted representations of learning, including both written and oral texts communicated through words, pictures, and symbols (see Chapter 4). Further, students have choices within these options that enable them to select the best representations of their thinking at the time. Thus before, during, and after reading and discussing, students are better able to demonstrate their thinking by drawing on their own strengths, experiences, and knowledge. Sharing their representations with others in their book clubs reveals the unique connections each individual makes with the text and the resulting constructed meaning. The variety of representations contributes to the diversity of the topics discussed and promotes more lively interactions. This encouragement of, openness to, and acceptance of diverse interpretations allows students to demonstrate their strengths and unique contributions to the group, building a sense of community.

STRIVING TOWARD LITERATE TALK

Traditional instructional practices focus on individualized reading development (see Chapter 9); however, a sociocultural perspective takes into account the social, historical, and cultural contexts influencing and defining learning. No reader exists alone; instead, each is part of a larger community of literate individuals (Fish, 1980) who discuss ideas, reactions, and beliefs about texts. To understand the norms of participation in a literate community, learners must actively participate in interactions focused on their constructed meanings of texts. As a function of participation in the community, individuals develop a taste for and appreciation of what the larger community defines as literary (Purves, 1990). It is within this community of readers that the teacher is able to present opportunities for students to make connections between their own experiences and texts. In communities, individuals know one another; value one another's contribution; focus on problem solving; share responsibility and control; learn through action, reflection, and demonstration; and establish a learning atmosphere that is both predictable and allows for choice (Short, 1990). To be empowered participants in a community in which they will become increasingly knowledgeable, readers must understand their active role in integrating the salient elements of the reading process in order to engage in literate thought. Therefore the community plays an essential role in literacy development. However, many educational contexts do not provide experiences that enable learners to construct concepts of themselves and their peers as literate members of a community. In fact, most classrooms are characterized by hierarchy, competition, and individualism (Short, 1990), so modifying the social context to one of equality, cooperation, and collaboration is difficult. Further, successful literature-based programs encourage individual interpretations and/or personal response; discuss literary elements; study authors, genres, and themes in depth; focus on ideas; draw connections between life experiences and texts; and examine multiple cultures and ethnic groups (O'Brien, 1991).

To begin the community-building process, the research team observed students participating in their book clubs and analyzed transcripts of their discussions. These analyses of early conversations revealed many examples of statements that might have reflected literate thinking, but speakers needed to expand or clarify their ideas for their peers to make connections between their talk and the larger conceptual issues they were considering. Further, observations revealed that students' difficulties with conducting their own discussions fell into two categories: *how* they interacted with one another and *what* they chose to discuss.

The transcripts of early book club discussions revealed a mixture of informational and interpersonal comments. In some groups, supportive treatment among peers existed early in the first year before instruction; sometimes the content resulted in literate discourse. At the same time, many groups faltered in their efforts to become a community. Their struggles varied from interpersonal problems to difficulty maintaining a conversation of substance to a combination of the two. Some examples help illustrate this.

The following group's manner of interacting is positive, since members are successful in getting others to share their thoughts. However, there is little substance to their talk.

Jeffrey: How good did you predict?
Ashari: I predicted, I don't know. I knew, I read the story before.
Leanne: How about you, Jane?
Jane: The woodcutter sure was double dumb because all he would do is keep changing his mind. One thing he was wishing, he'd keep changing his mind.
Jeffrey: That's what you predicted? How about you, Leanne? How good did you predict?
Leanne: I predicted pretty good. There's just some parts that I was wrong.
Jeffrey: If you keep on doing it, you get really used to it. That's what I did. I didn't know nothing about the story. I predicted well. I didn't even look through the story about when she (*unclear*).

The members of this group support one another in many ways. As the self-appointed leader, Jeffrey begins on a positive note, asking all how *well* they predicted. After each member shares her impression of her prediction, Jeffrey moves on without judgment. Thus, *how* this group interacted serves as a model of support and encouragement. At the same time, the participants need to build on one another's ideas more, exploring their meanings and questioning their positions. This limitation resulted from *what* they discussed. Even though the group is engaged in a task related to the teacher's prompt to predict upcoming events, there is little substance. Jane's comment leaves the others to wonder what she is predicting. Leanne evaluates her prediction without sharing its substance with the group. Thus, while this group demonstrates the support present in some groups, their conversation lacks substance.

A second example demonstrates how some students engage in literate discourse but block others from the conversation. The following was taken from a fifth-grade group's discussion of the story, "They That Take the Sword." Three of the students, all males, are discussing what they would do if they were the main character while the fourth, a female, is ignored. The content of the conversation focuses on what each speaker thinks he would do if placed in the main character's position.

Damon: If I was Seth, I would have done what all the other Quakers did and go North.
Julio: Yeah.
Ling Chang: Yeah, but what if you got caught? You wouldn't have nothin.'
Damon: No, 'cuz if you're up North, you,
Ling Chang: I know but,
Julio: The South, but while you're tryin' to get up there and they know you're gone, and they like go huntin'.
Damon: The North won't, uhm,
Ling Chang: Once you go across the borderline, they'd be waitin.'
Kim: Hey, Hey.
Damon: But once they find out that you're not there, you'll already be uhm,
Julio: About five miles.
Damon: You'll be way ahead of 'em already.
Kim: I'm in the conversation, too.
Ling Chang: The only way they could beat 'em is like take a horse because if you just run then they could ride a horse with the dog.
Damon: Then how do you think the other Quakers got up there?
Ling Chang: 'Cuz they ran!

The boys' discussion is an interesting debate about how they might run to the North to escape the South's discrimination. Such content is aligned with Book Club's goal to encourage discourse surrounding engagement with texts. At the same time, not all members are contributing. Kim tries to enter the conversation twice, but, despite her clearly articulated sense of being left out, the boys are not willing to let her enter their conversation. Moments later, she tries again to participate saying, "Don't leave me out of the conversation," and seconds after that pleading, "Please, don't leave me out of the conversation!" Even though the boys say nothing overtly to silence her, they continue their conversation without acknowledging her presence. In analyzing several groups, our findings matched others (e.g., Alvermann, 1995/1996; Evans, 1994) that boys sometimes dominate peer-led discussions, silencing the girls. To stop this, students need to understand why such discourse patterns do not allow the group to benefit from the multiple perspectives of those present or support those whose contributions are important. However, just telling students to "encourage" their peers to participate is not sufficient.

Even though some members need to encourage others to participate in any community, many students are ineffective when they make specific attempts to invite peers into the conversation. For example, in the following brief exchange, Julio tries to get Damon to contribute.

Julio: It's your turn, Damon.
Damon: It's *your* turn, Julio.
Julio: Say somethin'.
Damon: It's your turn.
Julio: I already said somethin'.

As this short interaction reveals, Julio is trying to get Damon to participate; but because he does not have a repertoire of strategies for encouraging participation, he resorts to structured turn-taking, telling Damon to talk because it is his "turn," not because he is interested in Damon's ideas. Promptings such as simply "Say somethin'" without giving Damon suggestions for what to contribute do not provide adequate support to engage Damon in a conversation.

As we examined many early transcripts, we found that several groups resorted to the more traditional forms of turn-taking that characterize I-R-E discourse patterns but were seldom successful in sustaining conversations related to the texts. Instead, as with the group above, it resulted in a type of bickering as the reluctant peer tried to avoid comment or simply made a single statement before falling silent again. This form of "encouraging" participation is problematic for Book Club because it is ineffective, causing groups either to fall silent or to discuss unrelated topics. Even more important, these efforts frustrate all involved, detracting from a sense of membership within a community.

As the previous transcripts demonstrate, many book clubs struggle with including all members in the conversation. Another emerging issue is how some groups overtly try to silence some individuals and/or devote all their attention to procedural issues instead of talk about texts. The following transcript illustrates both of these situations occurring at the same time.

David: You are looking at that one question when we can't jump to another
     question without answering it.
Georgio: Shut up, David.
David: But we should answer that question first!
Georgio: Okay, we get the point.
Antonio: Shut up, man!
Maria: Why didn't it say anything about . . . why didn't it say anything
     about it at the beginning and the end?
David: Probably because it [was
Enrika: [Why don't you shut up?

This transcript reveals how some students try to silence others by being rude. David tries to participate in this discussion, but group members tell him to "shut up," demonstrating a lack of interest in his ideas. Such treatment does not foster a sense of community in which students can safely share differing perspectives; instead, it creates a risky environment in which some members are eventually silenced. Further, the content is limited to an argument related to procedures.

Together, these examples show the range of struggles across the classes. Some students are polite and supportive but do not engage in substantive interactions. Others conduct interesting, literate conversations but ignore some members. Still others are unsupportive and unproductive. Clearly, to facilitate the development of a sense of a community of readers and writers who share ideas, teachers need to provide instruction that explicitly demonstrates ways of supporting one another. Therefore, Book Club teachers provide explicit instruction on the reasons why all members should participate (they have valuable ideas to contribute), how to be effective when trying to encourage peers to engage in the conversation, and what constitutes a literate conversation about texts. In sum, analysis of transcripts of early book clubs became sources for identifying both existing limitations within the groups and examples to use for instruction. This knowledge influenced the ongoing refinement of the Book Club program.

CURRICULAR ISSUES

Using the existing strengths and weaknesses in the book clubs as a basis, the teachers began providing the necessary guidelines for successful group discussions (McGee, 1995). As the research team met and discussed the curriculum, we outlined three components of our instructional plans: (1) explicit instruction, (2) modeling, and (3) scaffolding.

Explicit Instruction

Explicit instruction refers to all those elements of discourse that Laura and Deb discussed candidly during Book Club. For the student-led interactions, the teachers explicitly addressed how expectations for these interactions differed from other kinds of school talk. First, they outlined Book Club's goals and purposes so that students understood why they were changing the learning context from the ones they had previously experienced. Laura and Deb explained how Book Club was engaging students in the literate discourse active members of a community engage in. As participants in this community the students increased their learning and enjoyment of reading, writing, and discussing texts.

A second aspect of the instruction focused on the *how* of participation in book clubs. To clarify this, Laura and Deb provided instruction emphasizing the differences between "school talk" and "outside-school talk." That is, they had students describe how they had traditionally participated in classroom discussions. Their answers revealed, sometimes with additional teacher prompting, that in most classrooms they could only talk when the teacher asked a specific question, that their response needed to be an answer to this question, and that they rarely had occasions to express their own questions or issues of interest. Further, they explained that, in school, only one person speaks at a time, no one interrupts, and everyone must talk when called upon. Finally, they noted that the person leading discussions is the teacher. Once students had listed these qualities of "classroom talk," Laura and Deb focused their attention on "outside-school talk," asking them about conversations at the dinner table, with parents, with other adults, and with peers. This led to students identifying how interactions outside school are often marked by overlapping talk, interruptions, talking when someone has an idea to share, and various members assuming responsibility for maintaining the conversation. Listing the contrasts between more traditional school talk and the students' other talk enabled Laura and Deb to clarify explicitly how they wanted students to interact during their book clubs.

The third factor identified for explicit instruction was the *what* of their conversations; that is, the content. As with interactional styles, Laura and Deb had students describe the substance of school talk during reading and compare it to the kinds of things they discussed when outside school. This discussion led students to create a list of school content, such as proving comprehension, staying focused on curriculum, and emphasizing consensus. The essence of talk outside school related to topics of interest, making connections to life, and debating opposing positions. As with the *how* of interactions, Laura and Deb made a list of contrasting ideas about the *what* of their book club discussions, clarifying that book club talk should be more like the conversations students have in other contexts; at the same time, however, it should be literate talk, focusing on the texts by pursuing (1) related topics students found interesting; (2) connections they were making across texts, to their lives, and to school; (3) expressions of their interpretations, even if they differed from those of their peers; and (4) content related to the school curriculum, such as literary elements (see Chapter 3).

Thus explicit instruction focused on fostering better conversations in the book clubs. The teachers achieved this by emphasizing the purposes for both the total program and for the small, student-led discussions. Further, they explained their reasons for wanting students to interact with peers in book club. Finally the instruction stressed the variety of content for their discussions. While explicit instruction was necessary, it was not sufficient. Instruction also included teacher modeling of desired interactions.

Modeling

A modeling component was included in the instruction because a sociocultural perspective requires educators to consider the need for students to have a social experience with the concepts they are learning. Vygotsky (1978) argued that learning occurs first on an external social plane between individuals, then is later internalized (see Chapter 2). Therefore teachers needed to model concepts for students in an external, social context before they could internalize them. For behavioral learning such as shooting a basketball, the modeling is clear; however, for cognitive acts, the modeling must reveal how the teacher is thinking through a concept. For the book clubs, the teachers demonstrated explicitly the thinking required for successful discussions, particularly analysis, synthesis, and problem solving. For this, the teachers illustrated how to analyze a discussion to determine what was going well and what needed to be improved. This modeled instruction included four focuses of analysis: (1) an adult-modeled book club discussion, (2) transcripts of their discussions, (3) audiotaped book clubs, and (4) videotaped discussions.

Adult-modeled book club. Early in the school year, adults (researchers on the original project) modeled a total of four different discussions for both Laura's and Deb's classes. In the first example, the adults clearly were not listening to one another speak. Instead, members read from their logs in round-robin fashion without contributing to one another's ideas. In a second example, two participants rudely interrupted one another. In the third, the adult panel demonstrated how some participants contributed ideas furthering the group's construction of meaning while others ended up contributing nothing of substance to the discussion. The fourth adult-modeled book club attempted to demonstrate the desired goals of a community in which all members shared their thinking when relevant and the substance was focused on issues related to the text.

After each modeled discussion, the teacher led an analysis with her own class. Each time she asked students to identify what the group had done well. The purpose of beginning with strengths, even with the obviously poor discussions, was to convey to students the need to look closely for strengths in any group. Once students had listed the positive aspects of a group, the teacher focused on what participants could improve. After this, the class engaged in the decision-making process of selecting areas to strengthen and problem-solving discussion of how to improve. Teachers guided this process, helping students focus on both the *process* and *content* of the discussion. Once students had analyzed one modeled discussion, synthesized the major issues, and identified the means to address the problems, the adults modeled another book club discussion.

Modeling book club discussions provided a relatively risk-free context in which students could closely examine participation in book clubs. Since those modeling the behaviors were adults, students knew the discussions were presented for instructional purposes. Thus critiquing the conversation was safe; criticism could not be perceived as personal attack. Once Laura and Deb thought students understood the modeled process of critique, they moved to the next phase–analysis of "blind" transcripts. (See Chapter 12 for an alternative means of providing a whole-class forum to observe and discuss student-led discussions.)

Analysis of transcripts. The second phase mirrored the first, except that, instead of having adults role-play a discussion, Laura and Deb used sections of transcripts from book clubs. The names on the transcripts were changed to pseudonyms so that students could not identify which peer group they were analyzing. The teachers used the transcripts much like a reader's theater–volunteers assumed roles, read through the transcript once, then read it aloud for the class. As with the adult-modeled book clubs, teachers initiated the discussion by asking what the transcribed group had done well. Once this was noted, the class identified areas that needed improvement, prioritized what the group probably should work on next, then discussed how the group could address the problems. All this was completed without ever identifying the specific group because the purpose was to model the *process* of identifying the strengths and areas for improvement within a group and planning a course of action. As students internalized this in a total-group setting, they began adapting it for their own book clubs. Once students seemed skilled at critiquing the blind transcripts, Laura and Deb moved into phases three and four, which included analyses of audio- and videotaped book clubs.

Audio- and videotaped discussions. The final two phases of the modeling of both the *how* and *what* of their conversations were very similar to the earlier ones since they, too, included explicit discussions about the strengths and needed improvements of various book club discussions. The major difference was that with the tapes, students could identify which peers were participating in the group. This had the potential to include personal attacks, but since the teachers had extensively modeled the necessary analysis process that identified both positive and negative aspects of the discussion and focused on the discussion, not on individual traits, they knew that students were well-prepared for constructive analyses. Both classes began with audiotaped discussions because this enabled students to focus on the talk alone, listening to tone and following the content. Once this activity had provided specific feedback to all groups, the teachers shifted to analyses of videotaped discussions, enabling students to examine body language that either encouraged or discouraged participation, clarification, elaboration, and/or debate.

Modeling the process of analyzing discussions took several months in both Laura's and Deb's classrooms. While taking up a significant amount of instructional time initially, time devoted to modeling decreased as students internalized the process. Over time, their book clubs continually improved and required less intervention from the teachers. Thus the entire team believed that modeling was an essential instructional component for helping students assume responsibility for leading their own discussions. At the same time, modeling was coupled with explicit instruction and with scaffolding.

Scaffolded Instruction

As with modeling, the teachers also incorporated scaffolded instruction to facilitate students' adjustments to the new expectations for participation in class discussions. This too required analysis, problem solving, and synthesis. Each day while students met in their book clubs, both Laura and Deb circulated among them. Early in the year, the teacher needed to stop frequently, join a group, and provide support so that they could continue their discussion. Sometimes students' conversation meandered to other topics and they needed help getting back to a conversation related to the book. Sometimes members were silent and peers needed help encouraging participation. Whatever the problem, the teacher joined the group only long enough to help them identify the problem and solve it (Hauschildt & McMahon, 1997).

FIGURE 5.1. Self-Assessment Sheet

Name _____   Book _____

Stepping Back

	Date	Date	Date	Date	Date
Did I read the assigned pages?					
If not, I will read the pages during . . .?					
Did I write in my log book before starting Book Club?					
Did I find any new words for my vocabulary sheet?					
Did I write any questions for the author?					
Did I write any questions for my group?					
Did I do a free choice?					
If yes, which one?					
Did I share during Book Club?					
Did I listen to others?					
My Book Club today was . . .?					

Important Comments
Date: _____
Date: _____
Date: _____

Then she left the group to continue circulating. As the year progressed, there was increasingly less need for the teacher to join groups for this purpose.

A second form of scaffolded support that both Laura and Deb initiated as students began assuming responsibility for their own discussions was the inclusion of a self-assessment sheet (see Figure 5.1). Generally, this sheet required students to analyze their own participation in the group, identify whether each member had done everything possible to foster a quality conversation, and plan for future problem solving. For students who needed additional help, Laura and Deb wrote specific notes to them either on the sheet or in journals, trying to help students assume responsibility for solving their own dilemmas (see Chapter 6 for a specific example of this with one student).

Thus the curriculum of Book Club included content that helped students focus on their own participation in the small student-led discussions. This was not the only curriculum that Laura and Deb taught, but it was an extremely important aspect in getting students to assume responsibility for their own discussions. While change takes time and any book club discussion could be better, all members of the research team noted significant improvement in the book clubs over time. The transcript that began this chapter as well as those in other chapters of this book reveal how well students achieved the overall goal of engaging in literate talk.

CONCLUDING COMMENTS

Small-group, student-led discussions about texts are the "heart" of the Book Club program. Within the program, teachers build social contexts in which students lead their own literate conversations related to literature. In such settings, students turn to one another for help, provide assistance to peers who struggle in constructing meaning from a text, expand their own ideas, and make connections between literature and their own lives. In their book clubs, students collaborate to create contexts in which all members contribute. These student-led discussions are key to the program, but such social settings do not occur naturally. Instead, they grow and develop with instructional support. This support requires an integrated approach to literacy instruction by including reading, writing, speaking, and listening. With this support, elementary children can and do become engaged in reading literature and in participating in literary conversations.

Learning to Be Literate

Reconciling Convention and Invention

GORDON WELLS

Teaching children to be literate has probably been the most basic objective of schooling since the institution was first invented. Indeed, the three R's constituted the total curriculum of the earliest public schools. However, things have changed in the last hundred years; not the least of these is the definition of what it means to be literate (Resnick & Resnick, 1977). No longer is being able to decode print to speech a sufficient criterion of the ability to read, nor even is "literal" comprehension. Literate students are expected to make connections to their own past and possible future experiences, including intertextual connections to other texts they have read; to draw inferences from what is written (or not written, that might have been), including the detection of biases of various kinds; and to evaluate critically the significance of what they read, giving justifications for their judgments. Similar changes have taken place with respect to writing. While the ability to observe the conventions of "standard" grammar, spelling, and punctuation continues to be important, a literate person is also expected to be able to compose texts that, through appropriate choices of genre and style, effectively achieve the author's purpose with respect to the topic and anticipated audience and, at the same time, speak with an authentic, personal voice. Furthermore, both as reader and writer, a literate person is expected to be able to use texts as tools for participating in both personal and collaborative knowledge construction and the development of understanding.

Not surprisingly, with such goals for literacy learning in view, the traditional method of literacy teaching, with its dependence on prepackaged curriculum content, its entombment in "basal" readers and worksheets, and its pedagogical emphasis on teacher-directed recitation and students' mindless practice of decontextualized "skills," has been found to be totally inadequate. As a result, there have in recent decades been a variety of attempts to give students a more active role in the process—by allowing them a greater measure of control over what they read and write and over the purposes for which they do so, and by seeking to integrate the formerly separate language activities of reading, writing, and talking. Nevertheless, despite the good intentions and enthusiastic commitment of the educators involved, these attempts have not always succeeded in achieving their overall objective, namely, that of creating classroom communities that support the sustained development of fully literate individuals.

There are doubtless many reasons for this—not least of which is the politicizing of some of the issues involved, such as the place of mastery of phoneme–grapheme correspondence in the early stages and the appropriateness of children's being encouraged to think for themselves and to be critical of beliefs and values in which some of their elders have a vested interest. However, the root of the problems encountered is not always external. In some cases, it may be found in the absence of a coherent theoretical basis for the changes that are recommended; in others, it is the piecemeal nature of the proposed innovations that leads to a lack of balance between *convention* and *invention* and to the continued focus on language as an end in itself rather than as a means for acting, thinking, feeling, and communicating in relation to all aspects of living and learning in and out of the classroom. A third possible source of problems is the separation between design and implementation that can easily occur when educational change is mandated from above and teachers are not encouraged to take major responsibility for planning, evaluating, and modifying classroom practices in the light of their knowledge of local conditions. I propose to examine Book Club from these latter perspectives.

THE PLACE OF LITERATURE IN BOOK CLUB

One widely recommended innovation is the use of children's literature (often referred to as "trade books") as the basis of the reading program. This is certainly an improvement when compared with a reading diet restricted to the doings of Dick and Dora and their ilk. Children are much more motivated to read when they are able to select what appeals to them; they also read more if they find the activity itself pleasurable. Schemes such as "Borrow-a-Book," in which children take books home to share with family members, or "Buddy Reading," in which children at different grade levels read together in pairs, are successful because, with a wide range of material from which to select, readers at different ages and stages of development can find books that both partners find interesting; they also enjoy the social interaction about books that these schemes involve. Furthermore, through giving thought to what would be suitable for a particular partner, children also begin to develop a more conscious awareness of the criteria for choice. Thus, if only for the greater pleasure that children gain from their reading, and hence for the development of a disposition to choose to read for this reason, the move to a literature-based reading program is surely to be recommended.

However, this change is not unproblematic. With children essentially designing their own programs on an individual basis, the organizational demands on teachers increase considerably. Of course, whatever the approach, children's progress should be individually monitored and instruction given systematically as needed. When the program was organized by the sequence of tasks laid out in a published scheme and children were assigned to relatively homogeneous groups, this responsibility was often off-loaded, to a considerable extent, onto the scheme itself. With an individualized literature-based program, however, this is no longer possible. Instead, teachers have to design their own method of monitoring and ensure that they apply it systematically. Unfortunately, this does not always happen and, as a result, in many such classrooms, some children slip between the cracks and do not receive the specific type of help that they need. One of the strengths of Book Club is that the monitoring of reading strategies, and the provision of appropriate instruction, is an explicit feature of the approach. I shall return to this below.

But just as problematic is the status of "literature" in the switch from basals to trade books. To make the change solely to increase the motivation to read is not sufficient to ensure that children will reap the benefits of engagement with literary texts—that is, texts that have been deliberately crafted as autonomous works of art. As is abundantly clear from many senior literature classes, the classics can be studied as if they were textbooks. A similar approach is also built into some of the brand-name "literature-based" basal reading series that have begun to appear for junior students; the selected passages may be chosen from works that have genuine literary value but, in the workbook exercises, the passages are mined, as before, for their "information" by means of the all-too-familiar literal comprehension questions, and literary patterns are made the basis for the routine practice of formal structures with little or no thought about their contribution to the aesthetic effect of the poem or story in which they appear.

Therefore, if we are serious about making literature the basis of the learning and teaching of literacy, we need to ask ourselves what exactly is to be gained from engaging with literary texts (Chambers, 1983). In my view, there are at least three benefits, each equally important. First, literature enables us to go beyond our individual, lived experience and, through the imagination, to know other possibilities—events, actions, and feelings—that deepen our understanding and extend our potential for responding sympathetically and intelligently to the situations that we actually encounter (Hoggart, 1970). Literature can thus contribute significantly to personal development and the formation of identity. Second, literature constitutes an important part of our cultural heritage(s). To know who we are, we need to know about our past. And by this I do not mean facts about the past so much as the values, beliefs, and concerns of previous generations, as these are expressed in the poetry, drama, fiction, and nonfiction that has come down to us, and in contemporary literature that re-presents these heritages in forms that are accessible to readers of today. Reading literature can thus help us to understand the relation of our individual life trajectories to the historical trajectories of the cultures that have formed us and that we, in turn, are forming. Third, literary texts are works of art; they are both unique embodiments of their authors' intentions and artifacts that are deliberately crafted through the use and transformation of the genre-related resources of linguistic form and patterning that the culture makes available (Bakhtin, 1986). Recognizing how these literary elements are being used adds significantly to one's aesthetic appreciation of a particular literary text; it also increases one's own repertoire as a writer. However, learning to recognize these elements and how they produce their effects is itself dependent on reading with aesthetic awareness and consciously developing one's own voice as a writer.

For children to reap the benefits of a literature-based program, therefore, more is required than a collection of trade books from which they can make individual choices. To begin with, care must be taken in assembling the collection to ensure that it contains books of genuine literary merit; attention to the known and likely interests of the particular class of children is also critical, as is sensitivity to the representativeness of the events and characters presented in terms of gender, class, ethnicity, and cultural heritage (Booth & Barton, 1991). Opportunities for children to explore the significance of what they read–its connections to their own experience and that of their families and communities, past as well as present–are also essential, as are opportunities to respond to what they read in terms of their developing understanding of the world and of their possible ways of being and acting in it. To read and write in these ways, most children need systematic guidance and assistance; and all need interested others with whom to dialogue about what they read and write.

In the preceding chapters, it is clear that the developers of Book Club are fully aware of all these requirements. But what I think is noteworthy is the manner in which Book Club attempts to meet them. In many literature-based programs, children are required to write a report on each book they read; in many classrooms, too, children keep a response journal. Here, the teacher tends to be the only partner, and writing the only mode of response (Swartz,

1994). In other classrooms, children may read with a peer, with whom they discuss the book they are reading together, or they may work in a group, studying the same novel and then together presenting a multimodal response to the rest of the class (Chang-Wells & Wells, 1993). In these latter conditions, making sense and evaluating the significance of what they read benefits from the input of peers, who often bring perspectives from diverse backgrounds. In addition, because the initial response is oral, it is more likely to be exploratory and negotiative than when it is made individually and in writing. However, despite the merits of reader-response activities that involve groups of students in purposeful booktalk, such approaches rarely encourage students to engage with what they read as literature in terms of more than the first of the three benefits outlined above, namely that of personal relevance (Chambers, 1985). Still more rarely do they attempt to relate all three in a program that simultaneously integrates reading, writing, and talking about literature with other activities in which the students are engaged, or to do so in an organizational structure that balances individual, group, and whole-class participation (Booth, 1994).

THE THEORETICAL FOUNDATIONS OF BOOK CLUB

It is this systematic comprehensiveness that I find noteworthy about Book Club, and I attribute it in large part to the solid theoretical foundations on which the program is built. In its general orientation, Book Club is inspired by Vygotsky's theory of learning and development, and by the work of those who have extended and developed it in recent decades. This theoretical rationale is presented in considerable detail in the preceding chapters, so it is not necessary for me to recapitulate it here. Instead, I shall add what are essentially a few footnotes to the earlier presentation of sociocultural theory, focusing on some of the tensions that it highlights and on the way in which those tensions are dialectically reconstructed.

Perhaps the most striking of Vygotsky's claims, in this respect, concerns the *social* origin of individual intellectual development: "All higher mental functions are internalized social relationships," he wrote (1981, p. 164). In our highly individualistic culture, the idea that intelligence is taken over from others rather than being genetically given at birth is at least disconcerting, if not self-contradictory. Yet when we read his explanation of how the social (intermental) becomes individual (intramental) through social interaction in the zone of proximal development, the idea seems almost self-evidently correct (Vygotsky, 1987, chap. 6). In general terms, Vygotsky argued that intelligence develops through participation in joint activities of various kinds, in which others – adults and/or peers – provide assistance that enables children to achieve more than they can manage alone and, in the process, make available models for children to take over and to construct as part of their own individual resources for further participation. Chief among these resources are various semiotic tools for joint and solo meaning-making, of which spoken language is the most versatile and ubiquitous. It is by learning to use language in its various social modes and functions when interacting with others, Vygotsky argued, that children come to be able to use speech "internally", as the mediator for their own thinking. It is in *this* way that children develop the higher mental functions and so become able to "enter into the intellectual life of those around them" (Vygotsky, 1987, p. 88).

More recently, Halliday (1975, 1993) has put forward a highly compatible "language-based theory of learning" from the perspective of social semiotics, in which he spells out in more detail ideas similar to those that Vygotsky only sketched. What Halliday emphasizes is the way in which, in learning to use the different modes of language (spoken and written) in the registers and genres appropriate for different activities, children also construct culturally given means of construing and interpreting experience, including experience gained vicariously through literature; furthermore, in this process of appropriation they themselves are transformed, as also, to some extent, is the toolkit of linguistic resources that is appropriated (Wells, 1994a, 1996). For both Vygotsky and Halliday, then, intellectual development is quite largely about learning to use the culture's semiotic resources in the course of purposeful activities with others in ways that both conform to cultural norms (allowing one to participate effectively) and express one's individual perspective (making a contribution that advances the activity and/or extends one's own, as well as the group's, understanding). For this development to occur, however, two conditions must be met: There must be clear demonstrations of these resources in use – models to be appropriated – as well as opportunities to use them for oneself in interactive situations that are challenging, while still being supportive. This relationship between cultural continuity and individual originality, between convention and invention, is well captured diagramatically in the adaptation of Harré's "Vygotsky space" (Figure 2.1); it is also the basis of the four constituent processes of the writing component of Book Club.

A similar productive tension between convention and invention applies also to reading, as is argued by Lotman (1988), a contemporary Russian semiotician in the sociocultural tradition. Every text, he proposes, serves two functions. The first is to convey the author's meaning as adequately as possible. In this function, the text acts like a conduit to carry meaning from one mind to another (although, of course, this is never entirely possible, for the reasons spelled out in Chapter 4). Lotman calls this the "univocal" function;

it is what is emphasized in traditional teaching of comprehension. Although inadequate as the sole basis of response, the univocal function does nevertheless fulfill one important purpose of written texts, which is to provide "a common memory for the group" (p. 35), that is, to contribute to the maintenance of cultural cohesion and consensus.

Just as important in Lotman's view, though, is the second function, which he calls "dialogic." When read in terms of this function, the text acts as what he calls "a thinking device." In considering what the text could mean and how to respond to it, readers use it as "a generator of meaning" (p. 40) and so enrich and extend their own understanding. (In passing, it should also be added that, in this way, a text can function as "the more knowledgeable other" in the reader's zone of proximal development.) However, for a text to function for a reader as a thinking device, the reader must recognize that more than one interpretation of the text is possible and that no one of these should be treated as *the* final and authoritative statement on the topic.

However, here there is an apparent paradox. The conventional meaning of a text (i.e., the meaning derived through the univocal function) is, at one level, the basis for the dialogic response that the reader makes to it; until the conventional meaning has been understood, it might seem, it is not possible for the reader to proceed to a personal interpretation. In practice, however, it is often *only* by engaging with a text dialogically–by bringing one's personal experience and current concerns to the transaction with it–that any coherent meaning can be made at all. Only then is it possible, by entering into dialogue with others about the different interpretations that each has constructed, to work toward a consensus concerning the conventional meaning.

Reading in this way, as an engagement in an ongoing dialogue, is of course a normal and natural way to engage with a text. As Bakhtin (1986) has suggested, responding to a written text, if only in an inner dialogue, is a necessary part of the act of comprehending. Furthermore, it is a natural continuation of the process whereby the text one is reading came into being. For every text has a cultural and historical context; it does not emerge, *ab initio*, from the mind of its author, but is prompted by the author's interactions with others, particularly with the texts of other writers that the author has read.

From reading the preceding chapters, it is clear that, in Book Club, both the univocal (conventional) and the dialogic (inventional) functions of written texts are given due attention, as well as the relationship between them. Indeed, to my mind, one of the strengths of this program is precisely that it is this dialectical relationship between the univocal and the dialogic functions of texts that is enacted in the organizational relationship between reading and writing and between the book club and community share components of the total program. And it is in the different modes of talk that weave these different activities together that the seeming paradox of the social origins of mental functioning is so satisfactorily resolved.

A TEACHERLY PERSPECTIVE ON BOOK CLUB

For most teachers who are wondering whether to introduce Book Club into their classrooms, however, the soundness of the program's theoretical foundations will not be the prime consideration. Initially, what matters most to practitioners is whether an innovative program is coherent in implementation. That is, do the authors describe it in such a way that other teachers can see how it might fit into their way of organizing the totality of curricular activities? On this score, the preceding chapters seem to me to be extremely helpful. They not only describe the way in which the various components have been articulated in several different classrooms, but they explain in considerable detail the pedagogical rationale for the suggested organization.

For me, the most valuable aspect of the presentation is the clear explanation of the rationale concerning when and why to provide explicit modeling and instruction. It is too often assumed that, in a program that values student choice and creativity, there is no place for the teacher to intervene with direct instruction. However, as the authors make clear, simply providing a well-chosen selection of reading material is not sufficient to bring into being an environment in which "students would develop the necessary literary knowledge and literacy tools to participate fully and effectively in talk about text" (Chapter 1). Since most students are unlikely to engage in such practices outside the classroom, they need to have the aims of the program explained to them, to be shown what constructive booktalk looks like, and to be introduced to a variety of forms that responses may take.

A second important feature of the preceding chapters is the emphasis on community and the many suggestions as to how teachers can, with their students, create a community that engages with literature in a spirit of open-ended exploration and inquiry. Reading should certainly be enjoyable; it should also feed the imagination in ways that enable students to envisage possibilities of acting and feeling that transcend their past and present experience. But it should also encourage them to question what they currently believe and invite them to explore aspects of the world with which they are barely familiar. Individual students may already have developed the disposition to use books as a means of extending their understanding in diverse directions, but there is no doubt that this disposition will develop most readily when it is made central to the practices of a classroom community that is organized around inquiry (Wells, 1995).

CONVENTION AND INVENTION:
THE INTERDEPENDENT GOALS OF EDUCATION

In our increasingly complex society, schools have become charged with a wide range of responsibilities, ranging from child-minding to gatekeeping. However, the principal goals of formal education remain the same: first, to induct each new generation into the values and practices of the wider culture and to equip them with the disposition, knowledge, and skills to participate as productive and responsible citizens; and second, by recognizing and valuing the diversity of talents, interests, and experiences among them, to enable all students to realize their full potential as unique, creative individuals. In the history of public education, these goals have often been treated as incompatible, and the first has been given priority over the second. From a sociocultural perspective, however, they are more appropriately seen as complementary. For without the opportunity to participate in the ongoing practices of the culture, there would be no basis on which individuals could develop their unique identities and potential for participation; and without encouragement of the diversity of individual creativity, society as a whole would be deprived of those contributions that enable it to be self-renewing in its response to new challenges.

It is just such a concern to achieve a dialectical interdependence between convention and invention that is, as I have suggested above, the most significant feature of Book Club, both in the authors' exposition of its theoretical foundations and in the organizational structure that they suggest for its enactment. However, what is perhaps even more significant is that, in the relationship between the two components, community share and book club, and the activities that are proposed as central to each, the authors offer us a model of education that might equally fruitfully be introduced in other areas of the curriculum as well.

Furthermore, the tension between reproducing conventional beliefs and practices because they have served well in the past, on the one hand, and encouraging the risk taking involved in inventing new ways of thinking and acting in response to the problems of the present and future, on the other, is not felt only in the education of those designated as "students." It is also just as critical in the preparation and continuing professional development of teachers. Indeed, if we hope to see this tension reconstrued as productive interdependence in the school experiences of children, it must simultaneously be so experienced by those who teach them. That is to say, teachers must be enabled and encouraged to construct their own practice-oriented theory of teaching by forging a dialectical relationship between the generalized, theoretical recommendations of external experts and the personal understanding that grows out of reflection on the practices for which they are responsible in their own classrooms (Wells, 1994b).

In this context, the final feature of Book Club to which I should like to draw attention is the manner in which the program was, and is being, developed. From its inception, it involved a collaborative partnership between university and classroom and, as the following chapters make clear, its continuing development is enriched by the experiences of classroom teachers who are adapting it to the specific situations in which they work. As every teacher knows, any program needs to be modified to suit the needs of his or her particular students, despite the claims of universal applicability that are sometimes made by curriculum developers; indeed, no program can be exactly repeated, even by the same teacher with the students in successive years. However, Book Club does not merely allow for modification. It is a program that deliberately invites teachers to be teacher inquirers as, in using it, they seek the best ways to enable their students to become literate thinkers, readers, writers, and talkers. And, as is made clear, this will most successfully be achieved if they engage their students with them in communities of literate inquiry.

Section II

Extending Research on the Book Club Program

The members of the original Book Club research team had a variety of interests and reasons for becoming involved in the project. The authors in this section extended the original research as they explored questions related to their own interests. Section II contains five chapters that explore critical connections to prominent aspects of education: special education, education for ESL students, education of at-risk high school students, assessment issues, and students' perceptions of their own literacy learning.

In Chapter 6, Virginia Goatley describes her research with students qualifying for special education services, synthesizing three studies. She explores numerous ways the students progressed in their talk about text and their abilities to share their ideas with other students. She focuses on the instructional support that was critical to the students' success in their book clubs. Carol Sue Englert provides commentary following the chapter.

In Chapter 7, Cindy Brock draws on three studies with second language learners participating in Book Club, students from such diverse countries and related language backgrounds as Vietnam and Mexico. Cindy describes the experiences of these students, particularly how their language involvement assisted them in "learning to mean in English." Following the chapter, Robert Rueda, provides commentary and raises questions for consideration for among those educators interested in second language learners' participation in Book Club.

In Chapter 8, Fenice Boyd concentrates on high school students' experiences within the cross-age literacy project that she developed drawing on Book Club to create a context for struggling high school students to learn how to read, write, and talk about text. The students participated in two settings: (1) the preparation seminar, in which the high school students work with peers, under teacher guidance, to prepare to lead book clubs with small groups of elementary students, and (2) cross-age book clubs, led by the high school students in the elementary classroom. The chapter focuses on the preparation seminar and its influence on high school students' abilities to engage in literate thinking. Following this chapter, Donna Alvermann provides commentary.

In Chapter 9, Tanja Bisesi and Taffy Raphael describe the Book Club Assessment Project, focusing on the development and implementation of a performance-based assessment to evaluate students' progress in reading, writing, and oral language. They trace the problems with the *misalignment* of traditional assessment measures and literacy development as promoted through Book Club. They then describe alternative approaches to assessment that better capture the range of students' literacy development. Elfrieda Hiebert's commentary follows the chapter.

The authors of Chapter 10 are Christi Vance, Justin Ross, and Jenny Davis, former fourth and fifth graders in Deb's and Laura's classrooms. They explain their perceptions and definition of Book Club, discuss their favorite components of the program, and offer suggestions to teachers. Working with Cindy Brock, the authors created a chapter that outlines what the students feel is important for teachers to know about Book Club to work successfully with all elementary students. P. David Pearson responds to Christi, Justin, and Jenny's chapter.

Together, these five chapters provide numerous examples and insights into students and their participation in Book Club experiences. As our society increases in its diversity and teachers face new challenges on a daily basis, we benefit from research focused on how to help *all* students and teachers be successful in the classroom. Even more important is the promise of Book Club for helping all students develop the language and literacy skills and interest in reading that will help them throughout their lifetime.

CHAPTER 6

Talk About Text Among Special Education Students

VIRGINIA J. GOATLEY

During my first visit to a Book Club classroom, Marty, a special education student, intrigued me as he interacted with his peers during a discussion of *Cloudy with a Chance of Meatballs* (Barrett, 1978). Marty actively led the discussion, asking questions of his peers and thinking about alternative events for the story. During that fall, I continued to observe Marty both in his regular education and special education settings, two contexts with sharply contrasting literacy activities. In contrast to his regular education Book Club literacy activities, Marty's resource room instruction involved spelling lists, basal reading, phonics worksheets, and boardwork.

The educational and political community continues to debate the merits of resource rooms, mainstreaming, and inclusion. Special education students, such as Marty, are mandated to engage in literacy instruction in the setting deemed the best option to assist their learning (Schloss, 1992). Reading theories that articulate a process made up of component subskills often become the foundation for instruction for students with learning problems. Literacy instruction in special education programs, whether self-contained classrooms or resource rooms, historically has emphasized isolated skills and tasks that are often disconnected from the children's experiences (Allington, 1991; Johnston & Allington, 1991). The literacy instruction has often attacked the perceived deficits of the learning-disabled student from a bottom-up approach to teaching reading strategies, rarely engaging children with meaningful, connected text.

In contrast, literature-based instruction programs, such as Book Club, recognize the importance of language opportunities for student learning and

119

value quality literature taught holistically, rather than instruction focused on isolated skills. Thus students engage in more complex, higher-order thinking, having real purposes to read, discuss, and critique quality literature. Since students identified as learning disabled may often have considerable language abilities, despite lower achievement scores, the oral language and strategies learned in Book Club suggest it may be an ideal setting for literacy learning—a place where students are able to use their language skills to increase their literacy abilities. In addition, the social opportunities to engage in literate discussions with peers allow mildly impaired students to benefit from discursive interactions that help enhance social skills development (D. Cullinan, Sabornie, & Crossland, 1992).

As described in Chapter 1, a sociocultural perspective provides the theoretical framework for Book Club, emphasizing language and learning as well as the social context in meaning-making (Bruffee, 1984; Vygotsky, 1978; Wertsch, 1985). This perspective supports changing instruction for special education students because it argues that meaning is constructed through the social interactions of members of a community. Providing special education students with experiences similar to their regular education peers, rather than providing instruction that further isolates them both academically and socially, is important to facilitate their literacy growth.

Calls for reform in special education literacy instruction stress the importance of providing a social context in which students participate in meaningful literacy activities (Dudley-Marling, 1994; Englert, Raphael, & Mariage, 1994). Programs using more holistic opportunities for special education students to engage in literacy activities are being developed to help students view reading and writing as something different from a set of isolated skills. For example, the Early Literacy Project (see Englert et al., 1994) was designed for resource rooms and inclusion models to provide special education students instruction focused on discourse interactions with language foundational to all literacy instruction. Literacy activities such as morning message, author's chair, and process writing, where students interacted with text in authentic and informative ways, were integral to the project. Gilles (1990) also worked with seventh-grade learning-disabled students in a setting that encouraged their responses to literature through the use of discussion groups. These students were engaged in thinking about reading in terms of their own backgrounds and connecting texts to their lives.

Through my research, I wanted to explore the potential of Book Club for students who had been labeled as requiring special education services. This chapter focuses on two issues: (1) How can the Book Club settings support special education students' opportunities to engage in meaningful academic talk with their peers? (2) What instructional support do teachers using Book Club need to provide quality literacy instruction for special education students in both special and regular education settings?

In this chapter, I begin by providing some details of the three studies I conducted, introducing the participants and specific focuses of the individual studies. Second, I describe trends that these studies revealed in students' abilities to engage in meaningful discussions with one another and their regular education peers. Third, I focus on the specifics of the instructional support that appeared to enhance students' successful participation in their Book Club communities. Together, these studies have helped me identify ways in which to celebrate special education students' successes in literacy development and the development of literate thinking through their Book Club participation. They have also helped me identify the important instructional support provided by both teachers and peers.

SPECIAL EDUCATION BOOK CLUB STUDIES

During my graduate studies, I conducted three studies focusing on special education students' participation in Book Club. As a member of the original Book Club project team, I had the opportunity to observe Book Club classrooms and was particularly struck by the participation of special education students such as Marty, whom I described earlier. Though varying in context–some conducted in resource rooms, others in mainstream settings–the studies detailed in Table 6.1 involved students who had been labeled as learning-disabled or educatively mentally impaired.

The first study, conducted in the spring of 1991, focused on a group of five students in a resource room setting (see Goatley & Raphael, 1992). The second study, conducted during the 1991–92 school year, was a case study of Stark, a student labeled learning-disabled who was mainstreamed into Laura Pardo's fifth-grade classroom (see Goatley, 1996; Goatley, Brock, & Raphael,

TABLE 6.1. Special Education Studies

	Study One	Study Two	Study Three
Name	Resource room	Case of Stark	Follow-up
Year	1991	1991–92	1992–93
Students	Hillary, Kaitlin, Robert, Cheryl, and Rashad	Stark	Greg, Patrick, Amber, and Parker

1995). Conducted the following year, the third study compared four main-streamed special education students participating in Laura's classroom during Book Club.

Study 1: Working in a Resource Room

The study of a group of five upper-elementary students (Hilary, Kaitlin, Robert, Cheryl, and Rashad) using Book Club in their resource room took place parallel to developing Book Club in the regular education classrooms the first year of the project. Both the resource room teacher and the Book Club project research team served as consultants as I regularly described my thematic units, literature selections, and instructional plans. I conducted two units: (1) a genre study of folktales similar to the one Deb Woodman used with her fourth/fifth-grade regular education Book Club classroom, and (2) a theme-based unit of disabilities designed to help students bridge personal experiences and the texts.

Over the two units, my data included audiotapes of their book club discussions, field notes of our sessions, and copies of students' reading logs. My analyses focused on (1) the nature of the students' interactions during book club discussions, (2) changes in their reading log entries over the two units, and (3) types of questions students raised and discussed. Students' interactional patterns over time revealed their increasing concern that each participant have the chance to be heard. Reading log entries showed a connection between the instructional support they received in developing a range of responses to literature and the variety of responses revealed in their writing. In addition, the analyses indicated students' increasing ownership of the way they chose to respond, moving away from raising and answering literal questions to raising and attempting to address personal responses and theme-related issues.

Study 2: The Case of Stark

By studying Stark, a fifth-grader mainstreamed for reading and language arts, I extended my research from the resource room to the regular education classrooms. My particular interest was how Stark interacted with the regular education students in book club discussions and community share. I also focused on the nature of his contributions and the degree to which he balanced his background knowledge and personal experience with information conveyed through texts. Stark was an active participant in both discussion settings. His contributions indicated his comprehension of story events, his personal response to the texts, and his determination to influence the topics of discussion in his book club. For example, during the group's reading and discussion of Paterson's (1988) *Park's Quest*, Stark provided historical information about the Vietnam War relevant to the novel, described his family's experiences related to the war, and directed the group's conversations.

Study 3: A Follow-Up Study

Since I was impressed with Stark's ability to participate during Book Club, I conducted a second study exploring other mainstreamed special education students' experiences. I wondered whether Stark's experiences would characterize other similarly labeled students or whether important differences might emerge in studying an expanded group. Using similar data-gathering and analysis methods, I focused on four students identified as learning-disabled: Greg, Patrick, Amber, and Parker. Two students, Greg and Patrick, were quite similar to Stark, assuming leadership in their groups and maintaining active participatory roles. While Amber did participate, she assumed no leadership within her group. However, Parker showed a different profile. Like many students in special education settings, he was frequently absent, making a sustained relationship with his peers difficult and detracting from a sense of community in his book club.

The instruction in Book Club was quite different from that in which special education students participated in their resource room. Both the movement toward literature-based instruction and the one for inclusive education led me to question whether the students benefited from holistic instruction in their regular education room. Of particular concern was the opportunity for the teacher and peers to listen to their perspective and for the teacher to provide appropriate assistance in a diverse room that included advanced readers, students attending gifted programs, second-language learners, and Chapter 1 students.

Together, the studies helped me address the two major issues of opportunity and support for special education students' participation in the Book Club program. Now, I will describe students' initial responses to literature and participation in Book Club, outline the instructional supports that encouraged their progress, and provide examples of their improved discussions.

STRUGGLES WITH *HOW* TO SHARE

While students had opportunities to participate in their book clubs and community share discussions, it was clear from the data that they did not initially understand "how" such participation might occur. Their difficulties included maintaining conversations (e.g., taking turns, staying on task, avoiding long pauses), encouraging other members to participate (e.g., including all group members in the discussion, responding to peers' questions, supporting others' comments), and attempting to understand the content of responses (e.g., asking for elaboration, clarifying responses).

In study 1, I thought one advantage to having a small group of special education students would be opportunities for them to participate actively in all discussions. In contrast to the regular education setting, community share involved only five students, so everyone had easier access to the floor. Similarly, since there was only one book club group in the room, I could always observe and provide appropriate and specific instruction. I found that eventually students did take the floor and participate, but they needed initial help and support with their participation.

Robert quickly became a leader, skillful at getting the floor and directing the conversation. When I examined who had the opportunity to speak or, more importantly, to be heard, Robert often asked and received responses to his questions. In contrast, Hilary was often silent. Such variety in participation, both in accessing the floor and in receiving follow-up discussion, is exemplified in the following transcript. Robert, Kaitlin, and Cheryl maintain a discussion to answer a question Robert initiates about the story setting, while Hilary repeats one question (Why are they best friends?) five times before she receives any response.

Robert: Where was this at?
Hilary: Why are they best friends?
Kaitlin: It was at his house.
Robert: No, it wasn't.
Hilary: Why were they best friends?
Cheryl: It was at Bear's house.
Hilary: Why were they best friends?
Robert: No. / What state was it you know.
Cheryl: What country?
Kaitlin: Were they in the country of Michigan or Oklahoma, Texas? / / Maybe they were in New York.
Robert: It was a state you know.
Hilary: Why are they best friends? / / Why were they best friends?
Robert: Because they were! / You have a best friend don't you? / / / That was a stupid question to ask.
Kaitlin: Because they like each other. Probably they live with each other then they just got another house.

When the others finally responded to her question, Hilary was unable to maintain a discussion about the topic. Robert's reply, his pause, and his negative evaluation of her question may have suppressed Hilary's further participation.

Similar to many regular education students (see McMahon & Hauschildt, 1993), Hilary's inability to participate effectively was apparent. This difficulty may have stemmed from a lack of understanding about conversational norms: that it is important to allow a conversational topic to play out before attempting to shift to a new topic. The difficulty may be attributable to age and gender. Hilary, a third grader, was the youngest in the group. The other students were in fourth and fifth grade, reflective of the resource room's containing students from grades 2–5. Others (e.g., Alvermann, 1995/96; Jett-Simpson & Masland, 1993; Tannen, 1990) have described how boys and girls experience conversations differently from elementary through high school settings. Regardless of the cause, the data suggest that for Hilary to participate in Book Club effectively, she needed support.

Stark's initial difficulties appeared to be closely linked to social issues in the classroom and in his book club. Like Robert, he established an early pattern of assertiveness and made many attempts to dominate discussions with his peers. However, he also devalued opinions other members of his group expressed, often disagreeing and focusing instead on what he thought to be the right answer. Many times, he simply yelled over others to express his view. In the following transcript from a discussion of *James and the Giant Peach* (Dahl, 1961), Stark thinks he heard Mei, a student from Vietnam, say "golf" instead of "God." He immediately notes her mistake and proceeds to make fun of her, until Jean and Andy suggest that Stark is not using appropriate language for book club.

Mei: *(Talking with Stark.)* I'm talking about what he said. He said God is a girl.

Stark: She said golf, she said golf, golf is a girl.

Mei: I did not.

Stark: Golf is a girl.

Jason: Golf is a ball.

Stark: She said, golf is a girl. *(Laughs.)*

Andy: Man, will you please stop that thing and quit [laughing and goofing off.

Mei: [Don't be mean at me, okay?

Stark: If that's not it, she said Gooooodd!!

Andy: She said God.

Jean: Not golf.

Jason: I know God, all right, let's just get to book club.

Andy: We'll argue about this after.

In this instance, Stark reveals his need to understand and appreciate the importance of how to share in ways that do not demean others and contribute to the conversation.

DIFFICULTY WITH "WHAT" TO SHARE

In addition to initial difficulties with *how* to share, students often were not sure of *what* to share about the literature they were reading. While *how* to share was closely tied to the book clubs, *what* to share permeated all components of Book Club. Within the Book Club program, *what* to share in writing and through discussions centered around differing readers' perspectives brought to the text, the variety of responses evoked by the text, making sense of the content of the text, and making connections between the texts and readers' lives. In all three studies, data revealed that the primary areas that students struggled with included: (1) multiple interpretations of a text (e.g., more than one answer to many questions), (2) moving beyond literal interpretations (e.g., sharing personal response, prior knowledge, and personal experiences; discussing their feelings about the text; evaluating the text), and (3) drawing on other sources (e.g., other books, movies, TV shows). They rarely used strategies such as elaborating on their written responses to further discussion or formulating appropriate clarification or expansion questions.

Students revealed numerous comprehension strategies, although their discussions almost always centered around literal interpretations of the text. Indeed, early in the year Kaitlin showed her awareness that the text was a source for answers. When she was unable to answer her own question and peers did not provide a satisfactory answer, she opened the text to find the answer.

Kaitlin: What kind of food do they [have in their house?
Rashad: [They got huge food in their house.
Kaitlin: *(Flipping through story.)* Let's go back to the story to find the answer.

Kaitlin's comments suggest that she knew the text was one source of information for answering questions. In fact, this exchange was typical of many early book club discussions in which students raised literal questions, seeking answers from one another first, and when that failed, turning to the text. While an important comprehension strategy, it was not sufficient for creating interesting and meaningful conversations about the books they read.

Stark provides additional evidence of the students' overemphasis on literal meanings. His early participation is illustrated in the two following examples, revealing both his willingness to participate and the nature of his contributions. During an opening community share, Laura asks Stark and his peers to review what had happened in the previous chapter. Stark successfully recounts the main points from the chapter he had read the previous day.

Laura Pardo: Remember we read about it yesterday? // How are they sleeping, we read about it yesterday? Stark. *(Chosen from one of three students with their hands raised.)*

Stark: The spider or the silkworm, is goin' to make a bed like, a cot or something, for everybody to sleep on.

Laura Pardo: Was it the spider or the silkworm?

Stark: Silkworm. *(A few others say silkworm at the same time.)*

Laura Pardo: It spun like a web, like a cot or hammock and they slept on it. How long do you think they can go on like that?

Stark: For a loooonnnng time. *(Others answer at the same time; however, Laura repeats Stark's answer.)*

Early in the year, Stark regularly participated in such comprehension and review discussions but was much less apt to share his personal ideas or value the experiences of others.

The following year, when I observed four students, Amber provided a contrast to Stark's quick engagement in community share and book club in the regular education classroom. Even though she had spent the previous three years in a holistic resource room program, she had difficulty interacting during her group's conversation. She was reluctant to participate and needed a great deal of prompting to share her ideas or written responses. It took most of the year for Amber to feel comfortable in her group, to learn to value her responses to the books, and to be actively engaged in a classroom that had many more students than there had been in her earlier resource room experiences.

Parker's experience also contrasted with Stark's. His difficulties at home led to irregular attendance, behavior-related problems, and eventual disciplinary action from the district office. His inconsistent and erratic behavior and attendance meant that he often struggled to complete reading and writing assignments, to keep up with the topics discussed during book clubs he missed, and to participate with his group on those days he was present. Thus Laura needed to provide additional support to facilitate Amber's comfort when sharing ideas and to help Parker actively participate. Strategies to assist all students, especially students such as Hilary, Parker, and Stark are detailed in the following section. I focus on instructional conversations among teachers and students that contributed to their successful participation.

INSTRUCTION TO SUPPORT
SPECIAL EDUCATION STUDENTS

My observations in Deb's and Laura's classrooms revealed that *all* students, not just those with special needs, required instructional support to advance their thinking, strategy use, and appreciation of and response to literature. This instruction was essential particularly for those students not used to engaging in academic discourse with their peers. Instruction focused on aspects related to how to share and what to share during book clubs and included emphases on multiple literacy areas, such as comprehension, understanding and identifying literary elements, and writing. This instruction occurred through the assistance of "more knowledgeable others," including both teachers and peers (Raphael & Goatley, 1994).

Teachers as More Knowledgeable Others

Instructional support for students in both the resource and the regular education classrooms involved explicit instruction, modeling, scaffolding, and facilitating (see Chapter 3 for further discussion of teachers' roles). Three examples from the research illustrate the different forms of instructional support special education students experienced: (1) explicit instruction, (2) scaffolded log entries and discussions, and (3) self-evaluation.

In the regular education classroom, Laura used her observations of students' book club discussions to reveal potential problem areas, then invited students to discuss these problems in subsequent community share settings. For example, as students discussed Craighead-George's (1983) *The Talking Earth*, several seemed confused at the way *burden* had been used in the book. Laura addresses their confusions explicitly during community share.

Laura: Someone gave the turtle a burden, and some of you may not have heard the word *burden* because I could tell some of you mispronounced it and some of you said right away "I don't know how to say this word." A burden is something that you have to carry that is heavy. And it doesn't mean, it can mean, something that is actually strapped to your back, but it is usually symbolic and it means that you have something heavy weighing on your heart. Maybe you know something that is a big secret and it is bringing you down. Maybe you have a guilty conscience about something *(she continues with different examples and ties them back to the turtle in the book and the Seminole Indians)*. Symbolic. It does not mean that the turtle has the problems and carries them all on his back, but it is just a representation of that.

Not understanding Laura's explanation, Amber asks for clarification, eliciting further clarification as the following exchange reveals:

Amber: What does symbolic mean?
Laura: It means, it is like when we were talking about that imagery, something means something else, it is a symbol. When something is symbolic, it takes the meaning of it. Does that explain it? *(Looking at Amber.)*
Amber: It stands for something else?
Laura: *(Nodding.)* It stands for something else. Like an equal, like two lines is a symbol for an equal sign. It is a symbol for something else.

Laura provided explicit instruction about symbolism to help students clarify their confusions about the texts. Her openness to students' questions was critical to meeting their individual and collective needs.

In addition to explicit instruction, instructional support occurred in the form of scaffolding students' use of specific comprehension and response strategies. For example, during the folktale unit, students read Aardema's (1975) *Why Mosquitoes Buzz in People's Ears*. Even though students realized story comprehension depended on remembering a sequence of events, they were not sure how to use their reading logs to help them do so. I initiated a sequencing activity, asking students to draw pictures and write related sentences. After teacher modeling and group practice, most students completed their own sequence chart of story events. However, Kaitlin responded by insisting she could not do it. With scaffolded instruction, I showed her how to use the book as a guide to draw the pictures; she then dictated the first five sentences and finally wrote the last five sentences on her own (see Figure 6.1).

A second form of scaffolding took a more general form. While it was sometimes useful to model a single specific strategy, I found that students sometimes needed reminders about the range of responses that existed and appropriate ways to interact (i.e., what and how to share). Thus I created this chart, based on students' initial needs:

Strategies for Participating in Book Clubs

How to Share

1. Maintain conversations without long pauses
2. Respond to questions asked by other participants
3. Elaborate response to include reason for answer
4. Challenge interpretations of story

FIGURE 6.1.   Kaitlin's Reading Log on Sequencing

5. Clarify ideas, questions, answers, and response
6. Stay on task
7. Include all group members in discussion
8. Take turns

What to Share

1. Elaborate written response to support discussion
2. Formulate questions for clarification and interest
3. Share personal response, prior knowledge, personal experiences
4. Use comprehension activities to construct meaning and support ideas
5. Move beyond literal interpretations
6. Discuss feelings about text
7. Relate text to other books, movies, and shows
8. Evaluate the text

A focus on the categories and examples within what and how to share helped students broaden their goals beyond traditional ideas of simply reading accurately from the text to interacting with one another and debating issues associated with the book. First, it helped students decide on a particular response or topic for their reading log entry or for their book club discussion. Second, it provided a guide to appropriate interactions during book club and community share. By focusing on the two categories of what and how to share, I encouraged them to move beyond traditional formats of simply reading for fluency and accuracy to interacting with one another to debate issues associated with their books.

Laura used a similar form of scaffolding in the regular education classroom, one that I observed Stark take advantage of on several occasions. Laura and her students generated a wall chart listing areas they thought worthy of improving. Each book club picked one or two specific areas and worked directly on those they had chosen. Stark's group selected such topics as "making sure that everyone has a turn to share" and "not interrupting each other" as aspects of discussion they needed to improve.

A third form of instructional support involved encouraging, supporting, and responding to students' self-evaluations. Laura developed a think-sheet designed to encourage students' self-evaluation of how they had interacted during group activities, the way they had used their reading logs, and the degree to which they read that day's text material. The think-sheet was one way for her to monitor students' progress and to gain insight into their opinions of the books.

Stark's self-evaluation sheet indicates his perceptions of his participation during *Park's Quest*. One day Stark got up and left his book club before they were finished with their discussion. On his daily self-evaluation sheet, Stark wrote that his book club had been "really bad," explaining that "Mei was dasing [bossing] me around." Laura questioned whether Stark's difficulty was due to an ongoing problem between Mei and him regarding how to use the reading logs in their group. Knowing this was a concern for Stark, Laura paid particular attention to his group the following day and later talked with him about how he might resolve the ongoing problem. Through daily written communication, Laura monitored each student's group, offering support when needed. The self-evaluation sheet allowed Stark to track his progress and monitor his interactions with peers. It was an important tool for Laura to assess her students continually, particularly those who might warrant special attention.

Peers as "More Knowledgeable Others"

"Knowledgeable others" are often adults, but in the Book Club program they were also peers. Over time, explicit talk about how and what to share encouraged the students' abilities to learn conversational norms for posing questions and exploring extended, multiple answers. Over the three studies, I found numerous instances of peers serving each other in instructional or generally supportive roles; these roles can be categorized as relatively "formal" support roles, such as serving as models or providing missing information, and relatively "informal" support roles, such as students within a book club using collective knowledge to solve a problem.

One example of formal support occurred during the first study when I invited three fifth-grade students from Laura's Book Club classroom to model a book club discussion for the resource room students. Bart, Chris, and Lissa intentionally showed problematic discussions (e.g., off-task behavior, straying off the ideas of the book to unrelated topic, not saying anything, interrupting). I started a conversation among the fifth graders and the special education students to summarize what had worked well with these book clubs and how they thought their peers could have improved their discussion (see Chapter 2 for another example of this). In combining their evaluative responses of the fifth-grade book clubs, the students verbally listed the following suggestions:

Things to improve

1. Robert: They played pencils and they ain't supposed to.
2. Bart: Well you see what we're supposed to do is, we're supposed to read our log and we're supposed to ask questions if we have any, and you see what we did, she just read and said, and I just read it and said, and he just read, we're done. See we're supposed to ask ques-

tions. . . . Supposed to ask questions, you know keep a conversation.

3. Cheryl: Well, she kept, um, Lissa kept telling them when to read and when not to.

4. Bart: Yeah, she [Lissa] kept on cutting people off and, you know, not giving people a chance. Like Chris didn't even say anything, "All right that's enough. Now it's my turn," you know.

Things they did well

1. Robert: They each read from their log.
2. Hilary: They read good.
3. Hilary: They write good.
4. Cheryl: Um, answering, answering the questions.
5. Bart: We took turns, we asked questions, stayed on task, no interruptions.

Formal support, such as modeling problems in actual book clubs and reinforcement from the fifth graders summarizing how to improve, enabled the resource room students to understand better the problems occurring in their own book club and to conceptualize possible solutions.

Another illustration of more formal support occurred during the third study with the four students mainstreamed into Laura's classroom. Due to scheduling related to special classes, Laura placed two of the learning-disabled students (Greg, Patrick) in a book club with two students who attended the gifted-and-talented program (Shawn, Christopher). Laura and I discussed this grouping, wondering how it would work with the inconsistent schedules of the four boys and wondering if any particular students would dominate the group. However, because Shawn and Christopher missed the beginning of Book Club on certain days while attending the gifted-and-talented program, Greg and Patrick had to keep them current on the story events, find the main ideas, share ideas about characters, and relate the importance of one chapter to another. In this manner, the students were engaging in many of the reading strategies assessed on the Michigan Educational Assessment Progress test and in sharing their ideas for the dual purposes of supporting their needs and the groups' best interests for success.

At other times, peers in the same book club revealed different knowledge levels, thus enhancing one another's interactions, writing, and reading. One instance of this occurred during the resource room study. For a brief period, students revealed an overlearning of the conversational conventions to the point that they explicitly took turns, never interrupting each other, which led to stifled conversations. As a group, they explicitly debated the necessity of continuing this pattern. In essence, they began to realize a potential compromise between two extremes, shown in the following transcript:

Robert: Why do we take turns? Why can't / don't we just talk out?
Kaitlin: Because it won't be all right to talk out when everybody else is talking.
Cheryl: Then you can't understand that person / what they saying.
Kaitlin: We like to talk about / like / if we had a Book Club // and we had to write something down / we could talk about it / we could talk about each other / like if / like if we want to talk / like if Cheryl asked what we're supposed to do we could tell her what we have to do.
Cheryl: Yeah / like if Hilary was telling when Kaitlin was talking and they won't be able to hear / to understand what they were saying.

These students showed their awareness of the need for common guidelines ensuring everyone a chance to talk. Our discussion of this led to the students' designing a map relating their perceptions of and purposes for Book Club: read, write, talk, take turns, share ideas, listen, ask questions, answer questions, and talk about what they like to do (see Figure 6.2). Students identified what was important to their learning through talk among themselves. Their emphasis on sharing ideas with one another helped improve the social skills involved in exchanging ideas and broadened their concept of literate talk.

INCREASED PARTICIPATION AND COMMUNITY

Over each school year, the special education students showed growth in their perspectives about literature, their confidence in sharing their interpretations with others, and their awareness of multiple purposes for discussing text. The resource room students demonstrated increased elaboration of ideas. For example, their thoughts became clearer when critiquing a story. In January, Robert wrote only, "I like the story." By March, he gave a reason for his evaluation: "I think that they wasys bust fard and thye like to thke afar igre." (I think they was best friends and took up for each other.) Kaitlin's evaluations also became more elaborated over the period. In January she wrote "it was foome and sad." (It is funny and sad.) By March, she not only provided an evaluation, but gave specific reasons for her thoughts: "I thak that the story is good. and I like whin Duck and bear are friends and bear mad cucas for Duck. and Duck did bear's dish so they mast be friends good good friends." (I think that the story is good and I like when Duck and Bear are friends and Bear made cupcakes for Duck and Duck did Bear's dishes. So they must be friends, good, good friends.) These changes did not simply

FIGURE 6.2. Perceptions of Book Club

evolve; they were guided by specific discussion of what they might write about and the importance of elaborating ideas when conveying them to others. The increased elaboration in their writing logs revealed more depth and led to extended discussions during book clubs.

After participating in book clubs for two months, the students showed growth in their interactions, elaboration of written work, and discussion of questions. Further, they began to include their personal experiences in both their written and oral response, consistent with my emphasis during community share. For example, to prepare for reading and discussing *The Balancing Girl* (Rabe, 1981), students examined the book's cover and made predictions about the content. The story is about a young girl participating in her school activities while using crutches and a wheelchair. Later, in his reading log, Robert drew a picture of a person and wrote "'Cause they are special like we are."

When asked why he decided to draw a picture, Robert said, "'Cause they are human beings too. 'Cause people like tease them, they are just like we are but only they can't do certain things that we can do. We special 'cause, everybody's special in the world." His answer revealed that his comprehension of the text was far removed from a literal level toward literate thinking and personal response.

Students' discussions also improved as they began to include topics related to, but not specifically mentioned in, the text. In contrast to earlier discussions, in the following transcript Kaitlin responds to two of Hilary's questions, using the text as well as her personal knowledge of the situation.

Hilary: How long has she been handicapped?
Kaitlin: Probably about 28 days. Probably in the story it says how long she has been handicapped.
Hilary: How do you think she sits?
Robert: In a wheelchair like she usually do.
Kaitlin: She has to sit like this. *(Shows a straight back.)* Does she like being handicapped?
Hilary: No. 'Cause she wants to get out of the wheelchair sometimes.
Kaitlin: Well she must / she can get this one / it's in the back. 'Cause my cousin has one. He is handicapped and he sets down and presses a button and he slides down on the couch so he can sit down.

Kaitlin and Hilary show evidence of valuing the relevance of one's own experience in interpreting characters' feelings. In addition, Hilary gains access to the floor, introducing her topics of interest, a difficult area for her earlier in the year.

In the regular education room, Laura played an important role in helping Stark go beyond literal interpretations and to value many ideas in his writing. While reading *Island of the Blue Dolphin*, Laura occasionally asked students to respond to the prompts eliciting information from the book and students' personal responses. Over time, Stark started to draw on knowledge of the events and characters in the story to compare these to his own life. In December, he wrote:

I dont like people to die. When someone dies I go do something fun so I dont have to remember what happen. It is real bad that karana friend died and she is in the dumpes.

In Stark's response, he reveals both his knowledge of an event that happened to the character Karana and relates story events to his own experiences. While it took Stark a few more months before he consistently responded to text in this manner, such activities seemed to provide him with continual reinforcement to expand his view of reading and written response.

CONCLUDING COMMENTS

Efforts to ensure that all students are learning to read and write require special measures. For those who qualify for special services, literacy instruction may take many forms. It is important that such students be exposed to and recognize a holistic and response-oriented view of literacy in addition to our ongoing understanding of the importance of other reading components (e.g., comprehension, fluency, word recognition). The students described in this chapter were fortunate to participate in Book Club, since it allowed them access to many important aspects of literacy learning, including reading quality literature, engaging in literate discussions, and expressing personal responses.

The students grew in their understanding of what and how to share during written response and book discussions. This holistic instruction provided a context that supported increased, quality interactions among members of a community. For special education students, language use facilitated their literacy growth. Their learning needs were quite similar to the needs of *all* of the students. The teachers played an important role in supporting students in the areas where they needed additional instruction or reinforcement for their continued progress.

Once they were socially engaging with other students in literate talk, they learned a variety of responses to text that were valued and encouraged. In this chapter, the outline of the instructional supports, early attempts at discussion, and later contributions to talk illustrate that such growth may need time and continual energy but that the results are worth the effort.

COMMENTARY

CAROL SUE ENGLERT

Ginny Goatley's examination of the effects of Book Club with special education students is systematic and informative. Her research provides convincing evidence of the powerful and beneficial effects of students' participation in book clubs. Three important implications that warrant serious consideration in the general and special education literature are embodied in her work.

First, in the rush to include students in general education settings, researchers and teacher educators often neglect to design frameworks that can guide teachers' decision making in developing instruction that is inclusive of all children. According to W. Stainback and Stainback (1990), inclusive and supportive communities in educational settings are characterized by the following traits:

1. Members support each other.
2. The leadership and supportive relationships in the community are reciprocal.
3. Members have access to the varied experiences, knowledge, problem-solving strategies, and cultural or linguistic diversity of the other members.
4. Support in the community is directed by the members and remains consumer-driven.
5. Support to the various members is temporary, with the eventual goal of developing independence.
6. Each member is viewed as possessing talents, with the combination of the distributed knowledge and talents in the group making it a vehicle for learning superior to that which could be accomplished by individuals working alone.

Ginny's description of special education students' participation in Book Club shows that it represents one framework that can support teachers in their efforts to construct literacy experiences that are truly inclusive and embrace the diversity of the members in the classroom. In Book Club, we see members asking genuine questions, describing their experiences, providing leadership and supporting each other, and constructively listening to and building on one another's responses as they jointly negotiate meaning that integrates their various experiences and perspectives. These processes and outcomes are the very essence of inclusive programs (S. Stainback & Stainback, 1992; W. Stainback & Stainback, 1990).

Second, Goatley reports that creating a supportive "community'" that is inclusive of its membership is not a spontaneous process. It requires thoughtful teacher instruction and feedback concerning students' use of the social and communicative skills that support dialogic and social interactions. Within this community, students need to learn how to cooperate and display encouraging behaviors (e.g., being attentive, approving, listening, questioning); how to share ideas (e.g., getting the floor, taking turns); how to provide support to one another (e.g., asking questions, uptake on ideas); how to engage in perspective taking; and how to resolve conflicts and solve problems. Instead of viewing these as impediments to the implementation of Book Club, the meaningful and functional context of Book Club should be viewed as affording unique opportunities to teach the very communicative and social behaviors that are the foundation of successful learning across the curriculum. Book Club instruction emphasizes the very attitudes and values that will undergird students' understanding and acceptance of individual differences, while developing the help and support mechanisms that will sustain all learners in all areas of the school curriculum.

Third, Ginny's research points to the central role of the teacher in creating and responding to the learners' zones of proximal development. Although some researchers tend to suggest that simply putting students in learning groups can increase students' academic performance, Ginny reminds us that the teacher has a complex role in monitoring and guiding literacy development. Teachers must provide children with access to the language and interpretative strategies for responding to stories and must monitor the discussions of groups for opportunities to contextualize knowledge, support or scaffold performance, and expansively respond to children's evolving states of knowledge to push the outer limits of the current knowledge of what children know about *how* to share and *what* to share. This ongoing assessment of individual differences is a central basis for the effective instruction of all students, but particularly special needs students. Thus Book Club provides teachers with the basis for recognizing and responding to the zones of proximal development as a means for accelerating the literacy progress of all students, including students who might be at risk of school failure.

The three aforementioned facets of Book Club make it a highly viable framework for teaching literacy to diverse learners. However, there is one caution that should be expressed in the face of the potential misinterpretation of Ginny's description of holistic instruction to all learners. Some readers may interpret this as a call to abandon reading skills instruction in favor of literature-based or whole-language programs. My personal experience with beginning readers tells me that it is not sufficient for students to listen and respond to literature. While this is an essential facet of the curriculum, the acquisition of reading skills depends on the opportunity for students to read literature themselves. Students must be given access to the word-recognition skills they need and the opportunity to employ these skills while reading— either reading alone or with a buddy. The instructional component of Book Club provides the setting for the introduction of these reading skills, yet teachers must proactively plan to ensure that each child receives opportunities to develop the appropriate reading skills and to apply them to texts at their developmental level. With this instructional facet, the Book Club curriculum can be completely responsive to and inclusive of all children.

CHAPTER 7

Exploring the Use of Book Club with Second-Language Learners in Mainstream Classrooms

CYNTHIA H. BROCK

During the summer of 1994, I taught in a six-week migrant summer school program in the Northwest. The first day of summer school, Adriana watched me with a beautiful but bewildered smile as I discussed classroom procedures with my 32 third-grade children. When I addressed her directly in English and she did not respond, it became apparent to me that she did not understand what I was saying. She did not speak English, and, unfortunately, I spoke her first language – Spanish – with only minimal proficiency. Later that morning, with the help of a Spanish-speaking bilingual assistant, I learned that Adriana and her family had just moved from Mexico to our semirural northwestern community. Over nine years, I had taught in public schools as an elementary classroom teacher in places as diverse as inner-city Los Angeles, south Florida, and rural Oregon. I had had many students who, like Adriana, did not speak English as their first language. I had taught children whose first languages included Vietnamese, Creole, Cambodian, and Spanish.

During the past few years, as I began delving into the literature pertaining to educating children who speak English as their second-language, I discovered that my own teaching experiences reflect a broader national trend in our public schools. The population of second-language learners served by American schools is increasing steadily and rapidly (Garcia, 1990; Genesee, 1994; Nieto, 1992). This trend means that regular education teachers must strive to meet effectively the educational needs of our rapidly growing population of second-language learners (Cummins, 1994; McKeon, 1994).

One of the most important ways mainstream teachers can meet the educational needs of second-language learners is to teach them to participate fully in their classrooms and school communities. Of course, this is much more complex than "merely" teaching children English. For second-language learners to be able to participate effectively in their classroom and school communities, they must "learn to mean" in English. That is, they must learn ways of knowing and effectively interacting in their classroom and school settings (Gee, 1990).

In this chapter I focus on *why* and *how* Book Club serves as an important context for helping second-language learners "learn to mean" in English. I begin by discussing the related research useful for understanding why the Book Club setting has the potential to support second-language learners. I then briefly describe three research studies my colleagues and I conducted to examine second-language learners' participation during Book Club (Brock, 1995; Goatley, Brock, & Raphael, 1995; Raphael & Brock, 1993). Then, drawing on the data from these studies, I discuss the importance of Book Club for second-language learners' development in three ways: (1) providing a context for guided literacy learning, (2) providing opportunities to experiment with language-in-use, and (3) providing a context for second-language acquisition.

BOOK CLUB AND SECOND-LANGUAGE LEARNERS: LEARNING TO MEAN IN ENGLISH

For Bakhtin, student learning is facilitated when: (1) Students and teachers effectively orient themselves with respect to one another in a conversation, (2) the perspective each speaker or writer brings to a conversation is valued, and (3) conversants realize that meaning does not reside in words; rather, it resides in the ways in which words are used in particular contexts (Bakhtin, 1986; Wertsch, 1991). Thus, in general, Bakhtin suggests that meaningful situated language use facilitates learning. I briefly address each of these three points in terms of engaging second-language learners in literacy instruction that helps them "learn to mean" in English.

First, for Bakhtin, understanding occurs when speakers effectively orient themselves to one another within an interaction. Bakhtin's idea has significant implications for working with second-language students who may enter mainstream classrooms from vastly different sociocultural contexts. His work suggests that merely attempting to impart literacy skills to students is not sufficient to help students develop in-depth understanding. Educators must pay considerable attention to students–their backgrounds and ways of thinking and reasoning–in addition to the concepts and ideas we wish to help them understand. Students' abilities to develop understandings are facilitated by our insights into their thinking and the ways we use language as a tool to guide and shape their thinking and understanding.

Second, the perspective each speaker or writer brings to a conversation must be valued. Moll and Gonzalez (1994) argue that it is crucial to consider second-language learners' backgrounds relative to school settings in general and conversational encounters in particular. They suggest that second-language learners bring rich cultural resources, or "funds of knowledge," to school encounters. "Funds of knowledge" are "historically accumulated and culturally developed bodies of knowledge and skills essential for household and individual functioning" (p. 443). Despite how these "funds of knowledge" shape children's worldviews, teachers rarely draw on them, creating unnecessary disadvantages for these students.

Third, meaning does not reside in words; rather, it resides in the ways in which words are used in particular contexts. Gee (1990) argues that a primary responsibility of mainstream teachers is to enculturate second-language students into a set of mainstream discourse practices. This notion of enculturating students into a set of discourses means more than focusing on the form of a language. According to Gee, simply teaching children the skills of reading and writing is not enough to help them become truly literate members of the mainstream culture. Gee suggests that "literacy does not reside somewhere in the individual brain" (p. 42). Rather, literacy is deeply related to and inseparable from social practices. Literacy practices involve much more than merely the mechanical skills of decoding words and producing written text–"they also involve ways of talking, interacting, thinking, valuing and believing" (p. 43). In short, then, teachers must help their second-language students understand these ways of talking, interacting, thinking, valuing, and believing in the mainstream discourse community in addition to teaching them the conventions of language and literacy.

Scholars such as Delpit (1988) and de la Luz Reyes (1992) address the importance of striking a balance between skills and process instruction for diverse learners. They argue that teachers must provide students with explicit guidance as they "learn to mean" in English and must give students the freedom to experiment with "language-in-use" in meaningful ways. Book Club provides an important context for literacy instruction for second-language learners because students can experiment with oral and written language daily in a nonthreatening environment that guides and supports their growth. Additionally, Book Club affords second-language learners opportunities to offer valuable support and insights to others. Thus second-language learners are not always the "helped"; sometimes they are the experts, the "helpers."

BOOK CLUB AS A CONTEXT FOR SECOND LANGUAGE: THREE RESEARCH STUDIES

With my colleagues on the Book Club Project, I conducted three research studies to explore the experiences of second-language learners as they participated with their mainstream English-speaking peers. The three studies include a case study of a Vietnamese girl, Mei, across her first three years in the American school system (Raphael & Brock, 1993); a case study of Mei and four of her fifth-grade English-speaking peers as they participated in book clubs related to a single novel (Goatley et al., 1995); and a case study of initiating Book Club with a third grade class—most of whom were bilingual in Spanish and English—during a federally funded summer enrichment program designed for children of migrant workers (Brock, 1995).

Mei: A Longitudinal Case Study

Mei immigrated to the United States with her family when she was in the third grade. Taffy Raphael and I conducted a three-year longitudinal case study designed to explore Mei's literacy learning from third through fifth grade while Mei attended elementary school in an urban K–5 school in a large midwestern city. While Mei's reading program was literature-based in all three grades, she participated in Book Club only during the fourth and fifth grades. Through the study of her experiences, we examined the potential of Book Club to provide an authentic and supportive environment for Mei's academic development. Findings revealed that Book Club was a valuable context in which Mei could experience meaningful opportunities to learn to use academic discourse to discuss texts.

Diverse Students in a Book Club Discussion: Case Study of a Group

In the spring of 1993, during Mei's fifth-grade year, Ginny Goatley, Taffy, and I conducted an in-depth exploration of one three-week book club group to examine the participation of diverse learners in literature discussions in a regular education setting. Specifically, we explored the children's use of strategies for drawing on their own knowledge and that of their peers as they socially constructed meanings relative to the trade book they were reading. This study provided insight into the value of diverse learners engaging in academic interactions with their regular education peers. Additionally, it highlighted some of the many and varied strategies that diverse learners like Mei employ to socially construct meaning.

Book Club in a Bilingual Third-Grade Summer School Program

During the summer of 1994, as mentioned in the opening paragraph, I taught in a six-week, federally funded program designed to provide academic assistance to children of migrant workers from a semirural community in the Northwest. Of the 32 students enrolled in my third-grade classroom, 27 were bilingual in Spanish and English, 1 spoke only Spanish, and the remaining 4 spoke only English. A bilingual (Spanish/English) assistant and an English-speaking volunteer worked with me daily. In this study I sought to explore how Book Club could be used to provide second-language students with opportunities to participate in classroom discourse. Findings revealed that a complex array of interconnecting factors (e.g., amount of time spent learning to participate effectively in groups, degree of English language proficiency, etc.) must coalesce to contribute to the construction of productive learning opportunities for second-language learners in book club discussions.

IMPLICATIONS OF BOOK CLUB RESEARCH FOR SECOND-LANGUAGE LEARNERS

Together, these studies of third through fifth graders who spoke English as their second-language provided insights into the potential of Book Club for helping their language, literacy, and general academic development: "learning to mean" in English. In this section, I discuss the implications of the research in terms of opportunities for guided learning, experimenting with language-in-use, and acquiring a second-language.

Book Club as a Context for Guided Learning for Second-Language Learners

In Book Club, both the classroom teacher and peers serve as guides to facilitate second-language students' learning. In this section I discuss two ways—one more structured and one less structured—that Book Club teachers can provide guided instruction for second-language learners. Next, I discuss how peers can serve as guides for second-language learners.

Guided learning: Teacher as guide. In working with second-language learners in Book Club, structured planning prior to a particular lesson helps us anticipate particular students' needs or focus on specific instructional goals. In contrast, sometimes needs arose within the context of a lesson, requiring us to spontaneously initiate guidance or support to ensure students' success. In this section, I focus initially on an explicitly structured lesson from the summer school Book Club program. I then draw on data about Mei to illustrate more spontaneous forms of scaffolding for second-language learners in Book Club.

I structured Book Club during the summer school program similarly to the structure described in Section I of this book, where a typical day involved reading, writing, book clubs, and community share. I included thematic units to embed different instructional focuses over the course of the program. On July 13, during our unit on forest ecosystems, I wanted to help my students make connections between their lives and those of the characters in the books they were reading and to help them understand ways to write about these connections in their reading logs. I explicitly created opportunities to support their development of connections through the four components of Book Club.

Connecting between students' lives and ideas in the text required that they comprehend and remember the texts' content. Thus I scaffolded their understanding and memory. I started with the writing components, asking the students to write a brief overview of the story we had been reading for the past two days, *The People Who Hugged the Trees* (Rose, 1990). I did this to remind them directly of the story *content*. I also asked them to write about how this story might have reminded them of others we had read to scaffold their thinking about the story *theme*. By scaffolding their thinking about both content and theme, I helped them identify potential points of connections between the texts and their own lives.

Next, in community share, I focused on scaffolding their understanding of what it meant to make such connections, using a response category called "me and the book." Displayed prominently was a description of this category:

> Sometimes what I read about a character or an event makes me think of things in my own life or things I remember from past experiences. I can write about what the character or the event or other ideas from the story make me think about from my own life or from my past experiences.

While I had introduced this category to them earlier, they had very little experience with the format. I began by asking students to draw on what they had written, saying, "Before we start the story today, how does this story remind you of other books we've read or ideas we've discussed before in summer school?" I intended the question to invite students to make connections both in terms of content (e.g., forests, ecosystems) and themes (e.g., caring for the land and for living things).

Ned made an immediate thematic connection, saying the story made him think about the word *caring* because the main character, Amrita, cared about her special tree. He also made a content connection, noting that we had been learning about how we should care for our forests. Roberto's connection was also based on both content and theme as he added, "Umm, this story reminds me of *The Giving Tree* because, um, Amrita loves the tree in the forest like the boy in the story of *The Giving Tree* book loved the tree in the beginning of the book."

Their responses provided me with an additional chance to emphasize another thematic connection. Roberto's reference to "the beginning of the book" was significant, since Silverstein's (1964) book *The Giving Tree* traced the changing relationship of a young boy and a tree over the course of the boy's lifetime. It depicted an early love changing to late indifference, a point relevant not only to their current story but to our earlier discussions of ecosystems.

This community share session provided multiple examples of intertextual connections, thus furnishing a critical basis for turning to the "me and the book" prompt that I wanted to emphasize that day. I returned to the displayed description, noting that "what we just did right now is what this prompt is about. The prompt says . . . "

During the reading component, I real aloud a section of the book that the class had previously read with partners. I chose to do this to further support their potential to connect between the text and their lives. Since they had read this with partners, I assumed they were somewhat–if not thoroughly–familiar with the content. By reading to them, they were free to let the words flow as they thought about ways they might connect to the ideas in the book. I then asked them to partner-read the next section, again to facilitate connecting both during the actual reading and during any spontaneous conversations that might occur as they read together.

I asked them to write again in their logs, this time explicitly connecting between the text and their own lives, working with their partners for help in content and form. When they had finished writing, they moved into the book clubs, fully prepared to engage in rich, meaningful discussions about the differences and similarities in the nature of their "me and the book" responses.

Overall, I had structured this lesson to provide guidance and scaffolding relative to their literacy learning through: (1) initial writing, (2) focus on community share, (3) read-aloud and partner-reading opportunities, and (4) texts and prompts I selected for emphasis. Many might notice that such instruction should not be unique for second-language learners but is relevant to all students. Yet there are features about my instructional framework that related directly to recommendations in the literature directed toward those particularly interested in second-language acquisition.

Hudelson (1994) recommends using a variety of strategies for promoting literacy development for second-language learners, some of which I incorporated into this overall lesson. First, she recommends encouraging collaborative writing. Children in my class were encouraged to talk with one another, share ideas, and work together while writing in their reading logs. This was especially important because the children spoke English with varying degrees of proficiency. Children worked together to translate directions and ideas from English to Spanish and vice versa, thus providing reading and language support for one another. Further, children were encouraged to write in the language they felt most comfortable using.

Second, Hudelson recommends reading aloud to children daily. On this day, like others, I read part of the current Book Club book we were reading aloud to the class. While I had clear reasons in terms of literacy instructional goals for the day, I also thought this was necessary because attendance at summer school was not mandatory and some children came sporadically. Reading and discussing previous parts of the story helped those children who occasionally missed summer school. Also, because the children's English proficiency varied, hearing parts of the story several times helped them become more familiar with the language and ideas in the stories. I also modeled both reading aloud with expression and discussing the story as it is being read aloud so that the children could incorporate these habits into their own daily oral reading with a partner.

Third, Hudelson recommends carefully selecting texts for second-language learners. Following her guidelines, I selected Book Club stories for our thematic unit (e.g., *The Giving Tree* and *The People Who Hugged the Trees*) that met the following criteria: (1) high level of interest, (2) rich content with clear illustrations, and (3) a tendency toward some repetition of words. While these criteria are not exclusively for second-language learners, taken together they provide guidance and structure for second-language learners to engage in the process of "learning to mean" in English.

In addition to the structured plans for guidance and support, Book Club teachers also provide spontaneous guidance to their students, as noted in the example below drawn from the case study of fifth-grade students in Laura Pardo's room (Goatley et al., 1995). Each day, as students engaged in their book club discussions, Laura roamed the classroom monitoring student progress and providing guidance when needed.

On June 3, 1992, Mei and her peers had been reading and discussing *Park's Quest* (Paterson, 1988) for two weeks. The book, about a 12-year-old boy named Park whose father was killed in the Vietnam War, centers around Park's experiences as he meets and visits his father's family for the first time and discovers his Vietnamese half-sister, Thanh.

The complex relationships among the characters created frustration for Mei and her peers as they tried to understand the novel's events. At the core of their confusion was the relationship between Park and Thanh. Park's father and Thanh's mother had had an affair while he was stationed in Vietnam, resulting in Thanh's birth. After reading the part of the chapter revealing this information, students express confusion, saying that this could not happen unless Park's parents had divorced and his father had married Thanh's mother. Only Stark, a student identified as needing special education services, appears to understand this situation. He states, "No, not married. He was two-timing his friends, if you get what I mean." As indicated by their comments, though, the other students still did not comprehend what Stark meant.

Mei: I don't get it. Wait, do you know he, he know that it's his sister-in-
    law, that it is his wife, [but not his wife, his brother's wife,
Jason: [I might be wrong. I might be wrong if, um, his
    uncle is his stepdad, but I don't know.
Jean: It is.
Jason: I don't know if it is or not because I don't, [I don't know the right an-
    swer.
Jean: [It is!!
Stark: Mrs. Pardo, let's ask Mrs. Pardo. She knows more about it than we
    do.
Mei: I don't know.
Stark: Mrs. Pardo! Mrs. Pardo! Can we ask a question? Thanh's dad is
    Frank?
Laura: No, Thanh's dad is not Frank.

As indicated in the above conversation, the students did not agree on whether Uncle Frank could be Park's stepfather. Finally, they solicited Laura's assistance. The conversation continued as Jean asked Laura if Frank was Park's stepdad and if Frank married his sister-in-law. Laura explained that Frank was Park's uncle and Thanh's stepfather. With this information from the teacher, the students then wondered whether Park's mother knew about Thanh and, if she did know, why she had not told Park.

Thus, although not a formal lesson with a planned focus, Laura provided important guidance to the children as they needed it in the context of their book club conversation. Further, this guidance provided information to the children that was imperative to make sense of the story's plot and theme.

Guided learning: Peers as guides. Not only teachers provide guidance to second-language learners in Book Club; peers also serve as important resources. I draw on the longitudinal case study to illustrate the importance of peer assistance during Book Club.

Mei, the focus of the study, sought assistance from her peers, in different Book Club groups, on many different occasions, and for a range of purposes over the two years she participated in Book Club. As illustrated in their discussion of *Park's Quest*, sometimes Mei sought assistance relative to concepts or ideas discussed in the stories. The following excerpt from an interview with Mei at the end of fifth grade confirms that she valued her peers' assistance in comprehending the literature:

> Well like, like when you're reading a book and I, and I'm starting with my Book Club group and sometimes, I don't even, I don't even understand something, I could ask at my Book Club group and then they told me something that I should understand. So, that's why I like Book Club.

Not surprisingly, since Mei was in the process of learning a new language, vocabulary was one area of special interest to her. Laura encouraged the children to keep a written record in their logs of vocabulary words they wanted to know, and Mei took this task very seriously. While she often used the dictionary to find meanings of words she did not know, she also asked peers for help, as the following book club transcript demonstrates. During this discussion, Mei consulted with peers about the meaning of a word from the book *Bridge to Terabithia* (Paterson, 1977). Jason asked her to identify the word she wanted to know, and the following discussion ensued:

Mei: Vancris, or something.
Jason: What is it? *(Jason asked with a confused tone of voice.)*
Mei: Vancrish. The word, V-A-N-Q-U-I-S-H. *(Mei pointed to the word in her book.)*
Jason: Oh, vanquished.
Mei: You know the word?
Jason: Yes. It means, it means like vanished. This word, I think that what the word is. Vanished means like . . . *(Jason proceeded to define the word* vanish *as "nothing there.")*
Tabitha: No, it's NOT vanished! This word turns out to be vanquished. VanQUished!

The children established that the word they were trying to define was *vanquish*, not *vanish*. However, none of them knew what the word meant. Since they all needed help with this word, they had to rely on an outside source for help.

This incident is significant for several reasons. First, Mei was voicing a legitimate concern to her peers: She had encountered a difficult word in the context of her reading and she wanted to know what it meant. Second, Mei's peers took her concern seriously and sincerely tried to help her. Third, since all children in the group needed additional help with the word, the experience validated Mei as a peer among equals despite her lack of fluency with English. Thus the students' book club provided a context of support as they engaged in discussions of personal significance.

Book Club as a Context for Experimenting with Language-in-Use

Van Lier (1988) suggests that classrooms encouraging learners' experimentation with language help promote second-language development. He also emphasizes the need for meaningful or purposeful language use to promote second-language development. Book Club can be a context for students to experiment with language-in-use in a meaningful and functional manner. That is, in Book Club children use language to write about and talk about issues and ideas that *they* choose and consider to be important.

Book Club serves as a context for students to experiment with language in many ways on a daily basis. First, second-language learners have the opportunity to experiment with spoken language when they talk with their peers in their book clubs. Second, students have the opportunity to experiment with written language as they make decisions about what they want to write in their reading logs.

Mei often had opportunities to experiment with language and she took advantage of them. The excerpt below comes from a book club discussion on October 8, 1991. Mei and her peers were discussing *James and the Giant Peach* (Dahl, 1961), about a young orphan boy who must live with two mean aunts. One day a man gives James a bag of magic that he accidentally drops under a peach tree, causing a giant peach to grow. James enters the peach and engages in many adventures with the creatures he finds there.

Mei and her peers (Stark, Jean, Art, Jason) were discussing James's situation with his aunts and trying to decide what they would do in his place—living with cruel relatives. The children then begin to discuss alternatives to running away. Jean comments that she would run away like James does in the book. Jason agrees. Note the interesting stance that Mei assumes in the segment below. She seems to be using language, primarily in the form of questions, to get Jason to elaborate on and justify the ideas he presents to the group.

Jason: I would go anywhere I wanted to, like the ocean or any places I
     wanted / I wanted to go.
Mei: We're not talking . . . If you're hungry, what you do?
Jason: Huh?
Mei: *(Repeating with her voice slightly raised.)* If you're hungry, what you do?
Jason: Would I want?
Mei: If you hungry.
Jason: Hungry?
Mei: Yeah.
Jason: Umm, I don't know / I could just come back.
Mei: You said you would run away and you run anywhere you wanted, but
     you don't have any place to go.
Jason: The ocean probably.
Mei: And how can you go, you go anywhere?
Jason: I can. I can if I knew how to make a / start a fire. I could make a fire
     and I could catch some fish.
Stark: *(Telling Jason how to go about starting a fire.)* Take, take two rocks and
     then smack them together really hard and spark it.
Mei: How can you, how can you catch fish?

In the segment above, Mei was not experimenting with the form of language (i.e., she was not asking what a particular word meant); rather, she was experimenting with facilitating interactions to push Jason's thinking. She repeatedly asked Jason to elaborate on and justify the ideas he suggested to the group. Thus Mei used her Book Club discussion to push and probe her peer's thinking; she used language in a functional manner to experiment with meaning.

As illustrated in the following example from my study of Book Club in the summer program, another way that second-language learners experiment with language is through writing in their logs. As an example, "wonderful words" is one of the topics children could choose to write about. As with all the prompts I used in my summer class, I wrote the guidelines for "wonderful words" on large chart paper and hung it where the students could see it to use it as a reference.

Find some really wonderful words – words that are new, crazy, or descriptive; ones you might want to use in your own writing; ones that are confusing, or whatever. Write down the word or words and share them with your book club group. You might want to write a short note about why you picked the word so that you can remember later. You might also want to write the page number where you found the word so you can find it again.

Roberto's log demonstrates how he chose to write about a "wonderful word" he had learned while reading *The People Who Hugged the Trees* (see Figure 7.1). In the story, the main character, Amrita, strove to save her special tree and the forest of which it was a part from the maharajah's axemen, who were ordered to cut it down. In addition to writing about the new "wonderful word" he had just learned, Roberto chose to draw a picture of Amrita trying to save her tree from the maharajah's axemen.

Prompts such as "wonderful words" gave children the opportunity to experiment with new and exciting vocabulary they were learning. However, the children did not always use the formal Book Club prompts to guide their writing. Instead, they experimented with written language in other ways. For example, one day Roberto began writing acrostic poems in his log. This was

FIGURE 7.1.   Roberto's Log Entry

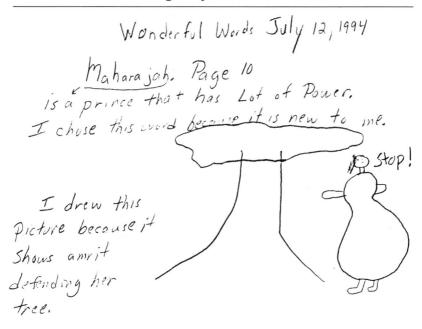

not something I had introduced to the children but something he had learned in school the previous year.

July 20, 1994

Forests   Trees

Fairly beautiful   Tropical trees
Only beautiful noices   Rain forest are wrisling with trees
Relaxing   Enourmus trees
Earth has lots of forests   Earth has lot of trees
Silent   Save our earth
Tropical Rain forests
Soft soil

Roberto's poetry experiments started a "rage" in the classroom. Other children followed his lead, including poems in their logs that drew on the stories and activities we engaged in throughout the forest ecosystem unit. Some children wrote acrostic poems like Roberto's, while others wrote more conventional poetry. All were engaged in meaningful language-in-use.

Book Club as a Context for Second-Language Acquisition

In the previous two sections I emphasized ways that Book Club provided a context for students to receive guided support from their teachers and peers, as well as a place to experiment with oral and written language in a functional and meaningful way. In this final section I emphasize two key points. First, second-language learners are capable of engaging in complex thinking and reasoning *while they are in the process of acquiring English*. Second, teachers must realize that second-language learners have important and valuable ideas and experiences to contribute to the class. The unique contributions they have to offer the classroom community can be capitalized on for the benefit of all students in the classroom.

During fifth grade, Mei was in her third year of attending an American public school. Technically, according to guidelines discussed by Collier (1989), it is unlikely that Mei would have reached academic proficiency in English. Typically, it takes a minimum of four years before children become academically proficient in their second language if they have gone to school in their home country. Nonetheless, even though Mei was still in the process of acquiring academic proficiency in English, the example and subsequent discussion below illustrates that she was quite successful at using a sophisticated array of strategies for interacting with peers in English.

As mentioned in an earlier section of this chapter, Gee (1990) suggests that being literate involves much more than merely "knowing" words; to be literate, individuals must know how to effectively use written and spoken language in various contexts in meaningful ways. To learn to use language effectively, children must have opportunities to practice it in meaningful contexts. Gaining access to book club discussions and maintaining control of the conversation was often difficult for participants when they discussed emotional issues. In one of their conversations, Mei wanted to talk about why Park, the main character in *Park's Quest*, called Vietnamese "killers." She used several strategies to gain access to the discussion. First, she interrupted the conversation. When that failed, she stated, "I have a question." When no one responded, she raised her voice, directly addressing the group. Then she tried overlapping speech. When none of these strategies "worked," out of frustration, she criticized the group: "Who's talking more?" Two of her peers acknowledged her desire to talk, providing her access to ask her question (Raphael & Brock, 1993).

Mei:　You guys, I have a question. Did, did you think like when, when Park you know what he said, he said all, all of the Vietnamese people are the killers. How, how come they be friends with Thanh?
Jason:　Dang man. [I would take that word back then.
Stark:　　　　　　[I'd be, I don't,
Mei:　But, but he, he be friends with her like when, when he don't even know that, that is his, his sister.

This segment exemplifies Mei's tenacity at making her position heard through the range of strategies she employed to gain the floor in the conversation. Not only did she feel she had a right to speak, she had a repertoire of tools to draw from to make sure that she was heard. While we cannot make a direct causal connection between Mei's strategy and her participation in Book Club, it seems likely that the daily opportunities she had to engage in meaningful discussions and the instructional support she received influenced her ability to use English in a functional, effective manner.

Not only did Mei develop sophisticated ways to "learn to mean" in English, she had many valuable contributions to offer her class during her Book Club discussions. Mei had the opportunity to act as "instructor" as a result of participating in Book Club. I draw on an excerpt from Raphael and Brock (1993) to illustrate this point:

> After several months in 4th grade, Mei began to talk more in small groups, but rarely volunteered during whole class discussions. In a January, 4th grade book club, Mei had begun to talk about her family's experience during and after the

Vietnam war. Her peers were interested, asked many questions and the discussion continued after other book club groups had ended. The other students drifted over to listen to Mei's group until she found herself talking in front of most of the students in her classroom. This was a positive experience on two levels. First, she was successful in directing her words to a general audience of listeners – making herself understood by many others. Second, she saw that her own knowledge and experiences were valued by and of interest to her peers. The effects of these efforts were seen in Mei's gradually increased participation in whole class discussions. (p. 184)

CONCLUDING COMMENTS

I have asserted that helping second-language learners "learn to mean" in English must be accomplished by balancing explicit instruction with opportunities for students to experiment with language-in-use in meaningful contexts. Book Club affords second-language learners these opportunities on a daily basis. In the book clubs, children have an opportunity to experiment with language in ways that are personally meaningful to them. As previously illustrated with numerous examples, students also engage in experiences in which both peers and adults can provide spontaneous minilessons during small- and large-group discussions. Whole-class community share provides a context for more explicit literacy instruction. I have argued that for second-language learners to be able to effectively participate in their classroom, they must "learn to mean" in English. Book Club can provide a valuable context for facilitating this.

With respect to the contributions that Book Club can make to our understanding of working with second-language learners, many experts (e.g., Cummins, 1994; Hudelson, 1994; Nieto, 1992) express urgent concern for the need to determine ways in which we, as an educational community, can best meet the needs of the increasing numbers of second-language learners in our schools. Scholars such as John-Steiner (1985) stress the importance of attending to the role that the regular classroom can play in fostering educational opportunities for second-language learners. Valdes (1992) asserts that effectively teaching second-language students "will involve much more than 'celebrating' cultural differences. . . . Addressing the needs of these students will demand carefully planned pedagogical solutions *based on an understanding of their unique characteristics*" (p. 86; emphasis added). Valdes argues that the educational community must vigorously pursue endeavors to learn about and promote literacy development for second-language learners.

In this chapter, I have discussed ways Book Club can be used effectively as a literacy program for second-language learners in mainstream classrooms. I conclude by introducing some important provisos for mainstream teachers of second-language learners to consider. The education of second-language learners is complex and controversial. I briefly introduce three issues especially relevant for mainstream teachers.

First, one goal for all teachers of second-language learners is enabling students to understand and use English effectively. Achieving this goal requires that teachers know about the process of acquiring a second language and about related pedagogical issues pertaining to educating second-language learners. Thus effective decision-making about literacy instruction for second-language learners requires examination of what it means to acquire a second language and how this knowledge can and should inform decisions about literacy instruction. A thorough discussion of these important issues is beyond the purview of this chapter; however, the reader is referred to both citations within this chapter and other resources listed in the Appendix.

Second, in concert with others who are concerned about effectively educating second-language learners (e.g., Genesee, 1994), I advocate the implementation of quality bilingual programs for second-language learners that afford children the opportunity to maintain and develop their first language and home culture while simultaneously learning the conventions of the dominant English discourse community. Unfortunately, however, the number of qualified bilingual teachers in this country is on the decline (Nieto, 1992). This and other factors (e.g., children who speak a wide spectrum of first languages in a given district) contribute to the difficulty of providing such educational programs for all second-language learners.

Finally, in many school districts it is common to have children who speak a variety of different languages in the same classroom at any one time. In other situations teachers may not teach students who speak multiple languages in their classroom at one time, but over the span of their careers, they may teach children who speak a variety of first languages. While it is important for teachers to strive to learn about the languages and cultures of the children they teach, it is not feasible to assume that teachers can become proficient in every language of the children they teach.

Book Club cannot be considered a substitute for quality bilingual programs with teachers proficient in the first languages of the children they teach. I would argue that it could potentially be an effective tool for literacy instruction in quality bilingual programs, but research would have to be conducted to substantiate this claim. What I am suggesting here is that Book Club can be an effective literacy program for second-language learners in *mainstream classrooms* where English is the primary medium of instruction. The work reported in this chapter directly addresses John-Steiner's (1985) concerns by illustrating ways that regular classroom teachers can play an important role in fostering educational opportunities for second-language learners.

APPENDIX: SUGGESTED READING

Office of Bilingual Education. (Ed.). (1989). *Beyond language: Social and cultural factors in schooling language minority children* (3rd ed.). Los Angeles: Evaluation, Dissemination and Assessment Center.

Peregoy, S. F., & Owen, F. B. (1993). *Reading, writing, & learning in ESL.* White Plains, NY: Longman.

Richard-Amato, P. A. (1988). *Making it happen: Interaction in the second-language classroom from theory to practice.* New York: Addison-Wesley.

Richard-Amato, P. A., & Snow, M. A. (Eds.). (1992). *The multicultural classroom: Readings for content-area teachers.* New York: Addison-Wesley.

Trueba, H. T. (1989). *Raising silent voices: Educating the linguistic minorities for the 21st century.* Boston: Heinle & Heinle.

I wish to thank Sarah Hudelson for her thoughtful comments on an earlier draft of this work.

COMMENTARY

ROBERT RUEDA

The beginning of this chapter describes a situation in which a teacher (in this case the author) finds herself able to communicate only minimally with a new student because of language differences. This is an increasingly common situation given the diversity now found in many classrooms, not only in states such as California and Texas but in many other places as well. In many cases, these students come from families in economically depressed circumstances and have not had access to many of the experiences that characterize the lives of middle- and upper-class students. Not surprisingly, school achievement in literacy and other areas is low. The question confronting schools is how to provide a learning environment that can meet these challenges.

Unfortunately, there is a long history in the educational literature documenting the failure to address this issue satisfactorily. A common but unfortunate practice with English learners has been to misjudge ability and potential based on surface features of oral language competence. This has often led to low-level and/or remedial instructional activities that serve to further diminish estimation of learning ability, resulting in a downward spiral of academic failure. One response to this diversity has been to engage in a simple "ethnicity- or language-matching strategy" under the assumption that if the teacher's and student's language and/or ethnicity is matched, achievement will automatically increase. However, not only are there shortages of teachers from diverse backgrounds, but simple matching of this type does not inevitably produce greater achievement.

Fortunately, there are an increasing numbers of examples in the literature—*including the description of the author's work with Book Club in this chapter*—that indicate that the above scenario is avoidable. Taken together, this chapter and other studies suggest some common features that promote literacy with English learners. Some of these include the following:

- Activating or supplying background knowledge that corresponds to the literature being read
- Establishing relationships between existing and new knowledge
- Providing an authentic context for literacy activities
- Making each student a contributing member of a literacy community
- Providing numerous opportunities to negotiate meaning

159

- Providing a context for high-level discourse around important problems
- Guiding and scaffolding participation, language use, and learning
- Providing a positive, accepting environment for differences related to language and culture
- Building on those cultural and linguistic resources in instructional activities

It is clear from this chapter that most, if not all, of these features are found to some degree in Book Club. Yet if interventions such as Book Club appear to be effective in promoting literacy, why are they not found in more classrooms? Some possible answers to this question illuminate some important issues meriting attention and directions for further inquiry.

One interesting aspect of this description of Book Club which raises an important issue is that, while Book Club has certain regular features or structural components associated with it, it would be difficult if not impossible to prescribe beforehand the teacher's role in an exact fashion. While this is clearly a positive feature, allowing the teacher to assist student performance on a moment-to-moment basis, some teachers find this ambiguity difficult.

It is also clear that a critical element for success in Book Club is the teacher's ability to monitor the interactional context as well as each student's current understanding, adjusting the activities and discourse accordingly. In effect, this redefines teaching as providing assistance so that it falls just above students' current levels of understanding and development. This represents a clear and important break from earlier, more traditional literacy programs and activities such as basal programs, which appear to have been compiled with the idea of making them "teacher-proof." This ability to monitor student understanding "on-line" and adjust one's output accordingly, referred to as responsive teaching, is not easily acquired.

These issues raise some interesting questions that might extend the work described in the present chapter. First, I believe we need to know more about how responsive teachers monitor ongoing classroom interactions with respect to their instruction and assessment. I wonder what it might take to enable teachers to engage in this type of instruction, whether as part of Book Club or other instructional models. That is, what types of professional development are needed to sustain this type of teaching?

On a more general note, the author commented that many features of Book Club promote the acquisition of literacy for all students, not just second-language learners. It would be interesting to more systematically investigate the specific features that currently exist or that might be incorporated that are especially valuable for students in the process of acquiring English. The author mentions some of these as collaborative writing, hearing stories read orally, and careful selection of literature. I wonder whether one or more of these are especially valuable for second-language learners. I also wonder about the role of parent participation and the optimal ways teachers can access and incorporate students' and their families' funds of knowledge. Book Club offers a ray of hope in the often dismal educational picture that surrounds students in the process of acquiring English, and more classroom-based inquiry is needed to explicate the theoretical and applied issues that might make these types of practices more accessible to a wider range of teachers and students.

CHAPTER 8

The Cross-Aged Literacy Program

Preparing Struggling Adolescents for Book
Club Discussions

FENICE B. BOYD

I have always been interested in adolescents who struggle with reading, writing, and schooling. When I taught these students, I based my instructional approach on the dominant belief underlying traditional literacy instruction. That is, I had students practice skills out of context and drilled them on those skills to help them become better readers and writers. My students used commercially published materials to develop comprehension strategies (e.g., getting the main idea, making inferences) by reading brief paragraphs and answering questions. They worked to improve their vocabulary skills by choosing the correct word or phrase for multiple-choice questions. I assumed that after mastering skills, students could read authentic literature, write for authentic purposes, and construct meaning for themselves in meaningful literacy activities. This approach was especially true for students who received "remedial reading" and other resource services. Eventually, however, I grew to realize that if poor schooling experiences (Fader, 1968)—where students are not participants in their own learning—had not worked for them through most of their schooling, an alternative approach to literacy learning was certainly in order.

RATIONALE FOR THE PROJECT

Traditional literacy instruction for low-achieving high school students has been criticized in recent years for its reliance on practicing decontextualized skills in isolation (e.g., Allington & McGill-Franzen, 1989), tracking into low-level literacy experiences (e.g., Applebee, 1991), and lacking opportunities for working with a variety of literary genres (Walmsley & Walp, 1990). Such instructional emphases, content, tasks, and expectations are not adequate for helping adolescents who struggle with literacy learning and schooling.

Historically, instruction in reading and writing has been based on behavioral theories that limited our definitions of success to the products of literacy activities (e.g., oral fluency, ability to answer literal comprehension questions) or, more recently, on theories of cognitive science that focus on individuals' reading and writing processes, without much attention to the social aspects of literacy development. This basis for instruction has been especially true for poor readers and writers, with programs that often mandate individual progress through skills-based instruction.

The past decade of reading and writing research has expanded the definition of *literacy* to recognize the inherently social nature of literacy events and to emphasize the contributions of social, linguistic, and cognitive processes to literacy learning (Bloome & Green, 1984; Green, 1990). In this reconceptualization of literacy learning, language use and meaning construction depend on various social dimensions in specific contexts (Beach, 1993). Such social dimensions include the participants' perceptions of responsibility, roles, needs, status, and motives.

The importance of emphasizing the social, as well as the cognitive, aspect of literacy learning has direct implications for research for adolescents and young adults who are not active participants in their own literacy learning. Kennedy, Jung, and Orland (1986) note the overrepresentation of students from diverse cultural and ethnic backgrounds in remedial and low-tracked programs. Other scholars (e.g., Au & Mason, 1981; Cazden & Leggett, 1981; Philips, 1983) document the differential treatment of diverse and minority learners in school contexts and argue that such differential treatment negatively affects students' reading achievement. For example, Cazden (1988b) provides evidence that minority children from New Zealand and the United States are discouraged from expanding on their thoughts. Similarly, Michaels (1981) reports that when the narrative styles of minority children differ from the expectations of white teachers, interaction is often unsuccessful and, over time, may adversely affect school performance and achievement. Such encounters with learning in schools often frustrate students when they learn that the background knowledge and experiences they bring to literacy learning are neither valued nor heard by their teachers and peers (Florio-Ruane, 1994).

As a participant in the Book Club project, I had opportunities to see young children of mixed academic abilities (i.e., high, average, and low achievers) engage in rich discussions around text. This inspired me to explore an alternative literature-based project with high school students who were not motivated to read and write. In my research, I have explored how high school students identified as having reading problems benefited from Book Club instruction in a cross-aged literacy program (Boyd, 1995). In this chapter, I describe the high school students' experiences as they worked together to prepare for sessions in which they would lead literary discussions with small groups of fifth-grade students. I address two key questions: What happens when low-achieving adolescents interact in an alternative contextualized literacy learning setting? What potential might this program have for helping students who are labeled "at-risk"?

OVERVIEW OF THE CROSS-AGED LITERACY PROJECT

My experiences with members of the Book Club team enabled me to learn more about literature-based reading programs and Book Club's potential to assist older students who have had impoverished literacy learning experiences. I consulted with Taffy Raphael and Susan McMahon about the possibilities of adapting components of Book Club to design and develop an alternative program for low-achieving adolescents. Their suggestions helped me design a project to offer these students opportunities to engage in an educative learning experience (Dewey, 1938). In this section, I provide an overview of five aspects of the Cross-Aged Literacy Program: (1) the development of the program contexts, (2) participant identification, (3) literature selection, (4) preparation seminar purposes, and (5) preparation seminar instructional focuses.

Developing the Program Contexts

In addition to considering the benefits book club might offer low-achieving adolescents, I considered previous research addressing advantages individuals receive from tutoring others. Research findings of cross-aged teaching programs identify potential, positive gains in several general areas for students who teach others: (1) motivation (Bloom, 1988; Dillner, 1971), (2) improved communication and social skills (Dollar, 1974), (3) increased opportunities for literacy learning (Allen, 1976; Cloward, 1967), and (4) development of positive attitudes toward school, teachers, literacy, and education (Dillner, 1971; Ellson, 1969; Granick, 1968; Paoni, 1971; Rosenshine & Furst, 1969; Snapp, 1970; Strodtbeck & Granick, 1972; Weitzman, 1965). Given the benefits cited in various tutoring programs as well as those related to Book Club, it seemed feasible to explore a project that merged Book Club and cross-aged literature discussion groups.

My goal was to enhance and encourage the literacy development of adolescents who were frustrated and poorly motivated to read and write by helping them to assume responsibility for the learning of younger children and, thus, themselves. I call this program the Cross-Aged Literacy Program. The Cross-Aged Literacy Program draws on the Book Club project (Raphael et al., 1992) and peer tutoring (Bloom, 1988; Topping, 1988; Wagner, 1982), extending and modifying both concepts. The Cross-Aged Literacy Program's language and literacy components are derived from Book Club (e.g., reading, writing, book clubs); the cross-aged nature of the program derives from peer tutoring.

The Cross-Aged Literacy Program consisted of two primary contexts— the *preparation seminar* and the *cross-aged literary discussion groups*—in which the high school students engaged in literacy activities. The *preparation seminar* is the context in which the high school students worked with me to prepare for their interactions with the elementary students. The *cross-aged literary discussion* provided a context for high school students to take leadership in implementing strategies learned for reading, writing, and discussing literature with younger students. I selected two schools (i.e., one high school and one elementary school) and talked with each of the administrators about their students' participation. The administrators identified one high school teacher and one elementary teacher willing to have some of their students participate in the study. The classroom teachers were involved by (1) discussing the possibilities of the program in assisting high school students, (2) recommending students who might benefit from the program, and (3) arranging students' schedules to accommodate both their regular class work and this project.

Participant Identification

The reading teacher and I selected four students who were enrolled in a high school reading-improvement course and who represented the heterogeneous mix of the school. All were ethnic minorities considered to be poor readers and writers with low motivation. Romel was a 17-year-old African American ninth grader who willingly, actively, and enthusiastically participated in social dialogue during the preparation seminar and the cross-aged literary discussion group sessions, often leading oral discussions with the younger children. Li Ping was a 16-year-old Vietnamese student, learning English as a second language during tenth grade. Lewis was a 16-year-old

African American ninth grader who tended to be less motivated to participate than either Romel or Li Ping in written and oral literacy activities. RaShea was a 14-year-old African American ninth grader who participated in the preparation seminar but refused to work with the fifth graders. In our first meeting, the teacher and I explained the purposes and expectations of the program, stressing that extra time and effort would be necessary. All four agreed to participate in the preparation seminar.

Literature Selection

I selected three books: *Song of the Trees* (Taylor, 1975), *Mississippi Bridge* (Taylor, 1990), and *Park's Quest* (Paterson, 1988). Scholars suggest that several factors (e.g., emotion, story understanding and liking, empathy with a certain character) influence how students engage a piece of literature (Black & Seifert, 1985; Golden & Guthrie, 1986; E. Hansen, 1986; Jose & Brewer, 1984; Mosenthal, 1987). I selected these novels because I wanted the students to read texts that might encourage rich discussions between both (1) the adolescents and me and (2) the high school and elementary students. In addition, since the high school participants for this program were minority students, I selected literature with multicultural themes and issues by and about people who are not part of the sociopolitical mainstream of the United States (Bishop, 1993).

Purposes of the Preparation Seminar

The preparation seminar had multiple purposes, from the theoretical to the pragmatic. The seminar provided an authentic context within which high school students interacted around texts that were interesting and personally meaningful but with reading levels that were comfortable enough for them to read independently. It is easy to sympathize with high school readers reluctant to be seen by peers reading books at a fourth- or fifth-grade level. Further, high school students with reading problems often have such a long history of reading practices equated with decontextualized skills that they lose sight of what sustained interactions with meaningful texts can evoke within themselves. The seminar activities centered around the texts that would be used with their fifth-grade literary discussion groups—groups they would lead. The high school students had a reason to study these texts—texts they might otherwise feel awkward reading and discussing with peers. Further, leading the younger students in discussions meant that they needed not only to read the story but to be able to identify important themes, to raise questions that would invite the younger students into the texts, and to provide support should the younger students run into difficulties.

Thus the theoretical basis for the preparation seminar drew on notions of proleptic teaching (Palincsar & Brown, 1984), building on the students' strengths and providing support so they could achieve goals that might have been beyond them if working independently. Reducing the difficulty of the text while encouraging them to read, respond, and create meaning for authentic purposes were two key areas of support. Others (e.g., Smith, 1988) have argued for the importance of being a member of the "literacy club," participating in real reading of real texts for real purposes. In the preparation seminar, students were treated as the literate individuals they were while also being challenged to push their literate thinking, using tools and strategies I introduced and reinforced.

The pragmatic basis of the preparation seminar reflected the importance of helping the high school students generate relevant background knowledge, understand the story's themes and content, and prepare questions or prompts to begin the literary discussions in the cross-aged setting. In that setting, I could work with the students closely to ensure that they were justifiably comfortable with upcoming interactions with the younger students. Further, students had the opportunity to collaborate in generating potential themes and topics, comparing experiences across their groups, and discussing solutions to any problems that arose with their groups.

In summary, I had four overall goals for the preparation seminar: (1) to encourage high school students' leadership and participation in the cross-aged literary discussions, (2) to plan, in collaboration with the high school students, for literacy activities and conversations for the cross-aged discussion, (3) to debrief the high school students after each of their cross-aged sessions, and (4) to monitor and assess the high school students' interactions and experiences in this alternative literacy instructional program.

Preparation Seminar Instruction Focuses

To achieve the preceding goals for the preparation seminar, I developed five instructional areas to help high school students in oral reading, comprehension, and literary response as they read high quality and engaging literature. The instructional focuses were reading, writing, discussion, lesson planning, and reflection/analysis.

Reading. In our preparation seminar, the high school students read on a voluntary basis. When they refused to read, I read orally, using the occasion to model fluency, intonation, and expression. Sloan (1991) suggests that when adults read orally to young children, this assigns a special role to reading, signaling to the child that adults find reading worthwhile and enjoyable. This notion is of similar concern for young adolescents who are less motivated to read. As our program and relationships progressed, the high school students eventually began to take more risks and read orally. They established a procedure of turn-taking by using a pause or the end of a section to change readers. I was excited when students showed this initiative because it demonstrated that they had gained enough confidence in themselves to take risks by reading orally to peers.

Writing. To encourage students to write in response to the literature, I drew on the concept of a reading log (see, e.g., Atwell, 1987; Fulwiler, 1982; Reed, 1988) and used ones similar to those described in Chapter 4. I prompted students' responses by asking them to draw on key issues or events in the story, to respond to questions that I raised, or to select from a range of options I described on a "reading log idea" response chart. I also encouraged students both to write and to use other forms of representation, such as drawings, character maps, and other visual formats. Through these varied writing log responses, I provided opportunities for them to respond personally to the texts, thus encouraging close reading and reflection. Doing so helped students prepare for later discussion in which they interacted around their differing responses to texts read.

Discussion. The discussion component provided a means to focus on key issues or events in the literature and to help prepare students for a literary discussion with younger children. My role during the discussion component was that of a facilitator, encouraging students to respond personally to the text and to engage in open-ended discussions with their peers and me before going to the elementary school. As we participated in our discussion, I modeled what their role and interactions might look like with the fourth and fifth graders. We conducted our discussions by: (1) reading response(s) from reading log entries, (2) asking questions, (3) asking students to clarify ideas and comments, (4) asking for predictions of upcoming events in the story, and (5) responding to one another's comments.

After the students had an opportunity to read, write, and personally respond to the literature, we reflected on our own discussions as a way to generate ideas and plan literary activities. This resulted in a different but interrelated phase of discussion, one in which the high school students brainstormed ideas for activities and planned literacy activities and tasks for the younger children.

Lesson planning. I expected the high school students to conduct discussions with the elementary children in ways similar to the discussions we had in the preparation seminar. To do so, we planned the lessons and procedures to guide them in facilitating a literary discussion with the fourth and fifth graders. The planning component of the preparation seminar began by talking about the reading, writing, and discussion activities in which we had engaged (e.g., who read, what they read, key issues raised, potential topics to discuss with younger children). Our planning for the cross-aged literary discussions centered on: (1) who would read orally at the elementary school, (2) the chapter(s) or section(s) to read, and (3) key questions, issues, and events from the literature to discuss. A variety of ideas emerged, specifically related to the key issues and events students might talk about in their small groups. After debating the discussion topics and developing questions, we made final decisions. The high school students wrote brief sentences in their planning logs to help remember the procedures for the activities with the younger children. For example, in his log, Lewis wrote:

5/6/93   Mis boyd is goin to read 15 mins
         there [they're] goin to write 5–10 minutes
         we can talk about 20 mins
         What was the probulm on the bus an how did you feel about
            the problem?
         What do you think about Jeremy?
         Why do you think all of the racism was goin on at that time
         Write all the questions on the bord and ask to do one or
            draw a pictures

Reflection/analysis. A final focus of the preparation seminar was reflection and analysis of the cross-aged interactions and discussions. I called this component "debriefings." I planned the debriefing phase to talk with the high school students about: (1) their roles and responsibilities in their small groups, (2) the strengths and weaknesses of the cross-aged sessions, and (3) their own learning as facilitators of cross-aged discussion groups with fourth and fifth grade students.

One important issue was the high school students' demeanor when interacting with the elementary children. I decided to confront this directly by providing them with a list of behaviors describing a good tutor (Pierce, Stahlbrand, & Armstrong, 1980). We read each of the 15 characteristics of a good tutor and discussed how those descriptions might be applied in a cross-aged discussion group. Further, I explained to the high school students that, because they were role models for the elementary students, they should remember to refer to the list when interacting with the children.

Roles and responsibilities related to both academic encounters and social interactions. To study and learn about themselves as facilitators and co-participants in cross-aged literary discussions, students viewed snippets of videotape of their discussions with the fourth and fifth graders. Either a student or I stopped the tape whenever we saw an event to discuss. After describing the event, we discussed its strengths to reinforce the positive and then its weaknesses to brainstorm ideas for improving.

Finally, students discussed how the various oral and written responses that the younger children shared either dominated, extended, or shortened discussions, enabling the high school students to learn strategies and skills they might use to help the children as well as themselves have productive literary discussions. This enabled the high school students to make connections between the elementary children's responses and the high schoolers' own literacy learning and social and cognitive development.

The instructional and debriefing focus of the preparation seminar gave the high school students an opportunity to develop their oral communication skills by discussing the literacy activities (reading, writing, discussion), tasks, and lesson plans. The debriefings gave the students a chance to reflect and critique themselves as learners and "teachers," and to rethink and reformulate their literacy activities before their next visit with the elementary children. Overall, the preparation seminar component offered opportunities for low-achieving adolescents to engage in literacy learning tasks and activities for meaningful purposes and to develop their planning, organization, and decision-making skills within a social setting.

ADOLESCENT STUDENTS' PARTICIPATION
IN THE PREPARATION SEMINAR

One of my primary interests in this project was how the preparation seminar contributed to the adolescents' ability to participate in the literacy activities characterizing Book Club. To understand this, I taped each seminar and wrote retrospective field notes. As I explored the data, three trends emerged, indicating changes in the adolescents' ways of participating: (1) increased interest in oral reading, (2) raising questions around text-based issues, and (3) sharing personal stories based on text-related issues.

Increased Interests in Oral Reading

When we began the preparation seminar, all four students were reluctant to read orally, saying only "I don't want to read." I drew three possible inferences from their refusals: (1) their fluency was poor and oral reading was a struggle; (2) they were embarrassed to read orally before me and others; and (3) they were unwilling to take risks. Since familiarity with the story was important for discussion, my only option seemed to be to read to them, even though I was concerned about both their reactions and the missed opportunity for their oral reading practice. I discovered that, instead of resisting my reading aloud, they appeared to enjoy following along silently. Further, I realized this provided me an opportunity to model features of oral reading such as fluency, expression, and intonation.

After several sessions of the preparation seminar, students began to volunteer to read orally. This seemed to have a domino effect—as one student took the initial step to read, another student followed. Initially, students who volunteered struggled both because their fluency was poor and because the book, Taylor's *Song of the Trees*, is written in black English vernacular and a Southern dialect. Students commented about the author's style; however, they did not give in to their struggle, choosing to continue reading but pausing to ask for assistance whenever they stumbled.

Through this experience, I began to see potential advantages in modeling text-based oral reading. Oral reading might be likened to a form of dialogue where there is interaction among the text, reader, and listeners. With this conceptualization of dialogue, I began to see evidence of Vygotsky's (1978) argument that the capacity for language use and development is contingent upon our social interactions with people. As I modeled oral reading in the preparation seminar, students gradually gained enough confidence and interest in this literacy activity. Their willingness to engage in oral reading activities provided an opportunity for what Dewey (1916) called "learning by doing." Students learn to read and write by reading and writing. Oral reading is a literacy activity that will increase opportunities for engagement in literary discussions for students identified as poor readers and writers. In addition, offering students occasions to engage in oral reading on a volunteer basis and in a "safe" learning environment ensures that they can become actively engaged (through reading or listening) with the text.

Raising Questions Around Text-Based Issues

Burbules (1993) notes that in a dialogue, questions might be asked for a variety of purposes. Types of questions include simple ones eliciting information, elaborate ones probing understanding, and others that challenge or critique. From simple to rhetorical, these forms of questions create a context to engage in dialogue for teaching and learning.

Similarly, literacy activities in the Cross-Aged Literacy Program entailed asking questions for a variety of purposes. The students and I asked questions requesting literal facts about the text, eliciting narrative responses, and challenging and critiquing students' understandings of and personal responses to the text. Our questions assisted in students' literacy development and modeled questions they might use as catalysts for discussions with the elementary children.

While observing the students' interactions in the preparation seminar, I noted how they raised questions as part of the dialogue, planning and deciding on the literacy activities they would conduct with the younger students. One activity began when students brainstormed oral literacy activities to facilitate their cross-aged discussions. As they searched through their trade books, they generated ideas about different places to stop the oral reading portion to raise questions and issues that emerged from the text to promote dialogue with the younger children.

In a section of transcript from the preparation seminar included below, students raise a question about the conflict a character experienced in *Mississippi Bridge*. Like *Song of the Trees*, the setting for *Mississippi Bridge* is rural Mississippi in the 1930s. Josias, the main character, had entered a building serving as both the local general country store and bus depot to purchase a ticket to Natchez Trace, where he had been hired to do some lumbering work. Josias proudly told the white men in the store about his luck in finding a job. However, his audience did not share his joy and let him know by intimidating him. Lewis, Romel, and Li Ping reacted to Josias finding himself in such a tense situation. Notice how Romel introduced a question and Li Ping offered support to help develop the question.

Fenice: Now, what question . . . what kind of question might you have the students respond to, that would spark some discussion about the conflict that Josias was in with the store people, and about Jo . . . I mean what Jeremy *(another character in the story)* might be feeling inside related to the conflict?

Romel: Why do you think that the um . . . the um white man got mad at Josias because what he had said?

Li Ping: What about the part that Josias lied to um Mr. Charlie? Right? Jeremy father, that he will have his brother somewhere?

Fenice: Okay, what about it?

Li Ping: She said that, he said that his, um, brother was sick and he coming to help him. He was lying about that to get away with Mr . . . Jeremy father, right?

Lewis: He was trying to git, 'cause he was 'spose to been going to 'git a job in Jackson.

Romel: He was gon' make more money than the white man.

Lewis: Yeah, he was gon' be making more money than the white man.

Fenice: So what about it Li Ping, what are you saying?

Li Ping: What should he do? Instead of lying and go away . . . I don't know.

It is interesting to note how the students raised their discussion questions. Burbules (1993) refers to a participation type of question he calls an "invitation," an open-ended request for opinions, beliefs, evaluations, interpretations, and elaborations. In the above transcript, Romel asked, "Why do you think . . . ," appearing to imply that he wanted to get other members' opinions. After Romel posed his question, the students opened the discussion by voicing their sense of the conflict among the characters, thus making an argument for the significance of their questions. For example, Romel's question implied that Josias (African American) was in a tension-filled situation because he shared his joy in finding a job during the Great Depression when it was hard for white men to find work. Romel's insight about the conflict between the two men in the store reflected his ability to use a text-based issue to develop questions for elaboration of ideas.

Li Ping continued by raising another question inviting opinions from her peers; however, she offered a different perspective on the same issue, raising the question from Josias's perspective rather than that of the antagonist and posing a challenge for Lewis and Romel. In addition, her question can be explored from another angle, since it appears to critique the character by noting the "backing down" approach Josias took when challenged. Li Ping's comment about Josias "lying and running away" suggests her reaction to the way Josias handled himself. The students decided to use Li Ping's question to explore the conflict of this event. As the next segment of transcript reveals, Li Ping's question created some tension in the group as I rephrased it.

Fenice: Li Ping's question . . . what else could Josias do rather than lie about the job he said he had. Okay, if I ask you that question, what would you say? What could he do?

Lewis: [He could um . . .

Li Ping: [He should not lie. He could . . .

Romel: He should have just told the truth.

Li Ping: Yeah, and say, *I could do better job than you are!*

Fenice: Okay, he told the truth at first, and the truth got him in trouble didn't it?

Romel: No.

Fenice: Yes it did.

Romel: Not really because, before . . . he had . . . naw . . . he got . . . I mean a white man . . . he was gittin' 'em all geaked up, and he was just like backing off, because a white man, he got loud, just a little bit, and 'den, he um turn it around, turn the um the whole story around.

Fenice: You said he could tell the truth.

Romel: Yep, and just let it be.

Lewis: He could stick with it.

Romel: Yeah, he just backed down . . . so he just changed it around.

Lewis: He could have stuck with what he was saying and said something like um, just because I'm black it doesn't mean I'm not equal to you, and that doesn't mean that I can't do the same things that you can do?

This discussion is an example of how the students discussed the circumstances surrounding a question they raised about an event in the story. Each one took a stance around the issue of Josias's conflict, stating he should not have changed his original story. Li Ping's comment was direct and specific, implying that Josias should have stood up for himself in the store. Romel expressed a similar opinion and elaborated on Li Ping's interpretation that Josias placed himself in a tension-filled situation when he changed his story. Lewis contributed yet another opinion, stating that he should not have changed his story when confronted by the men in the store.

In this example, Lewis, Romel, and Li Ping raised a question that resulted in a critique of Josias, implying that he did not do the "right" thing when he changed his story. Ironically, the students' critical stance suggested that they supported one another even though I attempted to complicate the discussion. Romel, Li Ping, and Lewis interacted with one another, contributing similar views in their dialogue. It appeared that the students used their knowledge and interpretations from the text to raise a question about a controversial issue, one that did not explicitly state anything about "truth" or when to tell it. However, the students used their notions of truth to support their argument – if Josias had told the truth, the problem would have been resolved. Rosenblatt (1983) suggests that an individual's reading of a piece of literature is a highly complex process because readers bring personal factors to literature that will affect interactions between the text and the reader.

Beach (1993) suggests that when students respond to text, they respond as members in a classroom community and impart perspectives acquired as members of families, social organizations, and neighborhoods. The opportunity to raise questions regarding issues imbedded in text offers students a chance to assume responsibility for their own learning and to contribute information in the classroom community. Occasions to talk and write about text have potential for helping low achievers develop competency in literary dialogue as they struggle to enhance and understand themselves as learners and become active participants in their own learning. Structured, authentic, and meaningful literacy tasks (i.e., preparation seminar) gave students a variety of ways to immerse themselves in discussions. Modeling and participation with an adult in dialogue first, and then co-participating with younger children in discussions, provided a context to learn more about the nature of educative dialogue when older and younger children read, write, and discuss literature.

Sharing Personal Stories Based on Text-Related Issues

I designed the social nature of the preparation seminar so that students would have a positive experience while they discussed the literature, planned the cross-aged activities, and participated in debriefings. Rosenblatt (1983) implies that creating a situation in which students have a vital experience during literature discussions may pose a dilemma for teachers when a separation emerges between the text and the issues relevant to students. However, in my role as teacher/researcher, I purposely attempted to help the students make connections between themselves and the literature. This was important because helping the students to learn how to make personal responses was not a goal of their high school reading-improvement course. For example, after the Taylor unit, we read *Park's Quest*, a book with characters whose experiences were similar to Li Ping's when she moved from Vietnam to the United States.

The next transcript is taken from a preparation seminar in which students were discussing *Park's Quest*. Park, the main character, could not understand why his mother refused to discuss his father, who had died in Vietnam 11 years earlier. He did not remember his father but was determined to find answers to his questions about him, so he visited his paternal grandfather in rural Virginia. Upon arriving, he met obstacles beyond his imagination. Instead of being welcomed as the long lost heir, he was taunted by a young girl, Thanh. Park encountered situations that prompted more questions before finding any answers.

The session began after I asked the students to write a response in their logs to what we had read. We brainstormed ideas by making suggestions for various issues or topics they might think about. Eventually, the idea of meeting an unknown relative for the first time emerged as an issue. As I explained the activity more fully, students appeared anxious to talk about it. In the transcript below, notice the overlapping talk, as Lewis, Li Ping, and RaShea attempt to tell their stories.

Fenice: I mean how would you feel if you had an uncle and you didn't even know that he was your uncle?

Lewis: I do. I got a *lot* of people in my family I don't know.

Fenice: Close relatives?

RaShea: Yep.

Fenice: Close relatives? *(Trying to confirm close as opposed to distant relatives. All students consent with an affirmative umm hmm.)*

RaShea: *(Inaudible but something about "my dad use to . . . ")*

Fenice: Well, okay now [listen . . .

Lewis: [I got people in my family that I just . . . I haven't even ever *seen!*

RaShea: I ain't never seen my daddy.

Lewis: I haven't . . . I have never actually met my grandfather on my mama's side.

Fenice: [See this is something that you can relate to in the text in your own experience. Park has . . .

Li Ping: [See . . . See . . . oh, I'm sorry.
RaShea: *(Laughing.)* She keeps saying see . . . see
Fenice: Go ahead, Li Ping. *(Li Ping whispers to me to go on and finish talking.)* I
was just going to say this is a personal experience that you just told me
about that you have that's similar to Park's. You can talk about that.

Students were seated with their reading logs and were ready to write a
response about an unknown relative. Before they began to write, however,
they seemed excited and anxious to talk. Lewis said that he had relatives he
had never seen before, emphasizing the word *lot*. When I asked them a
second time, stressing "close relatives," all students consented with an affirmative "umm hmm," suggesting that they have close relatives whom they had
never met. To acknowledge just how close an unknown relative might be,
RaShea stated with certainty that she had never seen her father. Lewis followed RaShea, specifically stating that he had never met his maternal grandfather. To let each student know their stories were important, I publicly acknowledged that, since what they had just said was personal and relevant to
the book, they could share with one another. Unfortunately, I spoke before
Li Ping was able to comment on her experience of talking to an unknown
relative over the telephone. Li Ping tried twice to gain access to the discussion
by speaking as I talked. RaShea acknowledged Li Ping by laughing and restated what Li Ping said. Li Ping remained anxious to share her story as I
continued to suggest how significant and relevant their stories were to the
chapters we would read from *Park's Quest*.

My domination of the conversation is important to note when considering students' discussions of texts. This book prompted Li Ping to make a
personal connection between text events and her life, one of my goals for the
preparation seminar. At the same time, my efforts to help students make
these links prevailed over Li Ping's attempts to share, thus potentially silencing her. Like many teachers whose goals include increased student responsibility for engaging in literate discussions, I temporarily derailed this in favor
of my own curriculum. This example demonstrates how important it is to let
students share their developing responses before intervening.

Students wrote brief sentences in their reading logs about relatives they
had never met. As they wrote their responses, they talked informally among
themselves, raising a geography topic. Lewis mentioned his cousins, whom
he had never met and who lived in a city 50 miles away from his home.
RaShea mentioned that she had relatives in states all across the country,
mistakenly stating, "I got relatives in all 46 states . . . 46, yeah." She hesitated
for a moment, appearing uncertain about the number of states in this country. Her statement turned the discussion into a debate among the students—
going back and forth about whether there were 46, 50, or 52 states. Students

eventually turned to me to settle the issue. Despite my response that there are 50 states, Romel remained uncertain, again stating that there are 52. They finished writing in the reading logs:

> *Romel*: I think that she going to talk to his other side of his dad's family. She going to be mad.
>
> *Li Ping*: when he first met his uncle, it made me remember when I first come to America I got a phone call from california, that was my uncle, I never heard of before, not even from my father, it confusion me, at first I though he was a stranger peson, who tryint to get me. it really scare.
>
> *RaShea*: I think Parks mother is going to tell him about his father and what he was like when he was alive and telling him how he passed away. I don't know my real dad I don't know if he's alive or dead.
>
> *Lewis*: i want to write about how park didn't know many of his fathers family just like in my family i have uncles and aunts that i don't know. and also he never met his grandfather the same as i have never met my grandfather on eather side of my family.

The discussion resumed as Li Ping anxiously asked to share her story first.

Li Ping: Can I say it first because I gotta leave in five minutes. Okay. Oh, I'm writing about his first meet his uncle.
Fenice: Um hm . . .
RaShea: Why you turning red?
Li Ping: Huh?
RaShea: Oh *(laughing)*, that's okay.
Li Ping: Oh, when I first came to America, and then I got a phone call from California, and he said um, his name was Tom, I think, and he said that he's my uncle, and I like *what!* It was my uncle? I never heard . . . I never heard before, even from my father. Never say anything. And I felt like *what?* I . . . at first I thought he was a stranger and trying to do something . . . to do bad thing about me or something, I was like huh? Uncle? And then he say, yeah. Never heard? I say no. And he said . . . and then I write a letter back to my father and ask if it's that true, and he say um hm. And . . . that's it. Scary.
Fenice: Is this uncle your mother's brother, or father's brother?
Li Ping: My father's brother.
Fenice: Your father's brother?
Li Ping: Umm hmm.
Fenice: And your father never told you about him?
Li Ping: Umm hmm. No one. But I don't know how he get my phone num-

ber. I think that my father give it to him or something. And he called up to me and ask if . . . ask if, um, is that okay to live over here, or I want to move over there? But no.

As Li Ping proceeded to tell her story, her tone and expression suggested she was surprised to receive a telephone call from an uncle who lived in the western United States. Attempting to open the discussion further, I asked Li Ping whether the uncle was her mother's or father's brother. She answered but never moved her story beyond the surprise of learning about her uncle from a telephone call. She implied that she was not quick to trust the person to whom she spoke. She told the group members that she wrote a letter to her father in Vietnam to confirm what the uncle said to her. She also conveyed to the group that her uncle wanted to know whether she would prefer living with him or continue to live with her adopted family.

Li Ping left the classroom for her appointment. The other students continued sharing stories during this intense discussion. The next segment of transcript is a continuation of the discussion that occurred after morning announcements. I resumed the discussion by asking Lewis to share his response. Notice how RaShea ignored my call for Lewis to share and proceeded to share her story.

Fenice: Let's get back, Lewis.
RaShea: I wanna go. I don't have um, I don't know my real dad, and I don't know . . . I don't know if he's alive or dead.
Fenice: You don't know your real dad?
Lewis: Just like Park don't know . . . doesn't know.
Romel: Yeah, she ain't the only one so . . .
Lewis: I know who my father is.
Romel: I know where he is . . . [lives but I don't know . . .
RaShea: *[I don't know that! I don't know nothin'!*
Romel: I don't really . . .
Fenice: Have you ever asked your mom?
RaShea: Huh? Yep.
Romel: [We suppose to see him this um . . .
Fenice: [Romel hold on a minute.
RaShea: She ain't gon' tell me. She told me already.
Fenice: Do you know why?
RaShea: No.

As I encouraged students to share their stories related to the text, they were all eager to talk. The vicarious experiences offered by literature can have a particularly significant effect when they are related to problems and conflicts intimately involving the reader (Rosenblatt, 1983). The students connected their stories and situations with Park's life. The links they made let them know as readers that their conditions are not unique. In the above transcript, RaShea anxiously stated that she does not know her biological father. When I restated what RaShea had said, Lewis compared RaShea's story to Park's, the character in the story, supporting her as she shared her experience.

After listening to RaShea, Romel entered the discussion, getting his personal story on the table, his voice filled with anger and emotion. It is interesting to note Romel's connection to and support of RaShea as he made his own story public, implying that he did not know his father as well. In the excerpt below, notice how he vented his frustrations about not being able to see his father.

Romel: *Stupid.* I don't either. If I *ever* meet my dad, that's too bad. I feel for him. *Stupid.*
Fenice: What do you mean that's too bad what you feel for him?
Romel: 'Cause /// you know, he coulda came to see [me, you know at least. I don't care if he did . . .
Lewis: [Made sure that he was alive.
Romel: Yeah, he alive, I know where he is. But um . . .
Lewis: I'm talking 'bout he coulda made sure that you were alive.
Romel: My grandmother came to see me but he can't see. Wait 'til I see him. He ain't be all these ten questions, it's just gon' be . . . straight-up questions. Then after that, I could leave. When I see him . . .

Romel began by yelling loudly and angrily "Stupid. . . . If I *ever* meet by dad, that's too bad." His comment refocused my attention, so I asked Romel what he meant, seeming to calm him enough to express his feelings, "he coulda came to see me."

This discussion illustrates the importance of providing low-achieving adolescents opportunities to participate in meaningful and purposeful conversations about books. Li Ping, RaShea, Romel, and Lewis participated in this conversation in ways that exceeded their engagement in traditional "remedial" reading instruction. They were emotionally involved in their responses (i.e., raised voices, overlapping speech), all desperately making asserted efforts to tell their stories. This discussion demonstrates that students made *real* connections to the book, linking their lives with Park, the main character.

All students, whether enrolled in gifted-and-talented or "remedial" reading programs, bring background information to literature. The opportunity to read literature and engage in meaningful and purposeful discussions should be experienced by all. Rosenblatt (1983) suggests that the reading of a particular work at a particular moment by a particular reader will be a highly complex process. The complexity of the interactions will affect the nature of the situation represented by the text as well as the reader. Li Ping's, Romel's, Lewis's, and RaShea's past experiences and present preoccupations resulted in spontaneous responses to *Park's Quest*. The exchange provided insight into the potential that low-achieving adolescents might bring when they are presented with opportunities to react to text.

CONCLUDING COMMENTS

The major purpose of the Cross-Aged Literacy Program was to study and understand what potential an alternative literacy context might have for the education of low-achieving adolescents, students who are often excluded from high-track or advanced placement courses in high school. The theoretical underpinnings of the Cross-Aged Literacy Program acknowledge the social nature of literacy learning and the constructed meanings participants build from interacting with one another and with texts in a social setting. In this chapter, I focused on my work with four high school adolescents, exploring how they actively participated in their own literacy learning in an alternative context. In my concluding comments, I address the implications for assisting educators in thinking about issues involved in the development of alternative instructional programs for adolescents who are frustrated with literacy learning.

This program gave low-achieving adolescents an opportunity to venture into reading, writing, and small discussion groups in a context that was different from their traditional literacy instruction. The program, curriculum, and materials were designed such that the participants engaged in meaningful and purposeful literacy experiences. Second, the students who participated in this project were placed into situations where they assumed responsibility for their contributions to the program as well as their own learning (e.g., read orally in class, answer open-ended questions, share ideas with others). Consequently, as students contributed in discussions and in sharing other ideas, they reinforced their peers' learning as well. Third, the Cross-Aged Literacy Program provides a context in which to raise issues for exploring the benefits of designing and implementing alternative literacy programs for adolescents who do not read.

Much of the criticism regarding literacy instruction for students who read and write poorly has been addressed by adopting a deficit model of reading and writing instruction. I chose to study an alternative literacy program with high school adolescents, presenting an alternative to the deficit perspective by looking at students' strengths as opposed to their weaknesses.

Students who find learning to read and write difficult bring varied, yet rich backgrounds to classroom communities. As educators, we must learn to help students connect their background experiences to literacy learning. When teachers and students create alternative literacy programs together, alternative ways of literacy learning evolve to become alternative ways of knowing what it means to read and write. Such possibilities provide a wealth of information for educators to further advance the literacy field and reach our students who are failing in the current educational system.

COMMENTARY

DONNA E. ALVERMANN

In Fenice's interpretation of a section of the transcript from the preparation seminar that involved students in reading and responding to *Mississippi Bridge*, she raised an issue I would like to explore a bit more broadly. The issue – that of looking at readers as being *discursively located* – is illustrated in Romel's and Li Ping's different perspectives on Josias's actions in response to the white men's attempts to intimidate him. By *discursively located readers*, I mean readers, like Romel and Li Ping, who interpret texts on the basis of the meanings available to them in a given place and time. That these available meanings are influenced greatly by one's values, beliefs, race, class, and gender (as well as any number of other historically situated sociocultural practices) is at the crux of my commentary. Specifically, I want to suggest that as literacy teachers we need to help students become resistant readers by teaching them to examine the sources of their available meanings.

To read resistantly is to read with a critical eye toward assumptions or "norms" that are often so firmly ingrained in each of us that they have become all but invisible and thus taken for granted. Reading resistantly involves, among other things, asking questions in alternative ways and maintaining a skeptical outlook on the messages authors convey, as well as the interpretations others draw from those messages.

In making the concept of resistant reading a bit more concrete, it is helpful to consider for a moment some alternative questions that might be posed if Romel and Li Ping's group were to meet again to discuss *Mississippi Bridge*. Romel might be encouraged to explore issues of race that discursively locate him as a reader. In addition to his question about "why the white man got mad at Josias," Romel might be prompted to ask questions dealing with the different views that can be produced by specific readings of the text. For instance, what does his small seminar group know about black men and their search for jobs in the present? Is this present-day situation any different from that described in the story, which is set in the Great Depression? Questions such as these help students to direct their attention toward how the availability of different meanings for a text will influence how they interpret the text.

Because I believe that individual readers are rarely the source or origin of their own meanings, it makes sense to me to view Romel, Li Ping, and others in their seminar group as discursively located readers. Viewing them in this way has several instructional implications. For instance, if I were to enter into a discussion with them as their teacher, I would encourage questions that explore how characters in a novel are constructed through particular information that is available to some members of their seminar group but not to others. I would also invite the group to consider how texts and readers are positioned through their membership in various discourse communities, with all their attendant discursive practices. Finally, I would call attention to some of those practices in order to help Romel, Li Ping, and others become resistant readers—readers who recognize that understanding does not necessarily entail accepting.

CHAPTER 9

Assessment Research in the Book Club Program

TANJA L. BISESI and TAFFY E. RAPHAEL

From the beginning of the Book Club project, members of the team raised concerns about assessing student progress. Some concerns related to evaluating the research project, while others related to detailing students' progress for parents, teachers, and the students' themselves. Increasingly, we became interested in how current research in assessment might help us develop measures aligned with the Book Club goals.

With Tanja's background and interest in assessment and Taffy's concern with continued development of the Book Club program, we began collaborating on the assessment strand. The original Book Club research team had documented student participation in Book Club, but they were concerned that the measures did not directly address students' literacy learning progress. Tanja was interested in assessment methodology and development. As a school-based speech–language pathologist, she had experience with both standardized, diagnostic tests and formative, instructionally oriented evaluation. This experience raised her concern about the value of available assessment formats and sparked her interest in alternative assessments. Taffy was interested in creating a system for demonstrating students' progress that would be consistent with the sociocultural perspective underlying Book Club. Over the three-year collaboration, we read about issues in aligning assessment practices with instruction, worked with Julie Folkert and Sara Bean (see Chapter 15) to pilot alternative assessment tools and procedures, and are involved currently in comparing assessment practices (e.g., portfolios, performance-based assessments, standardized tests) and their potential for informing students, teachers, parents, and administrators about students' progress in literacy learning.

In this chapter, we first discuss concerns with using only commercially available standardized tests to assess students' growth and achievement in the Book Club. Second, we describe the theoretical grounding and conceptual framework for our work, including the questions our assessment research addressed. Third, we describe the research that makes up the Book Club assessment strand.

STANDARD APPROACHES TO ASSESSMENT

How the educational community instructs and assesses students relates to its views of what it means to be educated. Within the last 50 years there has been a shift in the beliefs about what it means to be literate and about learning and instruction (Langer, 1991). These changes in basic assumptions about knowledge, learning, teaching, and literacy are represented in the Book Club curriculum. At the same time, while beliefs about literacy learning and instruction have changed, the principles and methods that shape assessment have remained relatively unchanged, resulting in *instruction–assessment malalignment*. This malalignment has contributed to many criticisms of standardized tests (e.g., Paris, Lawton, Turner, & Roth, 1991; Shepard, 1989) and to an emerging awareness of the need for more appropriate, alternative approaches for thinking about, examining, and evaluating students' learning (e.g., Au, Scheu, Kawakami, & Hermann, 1990; Paris et al., 1992; Valencia, 1990).

Traditional tests grew out of a need to assess mastery of discrete, isolated rules and skills in an efficient and cost-effective way (Langer, 1991; Shepard, 1989). They assessed convergent knowledge and relied on a set of standard procedures for administration and scoring, making them easy to give and tally. Despite standardized tests' inadequacies for assessing learning outcomes of programs like Book Club, they still are widely adopted as the primary assessment tool in education today.

Predictably, these tests contribute to students' emphasis on performance over learning and teachers' providing instruction on tested skills, rather than teaching in ways more consistent with their beliefs about literacy (Paris et al., 1992; Shepard, 1989). From the earliest days of the Book Club research project, we felt that neither the traditional tests (e.g., state-mandated Michigan Educational Assessment Program reading test [MEAP] or district-mandated reading tests) nor the categories on the district report card that Laura

Pardo and Deb Woodman were expected to use in 1990–91 provided the vehicles we needed to demonstrate students' growth in the range of areas that constituted the Book Club curriculum.

Standardized tests are limited for four reasons. First, they tap isolated, low-level skills, a problem particularly for instructional programs that seek to promote more complex literacy performances (Haladyna, Nolan, & Haas, 1991; Shepard, 1989). From the constructivist, holistic perspective of Book Club, literacy learning is a multidimensional, sense-making process including the interrelated development of the language arts. Available standardized tests neither examine nor promote aspects of such a view of reading. Second, these tests examine skills in decontextualized contexts rather than during authentic tasks and activities. While the Book Club teachers acknowledged the need for students to possess various literacy skills, they stressed the importance of learning and practicing these skills in the context of purposeful, text-based, sense-making activities (i.e., reading, writing, and talking about text).

Third, available tests ignore social aspects of literacy learning, being administered on an individual basis and independently completed by students. In contrast, Book Club teachers stressed diversity in sense-making and the role of interactive dialogue with other readers in the interpretation of text. Rather than portraying themselves as the sole authority on text interpretation, Book Club teachers acted as guides for students in the social processes of responding, discussing and negotiating meanings, and internalizing necessary tools for exploring multiple text understandings (Eeds & Wells, 1989). Fourth, many students are not motivated either to learn the skills tested or to perform well on decontextualized tests. Consistent with other research (e.g., Paris et al., 1991), the behavior we observed during standardized testing starkly contrasted with the highly motivated behaviors we noticed during Book Club instruction.

In summary, we coined the term *malalignment* to describe the situation we faced. Available standardized tests and traditional report cards align poorly with the goals of the Book Club curriculum. Scholars such as Tierney, Carter, and Desai (1991), Johnston (1989), and Paris and colleagues (1991) attribute this to a shift in the bases for our current curriculum from behavioral and information-processing perspectives on learning to sociocultural perspectives (see Chapter 1 for more extensive discussion of the theory guiding the Book Club program). Over the course of the Book Club project, we considered various solutions for demonstrating students' progress in meaningful ways, ranging from creating alternative report cards (i.e., changing the way in which students' progress was *reported*) to creating alternate forms of assessment (i.e., changing the ways in which teachers *gathered evidence* of student growth, such as portfolios or performance-based tests). In the next section, we describe the theoretical perspective that guided us in our efforts.

THEORETICAL PERSPECTIVE AND
CONCEPTUAL FRAMEWORK

Our desire to eliminate the problem of malalignment drove the creation of an alternative assessment system contextually sensitive to the Book Club program. As described in Section I of this book, Book Club is an integrated approach to literacy instruction centered around the small, student-led discussion groups from which the program takes its name. The assessment strand, like the program in general, is based in three theoretical perspectives: (1) a sociocultural perspective on learning, (2) reader-response literary theory, emphasizing personal response and literary analysis, and (3) the importance of curricular integration, emphasizing the interrelated development of language and literacy (i.e., reading, writing, listening, and speaking). While each of these perspectives is detailed in Section I, we consider each in terms of its relationship specifically to issues of assessment.

Sociocultural Perspective on Learning

We wanted the assessment to reflect the social constructivist principles (e.g., Gavelek, 1986; Vygotsky, 1978; Wertsch, 1985) in which the curriculum was grounded. From this learning and instructional perspective, knowledge is socially constructed in the context of collaborative, purposeful activities. Assessment tasks and materials must maintain their holistic nature while providing students multiple opportunities to demonstrate, internalize, and transform their knowledge and understandings. Book Club instantiates these principles through activities such as having students read complete novels and having them interact in a public–social domain during community share and book clubs. Given these principles and activities, we came to the conclusion that any assessment system that hopes to tap learning valued by and resulting from Book Club instruction needs to examine students' performance as they read, reflect upon, and talk about texts individually, in small groups, and in whole-class discussions.

Reader-Response Literary Theory

We wanted the assessment to reflect the program's reader-response orientation. This orientation emphasizes the transactional nature of reading (e.g., Langer, 1990a; Rosenblatt, 1991a), where readers play a central role in the process of constructing meaning, responding both aesthetically and efferently as their interpretations unfold. Book Club instantiates these principles through instruction in both text-oriented (e.g., prediction, summary) and reader-oriented (e.g., evaluation, self-in-situation) responses, while emphasizing the evolutionary, multidimensional, and intertextual nature of interpretation. We felt that assessment grounded in these principles should capture these aspects of readers' response to literature.

Curricular Integration

We wanted the assessment system to reflect our belief in the interrelated development of language and literacy. Because we believe that knowledge is acquired through social interaction and that the primary means of such interaction is through language, language is assumed to play a central role in learning (Vygotsky, 1978; Wertsch, 1985). In this way, language–both oral and written–becomes a tool for thought and mediates all learning. Not only does language mediate learning, but oral language and written language are interactive processes that support the development of one another as they each contribute to new forms of thought and learning (G. Wells & Chang-Wells, 1992). These principles are instantiated in the Book Club program through student response in multiple modes: Students read extended texts, speak and listen in large- and small-group discussions, and write in response logs. Thus assessment that aligns with these principles must tap students' use of all the language processes and the ways in which they support one another through reading, writing, and discussions.

These theoretical perspectives ground the performance-based assessment components: (1) students' public and social engagement during book clubs and community share, (2) individual reading as well as personal and literary response, and (3) written logs and oral discussions as support for reading. With these theoretical perspectives shaping the contexts and tasks defining Book Club instruction and the associated performance-based assessment, we turn to the conceptual framework and goals of Book Club that were the focus of our instruction and assessment.

Conceptual Framework

Consistent with our concern for aligning instruction and assessment, the conceptual framework guiding the assessment system was based on the instructional curriculum detailed in Figure 2.3. Thus the instruction–assessment components included: (1) language conventions, (2) comprehension strategies, (3) literary elements, and (4) response to literature.

Language conventions include knowledge of how our written and oral language systems work, from sound–symbol correspondence to conventions for interacting with others in response to text. Thus the assessment system required opportunities to examine students' progress from reading fluency to their ability to engage in sustained talk about text with peers across a range of settings, from whole-class to small-group discussions. Comprehension strategies include readers' ability to use their background knowledge and experiences to make sense of text, to process the text in meaningful and strategic ways, and to monitor their progress. Thus the assessment system required opportunities to examine students' ability to use strategies and monitor their sense-making while reading.

Literary elements focus on aspects of reading such as knowledge of theme, point of view, genres, and authors' craft. Thus our assessment system needed to provide vehicles for making students' knowledge in these areas visible through their writing and discussions of text. Finally, response to literature includes personal, creative, and critical response. Thus we expected our assessment system to provide windows into students' engagement with the texts they read, their ability to engage in a range of responses, and their ability to explain the sources of their response.

In short, the assessment research focused on creating a system to evaluate students' growth in those areas that constituted the Book Club curriculum. Identifying specific areas of students' progress and making those gains visible to parents, teachers, administrators, and the students themselves became the goal of the assessment research strand.

THE ASSESSMENT RESEARCH STRAND

Between 1990 and 1994, the Book Club project assessment strand consisted of three phases: (1) developing, adapting, and testing assessment tools to explore students' literary understanding, (2) developing, adapting, and testing ways of sharing information about students' progress with parents and administration, and (3) developing an assessment system parallel to the day-to-day Book Club program components. We briefly discuss the first two phases as background to a more detailed description of the performance-based assessment.

Assessing and Reporting Students' Processes of Literary Understanding

Initial research questions about the potential of Book Club participation to enhance students' response to literature led to examining two assessment tools: (1) a think-aloud process adapted from Langer (1990a) and (2) a parallel written version administered in whole-group settings. In both instruments, students were asked to read text segments from an informational article and a short story and respond as they read. For the oral think-aloud, students read and thought aloud to one of the researchers, who tape-recorded the session and occasionally prompted students to share their thoughts. For the written version, we divided the texts into sections, breaking at "natural" points (e.g., a point of suspense, a shift in topic) and asked students to write in a booklet what they were thinking, what they thought the text was about, and/or what they thought might happen next.

While both methods provided a window into students' processes of constructing meaning and interpreting the text, they also had serious limitations. The individual and somewhat artificial nature of the activity were at odds with the goals of the Book Club program (Bisesi, 1993). The students responded relatively independently (i.e., with one adult, sitting alone at a desk), which ignored the social nature of reading in preparation for and while participating in book clubs. Thus, while both tools had potential for demonstrating growth in response to literature and literary interpretation, they had serious limitations.

Sharing Students' Progress

While seeking appropriate assessment *tools* to demonstrate students' growth in Book Club literacy abilities, we developed and tested an alternative *means for sharing information* about students' progress with parents and administrators. Other researchers (e.g., Afflerbach & Johnston, 1993) have suggested that engaging in such development helps make visible the instructional content of focus and value in a literacy program. We developed a report card with the Book Club project team, including teachers and researchers (see Figure 9.1), that reflected the value we placed on strategies, comprehension, and expressive abilities while providing space for comments on other important aspects of students' literacy development, including response to literature, attitudes and dispositions, and general participation in literacy events. Teachers attached this report to the district report card each grading period, keeping a copy in the student's file. Parents expressed satisfaction at the range of information it provided, and teachers found it easy to use and adequate for their demands. In the third year, the Lansing school system changed its report card to one more compatible with Book Club goals and the attachment was no longer needed.

From the three-year pilot work with the think-aloud, written response task and the report cards, we had a clearer picture of what was lacking in the currently used and available tools. First, we needed a classroom assessment system that could document students' activities throughout the academic year and provide illustrations of a range of written and oral participation in components of Book Club. Second, we needed a tool teachers could use to illustrate growth on specific Book Club goals. Finally, we needed vehicles for sharing students' progress with other students, parents, and administrators.

FIGURE 9.1.   Report Card

Reading Abilities Checklist	Students' Name _____
	Teacher's Signature

Strategies	1	2	3	4
Predicting				
Sequencing				
Organizing				
Representation				
Identifying important ideas				
Refining/revising				
Drawing conclusions				

Comments: First Grading Period

Comments: Second Grading Period

Comments: Third Grading Period

Comprehension	1	2	3	4
Recognizes story themes				
Recognizes purpose				
Synthesizes information across text(s)				

Comments: Fourth Grading Period

Expressive Abilities: Oral	1	2	3	4
Evaluates text using specific ideas				
Ideas are expressed clearly				

Expressive Abilities: Written	1	2	3	4
Evaluates text using specific ideas				
Ideas are expressed clearly				

Key:
+ Excellent
✓ Satisfactory
– Needs Improvement

Reproduced with permission from the Book Club Project, Taffy E. Raphael and Susan I. McMahon, codirectors

These needs led to two strands of work: the portfolio project (see Chapter 15) and the performance-based assessment project described in the next section.

Creating a Performance-Based Assessment

The performance-based assessment project was designed to create a compromise between formal standardized tests such as the MEAP and the more informal, though contextualized, assessments derived from students' year-long portfolios. We turned to the literature on performance-based assessment for a potential alternative, since such assessments share features of both standardized tests (e.g., standards against which students' progress can be measured) and ongoing classroom-based assessments that are part of instruction (e.g., the data is gathered as part of a holistic instructional unit). We found that descriptions of performance-based assessments varied widely.

Most experts agreed that performance-based assessments should focus on student performance of tasks and activities that are of direct interest and "valued in their own right" (Linn, Baker, & Dunbar, 1991, p. 15), such as reading a novel, then talking or writing about it. Some (e.g., Wiggins, 1989) defined performance-based assessments as *authentic* assessments. Others (e.g., Farr, 1992; Feuer & Fulton, 1993) used the term *performance-based assessment* as an umbrella term to include specific assessment tools as well as portfolios. Still others (e.g., Abruscato, 1993; Stiggins, 1987) suggested that performance-based assessments consist of a standard set of activities that create the same measures of students' literacy progress across contexts. For example, students are assessed on their performance on a one-week unit, which parallels typical classroom instruction, in which all students read, write, and talk about the same books. This last definition generally describes performance-based assessments for large-scale purposes, yet we felt it was consistent with our smaller-scale assessment objectives.

Thus, we use the term *performance-based assessment* to describe students' activities and products (e.g., reading log samples, discussions, oral reading) from three standard, two-day Book Club "events." Students used an informational article for the first event, the second drew from the middle two chapters of the novel students read as part of their Book Club program, and the third used a short story. All texts related to the unit theme in the classroom. We designed the assessment to address student participation in the four literacy activities that made up the core of Book Club: reading, writing, book club, and community share. Each day, all participating students read the selection, created a written reading log entry, engaged in a book club discussion, and participated in a whole-class community share, thus standardizing the *activities* from which we analyzed specific strategy use and abilities.

We now describe the development and evaluation of this performance-based assessment. We worked closely with Sara Bean and Julie Folkert to examine students' learning outcomes within each of the four Book Club components in terms of language conventions, comprehension, literary elements, and response to literature as detailed in Figure 2.3. In developing the assessment, we considered the purposes of the assessment, texts used, and tasks to include.

Purposes. The performance-based system served dual goals of providing students, teachers, parents, and administrators with information about students' progress and providing insights into the effectiveness of the Book Club curriculum and relationship among performances across components. The research explored the feasibility of such a system in terms of both its administration and the value of its findings for use with the Book Club program. After establishing the purposes of the performance-based assessment, we developed the texts, tasks, and procedures.

Texts. The selection of three different forms of texts (i.e., informational text, short story, chapter book) parallelled the texts students read during Book Club and the kinds of reading performances in which students were expected to succeed, according to district and state guidelines. Within Book Club, several teachers had integrated their language arts and social studies instruction (see Chapters 11 and 14). Thus the informational selection represented the content-area reading that was part of their program. Trade books, usually in the form of novels, formed the primary texts used during Book Club. Students read novels such as Speare's (1983) *The Sign of the Beaver* and Reiss's (1972) *The Upstairs Room*. Selecting chapters from the middle of the students' novels provided a context in which they had developed some background knowledge, had worked together in their book clubs for at least a week, and were moving through and reflecting upon events in the novel. Finally, the short stories were illustrative of some of the picture books used in units. For example, *Hiroshima No Pika* (Maruki, 1980) was a picture book illustrating a relatively short story relating events on the day of the Hiroshima bombing.

In addition to their instructional validity, these three text types provided interesting comparisons from a research perspective. For example, we wondered whether events from the two narrative texts (i.e., the short story, the chapters) were both necessary or whether similar information would be gained from both. If the latter, then the performance-based assessment could be used with either the short story *or* the chapters. We also wondered whether students would respond differently to the informational and narrative texts. On the MEAP, students' difficulties with informational texts, but not with narratives, concerned the teachers.

In short, the purposes for the performance-based assessment were to create a system that would reveal students' abilities to read, respond to, and discuss both fiction and nonfiction selections. The research would provide information for teachers about students' progress, the Book Club program, and the performance-based assessment format. We constructed the tasks that comprised the assessment to achieve these purposes.

Tasks. Like other performance-based assessments (e.g., National Assessment of Educational Progress), we structured our assessment around an integrated instructional unit and with the four Book Club components in mind. Within the context of each two-day event, students participated in six basic Book Club activities: (1) reading portions of a text, (2) responding in writing to what they had read, (3) participating in a small-group text discussion, (4) sharing their groups' comments with the whole class, (5) evaluating themselves on their group participation, and (6) evaluating their journal writing. These six activities generated several samples (i.e., "artifacts") of their performance. Table 9.1 presents the artifacts collected during the six-day, performance-based assessment cycle.

As Table 9.1 details, audiotapes were available for analyzing students' participation in small- and large-group settings. We analyzed written responses through journal entries, examining students' ability to self-evaluate from their own appraisal of their book clubs and journal entries. Finally, to assess fluency, students read text segments orally.

In our pilot study, we collected writing samples from each student daily, since we felt their ability to express their personal responses to literature was a

TABLE 9.1.   Artifacts Collected Across Genres

Artifacts	Expository	Novel	Short Story
Small-group book club discussions (audiotaped)	1	1	1
Written journal entries	2	2	2
Whole-class community share (audiotaped)	2	2	2
Written small-group discussion self-evaluations	1	1	1
Written journal entry self-evaluation	Students selected one journal entry they thought was "best" of all they had written across the three genres to evaluate		
Oral reading sample (audiotaped)	1	N/A	N/A

critical goal for Book Club and collecting such samples was not difficult. Because of a limited amount of audiotaping equipment, we taped each book club once per two-day cycle, taping half the book clubs on the first, and the other half on the second day for each text (i.e., short story, informational selection, chapters). Students evaluated the taped book clubs, yielding three book club self-evaluations for each student. Students evaluated their six log entries at the end of all three performance-based events, selecting the one of the six that they felt was their best and writing an explanation of its quality. Finally, each student read one paragraph orally from the expository selection to provide fluency information.

PERFORMANCE-BASED ASSESSMENT ADMINISTRATION AND SCORING: AN ILLUSTRATION

To illustrate how the performance-based assessment worked, we turn to Julie's and Sara's classrooms during the spring of 1994, when they first used the system. At the time of the study, Julie taught fifth grade in a suburban school and Sara taught fourth grade in a rural district. Their implementation involved administering the performance-based assessment, then collaborating in the development of ways to evaluate students' performance. Further, since they were also using the portfolio system (described in Chapter 15), they were interested in comparing what they learned about their students' progress from the performance-based assessment relative to the portfolios.

Performance-based assessment administration occurred over three two-day events during a spring unit within which students learned about the impact of World War II on ordinary people. In both Julie's and Sara's classrooms, students read the same informational text and short story. The informational text consisted of three chapters from the Scholastic textbook, *The Day Pearl Harbor Was Bombed: A Photo History of World War II* (Sullivan, 1991). The short story was the picture book *Sadako* (Coerr, 1993), one that students read easily over the two days. Sara and Julie differed in their choice of novels. Sara's students read Lowry's (1989) *Number the Stars*. Julie's students selected one of three novels: *The Devil's Arithmetic* (Yolen, 1988), *The Upstairs Room*, or *Number the Stars*.

Students began the Book Club unit by reading from their novel, writing log entries, and engaging in discussion in book club and community share. After students had read approximately half their novel, the performance-based assessment began. Student interviews revealed that students did not perceive any difference between the performance-based assessment activities and Book Club. Students engaged in the first two-day event, reading the informational text that described some of the events in Europe during World

War II. The background and interest they had developed from their novels provided a basis for reading the nonfiction text. The next two-day event focused on their novels, while the last two-day event drew upon Coerr's book about Sadako, inviting connections between the experiences of ordinary citizens in Europe and those in Japan during and immediately following the war.

Because Sara and Julie were interested in the students' written response to these texts under different conditions, for each two-day event they varied the reading log entry. On one day, students chose how to respond. On the other day, they gave students a prompt to respond to before they could write their "free" response. Prompts included: "What trends or ideas do you notice that all three Axis powers display?" "What is Sadako trying to ignore and how is she reacting to it?" "Out of all the things that were happening to Hannah and the other Jews, what impacted the most and how did you feel as a reader?" Thus, over the course of six days, Julie and Sara gathered much information about students' oral reading, their small- and large-group discussions, and their written response to literature.

Developing scoring criteria was the next critical step. Working closely with Julie and Sara, we began by considering the goals of the performance-based assessment, emphasizing students' oral and written response to the texts they read. Our scoring efforts concentrated on the students' reading log entries and their book club discussions. We used community share discussions and students' self-evaluations as further information to support or raise questions about conclusions we had drawn from the information about their written and oral response. In this section, we focus on how we developed our "scoring rubric" for the written logs.

The rubric consisted of three levels of performance. For each level, we developed criteria, drawn from the framework outlined in Figure 2.3, to distinguish among students' work. For example, students earning the highest level for a written response, a 3, focused on major themes, drew evidence from the text to support their position, explored different responses invited by the text and linked them together in relevant ways, had an apparent purpose for their writing, had a focused and coherent response, and had a date on the entry. While a 3 response may not have addressed each criteria equally, together they provide an image of what a level-3 response would have.

In contrast, students earning level 1 had superficial entries with little reference to the text, no clear purpose, a string of trivial details, and a lack of coherence. Thus, our *rubric* has *performance levels* with *explicit criteria* that lead to a *score*. Table 9.2 summarizes the performance criteria for both journal entry and book club discussion rubrics.

We have two comments about the scoring rubric detailed in Table 9.2.

TABLE 9.2. Performance Criteria: Journal Entry and Book Club Discussion

Scores	Journal Entries	Book Club Discussions
3	• Focuses on major themes, issues, questions, or characters • Effectively uses evidence from text and/or personal experience to support ideas • Produces multiple, related, and well-developed responses • Writes for a clear purpose • Generates a well-focused, connected, and coherent response • Dates entry	• Focuses on major themes, issues, questions, or characters • Effectively uses evidence from text, content area, and/or personal experience to support ideas • Appropriately introduces new ideas • Builds/expands on others' ideas • Respects others' ideas • Talks for a clear purpose • Appropriately supports less active members of the group
2	• Focuses on secondary themes, issues, questions, or characters, or lacks detailed discussion of major themes • Uses little evidence from text and/or personal experience to support ideas, or use of evidence is less than effective • Demonstrates some sense of purpose for writing • Generates a somewhat focused, connected, and coherent response	• Focuses on secondary themes, issues, questions, or characters, or lacks detailed discussion of major themes • Uses little evidence from text and/or personal experience to support ideas, or use of eidence is less than effective • Demonstrates some sense of purpose for speaking • Build some on others ideas but may resort to round-robin turn-taking • Demonstrates some respect for others' ideas • Less than effective at introducing new ideas
1	• Superficial response with minimal reference to the text or personal experiences • A string of trivial textual details • Demonstrates no clear purposes for writing • Generates an unfocused, unconnected, and incoherent response • Does not date entry	• Superficial response with minimal reference to the text or personal experiences • Talks about trivial textual details or irrelevant personal experiences • Perservates on ideas—does not build on them • Does not introduce new ideas • Demonstrates no clear purpose for speaking • Speaks very infrequently • Raises hand before speaking and/or resorts to round-robin turn-taking

First, we used a 3-point, rather than 5-point, scale since the latter may be too easily associated with typical grading patterns (e.g., A, B, C, D, F). Second, we used a holistic rating scale that covered several dimensions or criteria since others (e.g., Freedman, 1979, 1993) have found that holistic scores are able to reflect how well writers develop and organize ideas while taking into account the whole piece. We use examples of students' reading log entries (i.e., journals) to illustrate the three levels of response to each of the three types of text (see Table 9.3).

Jamie's responses, listed in Table 9.3, earned the highest level of 3. Her first entry was written in response to the novel, *The Devil's Arithmetic*. Hannah, the main character of the novel, describes the workers in the concentration camp as monsters. In this entry, Jamie clearly and coherently takes issue with Hannah's beliefs. She starts by clearly stating her premise, "I don't think they are all monsters as Hannah said." She also draws on details from the text: "forced to be there, . . . forced by the Nazi monsters to work. . . . They do not choose to be cremated." Incidents from the novel are chosen to vividly and dramatically support her point. Further, the entry reflects several important curricular dimensions. Her entry suggests a degree of critical literacy in her use of evidence from the text to make her argument more persuasive, her personal response as she shares her feelings, her comprehension through her analysis of characters' beliefs, her summary of text information, and her apparent understanding of point of view.

Jamie's response to the short story, *Sadako*, reveals similar features. Her empathy with Sadako, as she sat in bed making paper cranes and hoping she would be well again, is very clear. The entire entry centers around the student's feelings (e.g., "I would be really scared. . . . I wish she could . . . get well") and the source of those feelings (e.g., Americans dropped the A-bomb). She also apparently understands the intersection between the myth of making 1,000 cranes to become well and the reality that the goal might simply raise Sadako's spirits and give her something to do while in the hospital. Like her novel entry in response to the chapters from the novel, Jamie's response reflects multiple curricular dimensions, including evidence of strategies for comprehension (i.e., question asking, summarizing), literary elements (i.e., understanding theme), personal response (i.e., sharing feelings), and critical literacy (i.e., support ideas with text evidence).

Jamie's entry in response to the expository text about Hitler's troop movement in Europe during the early years of World War II again reflects qualities detailed above. In this entry, Jamie makes her focus and her feelings clear within her first two sentences. Throughout the remainder of the response, she focuses on supporting her initial position by drawing on how other countries have reacted. Just as she feels "Hitler is such a Pig!" she relates to how Canada and the United States would feel if Hitler attacked. She seems

TABLE 9.5.   Scoring Guidelines: Journal Entries

3	2	1
Narrative: Novel		
I don't think they are all monsters as Hannah said. They are forced to be there and they have no control over what happens there. They are forced by the Nazi monsters to work. They do not practically starve each other to death, the monsters do. They do not choose to be cremated. The monsters do that to them. How can Hannah think such a thing? She and the others have done nothing wrong. They are forced to work. Why? The monsters?	I did like these two chapters because they didn't make sence to me. All of a sudden, Ellens parents were there, and I had no Idea were they came from. I think the book is getting boring now because there is nothing exciting happening. In the casket I don't think there will be a person in it, I also think it was rude for that soldier to hit Annmaries mom in the face	
Narrative: Short Story		
If I was Sadako, I would be really scared, and making those paper cranes would probably keep my spirits up. It would give me something to hope for, something to keep trying for. I mean, if she didn't have those cranes, what would she do all day? Sit and rot in her hospital bed? I wish she could have made the thousand cranes so that she could get well again. I wish the Americans had never dropped the A-bomb on Hiroshima, and none of this terrible disease stuff would never had happened.		Sadako had lukima. It's terible
Expository Nonfiction		
Before the End of May, 1940, Hitler's troops took over Czeckoxlovakia, Poland, Denmark, Norway, Belgium, Netherlands, and Luxembourg. Hitler is such a Pig! Even though he's trying to take over the world (and he came close in Europe) there is no way all people on earth would let him take over. Example: He invades Canada. Canada fights. The U.S. Helps Canada fight. U.S. gets Africa to help fight. Hitler stinks!	I used to think World War II was just a couple bombings here and there. I also thought he was just some big past military leader. Now I know he also ruled Germany as he was thier dictator. I was amazed when I found out that Jews were forced to work as slaves! Then I found out eventually, Hitler just started killing all the Jews!	It happened in March 1939, Germany took over the rest of Czeckoslovakia. The tiring six months of calm that followed the german quest of Poland that ended suddenly early in April, 1940. When Hitler's forces struck again, on June 9, 1940, the Norwagien Army surrendered to me germans.

to understand the power of developing her personal point of view (i.e., "there is no way all people on earth would let him take over"), while drawing on text information (e.g., "he's trying to take over the world [and he came close in Europe]"). This entry reveals evidence of success on dimensions of comprehension (i.e., organizes ideas to construct meaning), personal response (i.e., shares feelings), critical literacy (e.g., uses examples to illustrate points), and literary elements (i.e., her use of metaphor, "pig").

In contrast to a level 3, a level-1 journal entry reflected a superficial response without a clear purpose or even a date. These entries rarely offered insight into students' facility with the Book Club framework dimensions. Table 9.3 provides two illustrations, one each for a narrative and an expository selection response. The short story entry was written after Jay had read the first half of *Sadako and the Thousand Paper Cranes* (Coerr, 1977). The brief and superficial entry simply summarizes the story (i.e., "It's terible"). Jay's reasons for providing such a summary are not clear.

As Jenny's response to an informational text illustrates, length was not the primary characteristic of a level-1 response. Written in response to the chapters "Blitzkrieg" and "Retreat to Dunkirk," the longer entry is simply a string of trivial details pulled directly from the texts, without a clear purpose or personal interpretation.

The holistic score of 2 was more variable across entries than those characterizing scores of 1 and 3, due to the rather broad span of responses that were neither at the top of what would be expected nor so lacking as to be at the bottom. These responses tended to include two or more of the features listed in Table 9.2, including a focus on secondary themes, little or ineffective use of text for evidence of positions, and so forth. Further, while some entries revealed that students had gained knowledge about aspects of the Book Club framework, this was not consistent across entries.

Table 9.3 shows level-2 journal entries written in response to a narrative (i.e., novel) and an expository text. Tammy's narrative entry responding to *Number the Stars* has a clear purpose (i.e., to express her opinion of the chapters), but it is unfocused, with little evidence drawn from the text to support her opinions. Rather, it reflects a superficial list of her opinions of the chapter without analysis. While she included text-based information (e.g., "In the casket I don't think there will be a person in it."), her comment does not support a particular point. Ernie's expository entry, written on the second day of the expository text assessment, is his reflection on what he learned. He used the entry to clarify his understandings of the texts and organize his ideas to construct meaning but provided little personal response to or extended analysis of the text-based issues raised. His list of facts has little coherence or expanded explanation.

In summary, the scoring rubrics provided Julie and Sara with a means for evaluating their students' progress on Book Club–related response activities using a standard metric. When we each scored a set of students' responses and compared ratings, we reached over 80% agreement. Further, the process of evaluating students' responses revealed ways in which they had internalized aspects of the literacy curriculum reflected in the Book Club framework detailed in Figure 2.3. This provided teachers with insights into the effectiveness of their instruction for helping students gain strategies and ways of thinking related to reading and responding to texts. It provided a basis for assigning a grade to students for their report cards, as well as a potentially rich source of information for discussing students' progress over the year with parents. Finally, the process of gathering this information and developing a scoring scheme suggested that as an assessment tool, the performance-based assessment "event" was both feasible to implement and possible to evaluate.

However, our findings suggested modifications to the performance-based assessment format. First, since students' performances on the two narrative texts (i.e., the chapters, the short story) did not differ, the assessment now consists of two two-day Book Club events, one using the middle two chapters of students' Book Club novels and one using a thematically related expository nonfiction selection. Second, we eliminated the oral reading measure because it provided no additional information beyond teachers' ongoing evaluations of students' fluency. Third, the 3-point scale did not provide a sufficient band and we found ourselves using 1.5 and 2.5 so frequently that we have moved to a 5-point scale. Fourth, rather than attempting to score students' book club discussions using an individual rubric, we assigned a holistic group score since it was quite difficult for anyone other than the teacher to distinguish among the students' voices.

ONGOING RESEARCH

Our current research study explores the following question: What are the relative strengths of information provided through a performance-based assessment, through a portfolio system (described in Chapter 15), and through standardized testing? Our initial findings suggest that each form of assessment has distinct and complementary strengths and weaknesses for reflecting student growth and achievement (see Table 9.4) (Bisesi, 1996; Raphael, Wallace, & Pardo, 1996).

Performance-Based Assessment

The primary strength of the performance-based assessment is its ability to tap and to provide in-depth information about student performance on particular tasks (e.g., journal writing) that can be compared across time and students. This kind of assessment information could easily be used to monitor

TABLE 9.4.   Relationship Between Performance-Based and Portfolio Assessments

	Performance-Based Assessment	Portfolios
Strengths	• in-depth analysis • clearly defined scoring criteria and summative, quantitative precision • reliable scores • comparable results across students and time	• flexible data collection • ongoing picture of student growth and performance • formative results that are readily available • reduced labor intensiveness
Weaknesses	• reduced flexibility • labor-intensive data preparation • limited generalizability of performance • results not readily available	• little in-depth analysis of performance • few clearly defined, quantitative scoring criteria • no check on scoring reliability • result are not directly comparable across student and time

growth over time and across grade levels, potentially taking the place of other standardized forms of assessment. The performance-based assessment's clearly defined scoring criteria simplified our scoring task, increased our scoring consistency, and offered a well-defined picture of student performance on specific criteria at a given time. The process of developing specific criteria in collaboration with Sara and Julie influenced their future instructional/assessment practices in positive ways (e.g., they began to develop "target" performance criteria with their students in the classroom and focus on these targets during instruction and assessment).

Portfolio Assessment

In contrast, the primary strength of portfolios is their flexibility for addressing multiple tasks, artifacts, criteria, and goals on an ongoing basis. For example, Julie and Sara collected anecdotal notes on student performance and progress to supplement journal entry and discussion data. They also documented student progress on personalized, student-specific goals. In addition, portfolio assessment allowed teachers to construct evolving profiles of individual student growth on broadly defined performance outcomes. For example, Julie and Sara collected student journal entries weekly and surveyed them using a checklist targeting a limited number of assessment criteria. This form of assessment offered general, yet efficient, monitoring of student progress over time, providing teachers with readily available information on which they could base ongoing instructional decisions and helping students reflect on their own learning. Finally, while portfolio assessment is certainly complex, such information can be collected as needed rather than according to a prescribed, systematic procedure (e.g., standardized tasks, reliability checks).

The standardized tests provided information on a very narrow band of knowledge and, without the accompanying information from portfolios and performance-based measures, gave little indication of students' attitudes and dispositions, students' knowledge of response and analysis, students' engagement with literature, or future directions for instruction.

We are finding that classroom-oriented, performance-based and portfolio assessments possess the features listed in Table 9.2, which allow their combined implementation to complement each other. We are continuing to explore the ways in which these two forms of assessment can be used together for a range of assessment purposes (e.g., to direct instruction, for accountability) and to meet the needs of a variety of assessment audiences (e.g., students, teacher, administrators, parents). For example, Julie is using the performance-based assessment, administered during the fall and spring of the school year, as a piece of her students' portfolios. The results will be shared with parents during parent–teacher conferences as evidence of both entering abilities and progress during the year. Parents will also view portfolios for additional examples of student performance, allowing a broader picture of their child's ongoing participation in Book Club. Finally, Julie has adopted the spring performance-based assessment as a tool for her district's mandated "end of the year reading assessment." Along with teacher-generated narrative descriptions of portfolio performance, it provides school and district administration with evidence of students' progress toward school-level literacy goals.

CONCLUDING COMMENTS

Through our work on the assessment aspects of Book Club, we have become increasingly convinced that the current inconsistencies between instruction and assessment inhibit students' language and literacy development. As our research team became more immersed in the issues of assessment, we found ourselves also becoming more aware of issues related to instruction. As we developed rubrics to define students' progress, we were able to make our criteria more visible to other teachers interested in using Book Club and to the students with whom we worked. As both teachers and students became aware of the criteria, instruction became more focused. Such focus is critically important when working within a curriculum as encompassing as we hoped Book Club to be: integrating across the language arts, integrating the language arts with subject-matter study, learning to read as well as learning about literature, learning to respond to literature as well as to peers and teachers. By making goals and curricular components visible, by creating assessment practices that help teachers and students focus on important learning goals, and by creating rubrics that make performance expectations explicit, we move closer to the likelihood that what teachers intend to teach will be enacted throughout the curriculum and will lead directly to students' learning of important and meaningful language and literacy skills.

Through our ongoing and future work, we hope to explore further the strengths of classroom-oriented, performance-based assessment and its effectiveness when informing a range of assessment audiences (e.g., students, teachers, parents, administrators) of students' literacy progress. In addition, we hope to determine how performance-based assessment can more effectively be used in combination with other forms of assessment (e.g., large-scale standardized tests, classroom-based portfolio assessment) to help educators make better decisions about literacy.

COMMENTARY

ELFRIEDA H. HIEBERT

The situation that drew the attention of Book Club teacher-researchers to assessment is one that many of us have faced as teachers. We initiate a new set of practices in our literacy instruction. Our interactions with students inform us of the success of these practices. Our excitement turns to discouragement, however, when the new practices are evaluated with old tests. As teacher-researchers, we are prepared for the failure of the norm-referenced tests to capture the vitality of our students' reading and writing. What is less apparent is the need to prove the effectiveness of our new practices on the basis of norm-referenced test scores. I have described this dilemma in the teacher-researcher project in which I have been a participant (Hiebert, 1993). In that project, we arrived at a similar solution as that of the Book Club teacher-researcher group—we initiated new assessments to reflect the new practices. Because we had initiated a new set of assessments with the new instructional practices, we were able to combat questions about norm-referenced testing practices in the project.

For the survival of learning practices that teachers and students value, attention to the assessment dimension of new practices should be integral to the initiation of new practices. The Book Club teacher-researchers show us that there are three aspects of this integration of assessment with practice: (1) clarifying the goals of the practices, (2) identifying those literacy events that manifest those goals, and (3) summarizing students' progress on critical goals. The first two aspects are fundamental to the initiation of those activities that we usually describe as instruction and learning. Only the third involves activities that might be construed as the domain of assessment but, when viewed from another perspective, derive from teachers' expertise. I will highlight a point related to each of these aspects of the integration of assessment with practice from the experiences of the Book Club teacher-researcher group.

Clarifying Goals

Those of us who lived through the criterion-referenced program and testing movement typically cringe when we hear the word *curriculum*, since we associate it with the step-by-step scope and sequences of that era. A curriculum, however, merely means a clarification of the goals of a literacy program—the most essential aspect of program development. The Book Club teacher-researchers demonstrate that a curriculum that serves as the source for the day-to-day activities of students and teachers can be summarized in a handful of critical literacy goals—language conventions, comprehension strategies, literary elements, and response to literature. While teachers may give them different labels, these goals encompass the primary domains in literacy. Bisesi and Raphael point out another important distinction about curriculum—the emphasis that particular domains have at particular points in the development of literature expertise. The assessment of language conventions in the form of running records did not prove informative for these middle-grade teachers. For primary-level teachers, this domain will be prominent while another domain such as literary elements may be emphasized less.

Identifying Typical Literacy Events in Which Goals Are Manifest

Assessment occurs as part of the events in which literacy is used. If integrating what has been read into one's writing and discussions with others is what is valued in a literacy program, proficiency in these contexts should be assessed. When the events of daily classroom life are valued, teachers begin to see how various lenses can be directed at these events. When the benefits of different lenses are recognized, teachers do not need to choose between portfolio or performance assessment. Particular aspects of the valued literacy goals can be captured by portfolio assessments, while different aspects of these same goals can be viewed best through a performance assessment. The assessment technique does not become the goal but is used in service of literacy goals.

Summarizing Students' Progress on Critical Goals

It is in the summarizing of students' responses on tasks that teachers encounter an issue that has often been relegated to psychometricians, the psychologists who study the characteristics of tests. The fundamental issue has to do with the bases for claims about consistency in conclusions about students' learning. One of the reasons norm-referenced tests continue to dominate American literacy practices is because they are viewed as "objective" and "reliable." This form of objectivity is valued more than the definition of literacy underlying the test. Bisesi and Raphael demonstrate that, when teachers engage with one another in the same kinds of interactions as they facilitate among their students in Book Club, they are able to provide consistent summaries of students' progress on valued goals.

The portion of the chapter that deals with developing scoring criteria indicates that teachers began the process of scoring students' work by engaging in a critical form of interaction—talking about how particular goals were manifest in the context of students' actual work. Teachers have a vast store of knowledge about how particular goals are manifest in student work. When teachers have opportunities to share this knowledge base, their professional expertise can be recognized. This expertise was recognized in the form of "artifacts," or shared exemplars of student work that illustrated particular aspects of a goal. Once a group of teachers has shared and clarified their guidelines for decision-making about students' progress, teachers can use these artifacts and the accompanying way of describing these characteristics (the scoring scheme) independently and with their students. Through these artifacts and accompanying descriptions, teachers' expertise can be shared with others (including policy makers and parents). Periodically, a group of teachers will need to revisit their artifacts and descriptions of student progress. When a process has been followed such as that of the Book Club teachers, summaries of students' progress are not arbitrary but represent the reflective decision-making of professionals. The experience of the teacher-researchers in the Book Club project shows us that thoughtful summaries of student work derive from a shared vision of literacy and of the events that manifest this vision. Just as discussion is valued among students in Book Club classrooms, teachers' thoughtful assessments derive from their discussions with one another over an extended period of time, achievement, instruction, and policy.

CHAPTER 10

Students Speak
Book Club from Our Perspective

CHRISTI VANCE, JUSTIN ROSS, and
JENNY DAVIS, with CYNTHIA H. BROCK

INTRODUCTION

In this introduction, each participant describes the process of writing this chapter from his or her individual perspective. We constructed this introduction so that each of us could express our personal opinions about our engagement in the overall project. Even though Christi, Justin, and Jenny are the chapter authors, we begin with Cindy's discussion to provide an overall framework for describing our process when writing this chapter.

Cindy

This chapter represents the collaborative work among three students (Christi, Justin, and Jenny) with my guidance. We began meeting in May 1993 and continued to meet through the fall of 1994. We met over 30 times to complete the chapter. Two other adults also helped us: Laura Pardo, the students' former Book Club teacher for fifth grade, met with the children three times during the initial planning stages of the project. Taffy Raphael met with us twice to assist with the writing process and help make important decisions, such as order of authorship.

Throughout this entire project we strove to make sure that the chapter really was the children's work. To that end, as the primary adult participant, I did not ask the children about their perceptions of Book Club and then proceed to write the chapter. Rather, since I had only been involved in Book

The Book Club Connection: Literacy Learning and Classroom Talk. Copyright © 1997 by Teachers College, Columbia University. All rights reserved. ISBN 0-8077-3614-7 (pbk.), ISBN 0-8077-3615-5 (cloth). Prior to photocopying items for classroom use, please contact the Copyright Clearance Center, Customer Service, 222 Rosewood Dr., Danvers, MA 01923, USA, tel. (508) 750-8400.

Club during the last semester of the students' fifth-grade year, my role was that of "the teacher audience"—a term Jenny used when I asked the group what they wanted my role to be. I typically asked the students to talk about what they thought a teacher new to Book Club should know and taped these conversations. From transcripts of these discussions, the children identified key themes to guide their writing of the chapter.

The three children collaborated by negotiating the first half of the chapter with my assistance in revising and editing. The second half of the chapter reflects each different author's opinions about particular aspects of Book Club, such as some of their favorite things and suggestions they might give teachers who are thinking about implementing Book Club in their classrooms.

On occasion, if the children expressed a particular idea or concept they wished to communicate to their audience, Taffy or I shared words with them for their consideration. For example, when the authors talked about their desire to describe a "typical" Book Club lesson for their teacher audience, Taffy told them that such stories are often called "vignettes." Finally, readers might notice that the students occasionally chose their own words to describe Book Club components that differ from the terms described in the other chapters of the book (e.g., "class share" instead of "community share").

Christi

Writing this chapter was a long and difficult process. When we first started, we were unorganized. As we proceeded, we have become more organized. We did not know what we were doing because we had to find the right way to approach the chapter. We found the way by discussing what we liked about Book Club. Then we decided to take what we had talked about and make an outline of what we should include in the chapter. It took us quite a while to really begin the writing of the chapter. What has kept me going was knowing that this would get other kids to enjoy reading also. I knew this would help, so it kept me going.

Everything in this chapter was written by the three kids. At first, we decided what we should include, then we changed our ideas many times. This chapter shows that we thought long and hard about all of the things we wrote. I feel that we all have a different point of view about how we wrote this chapter, so I didn't think we should combine our explanations of the process.

Justin

In the beginning of the project it was kind of difficult because it took us a while to start everything in this process. We were not sure who should write what, what we were going to write about, and how we were going to write it. Like, how were we going to decide what to put in the outline? A difficult thing was that we did not know what information to include in the chapter. I think we all decided because we all agreed whether or not the outline was okay, and we all pitched in and got some ideas that we had written down.

We started out by talking about Book Club. I feel that Christi was the leader in many of our conversations because she had a lot of good ideas to contribute. Mrs. Pardo met with us several times the first summer we worked on this project. She helped us think about some important ideas for an outline. We also just talked a lot. After we talked, Cindy transcribed our conversations. Then we went over our transcripts and decided what ideas we liked and wanted to keep and what ideas we didn't want to keep. After we (the kids) went through the transcripts and decided what ideas we wanted to include in the chapter, Cindy took our ideas and compiled them into one big outline. Then we discussed the ideas again and narrowed them down to the information we wanted to include in our chapter outline. We revised the outline many times throughout the process of writing the chapter.

I wanted to include ideas in the chapter about how teachers got Book Club started and what kids do in Book Club. We were each given a notebook where we could write down our ideas, and I put my important ideas there. It was my idea to tell stories about how teachers might use Book Club in their classrooms. I didn't know they were called vignettes, though. Throughout the project, we have continued to write and revise our work.

I feel that I have had a lot of control over what I have written in the chapter. I used our outlines to guide what I wrote about, but sometimes the way I wrote was that Cindy and I talked and she asked me questions about what I was thinking and I wrote to answer her questions.

Jenny

This all started when I was in sixth grade and I talked with Mrs. Pardo, my former fifth-grade teacher. She told me that she was writing a chapter for the Book Club book. She also told me that some of the kids who were in Book Club might be writing a chapter in the book. I said that would be fun! Then a week or so later, Cindy called me and asked if I would like to help write one of the chapters for the book. She also asked me if I would work with Christi and Justin. I said I would like to work on the chapter with them to provide more ideas and information about Book Club.

Christi, Justin, and I did Book Club in fourth and fifth grade, so we knew how to have good conversations, and we knew a lot about Book Club. We worked as a team to write our chapter, but we didn't always agree on everything. We (the kids) decided what we wanted to write in the chapter. Cindy asked us questions about things that a teacher might ask us as we were writing our chapter. No one was really the boss. We all four worked together as a team.

We are three students (Christi, Justin, and Jenny) who participated in Book Club during fourth and fifth grades (1990–92). We were invited to work on this chapter during sixth grade, and we actually started writing at the end of sixth grade. We were invited to work on this project because we had participated in Book Club for two years and we know quite a bit about Book Club. Also, we did a good job when we participated in Book Club. We also believe that we were invited to write this chapter so that we can tell teachers about Book Club from kids' perspectives. That way, teachers can learn how kids feel about Book Club and what is important to kids in Book Club. At first, your students may not like Book Club, but as you go along they will enjoy it more. Most students think it's just another reading program that may be just as boring as the old one, but they'll learn something new. Do not give it up if the students do not like Book Club at first. It takes time to learn to do Book Club well.

In the first part of this chapter we explain our definition of Book Club. At the end of our explanation we present a vignette that gives you an example of how we did Book Club at the beginning of the year in fifth grade when we were reading the book *Tuck Everlasting* (Babbitt, 1975). Next, we tell you some of our favorite things about Book Club. Finally, we give you some general suggestions and ideas about using Book Club with your class.

BOOK CLUB: OUR GENERAL DEFINITION

Book Club is about reading, writing, talking in small groups, and having large-group discussions. The most important things about Book Club are that kids get to talk over the things they are reading, and they read trade books.

Reading

Book Club is really based around reading. We normally read chapter books that are literature books–not textbooks. Each day we usually read a chapter or two. The amount we read depended on how long the chapters were. We often read about a half hour or until everyone was finished. It depended on whether we had extra time to work on Book Club that day. We read many different kinds of literature books like fantasy, historical fiction, survival books, and folktales. We enjoy literature books instead of textbooks. Usually with textbooks there are a lot of questions at the end of each story. When we read textbooks we can't spend time enjoying the story because we are worried about finding answers to questions at the end of the story. We like literature books better because we can enjoy reading instead of having to look for answers to someone else's questions. In literature books we don't have to answer questions made up by the teacher or written at the end of the stories. Instead, we get to ask questions to our Book Club groups.

An advantage to being able to talk about literature books in our small-group book clubs was that we could ask and discuss our own questions about stories that we were interested in – not just the questions made up by teachers and textbook publishers. Often we asked the types of questions that are personal opinions, and there could be many possible answers to our questions.

Writing

While Book Club is focused on reading, writing is also important. We mostly did five types of writing in Book Club. We wrote in our reading logs, on our think-sheets, on "stepping-in" and "stepping-out" sheets, and on our evaluation sheets. The evaluation sheet gave our overall view of how our groups did each day.

Logs were where we wrote our thoughts, ideas, and feelings about a book or chapter we read. We did logs every day after reading. We did many different kinds of Book Club logs. (See section on "Favorites of Book Club" for examples of logs that we did.) When we did character maps we wrote about a particular character in the book. With "wonderful words" we wrote a word we liked and shared it with our group. Sometimes we drew a picture about what we read. Sequencing was putting events in the order of how and when things happened. For "author's crafts and special tricks" we wrote down what we wanted to share about what the author did in the story. When we did "me and the book" we shared something from the story that related to our life in some way. With critiquing, we told what the author could have done better or what the author did well. For "special story part" we found something in the story that we liked and shared it with a group.

"Stepping-in" sheets were what we did before we began a book. "Stepping-in" sheets were usually used to give us a place to include our ideas about what we thought the book was going to be about. "Stepping-out" sheets were just the opposite. These sheets were where we explained whether we liked the book. We explained our feelings and ideas about the book in "Stepping-out" sheets.

Even though writing is not the major part of Book Club, it is still important to teachers and students because it usually starts up the conversations in the group and helps to keep the conversations going. Writing in Book Club will help your students become better writers and thinkers because they will practice writing so much. These reading, writing, and thinking skills will help students forever. Writing is really mostly included so the students can remember what they were thinking while and after they were reading. Sometimes students can reread what they previously wrote to get new ideas for writing. Rereading what students have already written is a good way to bring more ideas to their heads.

Talking in Small Groups

Every day after we wrote in our logs, we got into groups chosen by the teacher and discussed what we wrote. We discussed other things, too. "Like what?" you might ask. Sometimes we critiqued the book; sometimes we asked questions like "How would you feel if you were the main character?" In other words, we put ourselves in the main character's place. We had guidelines—rules, that is—for our small-group book club discussions. First, we had to spread the different groups out within the room because if the groups were too close together they would disrupt each other. Then we could only talk with our group as a group. This means that we couldn't have a separate conversation with someone in our group while the rest of the group was talking about the book. Also, we couldn't talk with people in other groups while we were talking in our small book club groups. The other guidelines for our small book club groups were: (1) staying on task, which included talking about the book and not other unrelated things, (2) making sure that everyone had a chance to talk, and (3) of course, the regular classroom rules like keeping our hands to ourselves, taking turns, respecting others, and so forth.

At first when you have your students start talking in small book clubs, everyone may be equally quiet, but as you go on, a group leader will come. "What is a group leader?" Group leaders aren't picked—they just emerge. Usually someone who emerges as a group leader is someone who likes to talk a lot, take charge, and be the boss. A group leader can be good or bad. A good group leader usually starts and keeps the conversation going and gives everyone an equal chance to talk. For example, sometimes there will be a shy person in a group. A good group leader usually tries to change that and asks the shy person questions and tries to draw him or her into the conversation. A bad group leader will just keep talking and not give others a chance to talk.

Sometimes the group members may not like each other at first. They may or may not end up being friends. Even if students are not all friends, they should learn to get along with each other in their groups. Students need to get along in their groups because if they don't get along, they won't be able to have decent discussions about the book. Also, their grades for reading should partly depend on the quality of their book club discussions.

Large-Group Discussions

Usually a reading period included reading (e.g., silently, in partners, or following along with the teacher as she read aloud), writing in our logs, small-group book club discussions, and, finally, large-group discussions (or class share). "What is class share?" you might ask. Well, class share is when the students get back into their regular large group and the teacher asks the students questions about their small-group book club discussions, or she may ask the students specific questions about the story they read.

Sometimes during large-group time you can do activities to go along with the story, like skits or plays. When you do a skit or play, you give each group a chapter to act out, then you record the story as a movie made by your class. When we did group posters we got in a group and drew a picture about the story. This usually happened at the end of a book. One of our activities was making paper cranes. In fourth grade, we made origami cranes after we read the book *Sadako and the Thousand Paper Cranes* by Eleanor Coerr (1977).

We have given you a brief introduction about Book Club so that you will know our definition of Book Club. Now, we will give you an example of how a teacher could use Book Club with the kids in the classroom. In the vignette below, we share an example of one way that a teacher could conduct a Book Club session.

BOOK CLUB VIGNETTE

One possible way to conduct a Book Club reading class would be to have your students write in logs first, then read, then have small book club groups, and finally have class share. For example, at the beginning of the year in fifth grade, we were reading *Tuck Everlasting*. The teacher said to the class, "Why does the spring water make the characters live forever?" She asked us to write our predictions in our logs. She gave us about 10 minutes to write. Then she called on people to read their answers aloud. Next, she told us to read a specific chapter silently. She gave us about 20 minutes to read.

After reading, we got into our small book club groups. There were four or five people in each group. We discussed the chapter we read. Since *Tuck Everlasting* was one of the first books we read, we didn't know how to interact in small groups very well because we hadn't all done Book Club in the fourth grade and some kids were too shy to say anything. Some of the students didn't want to talk. Some kids weren't being serious at first; they were playing around too much. At first, some kids just didn't know how to carry on conversations or how to ask good questions.

Good questions give a group a lot to talk about. They promote conversations. We started to ask questions in our groups because our groups would sometimes be dead quiet. We learned to ask good questions by trial and error. Here are some examples of good questions that someone might ask other kids in a book club discussion about *Tuck Everlasting*. "If you had a chance to meet the main character in the story, would you? Why or why not? Would you want to be a character in the book? Why or why not? What makes the character so unique? Why?" These questions are good ones because they help kids to react to the characters in the book. By asking these types of questions, kids can't just say yes or no. They are going to have to talk more to answer the questions.

After talking in our book clubs, we went back to our seats and had a large-group discussion about our small-group discussions. Often in our large groups, we discussed ways that we might do a better job in our book clubs. For example, one time we talked about the importance of not cutting off others when they were talking. We also talked about how to communicate by helping others, sharing ideas, being fair, taking turns talking, and so forth. We also discussed the fact that round-robin reading of the logs does not make a very interesting conversation. Instead, the conversation is more interesting if we ask one another questions (e.g., "How do you like the book? What should the author do differently?") and just talk about our feelings and opinions.

FAVORITES OF BOOK CLUB

We had many favorites in Book Club, and we would like to tell you about some of them in this section.

Justin

When I was doing Book Club, one of my favorite things was that we got to get videotaped or tape-recorded and we got a chance to see ourselves on the videotape. Book Club overall is motivational. It is motivational not just because we get to write and talk in small groups but because we also got to do other activities like skits and plays. Talking was motivational because we were not just writing; we also got to talk.

One of my favorite things about talking is that we get a chance to talk to our friends and get ideas from others. We have a chance to say something really important, we get to tell what the author should do better, and we ask questions about the book. Books were sometimes hard for me to understand, and the teacher or other students helped me to understand the story. So, one advantage about the Book Club was talking with friends. Talking is important because you can say what you feel you want to say. This helps you learn to express your ideas and feelings.

Another favorite of Book Club is being able to discuss good topics. Good topics can come from good books, maybe even bad books because you can say what you don't like about the book if it was a bad book. An example of a good topic was when we were reading *Hatchet* (Paulsen, 1987) and we talked about the many ways that Brian was courageous. He was all alone, yet he was able to survive by finding food and shelter.

One of my favorite topics in Book Club was when we had the "God" discussion. This topic was a good topic because we were saying what we felt about the cloud men chapter in *James and the Giant Peach* (Dahl, 1961). One student said that God didn't exist and I said He did and we had a disagreement. Then he said that the Virgin Mary made the rocks fly to hit the peach and I said, "No, she didn't." Then I said, "Yes, she did if you want to have her do that." One good thing about the conversation was the topic.

Good books.   Some of my favorite books in Book Club during fourth grade were *Hatchet, Park's Quest* (Paterson, 1988), and *Bridge to Terabithia* (Paterson, 1977). *Hatchet* was my number one top book out of all of them because it was about survival and how Brian made himself do the impossible. Survival is my all-time favorite category of books. I like survival books because people can really make it on their own without any food or shelter. Plus, it can teach you a lot about nature and how it interacts with you. I admire characters in survival books because they actually really go out in the wilderness and just make themselves do things that they never knew they could do.

My next-favorite book was *Park's Quest*. In the book, Park found out that his dad had died over in Vietnam. One of the reasons I liked the story was because it was interesting the way he found out about his father and what happened to him. Also, it was interesting when he found out that he had a half-sister named Thanh.

One of the reasons I liked *Bridge to Terabithia* was because of how much Jess adored Leslie and the way she could really run for being a girl. They built a bridge across a stream and on the other side of the bridge they created a magical kingdom that they called "Terabithia." I liked the way that Jesse and Leslie were very good friends.

My favorite log.   I chose this log because it was written about one of my favorite books and Jenny and Christi drew a picture and I wanted to show something different because I wanted to show you that some people might like to write (see Figure 10.1).

FIGURE 10.1. Justin's Log Entry

NAME Justin   **DATE** 25 Mar.

I feel sad and good
the sad parts where when the
pilot died and Brian had to land
the plain but instead he crashes
it into the water and swims and
he is all alone in the wilderness
he has to make things and he
has to get food and water I don't
like when he gets ran over the
by the moos moose. I like when
he build the fire and at the end
I like when he gets the straight
sail he figure a lot. I like when
he found the save, and I hate
when he get poked from the porcupine.
and when the skunk came and spraid him
and he got it into his eyes

One of the benefits of logs is you can write a lot of important information from the book, and you can share a lot of information with teachers and classmates. I tend to write and I have a lot of writing in my logs. You can always write if you do not like to draw or think that you cannot draw. Sometimes, teachers will direct you about what to write. Mrs. Pardo did this for me at times. She often made us do prompts and after that we got to do free choice. On the day of May 8, 1992, I wrote this summary of *Hatchet* because I felt good about the story, and I was at the point where he got in the cave, made a fire, and got food and his hatchet out of the water. In my summary, I did a critique because the things I liked about the book were when he had something driving him to find everything he needed–shelter, fire, and food. The thing I hated is that the bears, the storm, and the raccoons interrupted him once he was doing great. I really like all of Paulsen's books.

Christi and Jenny

Some of our favorite Book Club books were *Number the Stars* (Lowry, 1989), *Tuck Everlasting, Island of the Blue Dolphins* (O'Dell, 1960), *Bridge to Terabithia, Park's Quest*, and *Sadako and the Thousand Paper Cranes*. We will briefly describe *Sadako* since it was one of our very favorite books.

Sadako and the Thousand Paper Cranes was about a Japanese girl named Sadako who had leukemia. She was a young girl during World War II. She had to stay in the hospital. Her best friend told her that if she made 1,000 paper cranes she would live. But she only made about 900 paper cranes and then she died. We think that *Sadako* is a good book to use to start Book Club because when you have a group of children, they can usually understand what they're reading in this story.

Favorite log–Christi. On this day I decided to draw a picture because I had a picture in my head about the story (see Figure 10.2). Normally, when I have a picture in my head I draw. I normally had a picture to draw. Some students don't like to draw as much as I do, but the ones that do enjoy it will have very interesting drawings like this one.

When you are reading, you get your own private movie in your head. Where do you think the movies about books come from? It's a person's own particular movie. Some books are much easier to get movies for. Like if I read a fantasy book, I would be able to get my own picture because I know it would never happen and if I read a historical fiction the movie will be boring like that time period. With a fantasy book, I could just laugh while we were reading silently because when I was reading, the words wouldn't be what I was laughing at; it would be the picture in my head.

FIGURE 10.2.   Christi's Log Entry

I drew a picture about when the cloud men hit the peach with a hailstone.

Favorite log–Jenny. I chose a log from the book *Island of the Blue Dolphins* because I like that book (see Figure 10.3). One of the reasons I like that story is because it is based on a true story. There really is an "Island of the Blue Dolphins"–only it has a different name in real life. Also, there really was a tribe taken from the island and a girl who survived on the island alone. I like the book because in the story Karana felt alone with nobody around and nobody to really talk to except her dog. I liked this particular log because

FIGURE 10.3.   Jenny's Log Entry

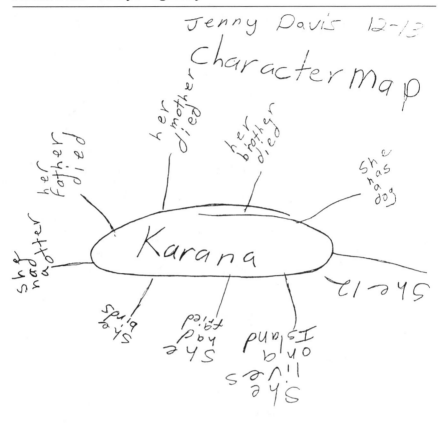

it tells a lot about how Karana feels. Also, neither Justin nor Christi picked this type of log to include in this chapter.

I did quite a few character maps on the main character when I was in Book Club. I usually did a character map if an author told a lot about a certain character. I enjoy making character maps to examine what I know about certain characters that interest me.

GENERAL SUGGESTIONS AND IDEAS FOR TEACHERS

Substitute Teachers

When your class has a substitute and you want your class to do Book Club, then we think we would let them have a Book Club group the same as if the regular teacher was there. If the students act up, then make them read the reading text instead of doing Book Club. You might be thinking that it would be difficult to do Book Club with a substitute. That is just your imagination. If the kids know how to do Book Club, it should be easy for substitutes to do Book Club with the class.

Book Club for Younger and Older Students

We think it would be really great for second- or third-grade teachers to use Book Club. You should use Book Club even with younger kids instead of reading textbooks and answering questions. We think literature books are a whole lot better than texts because they give more details and they tend to be more interesting. This makes for better book club discussions.

If you want to do Book Club in second grade and below, we would have the kids draw pictures and then tell what their pictures are about. In third grade and up to twelfth grade we would have kids do character maps, wonderful words, pictures, special story parts, me-and-the-book, and author's crafts. It is usually better to do more challenging things with older students.

CONCLUDING COMMENTS

We strongly encourage you to do Book Club with your students. Even though it will take your students a while to learn Book Club, please don't give up. Book Club really will help your students to be better readers and writers. If your students know how to read and talk to each other in small groups, they can do Book Club. It's not hard. Good luck!

COMMENTARY

P. DAVID PEARSON

Someday I would like to meet the student authors of this chapter, Christi Vance, Justin Ross, and Jenny Davis, so that I could thank them personally for providing me with such a powerful personal "reading" of Book Club as a "story" that they have lived through. After reading their account of and response to their Book Club experience, I thought to myself, "Why don't more of our accounts and evaluations of classroom materials and techniques include student voices?" After all, we would never think of evaluating cars, or television sets, or washers, or even new convenience foods without including, even relying on, the voices of the customers. Why don't we include the real clients of our educational system in more of our evaluations? I am quite sure I do not know the answer to that question. I am equally sure that Christi, Justin, and Jenny have started a new trend in educational evaluation!

From my perspective, the most important question to ask when judging the wisdom of including student responses is, What do we learn from students that we do not, could not, and would not learn from the teachers and researchers involved in Book Club? I think we learn a lot. Indeed, the remainder of my response is an answer to that very question – What unique understandings did I gain from the students?

The most important understanding conveyed by the students is that they do not see Book Club as something that teachers do *to* them but as an activity in which they wield a great deal of authority and responsibility for what happens and what they learn. They understand their role in making choices – about the books they read, about the discussions they hold, and about the ways in which they choose to respond to the texts they read. They understand their role in monitoring the content, quality, and fairness of their conversations about books.

A second important understanding I gained from the students is that they are quite aware of the social and cognitive consequences of classroom practices. In particular, their understanding of the differences between the factually driven discussions of basal selections and the theme-and-concept-driven discussions of Book Club is revealing. They clearly understand what happens to the talk among a group of students when you focus on the big ideas versus all the specific details. They also understand that it takes some getting used to when students move from one environment to the other.

222

And they reveal at least an implicit awareness of the importance of genuine response questions, questions for which any one student's response is as important as any other student's because the person who posed the question genuinely wants to know what individuals think about the question.

The social dimension is particularly salient in their comments. For example, they see the explicit advantage gained by working through a tough set of questions with one's colleagues. Contrast that attitude with the complaints we often hear from students when they are assigned group work or cooperative work groups. The difference with Book Club, I think, is that the students genuinely recognize that the response tasks they engage in are more respectful of human understanding and compassion than of content-based learning. And they know that the former traits are not necessarily reserved for the "good" students; insight can and does come from any and all members of the community. To learn, as an individual, that we have something to learn from our peers is one of the most important understandings we can come to as members of a species. It is nice to know that Book Club supports that insight and that it comes through to the students who participate.

A third key understanding that I gained by listening to Christi and Jenny and Justin is that students learn a lot from the books they read. And what they learn is not limited to insights about the human condition and how we relate (or fail to relate) to one another, although those are certainly key. The learning they gain can also be quite practical and factual, as when Justin talks about survival tips or Jenny talks about the "real-life" character of the *Island of the Blue Dolphins*.

Finally, I learned (or rather I was reminded) that students learn a lot about how a process like Book Club works. Because they do, they have feedback and advice to offer teachers about how, when, and with whom to use these processes. We would all do well to listen more carefully to their advice in these matters. We have much to learn from them. And, as I suggested earlier, we should all thank Jenny, and Christi, and Justin for starting a new trend in educational writing!

SECTION III

Teacher-Researchers in the Book Club Program

Section III focuses on research by elementary classroom teachers as they extend and examine the development of Book Club in their own classrooms. They discuss their implementation, adaptations, and modifications as Book Club evolved in their own classrooms. All were experienced teachers who pursued master's degrees in reading at Michigan Student University. The teachers were founding members of the Teacher Research Inquiry Group, a team of teachers who met regularly with Ginny Goatley and Taffy Raphael to discuss and reflect upon teaching and research. One of the many themes that united this group was trying to create a reading program that incorporated writing and oral language, that used literature as a basis for instruction, that emphasized personal response, and that facilitated our efforts to provide necessary instruction for students to enhance their literacy capabilities. Book Club became one model for devising such instruction in their classrooms. The chapters reflect their collaboration in terms of overlap among their goals, as well as their individuality as they adapted the program to meet the needs of their children, schools, and districts. A framework of teacher inquiry, literacy learning, and theory underlies all of the chapters in this section.

Laura Pardo, one of the founding members of Book Club, is in her fifth year of using Book Club with her students. In Chapter 11 she discusses reflective practice, presenting key issues that have arisen over the course of five years and how she has used these issues to become more reflective. Her chapter is followed by Dorothy Strickland's commentary on the role of reflection on teaching.

In Chapter 12, Pam Scherer, a third-grade teacher, discusses how she adapted Book Club for lower-elementary students. Pam discusses her major modification, combining the two discussion components of Book Club—book club groups and community share—into a "fishbowl" discussion. This integration of components facilitated her third graders' efforts to lead their own discussions. Lee Galda raises important issues for further consideration in her commentary on Book Club as an early elementary literature-based program.

Teaching first grade challenges educators to achieve a delicate balance between teaching phonics and decoding, whole language, and a love of literature. Kristin Grattan is such a first-grade teacher who also has adapted Book Club to fit lower-elementary students. In Chapter 13, she describes her language arts program, of which Book Club is one component. Following Kristin's chapter, Barbara Taylor highlights the important role a literature-rich environment plays in literacy development for young children.

In Chapter 14, Kathy Highfield and Julie Folkert describe the cross-curricular implementation of Book Club and social studies they created for their fifth-grade classrooms. They discuss both the process they engaged in as they combined the two areas and the units of study they created. Their restructuring of the Book Club program and the issues it raised are the focuses of their chapter. In a commentary following the chapter, Karen Wixson stresses the value of Kathy and Julie's adaptation of Book Club into an integrated unit.

Chapter 15 addresses the issue of assessment from the perspective of classroom teachers using Book Club. Julie Folkert and Sara Bean were teachers implementing Book Club who discovered that their existing assessment program did not align well with Book Club's goals and principles. They created an alternative assessment system involving portfolios and student self-evaluation and goal setting. This chapter describes the evolution of their assessment system, the issues that arose, and their own learning through the process. The commentary on this chapter by Kathy Au connects the work to others who have constructed classroom-based assessments.

Across the chapters in this section, one theme emerges with a powerful voice. *Teachers in the classroom* can and do *become actively involved in decision-making about their own teaching, which ultimately impacts their students' learning.* The teachers in this section exemplify dedicated classroom teachers who willingly spend their own time to look at themselves, their programs, and their curriculum, and strive to make changes that best meet the needs of their students.

CHAPTER 11

Reflective Teaching for Continuing Development of Book Club

LAURA S. PARDO

As teachers in inner-city schools, Deb Woodman and I have always looked for innovative ideas to use in our upper-elementary classrooms. At the beginning of the Book Club program, Deb was a first-year teacher who had substituted in my school for most of the previous year. I was a displaced middle school teacher at the elementary level for two years. Deb had a fourth/fifth-grade split; I was teaching fifth grade for the first time. These circumstances made us eager to use new methods to help our students learn. Through ties to Michigan State University and after several discussions with Taffy Raphael and Susan McMahon in the spring of 1990, we agreed to join the research team to study Book Club the following year.

By accepting this invitation, I had no idea the doors that would open for me. This chapter discusses the role of Book Club in helping me become a reflective teacher. I discuss what it means to be a reflective teacher, how Book Club supported and encouraged my journey toward becoming reflective, and how becoming reflective has influenced the way I continue to use Book Club in my classroom.

BEGINNING ON THE ROAD TO REFLECTION

The role of reflection in teaching has been discussed for a long time (see, e.g., Dewey, 1933; Feiman-Nemser & Featherstone, 1992; Schön, 1987). Dewey (1933) describes reflection in the classroom as "active, persistent, and careful consideration of any belief or supposed form of knowledge in light of the grounds that support it and the further consequences to which it leads" (p. 9). Strickland (1988) talks about the teacher as researcher in terms of studying one's classroom to gain understanding and to improve educational practice. She says, "teacher researchers use research to do a better job" (p. 756). For me, being reflective means I think about what I am doing, why I am doing it, and what adaptations are necessary. Being reflective means one is always learning to become the best teacher one can be.

I began using Book Club in the fall of 1990 with uncertainty and questions. Deb and I put a lot of faith in the research team, especially Sue and Taffy, and their expertise in the field of literature-based instruction. At the same time, we felt Taffy and Sue were putting a lot of faith in us, because Deb was a first-year teacher and I was teaching fifth grade for the first time. We contributed to the practical issues related to the program in terms of the ongoing life of the school; however, we relied heavily on the research team for issues related to literature-based instruction in general and Book Club specifically.

As the year progressed, I found answers to some of my questions about the Book Club program. These realizations began to occur as a result of Sue and Taffy's guidance and scaffolding. Both of them supported my learning but gradually withdrew explicit support as I became a more independent learner. Their scaffolding was like a wooden structure that provides support until the building can stand on its own (see Brown & Palincsar, 1989; Wood, Bruner, & Ross, 1976). Taffy and Sue supported me in many ways throughout the first year; however there were three specific areas that were crucial in helping me move toward reflective teaching: (1) learning to question, (2) understanding decision-making, and (3) keeping a journal as a means for recording my developing thoughts. It is important to note that Book Club provided the context within which this growth occurred.

Learning to Question

As I began to teach fifth grade for the first time, I continued using many of the strategies and methods I had used with my previous third-grade students, without much thought about whether or not these activities were appropriate for fifth graders. Having "experts" available for Book Club, I relied on the expertise and knowledge of the research team. At the beginning, I merely followed the team's suggestions and implemented methods I thought they wanted me to use. Over time, however, they helped me question my instructional decisions as I began to think about the developmental differences between third- and fifth-grade students, first in Book Club, then later in other subject areas. One way the research team prompted this reflection was their questioning during our biweekly meetings. Sue and Taffy asked us why we chose certain methods or why we decided to introduce one reading log entry before another. This prompting slowly enabled me to begin to question things for myself, as I developed my own sense of relevant questions and of situations that needed to be questioned. As I began to ask my own questions, Sue and Taffy pulled back their scaffolded support by questioning me less about my decisions. This was not something I had done on my own; it was only through modeling and scaffolded support that I began to see how and what to question.

For example, effective grouping was an issue we faced during the first year of Book Club. As a research team, we had made the decision early in the year to group the children heterogeneously. Yet as the year went on we began to question what *heterogeneous* meant. Initially the team had defined *heterogeneous* as mixed by gender, race, and ability. Through prompting within the research team, I began to realize there were other factors that might need to be considered when forming groups, such as attitude, personality, and motivation (Pardo, 1992). I studied these issues further, eventually presenting my findings at the National Reading Conference in 1992.

In learning to question my instruction and its effect on my students' learning, I was behaving in a manner consistent with the National Center of Research on Teacher Learning's (1991) agenda for research on learning to teach. They hypothesize that, "in order for teachers to alter these resilient beliefs, they must be introduced to an idea that is plausibly better and must be provoked to question their own experiences and to question the beliefs that are founded in those experiences" (p. 21). Book Club provided the context within which I could begin to raise some specific questions. Taffy and Sue modeled this process when they raised issues at our biweekly meetings. I soon began to understand the process of questioning, including the validity of my own questions. Yet I had to experience both the context and the process before questioning helped me alter my previous beliefs about learners and instruction.

Understanding Teacher Decision-Making

As I learned to question my instructional decisions, I began to understand the decision-making process and its relationship to student learning. I began to see how decisions were made and how those decisions could impact my instruction and ultimately my students' learning. Taffy and Sue helped me to look at instructional decisions by contemplating students' prior knowledge and experiences. For example, when the children began book clubs early in October, we found that they lacked the skills necessary to have meaningful, authentic conversations about the issues in the books (see Chapter 5; Raphael & McMahon, 1994). We looked at several factors, including our current instructional practices and the students' own knowledge, to make instructional decisions about how to help our students learn to talk in small groups. Sue and Taffy encouraged Deb and me to consider the traditional classrooms many of our students had experienced, and we realized that most students had not had much practice in student-led discussions.

Once we identified this as a key factor in students' ability to talk about text, we decided on several methods to encourage and help children develop needed discussion skills. The adult members of the research team modeled book clubs for the students by talking about their current read-aloud book. We audio- and videotaped the children in groups and let them listen to and watch themselves. We transcribed some of the tapes and then had the children act them out for one another. Finally, we taught discussion strategies (see Chapters 5 and 7 for more explanation of instruction on discussion strategies). Since I was actively involved in these decisions, I understood why they were made and how they could influence student learning. As more examples like this surfaced, Sue and Taffy continued to support me through this process, and eventually I shifted my instructional decisions to reflect my analysis of students' needs and the related goals. This was in contrast to making decisions based on resources, time, and scope and sequence—the kind of decision-making I had been involved in previously. I think Sue and Taffy helped me to focus explicitly on the decision-making process and its potential to effect student learning.

Keeping a Journal as a Means for Recording My Developing Thoughts

During the time I was learning to question and make educated decisions, Taffy and Sue also modeled personal strategies used by reflective teachers and researchers. I began to keep a journal, in which I noted my successes, failures, frustrations, and questions. I wrote at noon, after school, or at home, as I reflected on my Book Club lesson that day. I also engaged in conversations with the research team, where I was encouraged to discuss the things I had written about in my journal. We shared many dialogues about the issues and ideas that surfaced during Book Club, and each time I came away from these conversations with more knowledge. And finally, I realized that time is an important aspect of reflection, and I began to allow time to pass between things that happened in the classroom, a discussion of it, and the eventual decision concerning that event.

For example, in December 1990, my class did a biography study. The students read three different biographies—*Shaka, King of the Zulus* (Stanley & Vennema, 1988); *To Space and Back* (Ride & Okie, 1986); and *Peter the Great* (Stanley, 1986). I observed in my journal that while book club discussions were good, community share was awkward. The research team talked about this issue, and we agreed that the success of community share lies partially in the opportunity for students to draw similarities across books. Therefore, later in a similar unit in Deb's room, she chose two biographies of people (one about Jackie Robinson and the other about Glenn Cunningham) who shared common experiences, since both were athletes who had to overcome hardships before achieving success. Deb found that book clubs and community share went well because she could help the students make intertextual connections. In sum, I had identified the problem, the research team had discussed it, and time had passed for Deb to reflect on this experience before creating a successful biography unit for her class. My later discussion with Deb about this unit reinforced the process of making instructional decisions on the basis of students' needs. As an adult reader, I might be able to make connections across a number of biographies, but students need more explicit help. By being actively involved in the process of recording my thoughts and discussing them with other professionals, I reflected on my own instructional decisions and made better choices.

Practicing Reflective Teaching

During the years following the initiation of Book Club, Taffy and Sue did not regularly observe my class; yet the program became an integral part of my teaching and learning. I continued to have opportunities to talk with Sue and Taffy, through phone calls, e-mail, an occasional dinner meeting, and occasional observations of my class. Ginny Goatley spent time in my room the second year, following up some Book Club issues from the first year (see Chapter 7). I continued to have conversations with Deb about Book Club since we still taught next door to each other and shared common concerns. As I began on my solo journey of reflective teaching, I continued to rely on these relationships. However, I relied more heavily on my own classroom experience and my newly developed knowledge and confidence to make decisions.

DECISION-MAKING IN THE BOOK CLUB PROGRAM

During the next few years, as I began to teach more reflectively, my experience and knowledge levels expanded, and I moved forward in developing Book Club in my classroom. Of the many decisions I made, I have identified three major areas for discussion in this section: (1) selecting literature, (2) promoting and improving discussion, and (3) integrating subject matter.

Selecting Literature

In thinking about literature selection for Book Club, two main issues influenced my decisions: (1) how to select books with the greatest potential for discussion, and (2) how to provide students choice while maintaining quality discussions during community share. I wrestled with these dilemmas every time I selected a new book, but I never resolved them; rather, I made decisions that met my goals at the time. Lampert (1985) talked about this by arguing that, instead of solving problems, teachers must consider competing goals as they make instructional decisions in the midst of teaching.

Potential for discussion. The first literature selection issue was the book's potential for discussion. The research team felt that the books the children read needed to contain issues or ideas that encouraged and maintained detailed talk. Jason, a fifth grader in his second year of Book Club, reinforced this belief when he noted that while *James and the Giant Peach* (Dahl, 1961) was "fun to read, it isn't a good book for Book Club because there wasn't anything to talk about." Further, I began to notice that the most successful books were those that contained controversial themes and issues. For example, during the second year of Book Club, the students discussed several big ideas prompted by the books we read. During *Tuck Everlasting* (Babbitt, 1975), students debated the advantages and disadvantages to immortality, drawing on the experiences of the Tuck family. During *Bridge to Terabithia* (Paterson, 1977), Crystal raised the idea of Jess's guilt from not inviting his friend to share in an expedition with their teacher, an invitation that may have prevented the tragic accident. During another of Katherine Paterson's books, *Park's Quest* (1988), Mei, a Vietnamese student, expressed her anger at the way Vietnamese had been stereotyped as "killers." Because my students participated in such in-depth discussions about important themes and big ideas, it encouraged me to continue looking for books with the potential for controversial discussions.

Student choice. Student choice in literature selection is a topic of current research (e.g., J. Hansen, 1987; Routman, 1988; Swift, 1993). Many theories exist regarding the issue of choice, ranging from having all children choose all their books for reading instruction to having the teacher select a book for the whole class. Some of those who advocate children's choosing their own books for reading argue that choice increases desire and motivation to read. They believe children will pick texts that interest them, so they will be more likely to finish the book and understand its content. In my years of teaching elementary school, I have found this to be true with many of my students. So, even though we had decided to include books with common themes (e.g., the biography units) to facilitate discussions during community share, I still wanted to provide my students with some choices. At the same time, further reflection resulted in several additional questions in my journal. Does the entire class need to be reading the same book at the same time? If not, would I be able to find books that were similar enough to promote discussions during community share? As I began to consider these questions, within the umbrella of literature selection, I felt overwhelmed. I wrote in my journal; talked to Deb, Ginny, Taffy, and Sue; and gave it some time – the things I had learned to do during the first year of Book Club. I came up with several decisions based on these reflections.

First, I felt that all my students needed to be reading books that shared similar ideas to help them participate in the discussions. Second, since the "content" of good literature is a reflection of our humanity, the issues we face, what defines us as human beings (Probst, 1991), I wanted these broad themes to emerge through our whole-class community share and the students' book club discussions. I began to think of themes prevalent in literature and found that the issues reflecting humanity were the ones that tended to create the best opportunities for discussion. As I thought about how to combine the search for important themes with student choice, I explored ways to accomplish my goals. Either all students could read the same book, or the students could read different books with commonalities that promoted good discussion.

For example, Deb told me that she had used *The Weaving of a Dream* (Heyer, 1986) and *The Enchanted Tapestry* (San Souci, 1987) during a folktale unit the previous year. The whole class eventually read both books; each half of the class read one book, and then they traded. Because these two books are different versions of the same tale, this worked very well for community share discussions. These books also contained important themes, such as loyalty to family, honesty in dealing with others, and appreciation of beauty. This example showed me that it was possible to use more than one book at the same time if I chose carefully. However, students still had no choice if they all eventually read both books. Because this was problematic for me, I continued to look for further ways to manage this dilemma (Lampert, 1985).

As I continued to reflect, I realized that in order to meet my instructional and curricular goals, I needed to consider availability of literature, interest to students, and reading levels. My students might not take these into consideration if self-selecting their own Book Club books. Therefore I decided to offer students limited choices within three parameters: (1) book availability, (2) reading level appropriate for fifth grade, and (3) interest to most of my students. I accomplished this by asking students to select from a list of titles that met these criteria. This procedure worked well for me at that time, but I continue to revisit this issue each year and currently select a list of books to fit content area units (I will discuss this later in the chapter). What remains a constant criterion is the potential for discussion of important themes or big ideas.

Promoting and Improving Discussion

Since the research team felt that having good small-group and whole-class discussions was essential to Book Club, one of my goals was improving interactions. First, I looked at the grouping issue again to see if different configurations would impact book club discussions. Second, I evaluated the reading logs and the ways students responded in writing to assess their potential for encouraging good discussion. Finally, I looked at the role of community share in the program and tried to change or modify my role to see if I could raise the level of discussion.

Grouping. The issue of grouping looked different when I considered its impact on discussion. Deb had related that during the first year, when she had left several students together for more than one book, their discussions seemed better. So I began to experiment, leaving some students together for longer than one book or unit. As I observed and took notes about these "repeat groups," I began to see some advantages, and thus I began to use this grouping selection occasionally. Later I made this analogy in my daily reflection journal:

> In the workplace when two or three people work well together, management will strive to keep this combination of workers together. It promotes higher productivity and less problems. We should emulate this in the classroom. If two or three students work well together, we should consider letting them stay together for the same reasons. Creativity and productivity will increase, and children are learning a valuable life skill about working with others. Isn't this part of public education, to prepare children for the real world and a future work place?

What I further discovered was that by leaving some students together, I eliminated the "getting to know each other" period, and students continued with good book club discussions.

However, leaving some students together did not always promote better discussions because students formed cliques. This sometimes happened when the students who had been with each other during the previous unit were reluctant to allow or encourage new members to participate. At times, the repeat members already had a "system" or "style" of book club discussions, and new members found it hard to adapt. Therefore, I continued to change book club groups, making sure I maintained heterogeneity among gender, ethnicity, and literacy abilities. While I decided leaving some students together occasionally was a grouping option that might increase discussion, I used it sparingly. Allowing myself this option simply created more flexibility within grouping and helped to increase discussion among some of the book club groups. Without raising this question, talking to Deb, and my own reflection, I may not have realized this option existed.

Reading-response logs. I have reflected considerably on the use of the reading-response logs in promoting good discussions. Two specific issues I thought about were (1) the issue of choice as discussed above, and (2) the potential for the reading logs to impact students' later book club discussions. During the first year and in the early part of the second year, reading-response logs were teacher-directed. Two examples from my fall 1991 journal illustrate this. In response to a few chapters from *James and the Giant Peach*, I asked students: "What brave thing did James do in this part of the story? Explore a time when you have been brave." In responding to *Island of the Blue Dolphins* (O'Dell, 1960), I wrote the prompt: "Think about the friendship Karana had with Tutok. Think about some friendships you have had. Explain the feelings involved with true friendships, and describe how Karana might be feeling now that Tutok is gone." All of my students responded to these prompts. Therefore the children were responding in similar ways without variety or choice. Further, their book club discussions became predictable. If all students responded to the same prompts, the conversations reflected the similar content of their writing. Since I wanted my students to use the reading log in such a way that it would impact their discussions, I began to explore various kinds of written responses to encourage students to select their own response types each day.

At first, I was not sure how to reach this new goal, but in a conversation Deb related the following example from her classroom. Her whole class came up with the category they called "in the character's shoes" after reading *Number the Stars* (Lowry, 1989) and thinking about how they might act if they were Ellen or Annemarie. When using this choice of response, her children wrote what they thought they would do and how they would feel if they were the character in the story. Some children even drew a shoe, putting their response inside it, making the response more visual. I was impressed and intrigued by this process, and, even though I never introduced this category to my class, I did introduce the process of student-generated log options to give my students choice in their reading logs.

One way this played out in my classroom was when individual students decided to make this process their own. This was different from the way the "in the character's shoes" response was born, since Deb's whole class came up with that choice together. In my classroom, while reading *Bridge to Terabithia*, Jason noticed that the author named her chapters but that the reader could not predict by the title what a particular chapter might be about. He decided he would write about Paterson's titles, try to predict the chapter, and then explain what he thought she meant by the title after he read the chapter. This became known as "titles." When Jason created this response, he brought it to my attention, and I had him share it with his peers. This response type was added to the repertoire of responses my class could chose from when writing in their logs. I do not think I would have encouraged this kind of student input if I had not had time to talk to Deb and think about how this might look in my classroom.

During my observations of students using new log choices, I discovered that when students felt ownership over the process and product in their reading-response log, they were more likely to want to talk about it in their discussions. This confirmed what I had learned in other aspects of classroom teaching–when students have choices in their learning, they become more motivated and interested. Providing them with options for the reading log gave them a wider range of topics and ideas for conversations about the book. Since most children had answered the same prompts during the first year, the book club discussions had followed a predictable, structured path, one that the prompt had, in essence, predetermined. But when the children all chose different ways to respond, they began to have much richer and less predictable book clubs, some of which lasted up to 20 minutes and covered a barrage of topics, something I could not orchestrate by selecting my students' response types for them. Only by being critically observant, writing faithfully in my journal, talking with Deb and others, and reflecting on the issue of reading logs and discussion was I able to realize concerns and make changes therein.

Throughout my observations of the book club groups the second year, I also began to notice that fewer students relied solely on their logs for discussion in book club groups. As I observed further, I decided they were instead using their logs as a place to organize their thoughts and as a springboard to the discussion. I noticed many children coming to book club and talking freely about the story, something that had happened only occasionally the first year. I felt good about this development because getting children to discuss a story, instead of reading something they had written about it, was one of Book Club's goals. As I thought about why this happened, I decided to interview several of my students for more information. Their responses led me to believe that because students had choices and time to think and respond in writing, they felt more comfortable talking about the story and not simply reading from their logs as they had the first year. Jean made this comment in an interview in May: "Because you let us write about anything, then it's okay to talk about anything. Before, we knew we had to talk about the prompt." Upon hearing this and other similar comments, I made a commitment to myself to continue to give students log choices and ample time for writing to encourage new approaches to discussions. All of this was a conscious effort on my part. It did not simply evolve; it happened because of my observations, conversations with students and others, and my personal reflection.

Community share. The most important factor contributing to improved discussion was the change in my role during community share. I felt that my students were not used to a "community" of sharing but were more accustomed to teacher-led, whole-class discussions. I thought and talked about ways to get my students sharing and responding, rather than waiting for me to lead the conversation. During community share, I began modeling rather than leading to help my students understand and feel what a good conversation was like. I modeled several strategies, such as sharing without reading from the log, responding to what someone else had just said, questioning for understanding, and sharing personal experiences that related to the text. As part of the modeling I called on students or groups to share and encouraged them to talk from their heart. I began to hear students tell their peers, "just say it; you wrote it, so you know what you think; just tell us." In these ways, students began to talk more freely, first in community share, then during book clubs. As I reflected on my notes about this method of whole-class discussion, it made me think how my modeling resembled Taffy's and Sue's models of questioning earlier. I also began to realize that the ways that I learned something could have direct implications for the ways I asked my students to learn something, thus impacting my instruction further.

As students participated more actively in community share, I learned to step back, follow their lead, and listen to them engage in exciting, enthusiastic discussions. In addition, I encouraged livelier student talk by listening to the book club discussions that preceded community share, identifying interesting conversations, and using one of them to begin our whole-class conversation. For example, during *The Talking Earth* (Craighead-George, 1983), a book about the Seminole Indian tribe, I had played a tape of and furnished the words to a song called *Seminole Wind* (J. Anderson, 1992), which addressed some of the issues in the book. During book club, Bill and his group used the words to this song as the basis for their talk, as they tried to understand more about the Seminole tribe. At one point, they realized that the name of a famous Seminole chief is mentioned in the song, and Bill related additional information about this chief. I used this conversation to start community share that day, by asking Bill to share his knowledge about the Seminole chief. Situations like this enabled me to start interactions, then I stepped back, offering support as needed. Putting the direction of community share into the hands of my students and following their lead placed me in a new role—that of facilitator (see Chapter 2). I became more focused on my students and placed greater emphasis on the ideas that evolved from their groups and prompted further discussion. I began to see benefits from this decision as I continued to reflect on my teaching. Benefits included an increase in student talk, a decrease in teacher talk, and an increase in the quality of discussion during community share.

Integrating Subject Matter

As I continued to reflect on my teaching and the Book Club program, I thought about integrating subject-matter content. Curriculum integration has been gaining recent attention among researchers (see Alvermann, 1994; Lipson, Valencia, Wixson, & Peters, 1993) and teachers alike (see Chapter 14). When I looked at curriculum integration, I focused on two areas I had written about in my journal that continued to raise questions for me.

First, I noticed that some of my students were forming misconceptions about history and other content-area subjects during Book Club. This concerned me because it showed a lack of prior knowledge. Some of the Book Club books were historical fiction; however, just reading these books did not necessarily help students construct an accurate historical knowledge base. Therefore, I spent time helping students buiid a knowledge base to facilitate meaning construction while reading some of the literature. For example, in the biography unit mentioned earlier, I found my students had never heard of Peter the Great. Since the children had no prior knowledge of him or the time period in which he lived, they had no context within which to place the ideas presented in the text. At one point during the book, one group of children decided that Peter had 23 wives, when, in fact, he was married twice (consecutively, not simultaneously!). This group introduced the idea that he had multiple wives during community share when several other misconceptions became evident. Based on these discussions I decided to teach about Peter the Great's time period to help students better understand the story. One way I did this was by focusing specifically on comprehension, asking children a set of questions that could be answered by carefully reading the book. Their responses led to further discussions as the students and I worked through their developing ideas and began to build a common knowledge base.

Second, I found the original framework for the Book Club Program taking 60 to 75 minutes of class time a day. While I judged this to be time well spent, I was worried that I might be neglecting the content areas. I did not want to shorten the time for Book Club; since all elements of the program are equally important, I could not bring myself to cut anything. Because of the need to help build a knowledge base and the time this added, I began to look at alternative ways to integrate Book Club and content areas.

One thing that helped influence my decision came out of the collegial relationship I had formed with Kathy Highfield and Julie Folkert, who were using Book Club in their classrooms but integrating it with the social studies curriculum (see Chapter 14). Since I was reflecting on integration and several prior Book Club units had related to social studies (e.g., Native Americans, World War II), I began to discuss my ideas with Julie and Kathy. As I considered specific ways to integrate my curriculum, I decided that thematic units were an obvious approach. Current research also supported my decision (see Y. M. Goodman, 1989, for a review of research in this field). I also agreed with Pearson (1994), that "reading and writing must be contextualized, or situated, in authentic learning tasks" (p. 19). I believed that by integrating the Book Club program with subject-matter content, I could make learning more meaningful for my students. The next section will describe my reflections and decisions integrating Book Club and social studies.

Social studies and Book Club. As I pursued the idea of thematic units, I felt confident knowing Julie's and Kathy's program, which was similar to mine, had been successful with fifth graders. I was also motivated by evidence from my own pilot study of a unit on Native American lives. Therefore, after talking further with them and considering the issues I discussed above, I decided to teach my entire social studies curriculum through integration with Book Club. I planned my units, keeping in mind my social studies curriculum, the historical fiction available, and the prevalent themes related to humanity (see Figure 11.1). I continued to reflect on my practice and my student's learning throughout the process, always trying to monitor and adjust to make Book Club the best it could be.

As I look back at my decision to integrate social studies and Book Club, I believe both my students and I gained. I benefited from a new appreciation for my own decision-making ability and seeing the positive influence on student learning. My students gained a more thorough knowledge of the content and a deeper appreciation for the human side of the issues. My journal notes and reflections helped me understand how the students were improving in their use of reference materials. They also showed growth in presenting information both visually and orally, and in using newly acquired background information to help them understand and enjoy historical fiction during Book Club. Making decisions that led to a difference in my students' learning led me to value and appreciate my role as a reflective teacher. The remainder of this section describes my reflections during one particular unit during the 1993–94 school year, my fourth year of using Book Club in my classroom.

FIGURE 11.1. Integration of Social Studies and Book Club, Plan for the 1993–94 School Year

Date of unit	September/ October	October/ November	December	January	February/ March	March/ April	May
Unit Topic	Native Americans	Exploration/ Colonization	The American Revolution	Survival	The Civil War	World War II	Fantasy
Book Club literature	Sing Down the Moon— O'Dell	Sign of the Beaver— Speare	The Fighting Ground—Avi	Hatchet— Paulsen	Charley Skedaddle— Beatty	Sadako and the Thousand Paper Cranes —Coerr	Tuck Everlasting— Babbitt
Themes/issues	Prejudice, slavery, cultural heritage awareness	Persecution, freedom, new beginnings, friendships	War, death, patriotism, loyaly, growing up	Elements of self and survival, self-esteem and confidence	War, death, slavery, prejudice, friendships, loyalty	War, death, prejudice, friendships, family	Immortality, everlasting life, death

The Civil War unit. My class had spent several weeks studying the Civil War and the issues of slavery, racism, and prejudice. We had researched the Civil War in social studies by doing group research reports, reading *Charley Skedaddle* (Beatty, 1987) for Book Club, and viewing the movie *Roots* (Wolper, 1977). I had planned to end the unit after writing the reports, reading the book, and seeing the movie. However, as I reflected on the many written and oral interactions I had had with my class, I realized that some of my students still had a lot of questions about racism and prejudice. Further, as I reread my journal notes I was struck by the number of questions that students had raised across the unit and that I had listed but that we had not yet addressed. Also, during students' book clubs, I noted they questioned why people like Martin Luther King and Malcolm X needed to fight for civil rights when blacks had been freed during the Civil War. These interactions, my students' questions, and my reflections led me to continue with the unit, focusing next on the American South following the Civil War.

I chose three of Mildred Taylor's books for Book Club to help my students understand more fully the role the post Civil War period played in the issues of racism and prejudice. These three books are set in the rural, southern United States in the 1930s and reflect the feelings of a young black girl growing up during this time (*Mississippi Bridge* [1990]; *Song of the Trees* [1975]; and *The Friendship and the Gold Cadillac* [1989]). As we read these books, I continued to make observations in my journal, assessing students' connections and development of deeper understandings of the history of the civil rights movement. Through reflection, I became aware of my students' learning and I altered and adapted my instruction to meet their needs. I describe below several examples of how this happened.

Beginning **Mississippi Bridge.** The book *Mississippi Bridge* is about four young brothers and sisters who witness the boarding of a bus in rural Mississippi in the 1930s. As these children watch, some of their black friends board the bus. They are asked to sit in the back, but, when some white passengers want to board, the blacks are told to get off the bus to make room. As the bus begins its journey, it crosses a dilapidated bridge weakened by the rain. As the four black children watch, the bus plummets into the river below. The story continues by describing the rescue attempts and feelings of the four children. Prior to beginning reading this book, John wrote this prediction, "I think it'll be a fight for rights. Because they (the blacks) got kicked off the bus. Like the Rosa Parks thing. Because it wasn't fair at all. But she won't win because that's how it was back then." John's entry revealed to me that he was making a connection from the movie *Roots* (where even after the Civil War, southern blacks had to obey whites) to later class discussions about civil rights. I realized that he remembered information about the segregation of

whites and blacks on buses, specifically information about Rosa Parks. I believe John took this information and applied it to another bus situation. He
followed with a generalized statement, "But she won't win because that's
how it was back then," implying that he had learned that blacks had not
made political gains during this time period. His entry revealed that he had
synthesized his newly acquired knowledge and applied it to the Book Club
book.

While I was pleased that students were making these connections, I also
realized that it did not just happen—it required a lot of direct instruction,
modeling, and guided practice. I spent time modeling how to make connections and instructing students on specific strategies. We talked about using
prior knowledge constructed by reading books, watching movies, and studying specific content as resources when making predictions about a new text.
We practiced predicting by reading the information on the back of the book,
thumbing through the pages, and looking at the cover illustrations. I was
pleased to see evidence of my instruction in John's reading log entry. Being
observant and thoughtful about my instruction and its relationship to my
students' abilities and needs helped me take notice of evidence of student
thinking in their reading log entries.

***During* Mississippi Bridge.** During daily interactions in my classroom,
I overheard many conversations. These influenced me and helped guide the
direction of further instruction. I made many on-the-spot decisions as I listened to students discussing this controversial historical issue. For example,
at one point I heard a group of students discuss the way the white people in
the story were treating the black people. In this section of the transcript, the
children revealed their confusion over the way the blacks had to say "Yes, sir"
to the whites and the whites referred to the blacks as "nigger." Through the
course of our most recent research, we learned this was not only common
before and during the Civil War, but also well after. This conversation helped
me to understand that my students were still not clear about the relationships
blacks and whites had in the years following the Civil War.

Paul: They think, they can have slaves. And, owners be tellin them what
     to do. And make 'um say ma'am and sir. But that's stupid. Like we,
     [we said yesterday . . .
Patsy: [The war's over. Why should they have to say, oh . . . Mister and
     um, sorry sir?
Paul: Yah, that's what we was talking about, like yesterday.
Jonah: It's because . . .
Patsy: Why don't they call 'um by their names?

Jonah: Because back then, back then it's the way black people had to talk to white people.
Paul: Yup, Yup. That was bogue though, I didn't like that. Why didn't they just call 'um by they names? Some white people don't know they names. They be calling 'um nigger for the heck of it.

As I listened, I tried to see exactly what it was that was causing my students' confusion. Unlike some other issues that I could reflect on over time, this one needed immediate attention. I reflected on their discussion as I struggled to understand what had confused them. Patsy said "The war's over," referring to the Civil War. This story took place in the 1930s, and she had learned from our previous study that the Civil War was indeed over, so she could not understand why whites did not treat blacks equally. Jonah tried to help her as he responded to her, "back then it's the way black people had to talk to white people." He may have been drawing from his prior knowledge from the many books, movies, and reports he had had access to during this unit. This section of dialogue showed me that different students had different levels of understanding but that the group in its entirety still needed further information.

As I continued to listen to the same conversation, Jonah read from his log, identifying another topic for discussion. I was able to see evidence not only of their understanding of my prior teaching and their own prior learning, but also some gaps. My analysis of these gaps guided me as I planned how to continue instruction during this unit.

Jonah: Here's what I put, "Big Ma gets on the bus Josias goes to the back and Cassie wants a white's seat. She fusses and argues with Big Ma. Then the youngens stay in front of the general store."
Paul: This is another thing I don't like um, how when he wants to sit in the front, when the girl wants to sit in the front . . .
Patsy: [They should be able to . . .
Paul: [Yah, . . . instead of . . .
Patsy: [They didn't have those laws yet.
Paul: [. . . and anything . . .
Jonah: [but white people *still* think, they still own the black people.
Paul: And another thing I hate. Why do they call it white people's seats? It's a bus. It's for everyone to sit and have transportation, if they don't have cars to ride to places they need to go. Why don't everybody be there and sit where everybody else can [sit . . .
Raquel: [sit together.

Jonah: 'Cause nobody knows people should be treated equal. Until Martin
         Luther King was, No . . . [Until, um, . . .
Patsy: [That was . . .
Jonah: [. . . until Lincoln was elected president . . .
Patsy: [. . . that was way after
Jonah: [. . . then blacks was almost treated equally . . .

The information discussed here came directly from a book we had read
together about Martin Luther King and his fight for civil rights (Lowry,
1987). I could also see evidence from our research on President Lincoln and
his fight to abolish slavery. But when the children tried to tie these two ideas
together, I saw confusion. Notice that Patsy referred to "those laws." We had
read and talked about civil rights laws earlier, during the Martin Luther King
biography, and she was telling her group that blacks had to sit in the back of
the bus because this story (*Mississippi Bridge*) took place before the laws had
been passed, revealing her accurate understanding of the timing of historic
events. Together, their comments led me to think that some of the students'
confusions might be settled as they continued to talk.

Jonah's response indicated he had learned it is wrong to have separate
seats—"but white people *still* think, they still own the black people" (as if it
were still during slavery). This revealed to me that he, too, had made connections across historical periods. Later, Jonah made a second direct reference to
time—" 'Cause nobody knows people should be treated equal. Until Martin
Luther King," correctly placing civil rights laws into the context of Martin
Luther King's time period. However, Jonah then revealed his confusion
when he changed his reference to "until Lincoln was elected president."
Jonah knew that Lincoln freed the slaves and had concluded that Lincoln also
wanted equal rights for all people. Like Jonah, the group continued to struggle with this issue, still uncertain of the time frame. At the end of this excerpt
Patsy said, "that was way after" (the Civil War) and "then blacks was almost
treated equally." At this point, I felt that the confusion of events in history,
specifically related to Lincoln and King, had not been addressed well enough
in my classroom instruction earlier; then I made the decision to revisit this
point, beginning with our community share later that same day. However, I
continued to listen to their conversation, looking for other indications of
their understanding.

Near the end of this conversation I heard evidence of students making
further content connections.

Patsy: In our book, they said the Chinese were, uh . . . er . . . You know,
         our social studies um, homework, well they said, that . . .
Paul: [The Dutch and the Chinese.

Patsy: [. . . they workers, they were um, treating, the Chinese, differ-
ently . . .
Paul: [like dogs
Patsy: . . . because of their eyes.

In this section of the transcript, Patsy referred specifically to their social
studies book and their homework about prejudice. She related the information about Chinese people being treated unfairly because of the shape of
their eyes and made an indirect analogy to the unfair treatment of African
Americans. I was struck by the fact that students were able to make these
connections and yet not make others (like the Lincoln–King time period
relationship). However, this entire transcript helped me to think about the
ideas and issues surrounding civil rights and the Civil War that confused
my students. Having my students' learning directly influence my instruction
became one of the main benefits I have gained from reflecting on my students'
comments. As mentioned earlier, much of this reflecting happens during
classroom interactions so that I can tailor my instruction to meet the needs of
my students.

After the Mildred Taylor books. At the conclusion of these three
books, I asked the student to synthesize what they had learned. Stephen, a
child who has one Caucasian parent and one African American parent, wrote
a piece about Taylor's books.

> Mildred Taylor's books teach us lessons about life. The best lesson I
> learned was Not to have prejudice agant's any one couse of there color.
> It might hurt there felling. And one day they might Be rich and you are
> poor you might ask for money and they will say no couse of you hurt
> there feeling couse of preJudice. You should treat people like you want
> to Be treted. And If your white and rich and another person an't and
> there a different color and you start to teeze them you might get beat up
> and the wouldn't be fun. And If people start teezing you abut yor coler.
> Just say it isn't any differnt then your's

Stephen's entry revealed that he was still struggling with the issues of racism
and prejudice, even after extensive study. However, I felt that he had come
to terms with these ideas in his own mind, when, near the middle he wrote,
"You should treat people like you want to Be treted." And later he wrote,
"And if people start teezing you abut yor coler. Just say it isn't any differnt
then your's." During many book club discussions, I had witnessed Stephen
being the center of his group, almost looked on as an "expert" by his peers.
As I read Stephen's entry, I thought about the great controversy involved in

these books and began to understand the struggle Stephen had as he worked through these issues. This reflection helped to reinforce my belief that good literature with strong issues and themes helps develop children's thinking and influence their learning.

CONTINUING MY JOURNEY AS A REFLECTIVE TEACHER

I have now been teaching and reflecting on my instruction and student learning for four years. I have found it rewarding yet time-consuming. There are several things I do that seem to make the management of time and materials easier for me. I try to write in my journal daily. Frequently, I write when the children are writing in their reading-response logs or during my lunch hour. In my journal, I often take field notes of the students working in their book club groups, noting questions they raise, issues they talk about, and confusing or misunderstood passages they struggle with. I reflect on lessons taught and write questions I want to address later. I also try to take my journal home each weekend, to reread what I have written for the week and write in response to my observations. I write in the margins, or on the top, and I usually add a few new thoughts at the end of my reflection. My journal is a spiral notebook, and I keep the completed ones in a three ring-binder. I use several spirals each year.

For each of my students I keep cumulative folders in which I place copies of all reading-response logs, evaluation sheets, and any other relevant data. I use large hanging folders and keep them in milk crates. They stay at school during the year, so I refer to them when planning and making instructional decisions. At the end of each school year I take them home to use as I analyze my data further. I keep statistical and personal data, like test scores, family and personal anecdotes. I audiotape book clubs and an occasional community share or instructional lesson. I often listen to the tapes but rarely transcribe them.

I try to keep up my professional relationships with Deb, Sue, Taffy, Ginny, and other teachers. I find these outlets highly beneficial for my personal and professional growth. They serve as soundingboards, offer affirmation, and challenge my thinking as I try to make sense of the things I see in my classroom. I note their suggestions or ideas in my journal, so I can refer to them later as I reflect on issues that trouble me. I read teaching and research journals and try to stay current on books about teacher research and reflective teaching. One that has been particular useful is *The Art of Classroom Inquiry* (Hubbard & Power, 1993). Reading about other teachers' classroom research both makes me feel good about what I am doing and challenges me to think further and harder as they raise issues I may still be struggling with. Doing all of this concurrently is not always easy, but it is always worthwhile.

CONCLUDING COMMENTS

As I continue to use Book Club in my classroom and teach reflectively, I am reminded of how I felt at the beginning of this project. I was uncertain and had a lot of anxiety about the program. However, this has been one of the most powerful learning experiences I have had in my lifetime. I am truly thankful that the door to reflective teaching was opened for me through the Book Club program. I know that I will continue to be a reflective teacher as long as I am in the classroom. Now that I have traveled on this avenue, there is no other road for me to take.

Acknowledgment. I wish to acknowledge Deb Woodman of the Allen Street School for her early contributions to this chapter and for lending me examples from her classroom.

COMMENTARY

DOROTHY STRICKLAND

On reading Laura's chapter I was reminded, once again, of the hundreds of moment-to-moment decisions teachers make every day. The decisions involve what to teach, how to teach it, and how to adjust instruction to student response. Complicating the process is the fact that these decisions are made not only for the whole group, but for the small groups and individuals within it, and the realization that every decision has the potential to affect a host of decisions that preceded it. The teacher is indeed a creative problem solver, a role that has long been recognized in the literature. Certainly, our methods courses, curriculum guides, and instructional materials are based on informing teachers how to solve the problems associated with instructional decision-making. To Laura's credit, the description of her "journey" takes us far beyond the role of teacher as problem solver. As Schön (1983) might put it, she is a "problem setter"—a teacher who defines the decisions to be made, the ends to be achieved, and the means which may be chosen. "In real-world practice, problems do not present themselves to practitioners as givens. They must be constructed from the materials of problematic situations which are puzzling, troubling, and uncertain" (Schön, 1983, p. 40).

Of course, Schön was describing what reflective teachers do. Even as our field moves toward more holistic practice, however, the role of teacher as reflective practitioner remains less common in the literature than that of problem solver. At the pre-service and in-service levels, far less attention is given to helping teachers be more reflective about classroom practice than about what methods to employ. Perhaps the most valuable contribution this chapter makes is in allowing us to get inside Laura's head and share in her unique experiences. The combination of inquiry and reflection she describes can serve as a catalyst for action and discussion for teachers who are seeking to find their own voice in what they do.

Sharing Laura's introspection is valuable to the research world in many ways. Two of them stood out for me as particularly useful. First, as university researchers our tendency is to enter classrooms to observe specific phenomena. Even those of us who collaborate with classroom teachers and lean toward more qualitative or ethnographic techniques are highly focused in what we choose to observe, analyze, and describe. The critical role of the classroom teacher in these collaborations comes through very clearly in Laura's descriptions. The teacher is far more than someone to help execute the intervention. The classroom teacher's wisdom and perspective is invaluable in helping to truly contextualize the data. It is only the classroom teacher who sees and "feels" the effects of an intervention on the very culture of the classroom.

The second area in which I believe Laura's chapter makes a strong contribution is that of clarifying the distinction between surface-level alterations and genuine, thoughtful change in teaching practices. I wonder how often visitors have observed Book Club in Laura's classroom only to leave with the belief that what she does is simply a matter of putting books and students together in a circle and allowing them to talk. Of course, the real change is not easily discerned by the naive observer, one who is unfamiliar with the processes she employs and the theories and research upon which they are based. Real change emanates from philosophical shifts accompanied by much trial and error in the classroom; it is not easy to implement or replicate. The real danger resides in attempts by teachers to replicate overnight what they think is a simple procedural change or to think of change only as a new version of the old (e.g., Book Club as conventional reading groups using trade books rather than basals). Of course, any teacher's search for better instruction should be commended. It simply places a heavier burden on teachers like Laura to explain what they do on a deeper and more philosophical level.

CHAPTER 12

Book Club Through a Fishbowl

Extensions to Early Elementary Classrooms

PAM SCHERER

My third-grade students had been asked to write articles for our school's monthly newsletter. I was delighted when several children asked if they might write something about Book Club. The following is Jill's article.

> In Mrs. Scherer's class we do a little thing called Book Club. We do different books. After we get done with one book we do another. First we read one hole chap. Then we write about the chap. After that Mrs. Scherer calls four people into the middle of the room to share what they rote with the othe people. Then fter that the people call on the people in the addeeense for Questions or Quomemts.

Jill's description causes me to reflect on a number of questions: How did I come to include Book Club within my reading program? Why do I feel that Book Club is an exciting way to teach and learn? How have I modified Book Club to suit the needs of younger children? This chapter will focus on these and other questions about how I implemented a modification of Book Club in my primary classroom.

THE BEGINNINGS OF MY JOURNEY OF CHANGE

Like many of the contributors to this volume and participants in the Book Club project, I find that collaboration and conversations with my colleagues help me think about my teaching. My reflections on improving literacy instruction for my early elementary students led to my seeking opportunities to collaborate with colleagues and, eventually, to adopt a modified Book Club program. I was a participant in the Early Literacy Project (Englert, Raphael, & Mariage, 1994), a program emphasizing the importance of oral language, dialogue, and integration of language arts with content-area learning among young children. Further, I was enrolled in the Michigan State University Master's in Literacy Program, where I refined my theory of how children learn and found support to make substantial changes in my classroom. Finally, I was a member of the Teacher Research Inquiry Group (Goatley et al., 1994), where I often listened to conversations about Book Club among my colleagues teaching older children. Their discussions led me to consider ways I might implement such a program with my lower-elementary students. Book Club met many of my reading instructional goals: reading "real" literature, emphasizing writing, discussing books, and including personal response to literature. It offered a framework to incorporate instruction that capitalized on what I knew children enjoyed about books.

My previous teaching experience had been influenced by writers such as Y. M. Goodman (1978), Graves (1983), and Smith (1988), who emphasize the importance of using language for genuine purposes in meaningful contexts. I was captivated by Ashton-Warner (1964), who stressed immersing children in their own language. I learned that Vygotsky (1978, 1986) argued that children needed to be active participants in their own learning because their language use develops their thinking as well as communicates it. This language use to learn and communicate does not occur in isolation (Barnes, 1995), but within social contexts. This emphasis on language use led me to seek instructional programs that enabled me to create a stronger learning environment in my classroom. Book Club seemed to be such a program, since it provides opportunities for children to read and react to good literature; however, it was designed and implemented in fourth- and fifth-grade classrooms, so I considered how I could build on its strengths and those of my students. Further, how could I meet my district's mandates while still maintaining Book Club's components?

TEACHING TODAY: BOOK CLUB IN MY LOWER-ELEMENTARY CLASSROOM

For the past four years, I have taught second and third grades and a second/third-grade split in an urban school in Lansing, Michigan—the same school in which Book Club was initiated. The students walk from the surrounding area, a racially and ethnically diverse neighborhood serving both single- and dual-parent, lower-income homes. Many students receive federal support through breakfast and lunch programs and qualify for Chapter 1 services. Students tend to test either at or below grade level. Their academic difficulties seem to affect their motivation negatively. I have used Book Club with several classes, but in this chapter I focus on my experiences with a group of students I taught in both second and third grades from 1992 to 1994.

Reading in Book Club in My Third Grade

In my third-grade classroom, I have three major reading goals: (1) to emphasize reading as a meaning-making process, (2) to encourage personal response, and (3) to ensure all students access to texts we read and discuss. I also had three concerns that influenced my implementation. First, I needed to secure multiple copies of trade books. Second, these books had to be at a suitable reading level in terms of traditional measures (e.g., vocabulary, sentence length), as well as interpretability and interest. Third, the books needed to generate meaningful discussions and written responses.

Finding multiple copies of trade books. It is critical for each child to have a copy of a text. Physically holding the book, feeling the pages, and being able to see the text up close invite each reader to engage. I discovered three ways to meet this goal. First, my district supports a language arts center, which houses classroom sets of trade books across grade levels on a variety of topics. Thus I can secure many trade books for temporary use (usually about three weeks). Second, the school and local libraries provide other options related to the classroom set in terms of theme, genre, or author. I often use these as read-aloud texts. Third, I personally purchase individual or classroom sets of texts. Combining classroom sets with individual books, I can create a context for students to make interesting intertextual connections. When students are involved in meaning construction and personal response, they are able to make connections among the texts they are currently reading, ones they read in the past, and their own lives. Securing multiple copies of books helped me emphasize meaning construction, personal response, and ensuring access for all students. An example from my third-grade class will help illustrate how students engaged and began making intertextual connections.

When reading *Sadako and the Thousand Paper Cranes* (Coerr, 1977), students made connections to a previous book, *Charlotte's Web* (White, 1952). At first, these connections were literal. When they read that Sadako watched a spider crawl across the room, it reminded them of *Charlotte's Web*. While literal, these links became the foundation for more thematic connections that developed over time. As we progressed through the story, the students recognized a thematic connection when they commented that the two books were both about friendship and loss through death. Such connections revealed how these third graders were constructing meaning across texts.

A second way that including multiple copies of texts in my reading program proved beneficial was related to building students' background knowledge. While reading and discussing the book, students revealed their limited prior knowledge related to World War II. To address this and help them build this knowledge base, I found two nonfiction picture books to supplement our reading: *Faithful Elephants* (Tsuchiya, 1988) and *My Hiroshima* (Morimoto, 1987). While reading these, students began learning more about the effects of war in general and the bombing of Hiroshima in particular. Thus securing multiple copies of a variety of texts is critical to the way I conduct Book Club. However, simply having enough copies is not sufficient for younger students; one of the greatest challenges is finding interesting and thought-provoking books at an appropriate reading level.

Selecting books at a suitable reading level. I was concerned about the wide range of reading levels in my classroom. I knew I would have readers who had not succeeded previously, but I hoped that within the Book Club context they would become eager to read. After talking with Laura Pardo, I concluded that to have a common ground for whole-class discussions in the beginning, I should have all my students read the same book, leading me to select a book that met the reading level of the majority of my students. At the same time, it required me to identify ways to provide all students, regardless of reading level, access to the text.

There are a variety of ways to support those students who struggle with print. Just as Book Club advocates, my students read every day—alone, in pairs, or with individuals reading selected parts to the whole class. In addition, they also read along with a recording of the text, follow along as I read aloud, and participate in reader's theater performances. I assign specific chapters every day, but students can read ahead if they choose. Because they are not reading in isolation and because there is extensive variety in how to read, my students usually have little trouble completing the texts.

My students not only read each day, but also respond both orally and in writing. Based on observing their discussions and reading their logs, I concluded that my students were successfully comprehending the texts. Their discussions focused on key themes or ideas in the books. For example, when responding to *Charlotte's Web*, they focused on the ethical dilemma related to the value of a life, even that of the runt of a litter. When they read and responded to *Sadako and the Thousand Paper Cranes*, they wrestled with other problematic issues, such as the justification for war. Similarly, students' reading logs focused on meaning construction, interpretation, and response. They raised questions about fairness and justice, recorded events from their books, and identified favorite parts—all responses that suggested their understanding of the texts.

In addition to emphasizing reading as a process of meaning construction, interpretation, and personal response, I hoped to motivate my reluctant readers toward literacy and participation in a community of readers by selecting books that piqued their interests. My observations during Book Club provided evidence that through thoughtful book selection, I was achieving this goal as well. I observed my reluctant readers becoming some of my most enthusiastic participants. By the middle of the first semester, they frequently asked to take home the text we were reading, to practice reading, to get ahead so that they would have some background when they read during school, to catch up if they had fallen behind, or to be able to show their parents, guardians, or siblings that they were readers. They learned that they could write and talk about the texts just as well as, and sometimes better than, some of their more fluent peers. In short, providing access to print gave these students access to the *ideas* within, ideas to which they had strong personal responses and that they could understand once they had support for decoding.

Paul illustrated the success that resulted from emphasizing meaning construction over word-attack skills and providing support for struggling readers to have access to texts. Paul's first-grade teacher had considered retaining him but eventually decided he might benefit from promotion. His mother expressed concern about his reading ability during the first month of second grade, asking me whether I thought he should return to first grade. Many factors seemed to support her concern. Paul's standardized test scores placed him within the "at-risk" category. He had performed below grade level in both word recognition and fluency. Further, during one of my informal assessments, he described himself as a weak reader: "I am not a good reader. I miss a lot of words and don't read very fast but I like to listen to stories." While this data suggested that retention might be reasonable, I questioned whether it would be best. First, even though his test scores were low, they also revealed that his ability to answer questions about what he had read was at or above grade level. Further, in his quote above, he noted he liked hearing stories. In addition, he had already begun to appear comfortable with his peers in my classroom and enthusiastic about the book we were reading, willingly volunteering daily for book club discussions. We decided to keep him in my classroom.

Paul's access to interesting books during Book Club helped him actively participate in reading-related activities from the beginning of the year. I encouraged him, emphasizing repeatedly that he could read. While acknowledging that he might not be as fluent as some of his peers, I told him he was in fact a reader and supported this by giving him a chapter book comparable to those of his peers, ones in which the story was conveyed primarily through text. Finally, to validate that I believed he not only could read but also write and respond, I gave him blank papers to write his reactions on while he read.

Unlike the behavior his first-grade teacher observed, I saw Paul often making comments or asking questions that sparked conversations. For example, during *Charlotte's Web* he questioned whether Fern should love her father as much as her mother since her father was going to kill Wilbur, the pig. This led to a lengthy book club discussion about the morality of the father's actions and whether such a person deserves to be loved. Over time, Paul began to volunteer to read aloud for the group and to write thoughtful log entries that often served as a basis for discussion. While not the most fluent reader in the class, he began to realize there was more to reading than pronouncing words rapidly. As Paul progressed through third grade—also in my classroom—his attitude about his ability changed from that of a child who was embarrassed to one who was proud he could write and converse as well as his more fluent peers.

Books to provoke strong written and oral responses. Students' growth in their views of reading as a process of meaning construction, interpretation, and personal response, and in their attitudes toward reading as an activity to be valued and practiced, did not stem solely from the multiple copies of books at appropriate reading levels. To achieve these goals, books also had to evoke "strong" responses—responses where children asked difficult questions about the human condition or sought understanding about how or why people treat one another the way they do. For student-led discussions that were meaningful, the books they responded to needed depth.

Several thought-provoking books noted above illustrate the type I found valuable for Book Club. Books exploring the impact of war on the lives of ordinary citizens, such as *Sadako and the Thousand Paper Cranes, My Hiroshima*, and *Faithful Elephants*, led to discussions about justice, fairness, innocence, and responsibility. Similarly, books such as *Charlotte's Web* led students to consider issues of justice, friendship, life, and death. Books such as Holling's (1941) *Paddle to the Sea* raised questions about taking risks, exploring the unknown, and learning about faraway worlds. While I think it is critical for students to practice their fluency through reading books that are relatively easy, for Book Club I found that those books with thought-provoking content provided the "meat" needed to engage students in meaningful talk and written response. My early elementary children asked difficult questions and sought to understand complex issues. This is demonstrated in the following examples of written and oral responses from my third-grade students.

Even 8-year-olds are capable of asking questions adults have difficulty answering, as evidenced by Sean's entry related to the novel *Sadako and the*

Thousand Paper Cranes. In this story, Sadako survives the bombing of Hiroshima but later dies after contracting leukemia from exposure to radiation. Sean pondered, "Why do they have wars? Do people want to have wars? Leukemia is a terrible thing!!!! I will try to stop it!" Sean later shared this response with his book club, which prompted an extended conversation trying to clarify what leukemia is and the reasons for war. This also led to additional connections, such as a discussion about the Gulf War described on the evening news and one student's comments related to an uncle's dying from AIDS. Just as adults have serious questions and opinions, so do children.

In addition to asking difficult questions, third graders have strong beliefs about abstract concepts, such as what constitutes justice, that are elicited when reading thought-provoking books. An example of such a book is Richler's (1987) *Jacob Two-Two and the Hooded Fang*. In this story, a young boy is arrested for saying everything twice. He is found guilty of insulting a shopkeeper and taken away to a dreary children's prison. After reading the first two chapters, Sheri made the following comment to Tremaine during a book club: "I don't think it is fair to take him away. After all, he didn't do anything wrong. He just said everything twice. It is not right to put somebody in prison just for saying everything twice." As her comment illustrates, my students expect laws to be followed, but they also expect laws to be fair. Even at a young age, children have strong opinions about justice. Such comments are prompted by the depth of issues presented in literature.

So far, I have focused on the reading goals I addressed through Book Club in my classroom. In the next section, I describe how I encourage meaning construction, interpretation, and personal response through the writing component.

Writing in My Third-Grade Classroom

When I first considered adopting Book Club, I was optimistic about the way in which my students would handle the writing component because they already participated daily in writer's workshop (Graves, 1983). Since they were accustomed to choosing their own topics, I thought they would easily choose various types of written responses to texts. Also, since they were familiar with the writing process, I thought they would understand the difference between the reading log as a notebook for ideas in contrast to final, publishable works. Next, since they viewed themselves as authors who shared their writing via the author's chair, I thought they would be comfortable sharing their written responses during book club and community share. Further, as Graves would say, they were becoming "option-aware"; that is, aware of choices related to how and what to write, an awareness I thought would serve them well as they became familiar with the range of choices and purposes for written response to literature. Thus, while much about Book Club would be new to my students, I believed the reading logs would be one aspect with which they would be comfortable.

I wanted students to continue to use writing in ways similar to the workshop – to make choices, share ideas, and respond to peer's writing. However, I also wanted them to capitalize on the instructional opportunities that would support their development as readers through the written log component. For example, I taught students to note interesting or confusing words as a way of increasing attention to vocabulary building. I taught about traditional comprehension strategies, such as predicting or summarizing, as ways of recording ideas. I taught about interpretation and personal response, showing students how to draw intertextual connections, create character maps that gave insight into characters' motivations and backgrounds, and share ways in which the story reminded them of their own lives. In short, the logs and think-sheets within the writing component (described in detail in Chapter 4) provided numerous opportunities to teach literature response in Book Club in meaningful ways so students would enhance their understanding of and ability to write about books they read.

Instruction about how to use reading logs became critical for my students to bridge writer's workshop to their Book Club logs. Despite their experiences with process writing, many students' previous experiences with writing associated with reading led them to conclude that this writing merely proved comprehension of story events without including personal responses or pursuing topics that would be interesting to discuss later. Thus, while they were comfortable with the *idea* of written response to texts, I needed to model writing in response to literature. In the beginning, I maintained my own response log as a way of modeling different response types. This modeling included:

- Drawing a picture to capture what I was thinking or feeling
- Asking myself questions as I read
- Identifying memories of my life prompted by the story
- Writing predictions
- Retelling or summarizing a favorite story part
- Making connections to other texts

In addition to modeling various *types* of response, I also modeled personal response in different contexts.

One way in which I modeled personal response writing was through using the overhead projector. For example, while reading *Charlotte's Web* I often wrote entries like the following, based on my childhood: "When I was in third grade, we lived on a farm. My brothers and I used to swing from a rope high in the loft. We would build tunnels with the bales of straw and try to hide and scare each other. It was great fun!" In sharing this response, I underscored how events in the stories I read prompted me to think about my own experiences. In this case, Fern's visit to the barn brought back memories of playing with my brothers. I explained that by remembering my own experiences, I could picture what Fern saw when she went into the barn.

A second way in which I modeled personal response was through oral reactions as I read aloud. This thinking aloud as I read provided opportunities to make my thinking visible, which could serve as the basis for a written response. For example, when I came to a part of the book I found humorous, I paused, saying I would record this funny part in my log to remember. If I mispronounced a word, I paused, explaining that I had to reread this section to understand what was happening and to try to identify the word that had created the difficulty. Then I suggested that I record the word in my log for later clarification. Such modeling served two purposes: It helped students see examples of how one chooses what to write about, and it illustrated the strategies skilled readers use in understanding, interpreting, and responding to texts.

Because students' written log entries serve as prompts for their discussion, I have observed that, once they begin sharing these in their book clubs, they realize their personal responses are valid. While my support and modeling is necessary to help them begin to engage in more personal written responses, the responses and reactions of their peers are even more powerful. Initially, they watch my reaction to a peer's comment. My encouragement, my questioning to deepen my understanding of what they are saying, and my active listening and acceptance of their ideas serve two functions: (1) modeling the kinds of comments and questions they should ask one another and (2) helping reinforce the value of each personal connection to the text. In this way, I use students' comments based on their written log entries as powerful models of the range of possible responses.

To track their response and provide individual feedback, I have done two things. First, I collect their logs twice each week to read and comment on them, responding personally or asking questions about what they have written. I evaluate their responses and their apparent understanding of the story, as well as identify for future instruction the skills they need to develop or refine. Second, all students have a folder with all their reading logs, so they can review old entries, reread my comments/questions, and share them with parents or guardians.

The Book Club program creates an atmosphere in which a community of learners values everyone's opinions and helps others to expand and clarify oral and written responses. My students needed to build connections between writer's workshop and Book Club's written responses. I found that providing instruction facilitated students' success with responding in writing to the texts.

The Discussion Component in My Third-Grade Classroom: Into the Fishbowl

Kristin Grattan and I have discussed the difficulties younger students initially have engaging in meaningful discussions about books, regardless of the quality of the book or their level of interest. The initial discussion Kristin describes among her first graders (see Chapter 13) is similar to ones I witnessed initially in my classroom. While I was fairly confident that my early elementary students could be successful with the reading and writing components of Book Club, I doubted their ability to participate in student-led discussions because they had few prior experiences working in small groups and virtually none leading a discussion without the teacher's presence. However, as I described above, I had discovered that, when given the opportunity to read and write on their own, they exceeded my expectations. Therefore, I reasoned I could be underestimating their discussion abilities. After all, as Paley (1986) has so eloquently described, anyone who has spent time around young children knows they love to talk. I decided to try the groups using the upper-elementary model.

I divided children into groups balanced by ability, gender, and personality types (e.g., leaders, followers, dominators). I talked briefly about what a discussion is before creating six groups of four or five children each. Then we established that we would use our "quiet" voices so that all groups could hear their members. The resulting small-group discussions failed miserably and continued to fail each time I tried. Sometimes students did not seem to know what to discuss, sometimes the noise level was out of control, and sometimes both problems occurred. I asked members of the Teacher Research Inquiry Group for suggestions. The ensuing discussion resulted in my learning two valuable lessons from the more experienced Book Club teachers. First, implementing Book Club requires time and patience. Second, as with the other components of the program, the teacher must spend time making expectations clear. In the case of student-led discussions, the teacher must clarify both *how to discuss* and *what appropriate responses* look like. Only when these are in place can book clubs become a reality. With these two points in mind, I decided to try another approach: Instead of having several groups discussing simultaneously, I would have one, focusing on talk that was responsive to all participants and to the text. To do this, I decided to combine book clubs with community share, using a technique called "fishbowl." That is, I would have a small group of students sit in the center of the room to discuss a topic as the rest of the class surrounded them listening (Fitzgerald, 1975).

Before introducing this idea to my class, I discussed it with the Teacher Research Inquiry Group, reminding them of my frustration with having so many children talking at once and my disappointment with the quality of their discussions. This conversation with others using Book Club helped me clarify how my concept of fishbowl, serving as a means of modeling small-group discussions by incorporating both book clubs and community share, differed from community share alone. With this clearly in my mind, I was better able to explain it explicitly to my class.

Introducing students to fishbowl. I began by arranging the classroom so the fishbowl book club was in the middle of the room, surrounded by their audience. I then asked four volunteers to form a book club and sit in the fishbowl while sharing their responses to the book we were reading. Since heterogeneous grouping was part of the Book Club program design, I selected a mixed group of students from those who volunteered, considering those factors noted above (e.g., leaders, followers, dominators). At first, the students sounded much like Kristin's class, taking turns reading from their logs, then looking to me for direction. I soon realized I had not provided the scaffolded instruction necessary for them to proceed on their own.

Providing instructional support. Since I was integrating book club with community share, I had to be careful not to interrupt their student-led discussions with instruction. Therefore, I decided that, while I would provide explicit instruction on my expectations for book club, I would never interfere with fishbowl interactions. Instead, I planned to include minilessons at another time during Book Club. If students looked to me for direction during fishbowl, I reminded them I was just another audience member who must not interrupt their conversation to make comments or ask questions. Such practices enabled my students to assume responsibility and ownership over the discussion.

With this clearly stated, I began planning instructional support for fishbowl, just as I had provided such support for using reading logs. I focused each lesson on either *how* to interact or *what* might be appropriate to include. For example, one problem relating to *how* to interact seemed centered on turn-taking. I decided to lead a whole-class discussion comparing turn-taking in which turns are determined in advance (e.g., counting off during games), to instances in which turns are less structured, such as during conversations on the playground or at the dinner table. Within a short time, students began to negotiate turn-taking.

I began noticing how my explicit instruction on both how and what to discuss began to influence their fishbowl discussions so that they were more like the book clubs of their older peers. They began to draw easily on their logs as a basis for conversations and to call on members of the audience to contribute ideas when appropriate. This larger audience group facilitated extended, lively conversations that students were able to sustain according to the upper-elementary model. With fishbowl, we all listened to the book club discussion and entered into it from the audience. Our whole-class discussions often provided a context for discussing the quality of the conversation so that students were learning how to evaluate a good discussion. For example, sitting in the audience made it clear to students that not everyone could talk at once. At the same time, it also was apparent that fishbowl members need not raise their hands before contributing an idea. This led to a discussion about what "overlapping speech" is and when it is appropriate, helping establish the difference between rude interruptions and excitement that leads to shared response. Further, students noted that discussions are two-sided: Someone says something and someone else responds. Participants can ask questions, agree with a point, or disagree, but silence does not create good conversations.

Thus, I have modified the discussion portion of the original Book Club model by integrating book club with community share to create fishbowl. This meets my needs as an early elementary teacher and, more importantly, the needs of my students while still maintaining the features and benefits of each Book Club component.

A fishbowl discussion. To illustrate how third-grade students can indeed conduct their own conversations related to texts after explicit instruction on both how and what to discuss, I have included a fishbowl discussion that is typical of many I have observed in my class: (1) It reveals students' definite ideas about the human condition; (2) students are passionate in their opinions; (3) the discussion is characterized by depth of thought; and (4) the discussion becomes a place to clarify ideas encountered in the text.

These students had just finished the first chapter of *Charlotte's Web*. A litter of pigs had been born, and Fern's father decided to kill the runt. Notice the ease with which the discussion begins, its natural flow as students comment on one another's ideas, and the substantive nature of the content.

Paul: All right, I'll go first. I wonder if she loves the pig more than anyone.
Mary: I think she should love her father and mother.
Paul: Yeah, maybe her mother but not her father.
Galena: Well, if she loves her mother, she can love her father.
Paul: No, she should not love her father because he is going to kill Wilbur.

Mario: Well, I think you should love everybody in your family. Fern can love her mom and dad and still love Wilbur.

Paul: No way! Fern's dad was going to kill Wilbur so now she should just love her mom.

Manual: Yeah, but her dad didn't kill Wilbur so I think she should just put all that behind her and go on.

Jolene: I don't agree with Paul. She should love her mom and dad even if her father was going to kill Wilbur. And there's something I don't get. Why did he want to kill Wilbur in the first place?

Manual: Fern's father did not think that she would take care of Wilbur so they were going to kill the pig.

Jolene: It is not right to kill something 'cause someone else might not take care of it.

Manual: That's not why they were going to kill Wilbur. It has something to do with the pig being the littlest.

Jolene: Well, that's even worse! Killing it because it's the smallest!

This fishbowl discussion illustrates that third graders are not only able to hold an interesting conversation, but they can also reveal empathy for others, even a tiny piglet. Jolene passionately pleaded for Wilbur's life, first because she thought it was wrong to kill a living animal, then with more outrage when she learned that Wilbur had to die because he was the smallest. While Jolene was outraged, Manual knew something about life on a farm and had a better understanding of the story, so he tried to clarify this for Jolene.

Despite using Book Club for several years now, I am continually struck by the quality and depth of these student-led discussions—a quality and depth of understanding I rarely found when simply asking comprehension questions. I often sit back in amazement as my third graders offer their thoughts about others' responses, asking interesting questions that I may never have thought to ask. While my students initially were hesitant to volunteer for fishbowl, it now is almost everyone's favorite time of the day.

CONCLUDING COMMENTS

I had sought a reading program that used "real" literature, emphasized writing and talking about books, and allowed direct instruction in reading skills and strategies while also emphasizing personal response to literature. I have found all these opportunities with Book Club. The program has provided a context in which I can meet my goals for sharing quality literature, creating authentic circumstances for student ownership, allowing personal oral and written response, and providing a place to fulfill the needs of my district's curriculum. Teachers who share similar goals for their students will be able to adopt, and adapt, Book Club. Perhaps most importantly, I have learned that as teachers, we must be patient as we consider the most appropriate forms of instruction for our students and create interesting learning contexts. I frequently remind myself that just as my students are in a process of reading and writing, so are they in a process of learning to discuss. Like my students, I am continually in a process of initiating and fine-tuning the best literacy curriculum I can create.

COMMENTARY

LEE GALDA

Like other good ideas, the idea of Book Club is one that many teachers want to "borrow" and use in their own classrooms. When Pam Scherer decided to try Book Club with her second- and third-grade students, she already knew something very important: She would have to understand the principles of Book Club and then modify the existing structures to suit the needs and abilities of her students. Her report of how she did this is a model of effective curricular change.

Because she is a good teacher, Pam is also an avid learner, and she sensed a *need* for a change in her teaching because she was closely observing her students and assessing her practice. She then sought out the ideas and suggestions of *colleagues* whom she respected. Simultaneously, she examined the *knowledge* she had about how children became literate. She then examined Book Club as a model and *modified* it to fit her needs, continuing to make changes as she began implementing it. Given this, I assume that she will continue to *monitor* and *modify* her practices as she and her students grow in their literacy abilities.

As a model, Book Club offers advantages that many other classroom practices do not. First, it effectively links the English language arts—reading, writing, speaking, and listening—meaningfully, through children's literature. Second, it allows teachers like Pam to find a balance between decontextualized skill instruction and uninterrupted reading through mechanisms like the reading log. Third, it builds on the social nature of the classroom by providing opportunities for students to interact, but it does so in a structured manner because opportunities for whole-class and small-group interaction are part of each session. Fourth, it provides many opportunities for teacher demonstrations of the behaviors of fluent readers before, during, and after reading.

Despite these strengths, however, Book Club does not create a complete reading/language arts program, and Pam is well aware of this. The tension between selecting books that provoke engaged reading and interesting discussions and books that are accessible to struggling (or simply younger) readers is apparent. Sometimes Book Club needs to be supplemented with books that help developing readers build fluency. There is also a tension between teacher and group selection of books and individual interests. An independent reading program provides students with opportunities to pursue their own interests perhaps unrelated to Book Club. The same holds true with writing. While Book Club provides opportunities for understanding a text, reflecting on one's ideas through writing, and writing in a number of formats, time spent writing that is unrelated to Book Club is also an important part of a balanced language arts program.

Likewise, exploring the author's craft both within and outside the Book Club format is an important component of language arts instruction. While focusing on interesting ideas and powerful responses to engaging texts is a crucial first step, time spent considering how the author constructed the text, speculating on why he or she might have made particular decisions, and the effect of text structures, word choices, and so forth on the reader is also crucial. Intertextual connections, often first built through content, need to be built through style as well. Teacher demonstrations, interventions in book club discussions, and written response prompts can be devised to help children focus on the craft of the authors they are reading. For example, when Pam's students discuss Fern's love for her father and his attempted slaughter of Wilbur, the conversation could be pushed toward a consideration of why E. B. White began his book the way he did.

The careful balance between teacher direction and collaborative insight that is possible with Book Club means that teachers like Pam, ever alert for a "teachable moment," will have to make difficult decisions. Perhaps the most difficult balancing act of all for teachers is to remain quiet when their voices will intrude in the important business of the social construction of meaning and to intrude to nudge students toward an elaborated understanding of the role of the author and the effect of the text on their own responses. Discussions, like conversations, cannot be planned, and knowing if, when, and what to contribute to a Book Club discussion is a skill not easily learned.

Also, like any routine, it is easy to continue practices that are no longer necessary. Pam's fishbowl adaptation of small-group discussions may not be necessary once her students are adept at holding productive discussions. Perhaps students became increasingly able to manage independently. I wonder what support Pam provided to move her students toward independence. That is, how and when did she remove the scaffold of the fishbowl?

I also wonder how the children's responses changed over time and across texts. Did their intertextual connections continue to develop and become cumulative? For Pam's future research, an interesting exercise might be to go back to a previously read text and reread it, then compare the original and the later discussion to determine what is different and what remains the same. It would also be interesting to know how the group discussions influence children's individual responses across time and whether the reading logs offer any evidence of changes in response due to group discussions.

A literature- and language-rich classroom such as Pam's, with an open discussion format like fishbowl, presents opportunities for us to watch as children learn to build meaning in collaboration with their peers. If we watch and listen carefully, we cannot help but learn more about how children help themselves and one another become meaning-makers.

CHAPTER 13

They Can Do It Too!

Book Club with First and Second Graders

KRISTIN WALDEN GRATTAN

As a teacher-researcher who has used Book Club with early elementary students, I am convinced that the program is useful for students of any age. Over the past four years, I have modified the basic Book Club model based on the needs of my younger students. This chapter describes my Book Club odyssey, from my initial attraction to the program through first attempts to introduce my students to student-led discussions through the modifications I initiated as I used Book Club with first- and second-grade students. I end with an overview of Book Club with my most recent first-grade classroom.

MY ATTRACTION TO BOOK CLUB

In the mid- to late 1970s, I taught first, second, fifth, and sixth grades before leaving the classroom to raise my children. Between 1980 and 1988, I taught English as a second language for adult learners. During my time as an ESL instructor, I experienced the ways conversation and social settings enhance learning. I enrolled in several classes at nearby Michigan State University to update my credentials as well as learn about new instructional practices. When I returned to teaching elementary school in 1988, I spent the next two years in first-grade classrooms and, concurrently, returned to graduate school. I had always been interested in children's literature, and I wanted to study new trends and issues in this area, so I enrolled in the literacy master's program. It was during this course of study that I began to rethink my assumptions about learning in general and the teaching of literacy in particular.

In the 1970s I viewed reading as a solitary activity where students demonstrated their success through their ability to decode words. However, during the 1980s and 1990s, I began to rethink this. Over time, I have come to believe that reading is essentially a social activity. My changing stance has been supported by my experiences in the classroom, by what I was learning in the M.A. program through conversations with colleagues and professors, and through reading articles about literacy acquisition. For example, I read articles about Reciprocal Teaching by Palincsar and Brown that described how children's learning was enhanced through discourse about text. I was impressed by their argument that children need to be taught specific strategies to formulate, summarize, and clarify the material they read (e.g., Brown & Palincsar, 1989). I also read articles by G. Wells (1990a, 1990b; G. Wells, Chang, & Maher, 1990) that described how important talk about text is for encouraging "literate thinking." Wells also wrote about two responses to literature that I found interesting, an "outer-world" response, consisting of predictions and material aspects of the story, and an "inner-world" response, depicting values, feelings, and intentions. These seemed similar to the view held by Rosenblatt (1968), who described efferent reading as reading to find information and aesthetic reading as the reader's affective personal response to text. I thought that Book Club might provide an opportunity for my students to learn about aesthetic reading of literature.

I first heard about the Book Club program from Ginny Goatley, a fellow student. We often discussed her work as a research assistant working on the Book Club project in Laura Pardo's classroom. Ginny briefly described Book Club, which I thought was interesting, but I was more interested in a program tailored specifically to early literacy learning.

The next term, Susan McMahon was a co-instructor of one of my classes and I learned more about the Book Club program: its emphasis on quality literature and the instructional component that taught specific strategies that encouraged and valued students' personal responses to literature. I was becoming increasingly intrigued by encouraging students to read, discuss, and write about literature. I was also attracted by Book Club's recognition that learning occurs in social settings. As my professor the following term, Taffy Raphael described Laura's classroom and showed us segments of a videotape of her third-grade classroom (R. C. Anderson & Au, 1992)—a different classroom from that described in Chapter 11. This videotape greatly influenced my thinking about how effective co-operative groups and community share could be.

Finally, in 1993, I was one of the founding members of the Teacher Research Inquiry Group, a group of professionals from classrooms and the university who were interested in teacher research. Among the group were Laura, Kathy Highfield, Pam Scherer, and Julie Folkert, all of whom were interested in or using the Book Club program in their classrooms. Our monthly meetings gave me a chance to learn more about Book Club from my colleagues and begin to think about ways that Book Club could be used effectively with first and second graders.

FIRST-GRADE STUDENTS' DISCUSSIONS: THE CHALLENGES WE FACE

When I first initiated Book Club in my classroom, both my students and I were relatively naive about how to maintain meaningful discussion. The discussion that follows illustrates where my students and I began and lays a foundation for considering the kinds of changes I have seen in my students' discussion abilities over the four years I have used Book Club. This discussion among a group of first graders occurred late in the spring of 1992, the first year I had introduced Book Club to my students. These students had participated in many teacher-led discussions and had been encouraged to respond to the literature they read and heard. Though I had not taught them specific ways of responding or strategies for maintaining a discussion on their own, I had hoped that the other classroom experiences would provide a sufficient basis to support their independent discussion.

I assembled five students around a small table. In the center were a tape recorder and copies of Van Allsburg's (1981) *Jumanji*, a book I had just read to them. I explained that they would be discussing the book I had just read aloud. Amy spoke up right away: "I don't know what *discuss* means." I looked at the children seated around the small table and felt a twinge of misgiving, thinking to myself, "I don't know if this will work. I don't know if children this age can be expected to talk about a book without an adult to monitor and lead the discussion. What am I doing? Will this be a waste of time?"

Smiling brightly, I answered Amy. "That's a good place to start. What *does discuss* mean? *Discuss* means 'to talk about.'" The five of you will sit around this table and talk about the book I just read aloud. I will be here for a few minutes at the beginning, but I would like you to try to talk about or discuss the book without my help."

Mark nodded his head. "I'll go first." He looked at his literature log and read, "I wasn't thinking anything." Amy interrupted him with an air of authority: "This is reading, Mark, not discussing!" The other four members of the group ignored Amy's remarks and continued to read from their literature logs in a round-robin fashion, taking individual turns until each had read aloud his or her response. Amy interrupted each reader with the admonition: "This isn't discussing! This is reading!"

This discussion showed me that my first graders were not sure what to do when asked to discuss a book in a small group. Though I knew from my colleagues who used Book Club in upper-elementary grades that discussion content and format may be difficult for older students, I thought that my year-long emphasis on writing and literature had adequately prepared my students for leading their own discussions. I had had students write every day, familiarized them with a range of literature, and led discussions encouraging personal responses. While this had enabled my students to write interesting responses to my prompts and participate effectively in teacher-led interactions, it had not prepared them to lead their own discussions.

I learned that to implement Book Club effectively, I had to provide more explicit teaching. Just as my students needed guided practice, modeling, and explicit instruction in skills and strategies for reading and writing, they needed similar support to participate effectively in small-group discussions. Teacher-led discussions alone will not prepare children to lead their own interactions about books. I needed to think seriously about how the Book Club model could be adapted to help lower-elementary children learn how to respond to books and participate in student-led discussions.

MODIFYING BOOK CLUB TO MEET
THE NEEDS OF YOUNG STUDENTS

Despite the fact that Book Club had only been researched with students at the upper-elementary level, I was excited about the concept of using student-led discussion groups at the early elementary level. I had two basic questions: What current literacy activities in my classroom could I build on to include the Book Club components? What modifications of the components could I make so my first-grade students could experience Book Club? I reviewed the four basic components of Book Club that were designed to support the student-led discussion groups and compared them to my current teaching.

Three components—reading, writing, and community share—did not raise many concerns for me in terms of my students' ability to participate, since I already emphasized many literacy activities in my classroom (see Figure 13.1). My students read and wrote every day—sometimes in pairs, sometimes accompanied by a tape-recorded passage. I read aloud to my students daily, and I encouraged informal conversations about the literature I read. They also wrote daily during writer's workshop (Graves, 1983), and used their writing skills to respond to books I read aloud. During whole-group instruction I taught specific strategies and skills for reading and writing and modeled various responses to literature. Considering these aspects of my existing pro-

FIGURE 13.1. September and October Regular Classroom Literacy
Events

Literacy Event	Description	Times
Read around the room	Read bulletin boards, words and text hanging in room (including titles of books, children's names, rules, poems, songs, and chants displayed). Format is "echo" read followed by volunteers to read aloud.	Weekly to biweekly
Phonics program	Formal program combining penmanship and letter sounds	Daily
Morning message	Board message: Good Morning Room 102! It is [day]. It is [date]. [3–4 sentences about classroom and personal news] Group oral activity (model content representation, grammar, spelling), then messages typed into computer and printed for later illustration and reading.	Daily
Words we know	Students bring in words from environmental print, contribute to chart paper by copying or pasting (if from newspaper, magazine, box, etc.)	Several times a week
Writing workshop	Process writing emphasizing personal experience stories and drawings, movement from emergent to conventional use of print	Daily
Read-aloud	Teacher read-aloud from numerous books, some theme-related to Book Club books, others special interest, introduce author and illustrators, and so forth; students maintained response to the read aloud in a literature log.	Once to several times daily
Choral reading	Poems, chants on chart paper, read together. Followed by analysis of words and letter–sound correspondence	Daily
Take home books	Individual booklets of Choral Reading poems and chants, made for students to take home and read for signatures of who listened to them read. When they have collected a specific number of signatures, they return to school for a sticker.	3–4 per week
Sight words/basal reading program	Sight-word instruction based on those listed in the scope-sequence of the commercial program adopted within the district. Often taught using flashcards hung in room in odd places. Students must read the word (or sentence) to enter the room.	Daily
Silent reading	Begins as structured choice from set of books on a table, lasting 5 minutes, evolves to 10–15 minutes of reading any book of their choice	Daily
Special events	Literacy events that vary over the year: baking and cooking on Fridays; reader's theater; puppet shows for retelling of read-aloud stories	Varies
Newspaper and magazine activities	Research to find letters, words, some content where appropriate	Varies

gram, I decided I could easily integrate the reading, writing, and community share components of Book Club.

My First Year Using Book Club at the First-Grade Level

As the above discussion demonstrated, my first graders struggled both with the concept of discussion itself and with understanding how to participate in student-led discussions. My other early attempts resulted in similar findings. For example, I once read aloud a predictable picture book, *If You Give a Mouse a Cookie* (Numeroff, 1985), a circular story sequencing events following a young boy giving a mouse a cookie.

After listening to the story, the children responded to the story in writing. After completing their responses, they joined prearranged small groups for discussion. Like their peers, these students tended to read, in round-robin turn-taking, what they had written on their response papers. Their responses simply listed what each liked or disliked about the book without responding to one anothers' comments.

As I analyzed their discussions from these early book club experiences, I tried to understand what contributed to students' difficulties. One explanation related to my instruction. It became clear that, although I had encouraged literary discussions throughout the year, I had never been explicit about my expectations. I thought about Duffy and Roehler's (1987) stress on explicit teaching and realized that I needed to define *discussion*, explain participation, and clarify its importance.

Just as Laura has done with her older students (see Chapters 5 and 11), I began to teach discussion techniques explicitly. Together, my students and I created a definition of discussion and listed some basic rules to follow:

Discussion Guidelines

- Accept and respect what others say
- Respond by listening, asking questions, or making comments
- Look at the person who is talking
- May interrupt, but with courtesy

I also realized I could help students connect their literature discussions to the variety of discussions they engaged in throughout the day.

My initial efforts with Book Club in first grade led to somewhat improved conversations, so I felt confident that I could be successful with more reflection on my past instruction. I spent the summer analyzing some of the discussions and planning for the following year. As part of my analysis, I thought about the differences in the texts that I read over the year. Some books, such as *If You Give a Mouse a Cookie*, had simple story lines and, while easily understood by young students, offered little in the way of thought-provoking issues. Others, such as Naylor's (1991) *Shiloh*, were more complex and beyond the reading level of my first graders but seemed to lend themselves to debates over controversial issues. In fact, my students had initiated many spontaneous conversations in the whole-class setting during some of the read-aloud books. In my journal I noted, "Maybe the failure of some of my early Book Club discussion groups was not only the result of my students' inexperience in discussing the literature, but due to the basic simplicity of the plot and the lack of interesting characters in the selections I had chosen to read. What if I began the year with a great novel, one that would probably promote spontaneous conversation about the motives of the characters or the turns of the plot?"

Since most of the texts students could read independently did not contain the complex plots and characters that would promote the discussions I envisioned, I decided to base my next attempt using Book Club solely on read-aloud novels dealing with debatable issues. My decision was supported by discussions with colleagues who were using Book Club with somewhat older students (see Chapters 11 and 14). As I planned my curriculum for my second year of Book Club, I focused on four areas: (1) literature response logs, (2) directed discussions related to read-aloud selections, (3) student reading of grade-level books, and (4) introduction of "fishbowl" (see Chapter 12).

Book Club Years 2 and 3: A New Grade and New Focus

Despite being shifted from first to second grade, I began my second year of using Book Club building on what I had learned from my first graders. As a class, we began by working together to define *discussion*, describing how to discuss and sharing ideas about why interactions about texts were important. Second, we created rules to guide our discussions. Third, I read chapter books for the Book Club discussions. Fourth, I gave my students literature response logs and asked them to create (i.e., write or draw) a written response at the end of each chapter I read. I hoped such guidance prepared students to engage in their own discussions about texts.

Literature logs for early elementary students. I remembered that students at the upper-elementary level used literature logs to record their ongoing feelings, thoughts, and predictions about the books as they read them. I felt written logs were important because they also provided me with records of the students' understandings. I remembered that Laura often used whole-class writing prompts to help students focus and specifically to teach students various ways to think about and respond to texts. I used literature logs in the same way with my lower-elementary students. Like the upper-elementary teachers, in addition to free-choice responses I used prompts to encourage students to notice and reflect on certain literary elements, such as setting or characterization, and make connections between their own lives and the texts. Specific prompts often provided a focus for students to begin writing; however, gradually, they no longer needed them. As they became more involved with the story, they tended to use their literature logs to clarify their understanding of the story as it unfolded (Farris, 1989).

Before I began formal evaluation of the quality of the student-led discussions, I let them practice for three weeks, using the literature logs as a basis of the book club discussions. When I began observing the small groups, I was reminded of Amy's comment: "This isn't discussing! This is reading!" While the second graders' literature logs contained many interesting ideas, the small-group discussions did not reflect them. Instead, students read their entries in a round-robin fashion, without interaction or response. I returned to my earlier inquiry question: How could I more explicitly guide my students to take responsibility for leading discussions about the books we read?

Initiating directed discussion with literature logs. I was concerned that, while students had developed interesting ways of responding in writing, they did not convey them to their peers during their discussions. Further, they did not connect their responses to those of their peers. As I reflected on this, it appeared that students needed more guidance for sharing personal response in a small group. Thus I decided to incorporate literature log sharing into community share. In such a setting, I could both monitor and model how to value and react to the students' responses. I defined this as "directed discussion."

During directed discussion, I asked students to volunteer to read their literature log entries aloud and invited others to respond with observations, comments, or questions. With my guidance, they practiced the conversational rules we had established to promote better discussions, sharing their thoughts and feelings about a novel. The example that follows illustrates direct discussion.

I read *Shiloh* to the students, one chapter per day. Naylor tells a moving story about Marty and his struggle to remain true to his family's values, as he secretly takes care of a dog he thinks is being mistreated by its owner. Marty agonizes over every decision he makes. Students' literature response entries varied greatly, from descriptive pictures to evaluations of Marty's actions.

Early in my adaptation of directed discussion, I focused on predictions of story events and literary elements, such as tone, setting, and identifying main characters. During this phase, Goldie drew a picture of a dog with a

FIGURE 13.2. Goldie's Log Entry

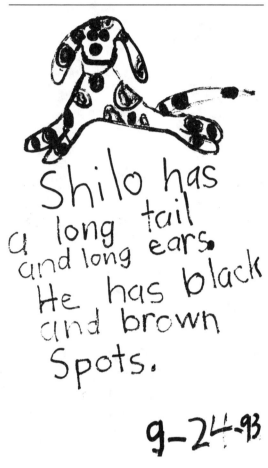

Shilo has a long tail and long ears. He has black and brown spots.

9-24-93

simple description (see Figure 13.2). Her entry reflects one of my focus points during direct discussion.

Later in the book, as events became more complicated, many issues emerged in students' responses, prompting debate about which path Marty should follow. The class became divided into two camps, those who believed that Marty should continue to hide Shiloh and those who felt that he should confide in his parents. Jessie's log entry (see Figure 13.3) suggests that it is worth lying to keep the dog's owner from taking and abusing the dog, while Sam's entry (see Figure 13.4) defines Marty's problem as having lied to his

FIGURE 13.3.   Jessie's Log Entry

It is worth it I think.
I don't hope Judd Travis
does not take the dog.

parents. During directed discussion, the whole class continued to debate this moral issue. Eventually, they decided that problems are easier to confront if they are not hidden, since hiding them is often more challenging than the original problem. This discussion was notably distinct from earlier ones because students responded by reacting to the content and debating the emerging issues.

FIGURE 13.4.   Sam's Log Entry

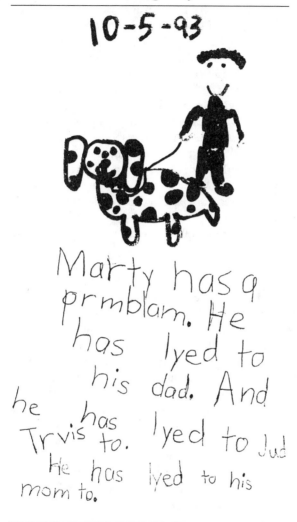

10-5-93

Marty has a prmblam. He has lyed to his dad. And he has lyed to Trvis to. He has lyed to Jud He has lyed to his mom to.

Independent reading and small-group activities. I was encouraged by directed discussions. Now that my book clubs, based on read-aloud selections, were underway, I turned to the question of how to facilitate students' articulation of responses to grade-level texts. Although I used a basal series required by my district for part of my reading instruction, I wanted to expand the instructional component to include literature that the students were able to decode independently. Because many of the books suitable for early second graders do not lend themselves to extensive discussions, I decided to encourage students to identify and discuss various literary elements, such as characterization, setting, and plot. I usually began with book talks about multiple books for which I had several copies. Then children chose which book they wanted to read. Once six people had chosen a book, it was considered a "closed group"; no other child could read that text at that time. The children read selections independently, and I provided each group a specific assignment to promote awareness of literary elements present in even the simplest of stories. Some of these were similar to responses used in upper-elementary grades: Draw the major characters and describe them, compare the book with another by the same author, make a poster advertising the book, or create a puppet show or skit to retell or change the ending of the story. I wanted to encourage children to read a selection independently, but I also wanted to encourage student interactions about books. Group discussions evolved because students had to work collaboratively to complete a group project to present to the class.

These activities helped the groups in two ways. First, they provided a focus and encouraged students to discuss books within the framework of specific assignments. Second, it provided opportunities to identify various literary aspects. Three months into the school year, I was pleased with the progress my class was making. They were participating in thoughtful, directed discussions during community share; they were reading grade-level texts independently; they were working with peers to identify specific literary elements; and they were creating projects to demonstrate their understanding of these elements.

At the same time, I was not completely satisfied. Although I felt that my modifications promoted student-to-student interaction and discourse about text, I still wanted to follow the original Book Club model that emphasized student-led discussions. I was faced with another question: How could I monitor and guide my students as they assumed responsibility for leading discussions about books? I was reluctant to place students into small groups to discuss a book since they still needed guidance, but I needed to help them take on responsibility. Pam told me about her idea of "fishbowl" (Chapter 12), which I began reflecting on as a means of addressing my concerns and the needs of my students.

Fishbowl in a second-grade classroom. In December, when the students were able to decode more sophisticated texts, I introduced fishbowl. After they read their books independently and wrote in their literature logs, I explained that four or five volunteers would sit at a table in the center of the room. Their role would be to talk to one another about the book they had read. The audience's role was to listen carefully. There were three empty chairs around the table. I explained that visitors from the audience could enter the discussion to add comments. I set no limits on how long the visits or discussions might last, but most fishbowl discussions lasted a total of five to ten minutes. Then the audience discussed and evaluated the small-group interaction.

During the first fishbowl, students relied heavily on their literature logs, so, the next time, I reversed the order of the written and oral responses. That is, I had the fishbowl occur before students had written anything in their logs. Interestingly, students seemed more eager to write after the discussion because they appeared to be thinking about the book in new ways. Fishbowl provided my missing component by enabling students to participate in small-group discussions. My modifications of Book Club were consistent with the original framework since I used reading, writing, and instruction to support student-led discussion groups. At the same time, grade-level considerations led me to make four basic changes not included in the original implementation: (1) I read aloud texts students could not read themselves to provide rich sources of ideas for discussion; (2) I drew students' attention to specific literary elements as a focus for their discussion when I incorporated texts my students could read independently; (3) I structured fishbowl to allow students to lead their own discussions with support; and (4) I asked students to write in their logs *after* discussion.

As I reflect on my journey of exploring and modifying Book Club to meet my classroom needs, I realize that it was a rather bumpy road. At the same time, it was personally and professionally rewarding. I was not always confident I would find answers to my questions, and I did not know where each discussion would lead; however, I discovered that modeling and modification resulted in emergent readers becoming better at articulating their responses to literature and entertaining new perspectives as discussions moved in unanticipated directions. I became closer to my students as we worked together to understand aspects of literature that were important to us. We valued one another's opinions and thoughts about the literature we read; their comments sometimes were more insightful than mine. Most importantly, they no longer looked to me for all of the answers. They contemplated and discussed issues important to them, constructing meaningful answers to their questions. Book Club had become a fascinating and purposeful way to teach reading, so I planned to use it in my future second-grade classrooms. Unfortunately, that was not to happen. When I returned the next school year, I was reassigned to first grade.

Book Club in Its Fourth Year: A Return to First Grade

As I began the year, I decided to use my modified version of Book Club with the first graders. One of my goals was to have fishbowl in place by spring term.

Identifying students' goals. I began by inviting my new students and their parents to visit my classroom the day before school started. I asked the children to fill out a survey (with help from their parents) listing what they hoped to learn in first grade and what they were looking forward to. I tallied the responses and found that the overwhelming majority indicated that they wanted either to learn to read or to improve their reading skills.

Initiating basic literacy instruction. Teaching 6- and 7-year-olds how to read is the first-grade teacher's greatest challenge. Children enter with a range of abilities, from beginning readers to children who still do not know the basic conventions of print. In addition to working with a range of abilities, I also have a range of content within literacy education to teach. Students need to learn about different genres; be able to compare and contrast different stories; make conclusions and predictions about the characters, setting, and plots; and learn about author's craft. I embed instruction about letters, phonics, and word families within meaningful texts related to their own lives and experiences. That fall, I returned to the literacy events I had stressed with my previous first-grade class (see Figure 13.1).

Within these literacy events, the reading instruction is twofold. I teach specific skills and strategies with both a basal reading program and many easy beginning-reading books. In addition, I provide children with opportunities to perform classic rhymes, folktales, poems and familiar songs. I find that such varied activities make learning to read meaningful and exciting.

Introducing literature study. While learning to read is the most difficult task facing first graders, I introduce literature study because it provides an alternative message. I want my students to know reading is more than the mastery of basic skills. I help them expand their definitions to include reflective and emotional response (Rosenblatt, 1968; G. Wells, 1990b).

As with the second graders, I found that the selections for the first graders must be sophisticated, containing well-defined characters and problems to prompt extensive discussions. Yet books worthy of discussion were beyond the ability of most first graders to read independently. Therefore I began to read aloud on the very first day of school. I chose the books for the excellence of the illustrations and the complexity of the plot. I often read the entire body of work by a certain author or books that centered on a certain theme or represented a certain genre. I chose books for the beauty of their language or for the pure enjoyment of their story. I read books for the pleasure it gave the children. I chose the subsequent discussions and activities to prepare students for the book club fishbowl discussions I envisioned for the second half of the year.

Introducing literature logs. I introduced my students to written response to literature in October. I gave each a small booklet, consisting of five sheets of paper stapled together. They wrote "My Book Log" on the cover. After I read a selected book aloud, they copied the title on one page and wrote or drew a response below. I let them chose the topic for the first several times, then began providing specific prompts, such as "What was your favorite part?" "Did this book remind you of anything that happened to you or someone you know?" "Draw and label the main characters." At the beginning of the year, most of the students were more comfortable drawing pictures, with one or two letters representing words. By December they were listing the characters and writing a sentence or two about the story. The level of response varied with the abilities of the children, but each of the students was able to experiment with different ways of responding to literature.

Introducing community share. Community share at the first-grade level was similar to the directed discussion I initiated with second graders; however, I had to model more since they frequently resorted to a litany of "My favorite part was . . . " comments. Whole-group sharing time provided me an opportunity to model and encourage a range of responses and an occasion for students to contribute their ideas.

Introducing student-led discussions through fishbowl. In January, we were ready for fishbowl. Since their fishbowl discussions typically lasted only about three to five minutes, this was an easy addition to our daily routine. Each small-group discussion was followed by visitors, then comments during a whole-group discussion related to the ideas brought up in fishbowl.

As I modified my teaching and implementation of Book Club over four years, I saw changes in how students engaged in literature discussions. A fantasy unit from the spring of that year illustrates how my modifications had come together. Students' discussions from that unit reflected higher levels of engagement, more meaningful exchanges among the students, and stronger connections across texts. Within one week, I read aloud four picture books and encouraged students to respond in both written and oral forms (see Figure 13.5).

On the fifth day of the unit, five volunteers—Liz, Pat, John, Jay, and Linn—eagerly moved to the small table for a fishbowl discussion. As soon as everyone was seated, Liz began.

Liz: *Hey, Al!* was like *The Magic Finger.*
Pat: I thought it was just like *The Magic Finger* because in *The Magic Finger* they turned into birds and then they turned back.

FIGURE 13.5.   Fantasy Unit

Day	Book Read	Plot Summary	Minilesson: Whole Group	Oral Response	Written Response
Monday	Louis the Fish (Yorinks, 1980)	A butcher who loves fish wakes up one morning and is delighted to find out that he has become a fish	(1) Elements of fantasy, emphasis on magical or fantastical happenings that change life of characters (2) Introduce chart of book title, characters, plot summary	Community share and fishbowl discussion	Prompt: If you could turn into something you love, what would you turn into? How would you feel?
Tuesday	The Girl Who Loved Wild Horses (Gobel, 1978)	Modern version of a Native American legend about a girl who becomes a horse	Add second book to chart	Community share and fishbowl discussion	Prompt: Free write
Wednesday	The Magic Finger (Dahl, 1966)	A girl who turns her next-door neighbors into small people with duck wings	Add third book to chart	Community share and fishbowl discussion	Prompt: Free write
Thursday	Hey, Al! (Yorinks, 1986)	A janitor whose life is boring travels to a island	Add fourth book to chart, as well as two fantasies brought in by two students	Community share and fishbowl discussion	Prompt: Free write
Friday			Add another fantasy brought in by student to chart	Fishbowl discussion: intertextual connections	

John: They didn't want to be birds in both books.

Liz: They didn't want to be birds in *The Magic Finger* because life was hard. They had to build nests and eat worms. Al wanted to be home.

Jay: *Hey, Al!* was like *Louis the Fish* because they both wanted a new life. But they were happy at the end.

Linn: Like *The Girl Who Loved Wild Horses* was happy. (*Britt and Van, two students from the rest of class who had been observing quietly, move to two empty chairs at the table.*)

Britt: Like Louis, when Al went to the sky he was happy at first.

Liz: They weren't happy in *The Magic Finger* when they were birds.

Van: In *The Magic Finger* and *Hey, Al!* they were happy at the end.

Jay: They were the same because at the end they change back to normal.

This discussion demonstrates the children's ability to participate in a quality book club discussion. Further, the content reflects a sophistication uncharacteristic of the book clubs from my earlier experiences with first graders who were unsure of what it meant to discuss a book. In the spring of 1995, my students were making intertextual connections among the four books, focusing on characters, plots, and themes. The modifications I initiated in Book Club helped my students know what constituted a meaningful conversation and how to interact with peers. It was clear that students were aware of and speaking confidently about a number of texts.

This discussion was different for a number of reasons. First, these students had had explicit modeling and teaching related to discussion techniques every day all year. Second, they responded to books in writing every day. Third, they shared their responses with their peers. Clearly, they had learned a lot. However, not only did the children's ability to respond change dramatically in four years, but so did I. I changed the way I value, teach, and model ways of responding to and discussing a story. The first time I tried Book Club in 1992, I did not provide examples of what a discussion was or give them opportunities to practice. I have found that a successful Book Club requires a great deal of explicit teaching at any level, particularly at the early grades.

COMMENTARY

BARBARA M. TAYLOR

Kristin Grattan's chapter about using Book Club with first and second graders has a lot to say to us about learning. I was struck by three very different but important points that were made as her story unfolded.

First, the descriptions of what Kristin's students accomplished reminds us that although children in first and second grade may be regarded as little kids who cannot do very much, this is really an unfounded viewpoint. With sufficient modeling, guidance, and support – ingredients that Kristin reminds us are essential – 6-, 7-, and 8-year-olds can learn to write a variety of responses to literature in their literature logs. They can be taught to carry on sophisticated conversations about books (McGee, 1992). The description of the seven children in Kristin's class comparing *Hey Al!*, *The Magic Finger*, *Louis The Fish*, and *The Girl Who Loved Wild Horses* was impressive. It served as a powerful reminder that primary grade children can engage in many challenging activities if we teach them well, give them a chance to try, and have high expectations for them.

One way to extend the fantasy unit outlined in Figure 13.5 would be to increase the number of prompts calling for aesthetic response. Although important, discussions on elements of fantasy and intertextual connections are likely to evoke different responses in children. Questions like "How did you feel when the girl turned into a horse at the end of *The Girl Who Loved Wild Horses*"? and "What or whom do you like to pretend to be when you are playing?" would tend to evoke personal, aesthetic responses, thus helping students learn to adopt an aesthetic stance toward literature (Rosenblatt, 1991a; Zarillo, 1991).

A second important point about learning that came out in Kristin's chapter is that learning how to do something new as a teacher takes time. Kristin describes in detail the evolutionary process she went through as a teacher to get her first- and second-grade students to the point where they were successful participants in the Book Club program. She was patient with her students and herself, but she also kept looking for new ways to improve as a teacher using Book Club. It is important for us to realize, or be reminded, that as we embark on major curricular changes as teachers, we must be patient. A new way of teaching will not fall into place overnight, or perhaps even over the course of an entire school year. Kristin's journey with Book

Club took place over four school years. Her persistence was truly commendable. She also points out the importance of having a teacher support group during the change process. As she met regularly with colleagues in the Teacher Research Inquiry Group, she was able to share ideas, learn about new techniques from others, and gain support for variations of Book Clubs that she wished to try with her primary grade students.

The third, and perhaps most important, point about learning that was so well communicated in Kristin's chapter deals with the benefits of learning within a social setting. Just after I read Kristin's chapter, I happened to read a somber article in *Science* entitled "Electronics and the Dim Future of the University" (Noam, 1995). This piece focused on the value of "mentoring, internalization, identification, role modeling, guidance, socialization, interaction, and group activity" (p. 249) as opposed to information dissemination in the university setting. In fact, the author of the article took the position that for universities to remain strong centers of learning they must recognize the importance of and take advantage of the communal aspects of learning that can take place in the classroom. I was struck by the fact that a similar message was coming out loud and clear in Kristin's chapter about the learning of first- and second-grade children. Kristin relates that she was initially attracted to Book Club in part because of its basic stance "that learning occurs in social settings." In her chapter, she provides many wonderful examples of how her students grew in their abilities to learn from one another as they participated in Book Club discussions.

I would argue that learning alone and learning together are both important. However, it is perhaps in the arena of learning within a social setting that we can accomplish the most as teachers (Johnson, Johnson, & Holubec, 1993). We should consistently take advantage of the social interactions that we can set up within our classroom community to enhance our students' learning. As Kristin tells us her story of implementing Book Club with first and second graders over four school years, we are reminded that teaching students to learn together takes time. We are also reminded that it is worth the effort because of the rich learning that takes place.

CHAPTER 14

Book Club

The Content-Area Connection

KATHY HIGHFIELD and JULIE FOLKERT

Recently thematic instruction has received increasing attention for its potential to help students seek connections across the school subjects, making their learning more meaningful. We have been involved in teaching through thematic units in social studies and literacy for the past three years, using Book Club as a framework for our program. In this chapter, we describe how our thematic teaching evolved and describe the thinking involved in integrating Book Club and social studies content.

CREATING A COLLABORATIVE RELATIONSHIP

We have worked together for the past four years, initially as graduate students in Michigan State University's master's program in literacy instruction, then as members of the Teacher Research Inquiry Group (Goatley et al., 1994). Our friendship and shared professional interests have made our collaboration an important part of our teaching.

When we entered the literacy master's program, we both had ideas and interests we hoped to develop through our coursework and interactions. We read about various theories of student learning, such as behaviorism, naturalism, cognitive science, and social constructivism (R. C. Anderson & Pearson, 1984; Gavelek, 1986; K. S. Goodman, 1976; Harker, 1987; McCarthey & Raphael, 1992; Pearson, 1994), developing a better understanding of the history of literacy instruction. We were attracted to and felt most comfortable with the precepts of the sociocultural perspective, resulting in our examination of our own teaching. Since students learn through social interaction, we decided to provide classroom contexts where discussion of ideas and learning is the accepted norm. We were dissatisfied with the existing reading programs in our schools, which tended either to emphasize teaching discrete skills or to deemphasize instruction, simply encouraging students to read more widely. As we began to think about how our practice fit our beliefs, it led to a search for different ways of organizing and teaching reading.

Because we were open to different ways of teaching, we were drawn to the idea of using the Book Club program when it was first introduced in our coursework because of the way it illustrated sociocultural principles. We liked the idea that Book Club emphasizes the instructional role of the teacher as a more knowledgeable other. We were also impressed by the idea that within each Book Club setting were all five aspects of the language arts: reading, writing, speaking, listening, and thinking. Therefore it provided a framework for teaching literacy that aligned with our beliefs about learning and the role of the teacher.

At the same time, even though there were many things about the original Book Club program we were attracted to, we were also concerned about the lack of connection between reading instruction and other content areas. As we car-pooled during the spring semester of 1992, we talked about ways Book Club could be used to teach literacy to our fifth graders and how we could effectively merge Book Club with content-area instruction, specifically social studies. We decided that Book Club seemed to value teaching thematically, using both an intradisciplinary approach, "themes developed to integrate the language arts" (Lipson, Valencia, Wixson, & Peters, 1993), and an interdisciplinary approach, themes developed to integrate content with literacy learning (McMahon, 1994). At the same time, we thought the Book Club program as initially implemented was strongest in integrating the language arts and did not provide a formal structure for integrating other content. Thus we decided to work together to create an interdisciplinary structure that supported students' Book Club activities but also fostered an understanding of social studies content. We were encouraged to pursue a Book Club model as a framework for our integrated unit because of three aspects already included within the program: (1) teaching thematically, (2) providing opportunities for students to learn important historical concepts, and (3) creating a community of learners.

The collaborative approach we used to implement Book Club in our fifth-grade classrooms was multifaceted, including discussion, support, and trust. Our collaboration as teachers included frequent discussion about our practices, various educational theories, dilemmas in the classroom, and our accountability to peers, supervisors, parents, students, and the community. We gave each other mutual support by discussing common problems. Our shared theories and beliefs about student learning and the role of the teacher provided a trusting atmosphere in which to ask tough questions about our practices as well as an openness to each other's ideas and suggestions for improvements. This collaboration facilitated professional growth and reflection in an atmosphere in which we took risks to improve our literacy instruction.

Second, we wanted our students to identify personally with history and learn three important historical concepts: (1) Make connections between current and historical events, (2) make connections among events within a time period, and (3) see history as real events happening to real people. These concepts are imperative to promote an understanding of history that extends beyond the historical events themselves. Third, we shared a goal of creating a community of learners in our classroom (G. Wells, 1990a). We envisioned a comfortable, safe environment for learning and risk taking in which all learners had specialized knowledge to be valued and shared.

MAKING BOOK CLUB OUR OWN

To explore the possibilities of integrating Book Club with social studies content, we began our first interdisciplinary unit in the spring of 1992, focusing on World War II. This topic met our criteria for relevance across four critical areas. First, since the topic was part of the school curriculum guide for fifth-grade social studies, it had curricular relevance. Second, several of our students had expressed interest in this time period because family members had participated in or been affected by World War II; thus it was a topic relevant to students. Third, it was relevant in terms of literary quality because many excellent fiction and nonfiction texts have been written about this time period. Finally, we were personally interested in reading and discussing books about this historical period.

We began our interdisciplinary unit using the Book Club framework that Susan McMahon (1994) had described, in which fifth-grade students read and discussed novels such as Coerr's (1977) *Sadako and the Thousand Paper Cranes* and picture books such as Maruki's (1980) *Hiroshima No Pika*. Like those students, ours were excited about the topic and engaged in discussion. However, we were concerned about their lack of relevant background knowledge, which contributed to what we believed were rather simplistic views of major historical events. For example, while reading *Sadako and the Thousand Paper Cranes*, Julie found that a group of students lacked sufficient background knowledge to adequately analyze the events leading up to the bombing, stating without qualification that it was a justified retaliation for the bombing of Pearl Harbor. This example, and others like it, led us to consider that our students lacked important background information to discuss meaningfully and thoroughly the issues they encountered in literature. To develop this background knowledge, we felt students needed to research related topics.

As a result of the pilot work with the World War II unit in spring 1992, we developed a plan for the following year that involved a series of interdisciplinary units connecting literacy instruction with social studies content learning. Each five-week unit included two weeks of research followed by three weeks of Book Club. Our plan had four goals. First, the two-week research unit immediately preceding the novel units provided opportunities to expand background knowledge related to the social studies topic. Second, we hoped students would learn relevant research skills in a meaningful context. Since they were seeking information related to texts they would be reading in Book Club and since they would be sharing their knowledge with their peers, they had a meaningful reason for completing their research reports. A third goal was to create a context in which students learned how to support their particular perspective by gathering information from a range of sources. Fourth, to meet our goal of creating a community we had students work in cooperative groups on topics related to the novels they would eventually read. In such groups, they developed expertise to share with peers, contributing to and underscoring the idea of a "community" of learners. All four of these goals–building background knowledge, developing independent research skills, developing support for one's point of view, and creating a sense of community–seemed consistent with recommendations to promote students' higher-level literate thinking skills (G. Wells & Chang-Wells, 1996) and students' ownership (Au, Scheu, Kawakami, & Herman, 1990).

We conceptualized this integration as two phases within our intradisciplinary approach: phase I–research, phase II–Book Club. During the research phase, the social studies content was in the foreground while the language arts remained in the background, being stressed within the context of research on history. During the Book Club phase, the foreground and background shifted so that the content provided the foundation and support for literature-based discussions. Here, the issues and history were stressed within the context of reading, writing, speaking, listening, and thinking. Further, the foundation of the Book Club program is the student-led discussion groups (Raphael & McMahon, 1994). We agreed that this was crucial to learning in a sociocultural setting. The research process, historical content, group-work skills, and problem-solving strategies would support and extend the book clubs by building background knowledge and supporting positive group dynamics so that students could effectively and thoughtfully discuss complex, real-life issues.

Our plan to incorporate a research component with a Book Club unit had several purposes. The research process had two goals. First, it provided an opportunity for building common background knowledge to facilitate the student-led discussions and their constructed meaning from the literature. Second, it provided a structure in which students could develop group and problem-solving skills that were necessary in their student-led discussions. Eventually, students realized the importance of the research phase, as illustrated in Dennis's response journal, where he alluded to his enhanced understanding and enjoyment of the novel's content: "This story is really really cool after you learned about the revilutionary war and It comes together more easy." Other students' written responses, much like this one, reinforced our rationale for integrating social studies instruction and Book Club.

INITIATING INTERDISCIPLINARY UNITS IN BOOK CLUB

The 1992–1993 school year marked the first full year of our integrated Book Club/social studies program. The success of the pilot project led us to focus on the thematic integration of historical eras in our country's history (e.g., colonization, Revolutionary War, Civil War, World War II). There were three phases to initiating these interdisciplinary units: (1) teacher planning to narrow the topical focus, (2) teacher–student collaboration for outlining and assessing the research within each topic, and (3) transferring ownership from teachers to students.

Narrowing the Focus

We needed to narrow the focus and number of the thematic units for two reasons. First, we wanted to provide logical links between our social studies curriculum and Book Club. Second, we wanted to ensure that Book Club did not become limited to what we were studying in social studies. During Book Club, we wanted opportunities for students to read a variety of genres and authors; in social studies, we were focusing specifically on our country's history. Thus linking historical fiction with social studies research made sense but could not be allowed to take over Book Club. Because we realized we could not "cover" all topics related to American history in any meaningful way, we adopted the notion that depth was better than breadth (Brophy, McMahon, & Prawat, 1991). That is, we concluded that our students would understand history better if we delved deeper into fewer major time periods than if we briefly read and discussed several. As we stated above, we wanted students to make personal associations to historical events by connecting these to current happenings, by relating historical events to one another, and by seeing history as real experiences happening to real people.

We knew we could not do this without limiting the topics we introduced across the year. Further, an organizational structure that restricted the time periods provided us more flexibility and facilitated our goal of including thematically linked material.

We decided to develop four thematic units, one in each marking period, linking Book Club and social studies. Since we generally had seven different units in Book Club over the course of the year, this left three units open to draw upon genres and authors unrelated to the social studies curriculum. The Appendix details the four historical eras we drew upon from social studies, as well as the books that we identified as relevant to each historical era: (1) colonization–exploring relationships between the European settlers and the Native Americans; (2) understanding the Revolutionary War and the birth of a new nation; (3) the role of the Civil War in our country's growth and development; and (4) World War II–beyond the boundaries of our nation. We studied these in the first, second, third, and fourth marking periods, respectively.

The books that we drew on are listed in the Appendix and simply reflect "our choice." There are many other excellent books that relate to these historical periods. Our choice was influenced by (1) books that we had read, (2) books that we wanted to read based on reviews we had seen in sources such as *The Horn Book* and *The Reading Teacher*, and (3) books recommended in conversations in the Teacher Research Inquiry Group. Once we were clear on the themes and the books we would draw on, we began the process of planning the research.

Outlining and Assessing the Research

After dividing the year into four historically based time periods, we decided to develop a research outline for each unit, with students' input. As teachers, we had particular goals we expected students to achieve. For example, in the first unit, on the colonial period, there was certain specific information we expected students to understand: (1) geographic regions, (2) aspects of the culture, and (3) information related to daily life. Further, we identified specific skills we planned to emphasize, such as note taking and writing expository texts. At the same time, since we feel strongly about students' choice and ownership over their learning, we shared with them the responsibility of formulating these outlines at the onset of each unit. We began by brainstorming and listing, as a total class, what would make a good final report. In the beginning of the year, during the unit on the colonial period, students brainstormed several ideas, including relationships between settlers and Native Americans, maps of the time period, and traditions (see Figure 14.1). Together, our instructional goals and the students' interests resulted in

FIGURE 14.1.   Native American Cultures—Research Project

GROUP MEMBERS:

The name of your tribe is _____
The name of your clan is _____

1. Regional information
- Climate
- Plants
- Animals
- Agriculture—soil type
- (What crops were grown?)
- Natural Resources
2. Culture
- Myths and legends
- Traditions
3. Daily Life
- Games
- Travel
- Types of homes/dwellings
- Types and examples of clothing
4. Relationships
- Trading
- Settlers/explorers
5. Map
- Incorporates information found
6. Note cards
- Turned in
- Accurate information following format

Comments:

an outline to guide them as they prepared their final report. Once we had established our goals for the unit, we turned our attention to assessment to establish clear criteria and expectations for student success (see also Chapter 15).

We began with the class-generated outline that clearly defined the content that was necessary in each section of the report. Then, through instruction, we clarified the expectations for success, always involving students in the process of establishing assessment procedures. Next, we provided examples of student work from the previous year, analyzed them, discussed their strengths and weaknesses, and developed criteria for their reports. This process led to specific criteria for assessing their final research projects.

This process of analysis, discussion, and goal setting has become a regular attribute of our daily classroom activities. We recognize that it is necessary to have an assessment system that ensures, monitors, and documents student progress. To do this, we establish criteria aligned with our goals and instruction. With our guidance, students develop the ability to analyze their work critically, set their criteria for grading, and come to consensus as a whole class (Stanford, 1977). This process is possible for us because we view assessment as an integral part of instruction (Valencia, 1990). Since both teacher and students establish and agree on the criteria, students are able to self-assess their work and reflectively understand the process of grading. Then we are better able to assess objectively the important components of each project. This demystifies the grading process and supports our beliefs about assessment.

Transferring Ownership

We structured our units over the course of the year so that there was a gradual transfer of ownership from teacher to students (Pearson, 1985). We view this transfer as a type of scaffolding, with students learning the content of history to support their book club discussions. As the year progressed, the criteria we set became more and more difficult, building on each unit, so that for the last unit students chose and defined most of the content.

In the beginning of the year, our outlines were highly structured and specific, but as we noticed increasing ownership and responsibility for learning among the students, we left more choices to individuals. In the second outline, they chose one topic to be an "area of expertise," meaning students could choose any aspect of the Revolutionary War to research, such as uniforms, weaponry, famous people, survival skills, or music of the era, to gain expertise. As the year progressed, students were able to research more complex topics, creating a high level of excitement and motivation. By the end of the year, Julie's class decided to create student videos that specialized in varying issues related to a common theme: "If we don't learn from history, we are condemned to repeat it." Each group of students then chose a sub-topic related to the war, such as (1) women in the workforce, (2) genocide, (3) the atom bomb, (4) stereotyping groups of people, and (5) background for U.S. involvement in the war. Groups researched general background information on their topic, developed an opinion related to the issue, and connected it to an event in the last ten years of our history. Next, they determined whether we, as a society, have grown and learned from our experiences or whether we have repeated the same mistakes. This provided a limited amount of structure for students while still allowing enough flexibility to make it meaningful.

TEACHING RESEARCH SKILLS

For students to develop a common knowledge base that supported and extended Book Club discussions, we found that they needed instruction in research skills. We encountered students' weaknesses in terms of their (1) use of library resources, (2) acquisition, interpretation, and synthesis of information, and (3) awareness of the availability of diverse resources. In this section, we discuss these three weaknesses and how we addressed them.

Use of Library Resources

Even though students in Kathy's school had used the library on a regular basis, she discovered early in the fall that they really did not understand how to use its resources effectively. When she asked her class how many of them knew how to use a card catalogue, only half of them raised their hands. Further questioning revealed that only a few students could explain the card catalogue's purpose and apply its use in an authentic research situation. Even though studying the card catalogue had been part of the previous year's curriculum, students had not learned to use it consistently for real purposes. Because we viewed the research as a means to an end rather than an end itself, we combined the historical research with the Book Club framework so that students had authentic reasons for conducting research and using library resources.

Since Kathy's students expressed a lack of understanding about how to effectively use the library, she decided to provide explicit instruction using a variety of sources, beginning with the card catalogue. First, she familiarized the class with the layout of the library, noting key resources. Then she modeled how to use the card catalogue, provided guided practice, and encouraged peer tutoring when necessary. This modeling and observation of their progress over time helped students build the research skills required to develop their background knowledge for reading and discussing upcoming novels.

Interpreting and Synthesizing Information

Unlike the students in Kathy's class, those in Julie's class had a foundational understanding of acquiring information in a research setting. However, even though Julie's students could effectively use the library, they shared other areas of weakness with Kathy's students. We discovered that students in both classes had difficulty interpreting and synthesizing the information. For example, they copied text directly from the reference without understanding or being able to explain what they had written. We felt their lack of understanding would inhibit their interpretation of the novels, picture books, and expository texts they would read later during Book Club.

Therefore Julie guided students to focus on their purposes for research. As a whole class, they selected a topic related to the time period being studied. They defined and generated a "key question," an open-ended question answered by synthesizing many resources supporting different perspectives. For example, "When did the Civil War start?" is not a key question because it can be found in one source. "What were the events that led up to the Civil War?" is an example of a key question.

Julie began her instruction on synthesizing information by reading aloud an article on Native Americans, which she also displayed on the overhead projector, then focusing on finding the answers to a key question. Instead of copying sentences, she modeled paraphrasing and rewording concepts in the text. She included suggestions from the class to demonstrate many examples of rephrasing information. This showed students that there are numerous ways to paraphrase, not just one acceptable answer, and underscored the process of combining information in expository text with preexisting knowledge.

Next, she provided students four different articles on the same topic to practice finding information on their key questions and paraphrasing. They shared their findings, which further illustrated the diversity of their paraphrasing. Students learned to (1) understand various perspectives, (2) synthesize and organize ideas, (3) reword difficult text into their own words, and (4) use writing to express and explore their findings.

Another example to achieve the same goal occurred in Kathy's class. Students chose an excerpt from an encyclopedia to practice paraphrasing. As a group, they rewrote a section of text in their own words, extending it with their existing knowledge. Students then shared the encyclopedia's version and their paraphrased version with the class. Using these examples, they analyzed the differences between student talk and booktalk. Their understanding was visible in later expository writing.

Higher-order thinking is an important goal for all learners and, as such, was important within Book Club. Students also learned varying perspectives involved in complex issues, which helped them understand others' viewpoints when reading about, considering, and discussing issues (e.g., racism, slavery, poverty) in book clubs. By reading, paraphrasing, and synthesizing information related to their key questions, students were developing the literate thinking essential to Book Club.

Utilizing Diverse Resources

Another weakness we saw in our students' research skills was their reliance on basic reference tools, such as the encyclopedia, and limited problem-solving abilities when they could not find information in the first resource they checked. For example, one group's topic was "the role of women in World War II." They began with the encyclopedia, then searched the card catalogue under "W" for women. When they did not find texts under this heading, they decided this was not a researchable topic. Their lack of familiarity with specialized reference tools, such as books of famous people, biographical dictionaries, almanacs, and CD-ROMs hampered their ability to research all available resources. Therefore we decided that students needed concrete and foundational knowledge about the research process before they began. Further, we expanded the available school resources with books from the public library and our own collections.

Julie helped her students acquaint themselves with resources other than the encyclopedia through a cooperative group activity. She gave each group a reference tool such as a biographical dictionary, requiring them to analyze it and teach its organization and potential uses to the rest of the class. Also, she asked them to find information connected to the upcoming research project on the Civil War. After sharing their findings, they engaged in a scavenger hunt through various reference materials to answer five questions. This created excitement and helped them locate information on the Civil War that would also be useful when constructing meaning from fiction and when explaining key concepts in book club discussions.

Because students helped determine topics to study, there was a great deal of ownership built into the research project, sparking motivation and interest as well as encouraging use of library resources. This work prior to Book Club built background knowledge and provided practice in skills, strategies, and higher-level thinking that enhanced book club discussions. Students' presentations of their specialized information to the class increased the knowledge base of the whole group, leading students to value one anothers' expertise, seek peer help to solve problems, and explore issues discussed in book clubs.

EVIDENCE OF INTERTEXTUAL CONNECTIONS

After students developed a research base, they were ready for the book clubs (see Chapter 5). Through literature, we began to see students linking historical events and concepts together in meaningful ways, an important aspect of historical learning. For example, during the World War II unit, while reading *Number the Stars* (Lowry, 1989), Al wrote: "I think if things get really bad for Ellens family they could sneak out of Copanhagan and go to AnneMarie's uncles house. Then they could build a raft and float across the river to Sweden like how Cuban people floated to USA. Then they could be free." Through this log entry, Al demonstrated his understanding of the dilemma Danish Jews encountered by comparing the main characters' situation to a then-current event – the Cuban exodus to Florida.

A second important aspect of historical learning is the ability to link historical events across time periods. After reading *Number the Stars*, Amy's log illustrates her thoughts connecting World War II to events surrounding the Civil War: "This book was the best one we read in book clubs so far. This book reminded [me] of the Underground Railroad. How they hid them. Everyone risked their lives either for themselves or someone else. I would recommend this book to anyone who wants to read about and learn about World War II."

HISTORY COMES ALIVE THROUGH BOOK CLUB

The culmination of meaningful historical and literacy learning was evident in Julie's classroom at the end of the year. Students became engrossed in studying the bombing of Hiroshima during World War II. They read *Sadako* (Coerr, 1993), *Hiroshima No Pika*, and *My Hiroshima* (Morimoto, 1987), all of which examine the war from a Japanese perspective. They also read *The Day Pearl Harbor Was Bombed* (Sullivan, 1991), which portrays an American perspective. At the same time, students discussed the controversy surrounding the Smithsonian exhibit on World War II, including the veterans' argument that the exhibit did not illustrate the American perspective. To culminate the unit, Julie asked her students to list the pros and cons surrounding the issue and come to a decision as to which side they personally supported.

This activity had three outcomes. First, students synthesized information they learned from their research, novels, picture books, informational text, current events, and book club discussions. Second, they assessed their own conceptual change that had occurred throughout the unit through re-reading their response journals. Third, they demonstrated knowledge of various perspectives on a single issue and constructed their own informed beliefs.

During community share, a minidebate broke out because students felt so strongly about their own perspective. As the discussion became more and more heated, they asked to have a debate. Since it was the last week of school, Julie reluctantly explained to her students that they would not have sufficient time. However, their enthusiasm and the high level of ownership led Julie to agree to the debate if students assumed responsibility for preparation. They agreed. Independently, the class decided to debate the pros and cons of using an atomic bomb to end World War II. Students divided themselves into teams and planned time to research and gather evidence to support their side. They decided to write essays to solidify their thinking and to build their case. Students agreed that they would use recess to practice developing their arguments and use class time only for the debate.

During the debate, students demonstrated their learning and argued persuasively for their side of the issue. Here, book clubs had a profound effect on motivating learning and enhancing the classroom as a community. Students launched into a higher level of engagement with the historical content than either of us had imagined possible prior to implementation of Book Club in our curriculum.

CONCLUDING COMMENTS

For us, Book Club became a framework that we could modify to meet our instructional needs and those of our students. Adopting a sociocultural perspective on learning provided us the concepts that enabled us to understand our professional needs for a collaborative environment with peers, to modify curriculum in any way that allows for meaningful learning for our students, and to foster greater student ownership over their own learning process. By modifying Book Club so that we could integrate our literacy and social studies curriculum, we were able to teach thematically, provide students opportunities to understand key historical events on multiple levels, and create a community of learners. We are happy with our efforts but not complacent. We continue to grow professionally, still questioning our practice and making modifications in our instructional programs.

COMMENTARY

KAREN K. WIXSON

Kathy's and Julie's extensions of Book Club offers a very reasonable way to begin integrating language arts and social studies curriculum and instruction. By putting social studies content in the foreground and language arts in the background during the research phase and language arts content in the foreground with social studies in the background during the Book Club phase, they insure an appropriate emphasis on both language arts and social studies content. The result is a series of well-balanced units that attend to the important content of language arts and social studies and the important connections between these two areas.

Kathy's and Julie's units embody several important features of quality integrated instruction. Most notable among these, I think, is the careful attention to the purposes and goals of their work at every level of development. First, they clearly articulated their personal goals/philosophies for teaching and learning. This is an important foundation for the decision-making that must occur in the development of integrated instructional units. Second, they have general goals for teaching language arts and social studies that guide their instruction and allow them to determine which content is important. Finally, they have specific objectives for each of the units. This is an absolute necessity for developing activities that are relevant to their content goals and consistent with their philosophy of teaching and learning.

There is a system at work here. Each level informs the next, resulting in coherence among the parts. This system insures that the learnings to be integrated are worthwhile in themselves, as are the connections between the subjects. The result is work that promotes an integrated knowledge base, not simply correlated activities.

I am also struck by the relations between their instruction and work I have been involved in to develop Michigan's new content standards in English language arts. I see many of these content standards in their units, some more strongly than others—which would be expected from any single set of instructional units. For example, the research component of their units relates directly to the content standard on "research and inquiry" and the Book Club component is directly related to the "literature" standard. In addition, students' ability to critically analyze their work, set criteria for grading, and come to consensus reflects attention to the standard on "critical standards."

Certainly there is also evidence of "skills and processes" and "genre and craft of language"; however, I am hard-pressed to imagine language arts instruction that does not touch on these content standards. I am particularly impressed with the manner in which their units exemplify the "depth of understanding" standard. This standard is often neglected in favor of coverage or because topics are selected primarily on the basis of teacher interests. The criteria they have established for identifying the focus of their instruction are extremely valuable in ensuring an emphasis on substantive content and deep understanding.

CHAPTER 15

A Portfolio Approach to Book Club Assessment

Navigating Instruction and Monitoring Student Growth

JULIE FOLKERT and SARA BEAN

In this chapter, we describe our research into the development of an assessment system to accompany Book Club, the program we now are using for reading instruction in our fourth- and fifth-grade classrooms. We have worked together since 1993, initially as students completing the literacy M.A. program at Michigan State University and later as members of the Teacher Research Inquiry Group and the Book Club project. While completing the master's program, we developed our philosophy of literacy instruction and learned about different theories and instructional models. We both found value in constructing knowledge collaboratively. We read many chapters and articles relating to the theoretical view of social constructivism (e.g., Gavelek, 1986; Vygotsky, 1978), which seemed to fit our beliefs about literacy instruction. Over time, our teaching had become more student-centered, promoting more student interactions, teaching using broad themes, and initiating more conscious teacher mediation. Not surprisingly, when we learned about Book Club, we thought it would work well in our classrooms, and it is now at the center of our language arts program. Each day, we focus on literature through the Book Club components. Students are given many opportunities to respond to text in a variety of ways. Through participation in both book club and community share discussions, our students are able to build on and refine their own views of the text, become more effective communicators in their writing and speaking, and develop active listening skills.

During the first year that we used Book Club, we relied on assessment tools that we had previously used, as well as adopted ones we had read about in journals such as *The Reading Teacher* and *Language Arts*. We used these tools to assess students' comprehension, discussion abilities, and strategy use.

For example, to assess their ability to comprehend and make connections to the text, we analyzed their journals and made comments periodically. To analyze the connections they were making across books and themes and their discussion skills, we listened to audiotaped student-led discussions and took anecdotal notes during book club and community share discussions. To interpret strategy use and comprehension, we periodically used think-alouds. Students used self-assessment procedures to analyze the improvement of their discussions over time. These informal tools provided feedback about students' growth, but parents, students, and administrators held the tools of the district and state in much higher regard. Thus we also administered required standardized tests, including the Michigan Educational Assessment of Progress (MEAP) – a criterion-referenced test given to all fourth-grade students to assess their reading and math abilities – and district-level end-of-the year reading tests measuring decontextualized skills use. While providing information about how well our students could use skills in isolation, these tests did not inform us about student growth in oral and written response or student thought processes, important focuses in Book Club.

While completing our coursework at Michigan State, we began to discuss our frustration regarding the inconsistencies between what the mandated assessments measured and our goals for Book Club instruction. We also lacked formal evidence to verify the growth we saw through the use of Book Club. We decided to take an assessment course during our final summer term and agreed to develop a portfolio system collaboratively that would more systematically document student growth related to the Book Club goals.

In this chapter, we focus on our development and implementation of a portfolio assessment system to document student progress and provide accountability for our instructional decisions. The chapter is organized around three processes related to our development of a portfolio approach: (1) assuming our ownership over assessment, (2) encouraging student ownership, and (3) finding a balance between teacher and student ownership. In each of these sections, we describe ongoing procedures, including our planning, implementation, analysis, and modifications.

TEACHERS TAKING OWNERSHIP
OF THE ASSESSMENT PROCESS

A portfolio approach to literacy assessment enabled us to gather information and identify our instructional goals, creating an interwoven system in which instruction and assessment worked together. This is in contrast to the more traditional forms of assessment that may drive instruction (i.e., teaching to a test), or have no correlation with the instruction that occurs within the classroom. "A literacy portfolio is a purposeful collection of student work and records of progress and achievement collected over time" (Valencia, in press, p. 3). Taking ownership of this process, we chose a collection of artifacts that reflected progress toward our literacy goals. Once we chose our direction, we began to plan a structure for assessment.

The Planning Process

As we began planning our portfolio system, we laid out four key phases. In the first phase of planning, we focused on aligning those reading outcomes required by both our district's curriculum and Book Club. In the second phase, we examined those Book Club goals that the curriculum guide omitted. In the third phase, we created a list of outcomes integrating goals from the curriculum guide and Book Club. Finally, we designed assessment tools to monitor growth in all the outcome areas. Throughout these four phases of planning, we collaborated closely.

We had two purposes for beginning with an alignment between the district's and Book Club's goals for reading instruction. Initially, we had planned to group specific Book Club objectives with our own district's curricula; however, when we listed the objectives from the district curriculum guide, we were overwhelmed by the number of superficial, isolated objectives, reflecting the "basalized" approach to reading instruction that we were consciously trying to improve. Therefore we began by integrating the basic skills listed in the district guides into contextualized activities using literature as a basis for instruction. For example, instead of a laundry list of skills taught in isolation, we created a "bank" of strategies for students to draw from.

Reading Strategies

Prereading Strategies

- I thought about what I want to find out.
- I got a dictionary in case I hit a roadblock.
- I asked myself questions about the article.

- I thought about what I already know about the topic.
- I made myself comfortable.

During Reading

- I asked questions as I went along.
- I read slowly and carefully.
- I paid attention to what I was reading.
- What I hit a roadblock, I reread part of the sentence or article to make sense out of it.
- When I couldn't figure out the meaning on my own, I talked to someone about it.
- I broke words into pieces to figure out their meanings.
- I connected what I was reading to something that had happened in my own life.
- I used pictures, graphs, and charts to help me construct meaning.

After Reading

- I thought about what I read and the strategies I used to solve comprehension problems.
- I checked to make sure my questions were answered.
- I couldn't find answers to my questions, so I found another resource.
- I went back into the text to find an answer.
- I brainstormed ideas with someone.
- I combined new information with things I have read or heard.

Students used this guide to become metacognitive about their strategy use. We also used it when we met individually with students, having them "think aloud" as they read and recorded the various strategies they used. This list of strategies from which students could chose while reading illustrates one concrete example of how we aligned the district's and Book Club's goals in a contextualized manner. This process of alignment helped us address essential skills in meaningful, contextualized ways.

The second step in planning our new assessment system was to identify those goals emphasized in Book Club but omitted in the district's curriculum guide. For example, one of the largest components of Book Club is the oral discussion initiated in both the book club and community share discussions. The district curricula addressed oral language only in terms of students' ability to present information to a group, with no attention to interactive dialogue in which speakers react to comments from others and, in turn, listen and respond to this reaction—essential elements of any group discussion. Also,

Book Club stresses students' engagement in higher-order thinking, such as analysis, synthesis, and evaluation. However, the existing curriculum guide virtually ignored this, focusing more on evidence of skill and strategy application. As a result, students' past literacy experiences led them to define *reading* as applying skills and proving comprehension. We committed to helping them restructure their definitions in order to promote higher-level thinking in response to the text.

Once we had completed the first two steps, we identified outcomes that would guide our construction of assessment measures. The Book Club components of reading, writing, community share, and book club led to our three categories of "reading," "written response," and "discussion" for organizing our four general outcomes:

Attitudes: Students' personal feelings and motivational characteristics regarding literacy

Strategic processes and skill development: Specific skills and strategies applied when engaging in any of the four language processes (reading, writing, listening, and speaking)

Constructs: Students' appreciation of themselves as effective communicators who identify personal goals

Content knowledge: The knowledge base students construct and students' identification and critique of literary devices

Figure 15.1 is an example of the outcomes we created that aligned the district objectives with our four established outcome areas.

Our final step in designing our new portfolio assessment was to design tools that measured our desired outcomes and monitored students' growth in each area. We were confident we would be successful because we had decided what areas we were going to assess prior to developing them, since the most important factor guiding us was insuring that the tool appropriately assessed the desired outcome (Worthen, 1993). With these in mind, we examined portfolio samples and checklists, analyzing the structure, the elements, and the ease of the documentation process. From those samples, we created a form that met our needs. Our form included the tool, its purpose, and a description (Figure 15.2). To hold ourselves and our students accountable, we summarized how we assessed each area. The reading-response log that we developed (Figure 15.3) enabled us to visualize our goals and monitor students' progression over time.

After creating our outcomes and measurements, we created an implementation schedule to stay focused and assess our progress, collecting information from various areas at appropriate levels (Valencia, 1990). This is de-

FIGURE 15.1.   Sample Outcomes

Attitude	Strategic Processes/Skill Development
* Students will show personal feelings and motivation about literacy. Reading: Student chooses to read Book Club novel during free time. Writing: Student is actively involved in making personal choices of how he/she will respond to text. Oral discussion: Student shares ideas and opinions during student-led discussions.	* Students will exhibit constructive comprehension of text. * Students will exhibit the use of appropriate writing processes and conventions. * Students will participate in the social aspects of literacy. Reading/writing: Student makes connections between the text and his/her own life. Writing: Student uses events from the text to organize his/her thoughts and opinions in the response log. Oral Discussion: Student expands on peers' thoughts and opinions.

Constructs	Content Knowledge
* Students value literacy as a mode of communication that incorporates all language processes. Reading: Student appreciates the variety of other members' interpretations of text. Writing: Student values the response log as a tool to organize his/her thinking. Oral Discussion: Student believes that discussing his/her reflections brings meaning for the entire group.	* Students will identify and critique various literary devices Reading: Student compares/contrasts the different genres of literature. Writing: Student applies the elements of story structure within his/her own writing. Oral Discussion: Student discusses the devices used by the author and their impact on the story.

picted in Figure 15.4. This was our plan for implementing portfolios in our classrooms.

The Implementation Process

We began the next school year feeling both confident and excited about implementing our new portfolio assessment. In addition to communicating the new assessment system to our students and colleagues at the school,

FIGURE 15.2. Assessment Form

Tool	Purpose	Description
Think-aloud	Assess student thought process during reading. Looking for point where meaning-making breaks down.	Students explain their thought processes at pre-established points. Teacher takes notes during this process.
Kidwatching	To assess student's performance in an informal setting to solidify other forms of assessment.	Observe students' attitudes and behaviors within the classroom setting during their discussions with others.
Anecdotal notes	To document observations.	Teacher jots down notes in a notebook or on cards during instructional activities to reflect on at a later time and to illustrate growth and change.
Reading attitude survey "Garfield Study"	To assess students' attitudes about reading.	Students choose from a pictorial representation of attitudes to compare to their own feelings about their response to given scenarios about reading.
Interviews	To gain student's reflections regarding their beliefs and feelings about various aspects of literacy.	Meet with student individually with targeted questions that fill gaps in your understanding of the child.
Running records	To check student's fluency (for less skilled readers).	Student reads orally as teacher documents miscues.

educating parents was crucial. We began by writing letters home communicating our rationale for implementing portfolio assessment, our goals, and our plans for achieving them. This letter addressed issues we predicted parents might raise and the relationship between the portfolios and the district's existing evaluation tools. We also suggested parents continue to communicate with us about their child's literacy development and their willingness to participate in the portfolio process. One way to facilitate this was a survey we

FIGURE 15.3.   Reading-Response Log

Name: _____   Novel: _____   Date: _____

Journal Entry Choices:

	Low Degree	Med. Degree	High Degree	Doesn't Apply
1. Makes connections between text and real world				
2. Makes reasonable predictions				
3. Summarizes story				
4. Puts story in correct sequence				
5. Develops characters				
6. Analyzes characters' actions				
7. Uses a variety of vocabulary				
8. Takes story events beyond the text				
9. Asks appropriate questions				
10. Discusses the setting's impact on the story				
11. Identifies problems and ways to solve them				
12. Relates the mood with the events of story				
13. Identifies author's purpose				
14. Compares story with genres or stories previously read				

Comments:

FIGURE 15.4. Implementation Schedule

TOOLS	Sept.	Oct./Dec.	Jan./Feb.	Mar./April	May/June
Parent letter	X				
Attitude survey	X				X
Introduce Book Club	X				
Modeling various responses	X	X	X	X	X
Modeling appropriate group behavior	X	X	X	X	X
Interviews (ongoing as needed)	X	X	X	X	X
Collecting and assessing response logs	X	X	X	X	X
Anecdotal notes	X	X	X	X	X
Audiotaping	X	X	X	X	X
Self-assessment questionnaire	X	X	X	X	X
Peer assessment	X	X	X	X	X
Analyzing journal responses			X	X	X
Performance assessment					X
Created benchmarks					X

conducted at the beginning and end of the school year. This survey enabled us to understand parents' comprehension of and expectations for assessment, and we used this feedback to adjust our assessment measures. This diverse feedback helped us include parents and their ideas in various ways. For example, some parents read their child's portfolio monthly, while others preferred to see it only at conferences. Also, some parents with specific concerns about their child's literacy development encouraged us to gather additional data. An unpredicted outcome of our changing the assessment measures in our classroom was increased input from and communication with parents.

In conjunction with our ongoing communication about our new assessment, we began implementing it. There were several components to our plan, ranging from samples of students' responses, to anecdotal records we kept during Book Club, to survey information about students' attitudes and beliefs. In this section, we describe part of this process by focusing attention on reading-response logs, anecdotal records, and students' self-assessment questionnaires.

Reading-response logs. The procedures for documenting student growth in writing responses to literature were simple. We collected their logs weekly and provided feedback through the checklist (Figure 15.3). Students stored the checklists and their logs in their portfolios. At the end of the marking period, Julie's students chose journal entries representative of their best writing to stay in the portfolio.

The instructional aspect of constructing quality log entries was also procedurally simple. To provide students with models that represented evidence of desired outcomes, we made copies of the best ones on transparencies, showed them to the class, and discussed the strengths and areas of improvement for each. We also brainstormed about how to achieve the goals we discussed. This process demonstrated to students what the outcomes were and how to achieve them. A specific example will demonstrate this.

Our desired outcomes for a personal response entry in their logs included three components: affective response, a connection to personal life, and an analysis of some aspect of the story. One example of how a student began integrating these is from Julie's class as they read *Tuck Everlasting* (Babbitt, 1975). Jenna, the author of this entry, was a below-average student who rarely made personal connections among the text, her life, and/or earlier discussions. However, she seemed highly motivated when reading about the Tucks. In her log, Jenna illustrated an integration of these goals when she responded to the main character's contemplation about drinking from a fountain of youth.

> This chapter was realy sad it made me think of my grandma Clayton. ("Honey", she died last year, but I still miss her so much) I know how Winnie wants to be comforted because I have something special I use when I feel like that. I guesse it might be hard to "save" Mae but she will still live because; she drank from the fountain! But then everyone will think she is a witch.

Prior to this, Jenna either summarized story events or related a personal opinion or experience without connections to the text. This entry shows her progress because she made a connection between Winnie's feelings and her own. Further, she goes on to analyze how the main character's dilemma (feeling responsible for Mae's capture and the potential revelation of the Tucks' secret) would impact the outcome of the story.

Anecdotal records. We took anecdotal notes as we observed students' book clubs to provide documentation about participation and discussion topics (Routman, 1991). Each book club was audiotaped twice each week, and we generally listened to those groups we had not observed in class. Tapes also proved helpful as records of discussions we had not heard in their entirety. The following scenario is a common example of how Julie used the combination of anecdotal notes and audiotapes to document book clubs.

During the study of the novel *The Sign of the Beaver* (Speare, 1983), Julie overheard one book club discussing their opinions of a case where parents were charged for leaving their young children alone while they went on vacation. Jon, a student who had not taken on much leadership in previous group sessions, was questioning the others about how they felt about the issue, stating his parents always had a baby-sitter or a relative stay with the children when they went away. Since this group was being taped, Julie listened for a few minutes before focusing on another group, planning to listen to the tape after school. However, before moving to another group, Julie listed two questions that would guide her when listening to the tape. First, how was the "home-alone" discussion connected with the text? Second, what was Jon's role throughout?

After listening to this tape, Julie decided to transcribe a portion of the discussion as evidence that students were personally responding to the text, connecting it to issues that were currently impacting their lives (fears of being alone/home-alone cases), and as evidence of a shift in group dynamics.

Nate: I can't believe Matt's dad left him alone in the middle of nowhere with a gun.
Sarah: I would have been really scared. I couldn't protect myself like [that
Jon: [But his dad taught him how to use the gun. He wouldn't have left him if he didn't think he could handle it.
Tanja: But Matt isn't telling his dad he is scared, and I think he is scared, don't you? (*Overlapping talk, students agreeing Matt is scared.*)
Jon: Yeah, but I would have been more scared to try to find my way back to get the rest of the family. Matt had to do one thing and staying at the cabin was the safest.
Tanja: Why didn't they bring someone older with them to help, so he wouldn't have to stay alone?

Nate: Probably there wasn't anyone who wanted to go that far away to make someone else's house. They had to do it.

Jon: It was different then too. There wouldn't be bad people around like there are today for Matt to worry about.

Sarah: Still my parent wouldn't let me do that.

Jon: No

Nate: Mine would *(laughter in the group)*

Tanja: Yeah, right!

Jon: Excuse me! Mine wouldn't either, let me stay by myself or they would get into trouble like those people in Chicago if they did.

Toward the beginning, Nate seemed to lead, bringing up issues to discuss. The leadership then transferred to Jon as he connected the "home alone" syndrome. This discussion seemed key for Jon because it seemed to boost his confidence and increase his participation. Julie placed a copy of this transcript in each student's portfolio as an example of personal response. It also served as a specific illustration of Jon's progress in participating in book club for his parents to see.

Julie's anecdotal note led her to listen more closely to the tape. This closer analysis enabled her to find evidence of a student's progress in oral language use, something that is difficult to document. Without using anecdotal records, she might have forgotten her questions related to this conversation and missed an opportunity to note growth in a concrete way.

Self-assessment questionnaire. Another measurement we included was a student self-assessment questionnaire, completed after book clubs:

Book Club Questionnaire

Name: _____   *Date:* _____

1. What strengths do you bring to Book Club?
2. Were your opinions and ideas valued and respected by other Book Club members?
3. Did listening to others' opinions and ideas help you understand the novel? How?
4. How did you help others come to a better understanding of the novel?
5. What are your thoughts and opinions about Book Club at this point in the year?

Students identified their successes, failures, and future goals. Jon's questionnaire, prior to reading *The Sign of the Beaver,* showed that he did not value

Book Club and he thought others did not value his opinion. After the successful Book Club experience noted above, he wrote, "I helped to keep the group talking and talked about the things the group liked. People started to ask me questions and I helped them to think about the book more. This helped me think more too." Thus this questionnaire provided additional evidence of the change in Jon's attitude and confirmed Julie's observation that he had participated more than in the past.

Evaluating Our Implementation

After collecting a considerable amount of data, we began to determine each student's strengths and areas for improvement. We also assessed how the entire class was proceeding. This part of the process enabled us to decide on future instruction at both whole-group and individual levels. Our assessment of this data resulted in two observations about our new assessment process. On one hand, we were pleased with the information we were gathering; on the other, we thought students needed to assume more active roles. Even though they reflected on their growth and goal setting, we analyzed and interpreted it, thus controlling the process. As evidence of their lack of ownership, we noticed that they never consulted their portfolios, only filed information. Our portfolio system was out of balance with our philosophy of instruction, so we began to restructure the system to make it a more authentic part of students' learning.

ENCOURAGING STUDENT OWNERSHIP
OF THE ASSESSMENT PROCESS

Critical to Book Club is the assumption that students can assume more responsibility in their learning than they currently take on in many classrooms. The most obvious example of this is the student-led discussions, or book clubs. We wanted to develop an assessment process that reflected more student responsibility. To this end, we identified two different processes that involved students immediately in the assessment process while simultaneously supporting our instruction in key abilities related to Book Club: (1) creating "targets" and (2) analyzing and reflecting.

Creating Targets

Based on an in-service focused on performance-based assessment, we adopted the idea of creating "targets" (Stiggins, 1987). Targets are the goals and the explicit criteria that describe how to achieve them. Key to this assessment is students' involvement in forming criteria within the targets, thus encouraging student ownership.

We began working with students to create targets for various types of journal responses and discussions. For example, Julie's class created a target for how to create a quality character web. Julie asked students to identify criteria describing a web that exhibits a high quality of analysis. After much debate and discussion, they agreed upon the criteria that would describe a 5, a 3, a 1, and one that missed the target totally. Julie then told the class that she expected them to try to construct character webs that met the criteria for a 5.

As an example of how this helped students become better writers by assessing their own work, we look at one example from the class. Jamie created Character Map A (illustrated in Figure 15.5) prior to the class's establishment of criteria. Her web includes limited information, demonstrating little analysis and a lack of depth. In contrast, the day the class created the criteria, Jamie constructed Character Map B (illustrated in Figure 15.6). This web is more explicit and insightful, revealing a stronger understanding of the character and his relationship to story events. As this example shows, targets were beneficial because they provided guidelines for success.

A second set of targets we worked as a class to construct related to book club discussions. For example, one of the key targets was maintaining a discussion focused on ideas related to the text. We wanted students to make connections between the topics they raised (personal responses, issues raised

FIGURE 15.5.   Character Map A

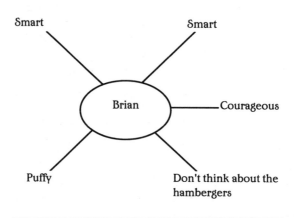

FIGURE 15.6. Character Map B

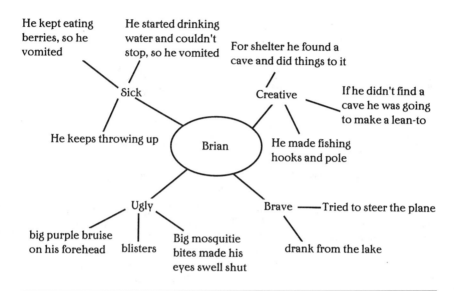

in the text, or ideas prompted by the text) and events in the books. We began by asking students to brainstorm what characterized a good conversation about a book, eventually creating a chart of their ideas (e.g., talking about the book, looking at the speaker, keeping everyone involved). Then we asked them to describe their responsibility in creating an on-target book club. As with the character web, we placed the criteria on a continuum from 1 through 5 and missing the target totally. Students then used this target to assess their own group, rather than merely depending on the teacher's checklist.

Because the students were involved in developing the criteria, they took more ownership in keeping their group on-task, assessing the attributes of their discussion, and developing a rationale for their self-rating. John, an above-average reader and a leader in his book club, used the criteria within the target as he assessed his group's success while discussing *My Brother Sam Is Dead*. His target illustrated how he used the criteria to reflect on his group's discussion, providing an example to support his rating (see Figure 15.7). Teaching students to provide specific evidence within their targets was time-consuming; however, we saw tremendous growth in students' ability to critique themselves and improve their discussions.

We began keeping the target criteria along with our other assessments in

FIGURE 15.7.   John's Self-Assessment

Target For Keeping Group on Task

1   2   3   4   ⑤

Writes in journal,
doodles, plays with pencil   (Listens to conversation)

Plays games with group member(s)   Asks members who are   } No one
                                             not on task to stop   was off
                                                                              task!!
Starts a separate conversation   (Begin a topic that
with group member(s) that has   is about the book)
nothing to do with the book
                                             (Ask non contributing   } All members
                                             members their opinion   } contributed
                                             about topic)

                                             (Respond to a topic that
                                             was brought up)

I feel I deserve a __5__ for keeping the group on task because __I__
started to debate on whether or not
Orover Hull was a witch. I also started
a conversation about the quote "Treason, Treason!"

---

the students' portfolios. Students began comparing their own assessments with ours and began using both to set goals for themselves. We plan to continue using this target-setting system but will create new targets each year, involving students in the process. Previous targets will be helpful only as models.

Analysis and Reflection

A second means of getting students more involved in the assessment process was guiding them toward reflecting on prior journal entries and discussions. Sara found that even after modeling and establishing targets for possible journal responses, some students continued responding in the same ways, without evidence of growth (e.g., drawing from a range of responses, expanding their formats). To address this concern, she began analyzing students' journal responses as a whole class. During community share, she projected sample responses on the overhead, focusing on various characteristics of strong and weak entries. Next, she had students read their own journals to find their "best" entry in relation to an established "target." On Post-It Notes® , they noted their reflections and analysis of the entry, placing the note on the page for future reference. In time, these modeling sessions and practice led to students becoming analytical about their responses, prompting better journal entries.

Becky was one student who quickly exhibited significant growth in the depth of her journal entries. Her attempt at writing a character analysis of Willy in *Stone Fox* (Gardiner, 1980) resulted in a summary of the story.

Stone Fox 2-1-94 Becky

Today little Willy got up early he was getting ready for the race. His eye was now swollen and he told Lester he bumped it this morning because he we nervus. I think Willy has a right to be nervous going against an Indian who hasn't lost yet.

I think Stone Fox should feel sorry for Willy now that he gave him that black eye. He should of just asked little Willy what he was doing there instead of just slapping him in the face.

Little Willy was right to say good morning and all that stuff to Stone Fox, because then maybe it would make him feel worse that he hit Willy.

I think Willy will get into an accident, maybe the sled will tip over tight when he's in the lead, and Stone Fox might feel sorry for him and help him up and let him win the race.

A few days later, Becky added a Post-It Note that revealed her analysis of this entry.

Character Development 2-3-94

I like this one b/c I talked about what happened to Willy and how he felt. It's more like a summary but it's close enough.

When she analyzed her entry against the target, she began to understand the difference between the assignment and her response. Three weeks later, after participating in a number of whole-group sessions analyzing the quality of and criteria for various responses, she completed a character analysis of Karana, the main character in *Island of the Blue Dolphins* (O'Dell, 1960). Her examples from the text and her additional ideas led to her description of Karana as strong and brave.

Island of the Blue Dolphins

Today Karana made weapon's to kill the wild dogs. She din't want to at first, but decided that it would be a good idea. I like Karana myself I think she's a very brave person. Also I think that like someone said I don't know who, but someone said, "I think that this is how it should go. I think that Ramo should've got into the canoe and paddled off to find the ship." I agree with them totally, because then Kamo would be alive and safe.

I also think that was a good idea of Karanaa to make weapons because she has to defend herself somehow.

Special story part!

p. 65 wherever I went during the day I felt secure with my new weapons and I waited patiently for the time when I could use them against the wild dogs that killed Ramo.

I think that this a special part b/c it tells me that Karana realy wants to get back at the wild dogs.

Later, she analyzed her entry and revealed her growing awareness of how to write a quality response.

Character Development 3-1-94

I talked about how Karana was brave and went against the laws and made weapons.
I also put a special story part that had to do with Karana breaking the laws.
I also explained why I thought it was a good special story part.
I also told that my special story part was good b/c it tells me that she really wants to get back at the wild dogs.

The changes in our assessment process addressed many of our concerns and resulted in students assuming more responsibility. However, this emphasis led to additional questions: If students engage in self-evaluation, set their own targets, and analyze the results, how could we be sure their targets sufficiently challenged them? What will lead to optimal success? These questions led us to our current work relating to performance-based assessment: setting benchmarks and establishing rubrics to guide teacher assessment using reasonable standards that balance student involvement.

FINDING A BALANCE BETWEEN
TEACHER AND STUDENT OWNERSHIP

After being successful in promoting student ownership over the assessment process, we recognized the need to create a system to better understand each student's success in achieving each outcome. Our extensive data made apparent that students were working at various levels. While we knew they were progressing, our data did not indicate the degree of growth. We realized we needed to define what constituted "quality work." Therefore, we have been working with Tanja Bisesi and Taffy Raphael to create a holistic system that outlines the qualities of various performance levels in each of the Book Club components. We have begun to create benchmarks that state various levels of performance, serving two purposes: (1) to document expectations of responses at various intervals throughout the year and (2) to guide students along the continuum to their optimal level of performance. Because the levels of performance are more explicitly stated, we have a clearer direction and can provide assistance to each student in achieving the program's goals (see Chapter 9 for more detail about assessment).

CONCLUDING COMMENTS

Throughout this process, a metamorphosis has occurred in our portfolio system. Each phase has been imperative to reach the point where we are now. We had to solidify our thinking before we could provide an arena in which all students could take part in the assessment process. As we reflect on the evolution that has occurred, we continue to look forward. We plan to analyze portfolios to establish benchmarks for types of responses at various points in the year. As our portfolio system continues to grow and change, we want to ensure that "the main purpose of assessment [is] to provide teachers and students with information useful in promoting students' growth in literacy" (Au, Scheu, Kawakami, & Herman, 1990, p. 575).

COMMENTARY

KATHRYN H. AU

Julie Folkert and Sara Bean's chapter is a wonderful teachers'-eye view of some key assessment issues in the language arts field. The start of their journey followed a pattern I have found to be familiar. They began by making changes in instruction that seemed beneficial to their students, providing them with rich experiences centered on Book Club. Soon they discovered that conventional forms of assessment, including standardized and basal reader tests, could not give an adequate picture of their students' learning. To address this problem, they set about developing their own portfolio assessment system.

In many cases teachers begin by collecting lots of student work in folders or by implementing numerous checklists. The initial focus on assessment activities, rather than on the purposes for assessment, often causes portfolio projects to founder. Julie and Sara avoided this pitfall by going through a three-phase process. They looked at the outcomes in their district's curricula, identified what they judged to be the major outcomes in Book Club, and found a way of meshing the two. They were sensitive to the requirements of their district, but they placed the district outcomes within the broader, constructivist framework of Book Club. Having outcomes in mind, they were in a position to seek the tools and procedures that would best assess students' progress toward these outcomes.

One aspect of the change process that I wondered about is the struggles and dilemmas that both Julie and Sara faced in the contexts of their schools and district. I wondered how much pressure they felt to continue to conform to the requirements of standardized tests and other traditional forms of evaluation. I wondered how other teachers and administrators in the district reacted to their use of portfolios. Often this struggle to change leads many teachers to adopt established measures because the challenges presented by others are too overwhelming. I think Julie and Sara probably faced such problems but chose not to write about them. I am interested in hearing about this at some time.

One of the greatest benefits of portfolio assessment is that it offers the potential of having students take ownership of their own literacy learning. Julie and Sara described several approaches to involving students in the process of self-assessment. They had students listen to tapes of Book Club discussions; complete questionnaires about their successes, failures, and goals as

Book Club participants; participate in the development of targets, or criteria, for high-quality work; and analyze their journal entries and discussions. Then they went beyond process to ask about product: Were students performing at an adequate level? This is a key question. It is perfectly possible for students to exhibit high levels of ownership but be performing far below grade level in the strategies of higher-level thinking required for understanding and interpreting literature or writing on self-selected topics. I applaud Julie and Sara's call for a balance between student ownership and the need to meet a certain standard of progress.

Finally, I was impressed by the manner in which Julie and Sara informed and involved parents. They tried to tailor the use of portfolios to parents' differing needs for information about their children's progress. In the future, I hope they will write more about this tailoring, perhaps including some case examples of students and their parents. I have read accounts about individualizing assessment to meet students' needs but not those of parents, and I believe this would be a valuable addition to the assessment research literature.

References

Aardema, V. (1975). *Why mosquitoes buzz in people's ears*. New York: Dial.

Abruscato, J. (1993). Early results and tentative implications from the Vermont Portfolio Project. *Phi Delta Kappan, 74*(6), 474–477.

Afflerbach, P. P., & Johnston, P. H. (1993). Writing language arts report cards: Eleven teachers conflicts of knowing and communicating. *The Elementary School Journal, 94*(1), 72–75.

Allen, V. L. (Ed.). (1976). *Children as teachers: Theory and research on tutoring.* New York: Academic.

Allington, R. L. (1991). The legacy of "slow it down and make it more concrete." In J. Zutell & S. McCormick (Eds.), *Learner factors/teacher factors: Issues in literacy research and instruction.* (Fortieth Yearbook of the National Reading Conference) (pp. 19–29). Chicago: The National Reading Conference.

Allington, R. L., & McGill-Franzen, A. (1989). Different programs, indifferent instruction. In A. Gardner & D. Lipsky (Eds.), *Beyond separate education* (pp. 75–98). Baltimore: Brookes.

Almasi, J. F. (1995). The nature of fourth graders' sociocognitive conflicts in peer-led and teacher-led discussion of literature. *Reading Research Quarterly, 30*(3), 314–351.

Alvermann, D. E. (1994). Trade books versus textbooks: Making connections across content areas. In L. M. Morrow, J. K. Smith, & L. C. Wilkinson (Eds.), *Integrated language arts: Controversy to consensus* (pp. 51–70). Boston: Allyn & Bacon.

Alvermann, D. E. (1995/96). Peer-led discussions: Whose interests are served? *Journal of Adolescent & Adult Literacy, 39*(4), 282–289.

Anderson, J. (1992). *Seminole wind.* New York: BMG Music.

Anderson, R. C., & Au, K. (1992). *Literacy in the content areas* (Classroom Instruction Videotape Series). Champaign, IL: Center for the Study of Literacy.

Anderson, R. C., Hiebert, E. H., Scott, J. A., & Wilkinson, I. A. G. (1985). *Becoming a nation of readers: The report of the commission on reading.* Washington, DC: U.S. Department of Education.

Anderson, R. C., & Pearson, P. D. (1984). A schematic theoretic view of basic processes in reading comprehension. In P. D. Pearson (Ed.), *Handbook of reading research* (pp. 255–292). New York: Longman.

Anderson, R. C., Wilson, P. T., & Fielding, L. G. (1988). Growth in reading and how children spend their time outside of school. *Reading Research Quarterly, 23*(3), 285–303.

Applebee, A. N. (1991). Environments for language teaching and learning: Contemporary issues and future directions. In *Handbook of research on teaching the English language arts* (pp. 549–556). New York: Macmillan.

Ashton-Warner, S. (1964). *Teacher*. New York: Simon & Schuster.

Atwell, N. (1984). Writing and reading literature from the inside out. *Language Arts, 61*, 240–252.

Atwell, N. (1987). *In the middle*. Upper Montclair, NJ: Boynton/Cook.

Au, K. H. (1993). *Literacy instruction in multicultural settings*. New York: Harcourt, Brace, Jovanovich.

Au, K. H., & Mason, J. M. (1981). Social organizational factors in learning to read: The balance of rights hypothesis. *Reading Research Quarterly, 17*(1), 115–152.

Au, K. H., Scheu, J. A., Kawakami, A. J., & Herman, P. A. (1990). Assessment and accountability in a whole literacy curriculum. *The Reading Teacher, 43*, 574–578.

Avi. (1984). *The fighting ground*. New York: HarperCollins.

Babbitt, N. (1975). *Tuck everlasting*. New York: Farrer, Strauss & Giroux.

Bakhtin, M. M. (1986). *Speech genres and other late essays* (V. W. McGee, Trans.). Austin: University of Texas Press.

Barnes, D. (1976). *From communication to curriculum*. New York: Penguin.

Barnes, D. (1993). Supporting exploratory talk. In K. M. Pierce & C. J. Gilles (Eds.), *Cycles of meaning* (pp. 17–35). Portsmouth, NH: Heinemann

Barnes, D. (1995). Talking and learning in classrooms: An introduction. *Primary voices, K–6, 3*(1), 2–7.

Barrett, J. (1978). *Cloudy with a chance of meatballs*. New York: Macmillan.

Beach, R. (1993). *A teacher's introduction to reader-response theories*. Urbana, IL: National Council of Teachers of English.

Beatty, P. (1984). *Turn homeward, Hannalee*. New York: Troll.

Beatty, P. (1987). *Charley Skedaddle*. New York: Troll.

Beck, I. L., & McKeown, M. G. (1986). Instructional research in reading: A retrospective. In J. Orsanu (Ed.), *Reading comprehension: From research to practice* (pp. 113–134). Hillsdale, NJ: Erlbaum.

Beck, I. L., McKeown, M. G., & Worthy, J. (1995). Giving a text voice can improve students' understanding. *Reading Research Quarterly, 30*(2), 220–238.

Bereiter, C., & Scardamalia, M. (1987). *The psychology of written composition*. Hillsdale, NJ: Erlbaum.

Berghoff, B., & Egawa, K. (1991). No more "rocks": Grouping to give students control of their learning. *Reading Teacher, 44*(8), 536–541.

Bisesi, T. (1993, December). *Envisionment building: Diverse learners constructing meaning during reading of fiction and nonfiction texts*. Paper presented at the annual meeting of the National Reading Conference, Charleston, SC.

Bisesi, T. (1996, April). *The process of striving to meet the challenge: Developing and implementing a performance-based assessment for a literature-based classroom*. Paper presented at the annual meeting of the American Educational Research Association, New York.

Bishop, R. S. (1993). Multicultural literature for children: Making informed choices. In V. J. Harris (Ed.), *Teaching multicultural literature in grades K–8* (pp. 37–53). Norwood, MA: Christopher-Gordon.

Black, J., & Seifert, C. (1985). The psychological study of story understanding. In C. Cooper (Ed.), *Research response to literature and the teaching of literature* (pp. 190–211). Norwood, NJ: Ablex.

Bloom, S. (1988). *Peer and cross-age tutoring in the schools: An individualized supplement to group instruction.* Washington, DC: U.S. Department of Health, Education, and Welfare, National Institute of Education.

Bloome, D. (1986). Building literacy and the classroom community. *Theory into Practice, 25*(2), 1–6.

Bloome, D., & Green, J. (1984). Directions in the sociolinguistic study of reading. In P. D. Pearson (Ed.), *Handbook of reading research* (pp. 393–421). New York: Longman.

Booth, D. (1994). *Children's voices.* Orlando, FL: Harcourt Brace.

Booth, D., & Barton, R. (1991). *Stories in the classroom.* Portsmouth, NH: Heinemann.

Boyd, F. B. (1995). The Cross-Aged Literacy Project: An alternative instructional program for adolescents who struggle with literacy and schooling. *Michigan Reading Journal, 28*(4), 46–56.

Brock, C. H. (1995, May). *Organizing literature-based reading instruction for second language learners.* Paper presented at the International Reading Association Annual Conference, Anaheim, CA.

Brophy, J., McMahon, S. I., & Prawat, R. (1991). Elementary social studies: Critique of a representative sample by six experts. *Social Education, 55,* 155–160.

Brown, A. L., & Palincsar, A. M. (1989). Guided, cooperative learning and individual knowledge acquisition. In L. B. Resnick (Ed.), *Knowing, learning, and instruction: Essays in honor of Robert Glaser* (pp. 393–451). Hillsdale, NJ: Erlbaum.

Bruffee, K. (1984). Peer tutoring and the "conversation of mankind." *College English, 46,* 635–652.

Bruner, J. (1986). *Actual minds, possible worlds.* Cambridge, MA: Harvard University Press.

Bruner, J. (1989). Vygotsky: A historical and conceptual perspective. In J. V. Wertsch (Ed.), *Culture, communication, and cognition* (pp. 21–34). New York: Cambridge University Press.

Burbules, N. (1993). *Dialogue in teaching: Theory and practice.* New York: Teachers College Press.

Calkins, L. M. (1986). *The art of teaching writing.* Portsmouth, NH: Heinemann.

Cazden, C. (1988a). *Classroom discourse: The language of teaching and learning.* Portsmouth, NH: Heinemann.

Cazden, C. (1988b). *Interactions between Maori children and Pakeha teachers.* Aukland, New Zealand: Aukland Reading Association.

Cazden, C., & Leggett, E. L. (1981). Culturally responsive education. Recommendations for achieving Lau remedies II. In H. Trueba, G. Guthrie, & K. H. Au (Eds.), *Culture and the bilingual classroom: Studies in classroom ethnography* (pp. 69–86). Rowley, MA: Newbury House.

Chambers, A. (1983). *Introducing books to children.* London: Heinemann Educational Books.

Chambers, A. (1985). *Booktalk*. London: Bodley Head.

Chang-Wells, G. L., & Wells, G. (1993). Dynamics of discourse: Literacy and the construction of knowledge. In E. A. Forman, N. Minick, & C. A. Stone (Eds.), *Contexts for learning: Sociocultural dynamics in children's development* (pp. 58–90). New York: Oxford University Press.

Clark, K., & Holquist, M. (1984). *Mikhail Bakhtin*. Cambridge, MA: Harvard University Press.

Clifford, J. (Ed.). (1991). *The experience of reading: Louise Rosenblatt and reader-response theory*. Portsmouth, NH: Boynton/Cook.

Cloward, R. (1967). Studies in tutoring. *Journal of Experimental Education, 36,* 14–25.

Coerr, E. (1977). *Sadako and the thousand paper cranes*. New York: Bantam Doubleday Dell.

Coerr, E. (1993). *Sadako*. New York: G. P. Putnam's Sons.

Cohen, E. G. (1986). *Designing groupwork strategies for the heterogeneous classroom*. New York: Teachers College Press.

Collier, V. P. (1989). How long? A synthesis of research on academic achievement in a second language. *TESOL Quarterly, 23*(3), 509–531.

Corson, D. (1984). The case for oral language in schooling. *The Elementary School Journal, 81*(1), 458–467.

Craighead-George, J. (1983). *The talking earth*. New York: Harper & Row.

Cullinan, B. E., & Galda, L. (1994). *Literature and the child* (3rd ed.). Fort Worth, TX: Harcourt Brace.

Cullinan, D., Sabornie, E. J., & Crossland, C. L. (1992). Social mainstreaming for mildly handicapped students. *The Elementary School Journal, 92*(3), 339–352.

Cummins, J. (1994). Knowledge, power, and identity in teaching English as a second language. In F. Genesee (Ed.), *Educating second language children: The whole child, the whole curriculum, and the whole community* (pp. 33–58). New York: Cambridge University Press.

Cunningham, P. M., Hall, D. P., & Defee, M. (1991). Non-ability grouped, multileveled instruction: A year in a first-grade classroom. *Reading Teacher, 44*(8), 566–571.

Dahl, R. (1961). *James and the giant peach*. New York: Puffin.

Dahl, R. (1966). *The magic finger*. New York: Harper & Row.

de la Luz Reyes, M. (1992). Challenging venerable assumptions: Literacy instruction for linguistically different students. *Harvard Educational Review, 62*(4), 427–447.

Delpit, L. D. (1988). The silenced dialogue: Power and pedagogy in educating other people's children. *Harvard Educational Review, 58*(3), 280–298.

Dewey, J. (1916). *Democracy and education: An introduction to the philosophy of education*. New York: Macmillan.

Dewey, J. (1933). *How we think*. Chicago: Henry Regnery.

Dewey, J. (1938). *Experience and education*. New York: Macmillan.

Dillner, M. (1971). *Tutoring by students: Who benefits?* Gainesville: Florida Educational Research and Development Council.

Dixon-Krauss, L. (1995). *Vygotsky in the classroom: Mediated literacy instruction and assessment*. White Plains, NY: Longman.

Dole, J. A., Duffy, G. G., Roehler, L. R., & Pearson, P. D. (1991). Moving from the old to the new: Research on reading comprehension instruction. *Review of Educational Research, 61*(2), 239–264.

Dollar, B. (1974). *Learning and growing through tutoring: A case study of youth tutoring youth.* New York: The National Commission on Resources for Youth.

Dorris, M. (1992). *Morning girl.* New York: Hyperion Books for Children.

Dudley-Marling, C. (1994). Struggling readers in the regular classroom: A personal reflection. *Reading Horizons, 34*(5), 465–487.

Duffy, G., & Roehler, L. (1987). Improving classroom reading instruction through the use of responsive elaboration. *Reading Teacher, 40,* 514–521.

Dyson, A. H. (1987). The value of "time off task": Young children's spontaneous talk and deliberate text. *Harvard Educational Review, 57*(4), 396–420.

Dyson, A. H. (1993). *Social worlds of children learning to write in an urban primary school.* New York: Teachers College Press.

Dyson, A. H. (1996). Faces in the crowd: Developing profiles of language users. In B. M. Power & R. S. Hubbard (Eds.), *Language development* (pp. 110–116). Englewood Cliffs, NJ: Merrill.

Eagleton, T. (1986). *Literary criticism.* Minneapolis: University of Minnesota Press.

Eder, D. (1986). Organizing constraints on reading group mobility. In J. Cook-Gumperz (Ed.), *The social construction of literacy* (pp. 138–155). New York: Cambridge University Press.

Edwards, D., & Mercer, N. (1987). *Common knowledge.* New York: Methuen.

Eeds, M., & Peterson, R. L. (1995). What teachers need to know about the literary craft. In N. L. Roser & M. C. Martinez (Eds.), *Book talk and beyond* (pp. 10–23). Newark, DE: International Reading Association.

Eeds, M., & Wells, D. (1989). Grand conversations: An explanation of meaning construction in literature study groups. *Research in the Teaching of English, 23*(1), 4–29.

Ellson, D. G. (1969). *Report of results, tutorial reading program.* Indianapolis Public Schools, Indianapolis, IN.

Emerson, C. (1986). The outer world and inner speech: Bakhtin, Vygotsky, and the internalization of language. In G. S. Morson (Ed.), *Bakhtin, essays and dialogues on his work.* Chicago: University of Chicago Press.

Englert, C. S., Raphael, T. E., & Anderson, L. M. (1992). Socially mediated instruction: Improving students' knowledge and talk about writing. *The Elementary School Journal, 92,* 411–449.

Englert, C. S., Raphael, T. E., & Mariage, T. (1994). Developing a school-based discourse for literacy learning: A principled search for understanding. *Learning Disability Quarterly, 17,* 2–32.

Evans, K. S. (1994, December). *Three cheers for "girl talk": The roles of grade 5 gendered talk in literature discussions.* Paper presented at the annual meeting of the National Reading Conference, San Diego.

Fader, D. N. (1968). *Hooked on books: Program and proof.* New York: Berkley.

Farr, R. (1992). Putting it all together: Solving the reading assessment puzzle. *The Reading Teacher, 46*(1), 26–37.

Farris, P. (1989). Story time and story journals: Linking literature and writing. *New Advocate, 2*(3), 179–185.

Feiman-Nemser, S., & Featherstone, H. (1992). *Exploring teaching: Reinventing an introductory course*. New York: Teachers College Press.

Feuer, M., & Fulton, K. (1993). The many faces of performance assessment. *Phi Delta Kappan, 74*(6), 478.

Fish, S. (1980). *Is there a text in this class? The authority of interpretive communities*. Cambridge, MA: Harvard University Press.

Fitzgerald, S. (1975). Teaching discussion skills and attitudes. *Language Arts, 52*, 1094–1096.

Florio-Ruane, S. (1991). Instructional conversations in learning to write and learning to teach. In L. Idol & B. F. Jones (Eds.), *Educational values and cognitive instruction: Implications for reform* (pp. 365–386). Hillsdale, NJ: Erlbaum.

Florio-Ruane, S. (1994). The future teachers' autobiography club: Preparing educators to support literacy learning in culturally diverse classrooms. *English Education, 26*(1), 52–66.

Flower, L. S., & Hayes, J. R. (1980). The dynamics of composing: Making plans and juggling constraints. In L. W. Gregg & E. R. Steinberg (Eds.), *Cognitive process in writing* (pp. 31–50). Hillsdale, NJ: Erlbaum.

Freedman, S. (1979). How characteristics of student essays influence teachers' evaluations. *Journal of Educational Psychology, 71*, 328–338.

Freedman, S. (1993). Linking large-scale testing and classroom portfolio assessments of student writing. *Educational Assessment, 1*(1), 27–52.

Freire, P. (1973). *Education for critical consciousness*. New York: Seabury.

Fulwiler, T. E. (1982). The personal connection: Journal writing across the curriculum. In T. Fulwiler & A. Young (Eds.), *Language connections: Writing and reading across the curriculum* (pp. 15–32). Urbana, IL: National Council of Teachers of English.

Fulwiler, T. (1986). *Teaching with writing*. Upper Montclair, NJ: Boynton/Cook.

Galda, L., Shockley, B., & Pellegrini, A. D. (1995). *Talking to read and write: Opportunities for literate talk in one primary classroom*. Athens, GA: National Reading Research Center.

Garcia, E. E. (1990). Educating teachers for language minority students. In W. R. Houston, M. Haberman, & J. Sikula (Eds.), *Handbook of research on teacher education* (pp. 717–729). New York: Macmillan.

Gardiner, J. R. (1980). *Stone Fox*. New York: Harper Trophy.

Gavelek, J. R. (1986). The social context of literacy and schooling: A developmental perspective. In T. E. Raphael (Ed.), *The contexts of school-based literacy* (pp. 3–26). New York: Random House.

Gavelek, J. R., & Raphael, T. E. (1996). Changing talk about text: New roles for teachers and students. *Language Arts, 73*(3), 182–192.

Gee, J. P. (1990). *Social linguistics and literacies: Ideology in discourses*. London: Falmer.

Genesee, F. (Ed.). (1994). *Educating second language children: The whole child, the whole curriculum, the whole community*. New York: Cambridge University Press.

Gilles, C. (1990). Collaborative literacy strategies: "We don't need a circle to have a group." In K. G. Short & K. M. Pierce (Eds.), *Talking about books: Creating literate communities* (pp. 55–68). Portsmouth, NH: Heinemann.

Giroux, H. A. (1988). Literacy and the pedagogy of voice and political empowerment. *Educational Theory, 38*, 61–75.

Goatley, V. J. (1996). The participation of a student identified as learning disabled in a regular education book club: The case of Stark. *Reading and Writing Quarterly, 12*, 195–214.

Goatley, V. J., Brock, C., & Raphael, T. E. (1995). Diverse learners participating in regular education book clubs. *Reading Research Quarterly, 30*(3), 352–380.

Goatley, V. J., Highfield, K., Bentley, J., Pardo, L. S., Folkert, J., Scherer, P., Raphael, T., & Grattan, K. (1994). Empowering teachers to be researchers: A collaborative approach. *Teacher Research: The Journal of Classroom Inquiry, 1*(2), 128–144.

Goatley, V. J., & Raphael, T. E. (1992). Non-traditional learners' written and dialogic response to literature. In C. K. Kinzer & D. J. Leu (Eds.), *Literacy research, theory and practice: Views from many perspectives* (Forty-first Yearbook of the National Reading Conference) (pp. 312–322). Chicago: National Reading Conference.

Gobel, P. (1978). *The girl who loved horses*. Scarsdale, NY: Bradburg Press.

Golden, J. M., & Guthrie, J. T. (1986). Convergence and divergence in reader response to literature. *Reading Research Quarterly, 21*(4), 408–421.

Goldenberg, C. (1992/93). Instructional conversations: Promoting comprehension through discussion. *The Reading Teacher, 46*(4), 316–326.

Goodman, K. S. (1976). Reading: A psycholinguistic guessing game. In H. Singer & R. B. Ruddell (Eds.), *Theoretical models and processes in reading* (pp. 497–508). Newark, DE: International Reading Association.

Goodman, K. S., Shannon, P., Freeman, Y., & Murphy, S. (1988). *Report card on basal readers*. Katonah, NY: Richard C. Owen Publishers.

Goodman, Y. M. (1978). Kid-watching: An alternative to testing. *National Elementary Principal, 10*, 41–45.

Goodman, Y. M. (1989). Roots of the whole-language movement. *Elementary School Journal, 90*(2), 113–128.

Granick, L. (1968). *Youth tutoring youth: It worked*. New York: National Commission on Resources for Youth.

Graves, D. H. (1983). *Writing: Teachers and children at work*. Exeter, NH: Heinemann.

Graves, D. H., & Hansen, J. (1983). The author's chair. *Language Arts, 60*, 176–183.

Green, J. L. (1990). Reading is a social process. In J. Howell & A. McNamara (Eds.), *Social context of literacy* (pp. 104–122). Canberra, Australia: ACT Department of Education.

Haladyna, R., Nolen, S. B., & Haas, N. (1991). Raising standardized achievement tests scores and the origins of test score pollution. *Educational Researcher, 20*(5), 2–7.

Halliday, M. A. K. (1975). *Learning how to mean*. London: Arnold.

Halliday, M. A. K. (1993). Towards a language-based theory of learning. *Linguistics and Education, 5*, 93–116.

Hansen, E. (1986). *Emotional processes engendered by poetry and prose reading*. Stockholm: Almquist & Wiksell.

Hansen, J. (1987). *When writers read.* Portsmouth, NH: Heinemann.

Harker, W. J. (1987). Literary theory and the reading process: A meeting of perspectives. *Written Communication, 9*, 235–252.

Harré, R. (1984). *Personal being: A theory for individual psychology.* Cambridge: Harvard University Press.

Harré, R. (1986). Social sources of mental content and order. In J. Margolis, P. T. Manicas, R. Harré, & P. F. Secord (Eds.), *Psychology: Designing the discipline* (pp. 91–127). New York: Basil Blackwell.

Harris, V. J. (Ed.). (1992). *Teaching multicultural literature in grades K–8.* Norwood, MA: Christopher-Gordon.

Hauschildt, P., & McMahon, S. I. (1997). *Reconceptualizing "resistant" learners and rethinking instruction: Risking a trip to the swamp.* Manuscript submitted for publication.

Heath, S. B. (1991). The sense of being literate: Historical and cross-cultural features. In R. Barr, M. L. Kamil, P. B. Mosenthal, & P. D. Pearson (Eds.), *The handbook of reading research* (Vol. II) (pp. 3–25). New York: Longman.

Hepler, S. (1992). Picking our way to literacy in the classroom community. In C. Temple & P. Collins (Eds.), *Stories and readers* (pp. 67–84). Norwood, MA: Christopher-Gordon.

Heyer, M. (1986). *The weaving of a dream.* New York: Puffin.

Hickman, J. (1983). Everything considered: Response to literature in an elementary school setting. *Journal of Research and Development in Education, 16*(3), 8–13.

Hiebert, E. H. (1993). Lessons from a Chapter 1 project. In I. C. Rotberg (Ed.), *Federal policy options for improving the education of low-income students* (pp. 48–53). Santa Monica, CA: Rand.

Hillocks, G. J. (1984). What works in teaching compositions: A meta-analysis of experimental treatment studies. *American Journal of Education, 93*, 107–132.

Hoffman, J. V. (1992). Critical reading/thinking across the curriculum: Using I-Charts to support learning. *Language Arts, 69*(2), 121–127.

Hoggart, R. (1970). Why I value literature. In R. Hoggart (Ed.), *Speaking to each other* (Vol. 2) (pp. 11–18). New York: Oxford University Press.

Holdaway, D. (1979). *The foundations of literacy.* New York: Ashton Scholastic.

Holling, H. C. (1941). *Paddle-to-the-sea.* Boston, MA: Houghton Mifflin.

Hubbard, R. S., & Power, B. M. (1993). *The art of classroom inquiry: A handbook for teacher-researchers.* Portsmouth, NH: Heinemann.

Hudelson, S. (1994). Literacy development of second language children. In F. Genesee (Ed.), *Educating second language children: The whole child, the whole curriculum, the whole community* (pp. 129–158). New York: Cambridge University Press.

Hunt, I. (1964). *Across five Aprils.* New York: Berkley.

Hunt, P. (1991). *Criticism, theory, and children's literature.* Oxford, UK: Basil Blackwell.

Iser, W. (1978). *The act of reading: A theory of aesthetic response.* Baltimore: Johns Hopkins University Press.

Jett-Simpson, M., & Masland, S. (1993). Girls are not Dodo Birds! Exploring gender equity issues in the Language Arts classroom. *Language Arts, 70*, 104–108.

Johnson, D. W., & Johnson, R. T. (1990). Cooperative learning and achievement. In S. Sharan (Ed.), *Cooperative learning* (pp. 23–37). New York: Praeger.

Johnson D., Johnson, R., & Holubec, E. (1993). *Circles of learning: Cooperation in the classroom* (4th ed). Minneapolis: Interaction Book Co.

Johnston, P. (1989). Constructive evaluation and the improvement of teaching and learning. *Teachers College Record, 90*(4), 509–527.

John-Steiner, V. (1985). The road to competence in an alien land: A Vygotskian perspective on bilingualism. In J. V. Wertsch (Ed.), *Culture, communication, and cognition: Vygotskian perspectives* (pp. 348–372). New York: Cambridge University Press.

Johnston, P., & Allington, R. (1991). Remediation. In R. Barr, M. L. Kamil, P. B. Mosenthal, & P. D. Pearson (Eds.), *Handbook of reading research* (Vol. II) (pp. 984–1012). New York: Longman.

Jose, P., & Brewer, S. (1984). Development of story liking: Character identification, suspense, and outcome resolution. *Developmental Psychology, 20*, 911–924.

Keegan, S., & Shrake, K. (1991). Literature study groups: An alternative to ability grouping. *Reading Teacher, 44*(8), 542–547.

Kennedy, M. M., Jung, R. K., & Orland, M. E. (1986). *Poverty, achievement, and the distribution of compensatory education services.* Washington, DC: Office of Educational Research and Improvement, U.S. Department of Education.

Krogness, M. M. (1989). Reading, writing, rappin' and rollin'. In J. M. Jensen (Ed.), *Stories to grow on* (pp. 157–167). Portsmouth, NH: Heinemann.

Kucer, S. L. (1985). The making of meaning: Reading and writing as parallel processes. *Written Communication, 2*, 317–336.

Lampert, M. (1985). How do teachers manage to teach? *Harvard Educational Review, 55*(2), 178–194.

Langer, J. A. (1990a). The process of understanding: Reading for literary and informative purposes. *Research in the Teaching of English, 24*(3), 229–260.

Langer, J. A. (1990b). Understanding literature. *Language Arts, 67*, 812–816.

Langer, J. A. (1991). Literacy and schooling: A sociocognitive perspective. In E. H. Hiebert (Ed.), *Literacy for a diverse society* (pp. 9–27). New York: Teachers College Press.

Langer, J. A. (1995). *Envisioning literature: Literary understanding and literature instruction.* New York: Teachers College Press.

Lehr, S. S. (1991). *The child's developing sense of theme.* New York: Teachers College Press.

Linn, R. L., Baker, E. L., & Dunbar, S. B. (1991). Complex, performance-based assessment: Expectations and validation criteria. *Educational Researcher, 20*, 15–21.

Lipson, M. Y., Valencia, S. W., Wixson, K. K., & Peters, C. W. (1993). Integration and thematic teaching: Integration to improve teaching and learning. *Language Arts, 70*(4), 252–263.

Lotman, Y. M. (1988). Text within a text. *Soviet Psychology, 26*(3), 32–51.

Lowry, L. (1987). *Martin Luther King Day.* New York: Scholastic.

Lowry, L. (1989). *Number the stars.* South Holland, IL: Yearling.

Lucking, R. A. (1976). A study of the effects of a hierarchically-ordered questioning technique of adolescents' response to short stories. *Research in the teaching of English, 10*, 269–276.

MacClean, M. (1988). A framework for analyzing reader-text interactions. *Journal of Research and Development in Education, 19*(2), 16–21.

Maruki, T. (1980). *Hiroshima No Pika.* New York: Lothrop, Lee & Shepard.

McCarthey, S. J., & Raphael, T. E. (1992). Alternative perspectives of reading/writing connections. In J. W. Irwin & M. A. Doyle (Eds.), *Reading/writing connections: Learning from research* (pp. 2–30). Newark, DE: International Reading Association.

McGee, L. (1992). An exploration of meaning, construction in first graders' grand conversations. In C. K. Kinzer & D. J. Leu (Eds.), *Literacy research, theory, and practice: Views from many perspectives* (41st Yearbook of the National Reading Conference) (pp. 177–186). Chicago: National Reading Conference.

McGee, L. M. (1995). *Talking about books with young children.* In N. L. Roser & M. G. Martinez (Eds.), *Book talk and beyond* (pp. 105–115). Newark, DE: International Reading Association.

McKeon, D. (1994). Language, culture, and schooling. In F. Genesee (Ed.), *Educating second language children* (pp. 15–32). New York: Cambridge University Press.

McMahon, S. I. (1994). Student-led Book Clubs: Transversing a river of interpretation. *The New Advocate, 7*(2), 109–126.

McMahon, S. I. (1996). Student discussions about texts: Why student-led groups are important. In L. B. Gambrell & J. F. Almasi (Eds.), *Lively discussions: Creating elementary classrooms that foster engaged reading* (pp. 224–247). Newark, DE: International Reading Association.

McMahon, S. I., & Goatley, V. J. (1995). Fifth graders helping peers discuss texts in student-led groups. *Journal of Educational Research, 89*(1), 23–35.

McMahon, S. I., & Hauschildt, P. (1993, April). *What do we do now? Students' struggles with talking about books.* Paper presented at the annual meeting of the American Educational Research Association, Atlanta.

Mead, G. H. (1934). *Mind, self, and society from the standpoint of a social behaviorist.* Chicago: University of Chicago Press.

Meltzer, M. (1990). They that take the sword. In A. Durell & M. Sachs (Eds.), *The big book for peace.* New York: E.P. Dutton Children's Books.

Michaels, S. (1981). "Sharing time": Children's narrative styles and differential access to literacy. *Language in Society, 10*, 423–442.

Moll, L. C., & Gonzalez, N. (1994). Lessons from research with language minority children. *Journal of Reading Behavior, 26*(4), 439–456.

Moore, S. R. (1995). Focus on research: Questions for research into reading-writing relationships and text structure knowledge. *Language Arts, 72*(8), 598–606.

Morimoto, J. (1987). *My Hiroshima.* New York: Viking.

Morrice, C., & Simmons, M. (1991). Beyond reading buddies: A whole language cross-aged program. *Reading Teacher, 44*(8), 572–579.

Mosenthal, J. (1987). The reader's affective response to narrative text. In R. Tierney, P. Anders, & J. Mitchell (Eds.), *Understanding readers' understanding* (pp. 95–105). Hillsdale, NJ: Erlbaum.

National Center of Research on Teacher Learning. (1991). *An agenda for research on teacher learning*. East Lansing: Michigan State University.

Naylor, P. R. (1991). *Shiloh*. New York: Atheneum.

Nieto, S. (1992). *Affirming diversity: The sociopolitical context of multicultural education*. New York: Longman.

Noam, E. (1995). Electronics and the dim future in the university. *Science, 270*, 247–249.

Numeroff, L. (1985). *If you give a mouse a cookie*. New York: HarperCollins.

O'Brien, K. L. (1991). A look at one successful literature program. *The New Advocate, 4*(2), 113–123.

Odell, L., & Cooper, C. (1976). Describing responses to works of fiction. *Research in the Teaching of English, 10*, 203–225.

O'Dell, S. (1960). *Island of the blue dolphins*. New York: Dell.

Ogle, D. M. (1986). K-W-L: A teaching model that develops active reading of expository text. *The Reading Teacher, 39*(6), 564–570.

Paley, V. G. (1986). On listening to what the children say. *Harvard Educational Review, 56*(2), 122–131.

Palincsar, A. S., & Brown, A. L. (1984). Reciprocal Teaching of comprehension-fostering and comprehension-monitoring activities. *Cognition and Instruction, 1*, 117–125.

Paoni, F. J. (1971). *Reciprocal effects of sixth graders tutoring third graders in reading*. Unpublished doctoral dissertation, Oregon State University, Corvallis.

Pappas, C. C., & Brown, B. (1987). Young children learning story discourse: Three case studies. *The Elementary School Journal, 87*(4), 454–466.

Pardo, L. S. (1992, December). *Accommodating diversity in the elementary classroom: A look at literature-based instruction in an inner city school*. Paper presented at the 1992 National Reading Conference, San Antonio, TX.

Paris, S., Calfee, R., Filby, N., Hiebert, E., Pearson, P. D., Valencia, S., & Wolf, K. (1992). A framework for authentic literacy assessment. *The Reading Teacher, 46*(2), 88–98.

Paris, S., Lawton, T., Turner, J., & Roth, J. (1991). A developmental perspective on standardized achievement testing. *Educational Researcher, 20*(5), 12–20.

Paterson, K. (1977). *Bridge to Terabithia*. New York: Harper Trophy.

Paterson, K. (1988). *Park's quest*. New York: Dutton.

Patton, M. Q. (1985). *Qualitative evaluation methods*. Beverly Hills: Sage.

Paulsen, G. (1987). *Hatchet*. New York: Puffin.

Pearson P. D. (1985). Changing the face of reading comprehension instruction. *The Reading Teacher, 38*(6), 724–738.

Pearson, P. D. (1994). Integrated language arts: Sources of controversy and seeds of consensus. In L. M. Morrow, J. K. Smith, & L. C. Wilkinson (Eds.), *Integrated language arts: Controversy to consensus* (pp. 11–31). Boston: Allyn & Bacon.

Pearson, P. D., & Fielding, L. (1991). Comprehension instruction. In R. Barr (Ed.), *Handbook of reading research* (Vol. 2) (pp. 815–860). New York: Longman.

Philips, S. U. (1983). *The invisible culture: Communication in classrooms and community on the Warm Springs Indian Reservation*. White Plains, NY: Longman.

Pierce, M. M., Stahlbrand, K., & Armstrong, S. B. (1980). *Increasing student productivity through peer tutoring programs*. Austin, TX: Pro-Ed.

Probst, R. (1988). *Response and analysis: Teaching literature in junior and senior high school*. Portsmouth, NH: Boynton/Cook, Heinemann.

Probst, R. E. (1991). Response to literature. In J. Flood, J. M. Jensen, D. Lapp, & J. R. Squire (Eds.), *Handbook of research on teaching the English language arts* (pp. 655–663). New York: Macmillan.

Purves, A. C. (1990). *Indeterminate texts, responsive readers, and the idea of difficulty in literature learning* (Report Series 4.1). Albany: State University of New York, Center for the Learning and Teaching of Literature.

Purves, A. C., & Beach, R. (1972). *Literature and the reader: Research in response to literature, reading interests, and the teaching of literature*. Urbana, IL: National Council of Teachers of English.

Rabe, B. (1981). *The balancing girl*. New York: Dutton.

Raphael, T. E., Boyd, F. B., & Rittenhouse, P. S. (1993, April). *Reading logs in the Book Club program: Using writing to support understanding and interpretation of text*. Paper presented at the annual meeting of the American Educational Research Association, Atlanta.

Raphael, T., & Brock, C. (1993). Mei: Learning the literacy culture in an urban elementary school. In D. Leu & C. Kinzer (Eds.), *Examining central issues in literacy research, theory, and practice* (pp. 179–189). Chicago: National Reading Conference.

Raphael, T. E., & Englert, C. S. (1990). Writing and reading: Partners in constructing meaning. *The Reading Teacher, 43*(6), 388–400.

Raphael, T. E., & Goatley, V. J. (1994). The teacher as "more knowledgeable other": Changing roles for teaching in alternative reading instruction programs. In C. Kinzer & D. Leu (Eds.), *Multidimensional aspects of literacy research, theory and practice* (Forty-third Yearbook of the National Reading Conference) (pp. 527–536). Chicago: National Reading Conference.

Raphael, T. E., & Hiebert, E. H. (1996). *Creating an integrated approach to literacy instruction*. Ft. Worth, TX: Harcourt Brace.

Raphael, T. E., & McMahon, S. I. (1994). Book Club: An alternative framework for reading instruction. *The Reading Teacher, 48*(2), 102–116.

Raphael, T. E., McMahon, S. I., Goatley, V. J., Bentley, J. L., Boyd, F. B., Pardo, L. S., & Woodman, D. A. (1992). Research directions: Literature and discussion in the reading program. *Language Arts, 69*(1), 54–61.

Raphael, T. E., Wallace, S., & Pardo, L. S. (1996, April). *Assessing the literacy growth of fifth grade students: A question of realigning curriculum, instruction, and assessment*. Paper presented at American Educational Research Association, New York.

Reed, S. D. (1988). Logs: Keeping an open mind. *English Journal, 77*(2), 52–56.

Reeder, C. (1989). *Shades of gray*. New York: Avon.

Reiss, J. (1972). *The upstairs room*. New York: Harper & Row.

Reit, S. (1988). *Behind rebel lines*. Orlando, FL: Harcourt Brace Jovanovich.

Resnick, D. P., & Resnick, L. B. (1977). The nature of literacy: An historical explanation. *Harvard Educational Review, 47*(3), 370–385.

Richler, M. (1987). *Jacob two-two and the hooded fang.* New York: Bantam.

Ride, S., & Okie, S. (1986). *To space and back.* New York: Lothrop, Lee & Shepard.

Roehler, L. R., Duffy, G. G., & Meloth, M. S. (1986). What to be direct about in direct instruction in reading: Content-only versus process-into-content. In T. E. Raphael (Ed.), *The contexts of school-based literacy* (pp. 79–95). New York: Random House.

Rogoff, B. (1994). Developing understanding of the idea of communities of learners. *Mind, Culture, and Activity, 1*(4), 209–229.

Roller, C. M., & Beed, P. L. (1994). Sometimes the conversations were grand, and sometimes . . . *Language Arts, 71*(7), 509–515.

Rose, D. L. (1990). *The people who hugged the trees.* Niwot, CO: Roberts Rinehart.

Rosenblatt, L. (1968). *The reader, the text, and the poem.* Carbondale: Southern Illinois University Press.

Rosenblatt, L. M. (1976). *Literature as exploration.* New York: Noble & Noble. (Original work published 1938)

Rosenblatt, L. M. (1983). *Literature as exploration.* New York: Modern Language Association of America.

Rosenblatt, L. M. (1985). The transactional theory of the literary work: Implications for research. In C. Cooper (Ed.), *Researching response to literature and the teaching of literature: Points of departure* (pp. 33–53). Norwood, NJ: Ablex.

Rosenblatt, L. M. (1991a). Literary theory. In J. Flood, J. M. Jensen, D. Lapp, & J. R. Squire (Eds.), *Handbook of research on teaching the English language arts* (pp. 57–62). New York: Macmillan.

Rosenblatt, L. M. (1991b). Literature–S.O.S.! *Language Arts, 68*(6), 444–448.

Rosenshine, B., & Furst, N. (1969). *The effects of tutoring upon pupil achievement: A research review.* Philadelphia: Temple University Press.

Routman, R. (1988). *Transitions: From literature to literacy.* Portsmouth, NH: Heinemann.

Routman, R. (1991). *Invitations: Changing as teachers and learners, K–12.* Portsmouth, NH: Heinemann.

San Souci, R. D. (1987). *The enchanted tapestry.* New York: Dial.

Schloss, P. J. (1992). Mainstreaming revisited. *The Elementary School Journal, 92*(3), 233–244.

Scholes, R. (1985). *Textual power.* New Haven, CT: Yale University Press.

Schön, D. A. (1983). *The reflective practitioner: How professionals think in action.* New York: Basic Books.

Schön, D. A. (1987). *Educating the reflective practitioner.* San Francisco: Jossey-Bass.

Shepard, L. (1989). Why we need better assessments. *Educational Leadership, 46*(7), 4–9.

Shor, I. (1992). *Empowering education.* Chicago: University of Chicago Press.

Short, K. G. (1990). Creating a community of learners. In K. G. Short & K. M. Pierce (Eds.), *Talking about books* (pp. 33–52). Portsmouth, NH: Heinemann.

Silverstein, S. (1964). *The giving tree.* New York: Harper & Row.

Sims Bishop, R. (1992). Multicultural literature for children: Making informed choices. In V. Harris (Ed.), *Teaching multicultural literature in grades K–8* (pp. 37–53). Norwood, MA: Christopher-Gordon.

Sinha, C. (1989). *Language and representation*. New York: New York University Press.

Sloan, G. D. (1991). *The child as critic: Teaching literature in elementary and middle schools*. New York: Teachers College Press.

Smagorinsky, P. (1986). An apology for structured composition instruction. *Written Communication, 3*(1), 105–121.

Smith, F. (1988). *Joining the literacy club*. Portsmouth, NH: Heinemann.

Snapp, M. (1970). *A study of the effects of tutoring by fifth and sixth graders on the reading achievement scores of first, second, and third graders*. Unpublished doctoral dissertation, University of Texas, Austin.

Speare, E. G. (1983). *The sign of the beaver*. New York: Dell.

Squire, J. R. (1964). *The responses of adolescents while reading four short stories*. Champaign, IL: National Council of Teachers of English.

Stainback, S., & Stainback, W. (1992). *Curriculum considerations in inclusive classrooms: Facilitating learning for all students*. Baltimore: Paul H. Brookes.

Stainback, W., & Stainback, S. (1990). *Support networks for inclusive schooling: Interdependent integrated education*. Baltimore: Paul H. Brookes.

Stanford, G. (1977). *Developing effective classroom groups*. New York: Hart Publishing Company.

Stanley, D. (1986). *Peter the Great*. New York: Macmillan.

Stanley, D., & Vennema, P. (1988). *Shaka, king of the Zulus*. New York: Morrow.

Stiggins, R. J. (1987). Design and development of performance assessments. *Educational Measurement: Issues and Practices, 6*(3), 33–42.

Strickland, D. (1988). The teacher as researcher: Toward the extended professional. *Language Arts, 65*(8), 754–764.

Strickland, D. S., Dillon, R. M., Finkhouser, L., Glick, M., & Rogers, C. (1989). Research currents: Classroom dialogue during literature response groups. *Language Arts, 66*(2), 192–200.

Strodtbeck, F., & Granick, L. (1972). *An evaluation of the youth tutoring model for in-school neighborhood youth corps*. New York: National Commission on Resources for Youth.

Sullivan, G. (1991). *The day Pearl Harbor was bombed: A photo history of World War II*. New York: Scholastic.

Swales, J. M. (1990). *Genre analysis: English in academic and research settings*. Cambridge, UK; New York: Cambridge University Press.

Swartz, L. (1994). Reading response journals: One teacher's research. In G. Wells et al. (Eds.), *Changing schools from within: Creating communities of inquiry* (pp. 99–127). Portsmouth, NH: Heinemann.

Swift, K. (1993). Try reading workshop in your classroom. *The Reading Teacher, 46*(5), 366–371.

Tannen, D. (1990). *You just don't understand: Women and men in conversation*. New York: Ballantine.

Taylor, M. D. (1975). *Song of the trees*. New York: Bantam.

Taylor, M. D. (1989). *The friendship and the gold Cadillac*. New York: Bantam.

Taylor, M. D. (1990). *Mississippi Bridge*. New York: Bantam.

Tharpe, R. G., & Gallimore, R. (1988). *Rousing minds to life*. New York: Cambridge University Press.

Tierney, R. J., Carter, M. A., & Desai, L. E. (1991). *Portfolio assessment in the reading-writing classroom*. Norwood, MA: Christopher-Gordon.

Tierney, R. J., & Pearson, P. D. (1983). Toward a composing model of reading. *Language Arts, 60*(5), 568–589.

Tierney, R. J., & Shanahan, T. (1991). Research on the reading-writing relationship: Interactions, transactions, and outcomes. In R. Barr, M. L. Kamil, P. Mosenthal, & P. D. Pearson (Eds.), *Handbook of reading research* (Vol. II) (pp. 246–280). New York: Longman.

Topping, K. (1988). *The peer tutoring handbook: Promoting co-operative learning*. Cambridge, MA: Brookline Books.

Tsuchiya, Y. (1988). *Faithful elephants: A true story of animals, people and war*. Boston: Houghton Mifflin.

Tunnell, M. O., & Jacobs, J. J. (1989). Using "real" books: Research findings on literature based reading instruction. *The Reading Teacher, 42*(6), 470–477.

Valdes, G. (1992). Bilingual minorities and language issues in writing: Toward profession wide responses to a new challenge. *Written Communication, 9*(1), 85–136.

Valencia, S. (1990). Alternative assessment: Separating the wheat from the chaff. *The Reading Teacher, 44*(1), 60–61.

Valencia, S. (in press). Portfolios: Panacea or Pandora's box? In F. Finch (Ed.), *Educational performance testing*. Chicago, IL: Riverside.

Van Allsburg, C. (1981). *Jumanji*. New York: Houghton Mifflin.

Van Lier, L. (1988). *The classroom and the language learner*. New York: Longman.

Villaume, S. K., Worden, T., Williams, S., Hopkins, L., & Rosenblatt, C. (1994). Five teachers in search of a discussion. *Language Arts, 47*(6), 480–489.

Vygotsky, L. S. (1978). *Mind in society: The development of higher mental psychological processes*. Cambridge, MA: Harvard University Press.

Vygotsky, L. S. (1981). The genesis of higher mental functions. In J. V. Wertsch (Ed. & Trans.), *The concept of activity in Soviet psychology* (pp. 144–188). Armonk, NY: Sharpe.

Vygotsky, L. S. (1986). *Thought and language* (A. Kozulin, Trans.). Cambridge, MA: MIT Press.

Vygotsky, L. S. (1987). Thinking and speech. In R. W. Rieber & A. S. Carton (Eds.), *The collected works of L. S. Vygotsky: Vol. 1. Problems of general psychology* (N. Minick, Trans., pp. 144–188). New York: Plenum.

Wagner, L. (1982). *Peer teaching: Historical perspectives*. Westport, CT: Greenwood.

Walmsley, S. A., & Walp, T. P. (1989). *Teaching literature in elementary school* (Report Series 1.3). Albany: State University of New York, Center for the Learning and Teaching of Literature.

Walmsley, S. A., & Walp, T. P. (1990). Toward an integrated language arts curriculum in elementary school: Philosophy, practice, and implications. *Elementary School Journal, 90*, 257–294.

Weitzman, D. (1965). Effect of tutoring on performance and motivation ratings in secondary school students. *California Journal of Educational Research, 16*, 108–115.

Wells, D. (1995). Leading grand conversations. In N. L. Roser & M. G. Martinez (Eds.), *Book talk and beyond* (pp. 132–139). Newark, DE: International Reading Association.

Wells, G. (1990a). Creating the conditions to encourage literate thinking. *Educational Leadership, 47*(6), 13–17.

Wells, G. (1990b). Talk about text: Where literacy is learned and taught. *Curriculum Inquiry, 20*(4), 369–405.

Wells, G. (1993). Reevaluating the IRF sequence: A proposal for the articulation of theories of activity and discourse for the analysis of teaching and learning in the classroom. *Linguistics and Education, 5*(1), 1–38.

Wells, G. (1994a). The complementary contributions of Halliday and Vygotsky to a "language-based theory of learning." *Linguistics and Education, 6*, 41–90.

Wells, G. (1994b). Teacher research and educational change. In G. Wells et al. (Eds.), *Changing schools from within: Creating communities of inquiry* (pp. 1–35). Portsmouth, NH: Heinemann.

Wells, G. (1995). Language and the inquiry-oriented curriculum. *Curriculum Inquiry, 25*(3), 233–269.

Wells, G. (1996). Using the tool-kit of discourse in the activity of learning and teaching. *Mind, Culture, and Activity, 3*(2), 74–101.

Wells, G., & Chang-Wells, G. L. (1992). *Constructing knowledge together*. Portsmouth, NH: Heinemann.

Wells, G., & Chang-Wells, G. (1996). The literate potential of collaborative talk. In B. M. Power & R. S. Hubbard (Eds.), *Language development* (pp. 155–168). Englewood Cliffs, NJ: Merrill.

Wells, G., Chang, G. L. M., & Maher, A. (1990). Creating classroom communities of literate thinkers. In S. Sharan (Ed.), *Cooperative learning* (pp. 95–121). New York: Praeger.

Wertsch, J. V. (Ed.). (1985). *Vygotsky and the social formation of mind*. Cambridge, MA: Harvard University Press.

Wertsch, J. V. (1991). *Voices of the mind: A sociocultural approach to mediated action*. Cambridge, MA: Harvard University Press.

White, E. B. (1952). *Charlotte's web*. New York: Harper.

Wiencek, J., & O'Flahavan, J. F. (1994). From teacher-led to peer discussions about literature: Suggestions for making the shift. *Language Arts, 71*(7), 488–498.

Wiggins, G. (1989). A true test: Toward more authentic and equitable assessment. *Phi Delta Kappan, 70*(9), 703–713.

Wilson, P. (1992). Among nonreaders: Voluntary reading, reading achievement, and the development of reading habits. In C. Temple & P. Collins (Eds.), *Stories and readers* (pp. 157–179). Norwood, MA: Christopher-Gordon.

Wolf, S. (1993, December). *"No one had ever talked to her of things like this before."* Discussant presentation at the National Reading Conference, Charleston, SC.

Wollman-Bonilla, J. E., & Werchadlo, B. (1995). Literature response journals in a first-grade classroom. *Language Arts, 72*(8), 562–570.

Wolper, D. L. (Producer). (1977). *Roots* [Film]. Los Angeles: Wolper Pictures, Warner Home Video.

Wood, B., Bruner, J. S., & Ross, G. (1976). The role of tutoring in problem solving. *Journal of Child Psychology and Psychiatry, 17*, 89–100.

Worthen, B. (1993, February). Critical issues that will determine the future of alternative assessment. *Phi Delta Kappan, 74*, 444–448.

Yolen, J. (1988). *The devil's arithmetic*. New York: Puffin.
Yoricks, A. (1980). *Louis the Fish*. New York: Farrar, Strauss & Giroux.
Yoricks, A. (1986). *Hey Al!* New York: Farrar, Strauss & Giroux.
Zarillo, J. (1991). Theory becomes practice: Aesthetic teaching with literature. *New Advocate, 4*, 221–233.

APPENDIX: ADDITIONAL BOOKS USED

Colonization: Exploring relationships between the European settlers and the Native Americans

Historical Fiction:
Conrad, J. (1991). *Pedro's journal*. Honesdale, PA: Caroline House.
Dorris, M. (1992). *Morning girl*. New York: Hyperion Books for Children.
Speare, E. G. (1983). *Sign of the beaver*. New York: Dell.

Picture Books:
Bruchac, J. (1995). *Gluskabe and the four wishes*. New York: Cobblehill Book/Dutton.
Harrell, B. (1995). *How thunder and lightning came to be*. New York: Dial Books for Young Readers.
Sis, P. (1991). *Follow the dream*. New York: Knopf/Random House.
Yolen, J. (1992). *Encounter*. New York: Knopf.

Information Texts:
Freedman, R. (1987). *Cobblestone: The story of American Indian chiefs*. New York: Scholastic.
Freedman, R. (1992). *Indian winter*. New York: Holoday House.
Liptak, K. (1990). *North American Indian sign language*. New York: Watts.

Understanding the Revolutionary War and the birth of a new nation

Historical Fiction:
Avi. (1984). *The fighting ground*. New York: Lippincott.

Picture Books:
Longfellow, H. (1990). *Paul Revere's ride*. New York: Dutton Children's Books.
Polacco, P. (1990). *Just plain fancy*. New York: Bantam Books.

The role of the Civil War in our country's growth and development

Historical Fiction:
Beatty, P. (1987). *Charley Skedaddle*. New York: Marrow.
Paulsen, G. (1993). *Night John*. New York: Delacorte Press.
Taylor, M. (1976). *Roll of thunder, hear my cry*. New York: Dial Press.

Picture Books:
Levine, E. (1988, 1992). *If you traveled on the underground railroad*. New York: Scholastic.

Polacco, P. (1994). *Pink and say*. New York: Philomel Books.
Ringgold, F. (1992). *Aunt Harriet's underground railroad in the sly*. New York: Crown.
Winter, J. (1988). *Follow the drinking gourd*. New York: Knopf.

Information Texts:
Haskins, J. (1985). *The day Fort Sumter was fired on*. New York: Scholastic.
Meltzer, M. (1980). *All times, all people*. New York: Harper & Row.

World War II: Beyond the boundaries of our nation

Historical Fiction:
Coerr, E. (1993). *Mieko and the fifth treasure*. New York: G. P. Putnam's Sons.
Reiss, J. (1972). *The upstairs room*. New York: Crowell.
Yolen, J. (1988). *The devil's arithmetic*. New York: Puffin Books.

Picture Books:
Innocenti, R. (1985). *Rose Blanche*. Mankato, MN: Creative Education, Inc.
Tsuchiya, Y. (1988). *Faithful elephants*. Boston: Houghton Mifflin.

Information Texts:
Pettit, J. (1993). *A place to hide*. New York: Scholastic Inc.
van der Rol, R., & Verhoeven, R. (1993). *Anne Frank: Beyond the diary*. New York: Viking.

About the Authors

Sara Bean teaches fourth grade at Highmeadow Common Campus, a National Exemplary School in Farmington, Michigan. She received her master's degree in literacy education from Michigan State University. She is presently a member of a teacher-researcher group and has shared her research at both the state and national level.

Tanja L. Bisesi is a doctoral student in the educational psychology program at Michigan State University. She teaches courses for pre-service and in-service teachers in language development, educational psychology, and classroom literacy assessment. Her research focuses on classroom literacy assessment practices. She formerly worked as a speech–language pathologist in the public schools and other settings.

Fenice B. Boyd received her Ph.D. from Michigan State University. She is an assistant professor in the Department of Language Education at the University of Georgia. Her current research interest centers on developing alternative literacy learning contexts for adolescents who struggle with reading, writing, and schooling.

Cynthia H. Brock is a doctoral candidate in educational psychology at Michigan State University. She was a public school teacher for nine years, teaching in both large inner-city schools and in small rural districts. Her research interests include student learning in general, and literacy learning and instruction for second-language learners, particularly at the elementary school level.

Jenny Davis is a student at Everett High School in Lansing, Michigan. Her favorite subjects are English and social studies. She likes to read mysteries, survival stories, and nonfiction. Her hobbies include talking on the phone, shopping, and reading.

Julie Folkert is a fifth-grade teacher at Highmeadow Common Campus, a National Exemplary School in Farmington, Michigan, where she has been teaching for eight years. She received her master's in literacy education at Michigan State University in 1992. She is a part of a teacher research group; presents at local, state, and national conferences on the topic of assessment; and leads staff development within her district.

Virginia J. Goatley taught in preschool and elementary classrooms prior to her current position as assistant professor in the University at Albany–SUNY Department of Reading. Her ongoing research interest is with students who are experiencing difficulty in learning to read and write and the type of instruction that might support their literacy acquisition. Her Book Club research focused on special education students, and her current research project involves community support for emergent readers and writers.

Kristin Walden Grattan received a B.A. from Albion College. Her first teaching experience as an ESL teacher in first and second grades in Mexico City, Mexico, helped her understand the connection between language use and learning. She currently teaches first grade at Steele Elementary School in Mason, Michigan.

Kathy Highfield teaches fifth grade at Holly Elementary School in Holly, Michigan. She received her master's degree in literacy instruction from Michigan State University in 1993. Her classroom research interests have focused on integrating literature-based instruction with content-area subjects, the dynamics involved in student-led discussion groups, and the role that discussion plays in students' learning process.

Susan I. McMahon is an assistant professor of reading education in the Curriculum and Instruction Department at the University of Wisconsin–Madison. A former high school and middle school teacher, she is currently studying integrated language arts and social studies curriculum in the elementary grades as part of the National Research and Development Center on Improving Student Learning and Achievement in English. She also teaches graduate and undergraduate courses in literacy education and advises master's and Ph.D. candidates. She is active in several professional organizations and serves on the editorial boards of the Elementary School Journal and the National Conference Yearbook.

Laura S. Pardo was a classroom teacher for 13 years. She received her master's degree in literacy instruction from Michigan State University, where she continues to collaborate with colleagues. She is currently a consultant for Silver Burdett Ginn. Her research interests are classroom discourse, questioning, and inquiry-based learning.

Taffy E. Raphael is a professor of literacy education in the Departments of Teacher Education and Educational Psychology at Michigan State University. A former teacher of upper elementary grades, she is currently coordinating the master's degree program in literacy instruction at MSU, as well as teaching courses related to literacy instruction at the undergraduate and graduate levels. She is active in several professional organizations and serves on the editorial boards of professional journals such as *The Reading Teacher* and *Reading Research Quarterly*. She is coauthor of the recently published *Creating an Integrated Approach to Literacy Instruction*.

Justin Ross is a student at Eastern High School in Lansing, Michigan. His favorite subjects are social studies and math. He likes to read mysteries, survival books, and biographies. His hobbies include talking on the phone with friends, reading, and playing sports such as basketball, football, soccer, and karate.

Pam Scherer is currently the literacy teacher at Allen Street Elementary in Lansing, Michigan, where she has taught for the past 25 years.

Christi Vance is a student at Eastern High School in Lansing, Michigan. Her favorite subjects are math and orchestra. She likes to read fantasy books. Her hobbies include playing the viola, watching television, talking on the phone with friends, and reading.

Index